ALLYN AND BACON, INC.
Boston London Sydney Toronto

C. LAMAR MAYER
California State University
Los Angeles

EDUCATIONAL ADMINISTRATION AND SPECIAL EDUCATION

A Handbook for
School Administrators

Library of Congress Cataloging in Publication Data

Mayer, C. Lamar, 1927–
    Educational administration and special education.

    Bibliography: p.
    Includes indexes.
    1. School management and organization—United
States—Handbooks, manuals, etc. 2. Exceptional
children—Education—United States—Administration.
3. Exceptional children—Education—Law and legislation
—United States.   I. Title.
LB2805.M313   371.9′042   81–3586
ISBN 0–205–07555–X   AACR2

Printed in the United States of America
10   9   8   7   6   5   4   3   2   87   86   85   84   83   82

78220

Contents

iii

PART II: KNOWING THE FRAMEWORK FOR DEVELOPMENT AND OPERATION OF SPECIAL EDUCATION PROGRAMS

PART III: ADMINISTRATIVE MODELS FOR SPECIAL EDUCATION PROGRAMS AND SERVICES

and Monitoring the Budget • Matching Facilities and Student Needs •
Equipping and Supplying Programs • Summary • References • Court
Cases • Additional Suggested Readings

Introduction • What Do We Need to Know? • Getting the Data • Using
the Information • Reporting • Summary • References • Additional Suggested Readings

List of Figures

List of Tables

Foreword

What is it that makes a professional book worth reading? For the busy school administrator, the book must fill a need for information about school programs and must demonstrate an acceptable measure of scholarly competence. School administrators are interested in the theories on which education is based, but they are more immediately concerned with the know-how of school program operation. This book recognizes that concern with an appropriate "sprinkling" of theory and background and a wealth of practical information regarding special education programs.

The reader of this book will soon see that it is directed to the needs of working school administrators. It summarizes, in two chapters, the information administrators need to know about the characteristics of exceptional individuals and then provides an excellent overview of the framework of laws, regulations and policies that govern special education programs in the schools. This background information is then utilized in other chapters to deal with the "what and how" of administration of school programs for special education students.

Many books are directed to the generalities of a given topic, but do not get to the specifics that are needed by practitioners in the field. This book recognizes the generalities of program administration, but it also gives extensive attention to the specifics. Self-study checklists, definition of specific responsibilities of various administrators, examples of school board policies, forms for compliance reviews, and sample budget planning sheets are but a few of the many specific and practical helps included in the various chapters.

So one may come back to the original question, "What is it that makes a professional book worth reading?" and add another question, "Is this a book that school administrators should read?" I have attempted to answer the first question, and my answer to the second is an enthusiastic—*yes!* It is a comprehensive work in a field where most school administrators have a need for more information. Their time will be well spent in studying this material.

Dr. Richard T. Cooper
President, Association of California School Administrators
Area 5 Superintendent, Los Angeles Unified School District

Preface

Every minute of every school day in thousands of schools throughout the nation, school administrators are faced with opportunities and obligations to provide special education programs for handicapped and gifted students. Decisions are made, activities are initiated, parent conferences are held, and students are taught in the school buildings and in the district offices of thousands of local education agencies. At the same time, legislatures, courts, school boards, and numerous federal, state, and local agencies are busy writing, adopting, and implementing new laws, regulations, and policies for the operation of school programs.

Nearly four million individuals with exceptional needs are now being served in our schools' special education programs. These programs exist because educators and parents recognize that special education is a necessity for many students if they are to fully benefit from the school curriculum. But they also exist because a series of court cases and laws guarantees all students the right to an appropriate education at public expense. For some students, an appropriate education means special education programs and services.

This book is about students (children and youth) described as individuals with exceptional needs and the special programs and services that must be all or part of their school experience. It is also about the people who provide those school experiences, but it is written particularly for practicing school administrators or those people who are preparing for administrative positions.

Whereas most books that are written about administration of special education are directed toward special education administrators, this one is addressed to the general administrators—principals, assistant superintendents, superintendents, and other school and central office staff. It was written with the hope that the information provided about these programs will enhance the professional abilities of these administrators as they exercise program leadership. The ultimate goal is better opportunities for the students.

The author acknowledges with appreciation the patience of family members and colleagues during the months it took to gather information and write this manuscript. Thanks are also due to the typists, who worked evenings and weekends to help produce a readable document.

The author also appreciates the many professional people in special education and educational administration who provided helpful material and ideas. Among those who made many good suggestions concerning particular chapters are Drs. Gary Best, Rose Marie Swallow, and Abraham Ariel of California State University, Los Angeles; Jerry Thornton, Downey Unified School District; Jack Rouman, Montebello Unified School District; and Al Casler, Los Angeles Unified School District.

Finally, the author acknowledges with thanks the reviews of the manuscript prepared by Dr. Edwin R. Page, Executive Director of Special Programs and Student Services, Plymouth-Canton Community Schools; Dr. Donald Robson, Department of Administration and Curriculum, Purdue University; Dr. Charles Forgnone, Chairman, Department of Special Education, University of Florida; Dr. Jean B. McGrew, Superintendent of Schools, East Grand Rapids Public Schools; Dr. William Davis, College of Education, University of Maine; Dr. James H. Fox, Mansfield City Schools; and Dr. Arthur Wagman, Assistant Superintendent for Business Administration, Wayland Public Schools. Their constructive criticisms and suggestions were obviously based on extensive experience and knowledge of the field. Many of this book's strengths can be credited to their suggestions; its shortcomings belong solely to the author.

C. L. M.

I

Understanding the Scope of Special Education Programs

1

Educational Administration and Special Education: Who, Why, How?

"The functions of leadership are to be perceptive of needs and possibilities for change, to organize a field so that the work to be done will be clear and then to implement the new structures and processes."

(Reynolds 1973, p. 23)

INTRODUCTION

Since the day of the one-room schoolhouse, educators have been aware that the educational needs of certain children within their classes were not being met in the traditional school program. Some children did not see, some did not hear, some did not learn, some did not behave sufficiently well to allow them to succeed in school; yet, increasing numbers of these children were attending classes. They were made a part of the system by changing social forces that included urbanization, compulsory school attendance laws, mandatory educational provisions, and parental demand for inclusion of their children in the schools' programs. School systems have responded to these children's widely differing needs with a variety of approaches. Thus, they have changed the knowledge and skills required of teachers and school administrators.

The past decade has seen great emphasis placed on the idea of providing educational opportunities for *all* children. Weintraub and Abeson (1976, p. 7) describe the change as an educational revolution: "This revolution to establish for the handicapped the same right to an education that already exists for the nonhandicapped had been occurring throughout the nation, in state and local school board rooms, state legislative chambers, and, perhaps most importantly, in the nation's courts." This "revolution" has resulted in state and federal legislation mandating special education programs. It also has resulted in rapid growth in programs for exceptional children and for children who are less deviant from the educational norm but who still need special assistance. Organizational models for some exceptional children are looked upon as part of the regular school's offerings; other approaches may be seen as separate or parallel or special, but whatever the design, the number of children in many school districts who receive services from special education programs exceeds 10 percent of the total school population.

The new state and national legislation and the programs that have developed are being greeted with varying attitudes. Some describe these developments as "a bill of rights for the handicapped"; others describe them in highly critical terms. The movement to serve many of these students in regular classes (service in the least restrictive environment or mainstreaming) is receiving intensive scrutiny from teachers and teacher organizations and has generated a great deal of public interest.[1] Educators in general and the public at large are very positive in supporting the rights of handicapped students to an appropriate education, but are asking many questions, such as "How?" "Who is responsible?" "Who will pay for it?"

The involvement of such large numbers of children in various types of special education programs (and placement of these programs in regular schools) has created a need for school administrators who are knowledgeable about the educational needs of this segment of the school population. The need is not limited to the person who may be called the "director of special education." It is almost a certainty that any person preparing for an administrative position in the schools will have some degree of involvement with one or more special education programs. This involvement is required of the principal, the assistant superintendent, and the business manager just as it is required of the coordinator of guidance services, the director of testing, and the supervisor of special programs.

Following the premise that the success of any special program depends heavily upon knowledge and commitment on all administrative levels, this book is devoted to the tasks of (1) describing the scope and nature of special education programs, (2) discussing administrative roles in the organization and operation of these programs, (3) presenting organizational models for effective programs, and (4) proposing suggestions for action-oriented plans. This should serve as a practical handbook that provides suggestions and guidance for the daily tasks performed by school administrators.

NEW RESPONSIBILITIES AND A PROBLEM OF BACKGROUND

A knowledge of the programs one proposes to administer is crucial to the success of both the administrator and the program. Herein lies one of the greatest problems of many school administrators with regard to special education—superintendents, personnel directors, principals, and others have often had no formal training in special education, have limited experience in dealing with educational problems of the handicapped, and have minimal background in the area of giftedness. Conversely, most school administrators are well prepared by background and experience for giving direction to school programs for other students.

Current laws, court decisions, and the educational program changes of the last two decades place the educational administrator in the position of being responsible for a broad range of programs in areas in which he/she has no teaching experience and a limited background of knowledge. This problem has often been ignored or denied by those who feel that special programs are the responsibility of the director of special education. This, however, can never be a satisfactory solution. Special education administrators are not usually located at the school site, "where the action is." They are not in charge of budgeting, personnel, or district policy making. The special education administrator can and should assist in each of these functions as they relate to special education programs, but major responsibilities lie with general administrators. A more detailed discussion of specific administrative roles is included in Chapter 5.

INVOLVEMENT WITH THE TOTAL SCHOOL PROGRAM

Historically, educational programs for the handicapped student were initiated with the concept that "survival" in the mainstream of regular programs was impossible or highly unlikely. Since the need for educational opportunities was evident, separate residential or day programs were started. Later, special (usually segregated) public school classes were initiated. That administrative structure flourished until the mid 1960s, when the system began to receive serious challenges on the basis of research findings and legal actions by individuals and groups representing the handicapped. The civil rights movement, which began in the 1950s, eventually became a major force in obtaining civil rights for the handicapped. There has been a continuing effort to guarantee that these rights include access to educational programs. (See Chapter 4 for a more detailed discussion.)

While special education programs were small and segregated, teachers and administrators of general programs often felt that their responsibility for handicapped students ended when they were referred to the special education program. The children now had a specially trained teacher and administrator who assumed educational responsibility for them, since they did not fit into the traditional mold for classroom instruction. For some students the need was obvious, but in some instances the referrals to special programs reflected teacher need rather than student need.

Historically, a series of efficacy studies typified by reports by Johnson (1963), Goldstein, Moss, and Jordan (1964), and a highly significant article by Dunn (1968) challenged the quality of education for the mildly handicapped in segregated special classes. This research evidence, coupled with significant changes in the laws during the 1970s and general public sentiment against various forms of segregation, caused educators, parents, legislators, and the courts to take action to modify the administrative structure or models by which exceptional individuals were served.

The movement toward change was highlighted by court decisions such as the 1971 *Pennsylvania Association for Retarded Children v. Commonwealth of Pennsylvania* and state legislation such as Chapter 766 of the Massachusetts Education Code (1972).[2] These actions gave impetus to an already developing movement toward mainstreaming, but the passage of P.L. 94–142 by the 94th Congress assured that handicapped children would again become involved in the nation's general education programs (served in the least restrictive environment). These actions have again given a major portion of the responsibility for education of disabled students to the general administrator and the regular classroom teacher.

In some cases, the special education pendulum swung too far. Special education programs for some students were abolished, and the students were placed in regular classes where they were unable to cope with the curriculum or the standards for behavior. This procedure often proved to be even less successful than the other extreme, and certainly did not provide for the needs of the moderately or severely disabled individual. Nevertheless, the term "mainstreaming" came into very popular use, and a huge volume of professional literature relating to the mainstreaming concept emerged (see suggested readings at the end of this chapter). In other instances the pendulum did not swing at all, and handicapped students were served in segregated facilities or not included in any school program.

As mentioned above, mainstreaming has been misinterpreted by some people to mean regular class placement with *no* special services, but this is contrary to the larger social concept of being within the mainstream of life experiences, but having a diversity of needs, experiences, and services. Mainstreaming has more realistically come to mean that most mildly handicapped students are basically served in regular classes and are separated from their nonhandicapped peers only for special instruction or services that cannot realistically be provided in the regular classroom. This concept has led us to more accurate terms for the administrative delivery system now being utilized. The more commonly used terminology now emphasizes service in the "least restrictive environment" or, more positively, education in the "most appropriate placement." A concept statement adopted by the California State Board of Education in 1978 is helpful in arriving at an acceptable definition and understanding of the terms being used and their application in school systems.

THE LEAST RESTRICTIVE ENVIRONMENT AND MAINSTREAMING: THE CONFUSION AND A CLARIFICATION [3]

As the Right-to-Education for the Handicapped began to emerge as a critical issue in this country, the word "mainstreaming" came into popular usage as a method of implementing that concept. The word has many and varied definitions, but is generally accepted as meaning the placement of handicapped students into regular classrooms. It is this definition which has come to be identified with California's Master Plan for Special Education, and consequently many persons mistakenly assume that under the Master Plan all children with exceptional needs are to be served in regular programs. The State Commission on Special Education submits this paper to aid in clarifying the intent of the Master Plan for Special Education and the reality of the implementing legislation.

In January, 1974, the California State Board of Education adopted the Master Plan for Special Education as the blueprint for special education in this state. In October, 1977, Governor Brown signed AB 1250, which provides for phased-in, mandatory, statewide implementation of the Plan.

The word "mainstreaming" does not appear in the Master Plan. The phrase used is "least restrictive alternative" (called in P.L. 94–142 and hereafter in this paper, the "least restrictive environment"). This concept, specifically set forth in the Master Plan, had been operating in California and elsewhere for certain groups of special children over the past thirty years. It has often been termed integration or normalization. The time has now come to extend its proven benefits to all handicapped children.

Least restrictive environment is described in the third philosophical goal of the Master Plan as follows:

Public education must offer special assistance to exceptional individuals in a setting which promotes maximum interaction with the general school population and which is appropriate to the needs of both.

The rationale underlying this principle is that children's similarities as human beings are more important than their differences, and if education is preparation for life, then normal and handicapped children are best prepared in environments in which there is maximum opportunity for interaction and peer modeling. Qualities of understanding, acceptance, cooperation, and respect cannot develop if children are consistently isolated from each other in their formative years. The future of general and special education depends on programs that are designed to respond to the changing needs of all pupils!

The statement above asserts that any child who can best grow academically, emotionally and socially in the regular classroom must be provided with whatever assistance that child and his or her teacher need to facilitate that learning and growth. Least restrictive environment must be viewed in terms of the individual child's needs, not as an arbitrary "ranking" of settings, but as a variety of equally important options designed to meet differing needs most appropriately.

There are wide individual differences in children with exceptional needs. Some have disabilities so unique that their "least restrictive environment" may be a special class, center, hospital, nonpublic school or home teaching. Some have disabilities so subtle that, despite the external appearance of normality, they are best accommodated by varying combinations of instructional and supportive components.

The Master Plan concept incorporates accurate assessment, individual educational planning, flexible instructional components, and appropriate use of supportive services, nonpublic schools and agencies. Each placement assignment must be made on the basis of the child's needs and abilities, requires the consent of the parent, must never be considered permanent, and is to be reviewed at least annually to see if movement to a more appropriate environment is in order or if other educational interventions are needed. The Individualized Educational Plan (IEP) is the process which ensures that these steps will be taken.

Master Plan legislation requires support for teachers in these endeavors to better serve children. It provides for staff development programs; resource programs; designated instruction; program specialists to provide consultation, information and materials; and special equipment.

When children's needs are the primary concern, and ways to meet those needs are arrived at with professional expertise and with parental involvement and consent, disagreement over appropriate learning environments will be minimized.

THE NEED TO KNOW

A careful study of the preceding statement helps one to recognize that a wide variety of program arrangements are needed to meet the educational needs of different exceptional individuals. In reality, this should come as no surprise to a school administrator who, every day, deals with the problems of providing a wide range of programs to meet the needs of other students. The major point to be stressed here is that (by definition) exceptional individuals have characteristics and needs that are *significantly* different from the norm. In many instances exceptional traits are deficits that require special equipment, materials, scheduling, curriculum, and teaching techniques in order to be improved. These students have the same needs as their nonhandicapped peers, but they also have more intensive special needs.

A variety of different models have been presented in the professional literature and in state and local plans to describe the continuum of special education programs and services. At one end of the continuum are the programs that are most isolated or different. At the other end are the programs that provide the least special or different services. Severely handicapped students are served in the former programs, and the moderately and mildly handicapped are served in the latter ones. Numerous models and administrative structures explain the means by which the continuum of programs and services is provided by local education agencies (LEAs).[4]

The topics discussed in the preceding paragraphs (historical perspectives, legislation and court decisions as change agents, the mainstreaming movement, and the characteristics and needs of handicapped students) are all items that the administrator needs to know about if school programs and services are to function successfully. It should also be recognized, however, that knowledge about something does not ensure appropriate action. Burrello and Sage (1979, pp. 216–17) discuss the importance of the values of the key policy and decision makers and the need for administrators to develop the skills that will enable them to handle their special education responsibilities. These general areas of commitment to quality program operation and the knowledge and skills necessary for program operation form the basis for more detailed discussion and the process of self-assessment of program status.

ASKING THE RIGHT QUESTIONS

The process of developing, maintaining, and improving school programs usually begins with administrators, teachers, other professionals, parents, students, or community persons asking questions. This process helps provide the information and support needed for program planning, development, and operation. Following is a partial listing of major topics under which special education questions might be classified:

- Characteristics of the students to be served
- Legal requirements and district commitment for programs
- Assignment of program responsibilities
- Working with other agencies
- Administrative structure or models that are feasible for the district
- Procedures for identification and program assignment
- Parent and community relationships
- Personnel
- Resources
- Curriculum emphasis
- Evaluation of programs.

By utilizing the above topics and adding others that accommodate local need, one can develop a checklist that will assist leadership personnel in creative inquiry and in obtaining the answers that are essential for efficient operation of special education programs. Examples of format and questions may be found on the following pages. The first page provides an example of how the questions may be answered by a local education agency (LEA); subsequent pages suggest other self-study questions relevant to LEA operation of special education programs.

SELF-STUDY CHECKLIST: CHARACTERISTICS OF STUDENTS TO BE SERVED

Questions	Yes	No	Information/Action Needed	Source of Information	Person Responsible
1. Are all administrators aware of the type of educational disabilities found in our school population?	X			Student records, Counseling office records	Coordinator of Pupil Person. Services
2. Are we knowledgeable about the types of education-related disabilities (physical, emotional, social) for which school programs must provide?			X	District screening records	Director of Special Education
3. Do we have accurate information regarding how many students in each disability area are being served? Not being served?	X			Special education report	Same
4. Do our records show the age range numbers in various disability groupings?	X			Same	
5. Are appropriate persons in our district fully knowledgeable about the characteristics and needs of "our" kids? • School Nurses and Teachers—special health problems of individual students. • Teachers—learning characteristics and problems. • Bus Drivers—abilities of students to sit, stand, ride, step up and down. • Work-study Coordinator—occupational skills, physical stamina, social skills.		X	X	Staff meetings	Dir. of Spec. Ed. Coord. of Staff Training
6. Are nonhandicapped students learning about disabilities and how to relate positively with their handicapped peers?		X	X	Observation	Principals
7. Are we working to enhance the understanding of parents of both special needs and regular students about handicapped students?	X			Informal questionnaire	Teachers

Note: The questions and responses given are examples. Local districts should formulate additional questions pertinent to their needs.

SELF-STUDY CHECKLIST: LEGAL REQUIREMENTS AND DISTRICT COMMITMENT

Questions	Information/Action Needed			Source of Information	Person Responsible
	Yes	No			
1. Does our district have a written policy statement that commits it to providing opportunities for a quality education to all students with exceptional needs?					Supt.
2. Has the board of education communicated to school administrators, teachers, parents, and the community that it will operate (or participate in) programs for *all* students within its jurisdiction?					Supt.
3. Have administrative assignments been made to keep us informed of new policies, laws, and court decisions; are we monitoring our compliance?					Supt. Dir. of Spec. Ed.
4. Are we in full compliance with federal laws and regulations—particularly the Education of the Handicapped Act, P.L. 91–230; the Education for All Handicapped Children Act, P.L. 94–142; the Rehabilitation Act of 1973, P.L. 93–112—and the amendments to these laws and regulations?					Dir. of Spec. Ed.
5. Are we delivering school services as outlined in state laws and regulations for disabled and gifted students?					Principals
6. Does our district have well-developed board policies and administrative regulations for operation of special programs at the local level?					Supt. Dir. of Spec. Ed.
7. Are we in compliance with relevant court decisions?					Legal Counselor
8. Do we have a checklist of items that will help in self-evaluation of compliance with all provisions of the laws and regulations?					Dir. of Spec. Ed.

Note: Add or delete questions as needed.

SELF-STUDY CHECKLIST: ASSIGNMENT OF PROGRAM RESPONSIBILITIES

Questions	Yes	No	Information/ Action Needed	Source of Information	Person Responsible
Have administrative assignments been made so that the line of responsibility is clearly understood for the following:					
1. Screening and referral of students with special needs?					
2. Assessment of student characteristics and needs?					
3. Assignment/placement of students for special services or programs?					
4. Development of an individualized education program?					
5. Development of special curriculum requirements with appropriate scope and content?					
6. Development of effective teaching strategies?					
7. Counseling/consultation with parents?					
8. Arrangements for transportation?					
9. Budget development and control?					
10. Periodic evaluation of the individual student's progress?					
11. Program evaluation?					
12. Evaluation of professional staff?					
13. Data gathering and reporting to state agencies?					
14. Overall program coordination?					

Note: Add or delete questions as needed.

SELF-STUDY CHECKLIST: WORKING WITH OTHER AGENCIES OR INDIVIDUALS

Questions	Yes	No	Information/ Action Needed	Source of Information	Person Responsible
1. Have we identified all of the other public agencies that might assist or provide services to the district and/or to our students? Are lists available to appropriate persons?					
2. Have we identified all nonpublic agencies that might assist or provide services to the district and/or to our students? Are lists available to appropriate persons?					
3. Have we identified a contact person in the agencies listed above?					
4. Have we established agreements and/or working relationships with other agencies?					
5. Do we have procedures for informing parents of the services available from other agencies?					
6. Do our student records provide appropriate information about services, treatment, and therapy that individual students are receiving from other agencies or professional individuals?					
7. Are procedures established for obtaining parental permission for exchange of relevant information?					

Note: Add or delete questions as needed.

13

SELF-STUDY CHECKLIST: ADMINISTRATIVE STRUCTURE/MODELS FOR OUR SITUATION

Questions	Yes	No	Information/Action Needed	Source of Information	Person Responsible
1. Are administrators at the policy-making level familiar with the range and type of special education programs and services that are permitted or mandated?					
2. Have we considered the program needs of all special education students within our jurisdiction?					
3. Have we analyzed and compared needs and resources?					
4. Have we completed, or do we need to complete, arrangements for cooperative action with other districts/agencies?					
5. Are we providing the full continuum of services needed to meet the requirements for least restrictive environment?					
6. Do we have an identifiable model/structure that can easily be explained to others?					
7. Are there ways in which our programs could be organized for greater efficiency?					

Note: Add or delete questions as needed.

SELF-STUDY CHECKLIST: PROCEDURES FOR IDENTIFICATION AND PROGRAM ASSIGNMENT

Questions	Yes	No	Information/Action Needed	Source of Information	Person Responsible
1. Have we established procedures for identifying *all* handicapped children, ages _____ to _____, who may be in need of special education services?					
2. Have we established procedures to inform appropriate school personnel and the public about the district's identification, screening, and testing procedures?					
3. Are we obtaining informed parental consent for testing? Are parents informed about their rights?					
4. Are proper procedures being followed to assure confidentiality of information?					
5. Do our identification/assessment procedures include, when appropriate, assessment of academic progress, emotional development, psychomotor problems, reading skills, vision, hearing, and communication abilities?					
6. Are our time limits in accordance with federal and state code and regulations?					
7. Have we established, to the best of our ability, non-discriminatory procedures?					
8. Are teachers, principals, and parents informed as to the "who, how, when, why" of referral?					
9. Are the activities of our assessment and planning teams organized so that time is efficiently utilized?					
10. Are we utilizing the assessment information effectively in the process of educational planning?					
11. Are parents involved in all appropriate aspects of identification, assessment, and educational planning?					
12. Do we have an organized schedule to assure periodic re-evaluation of all students?					

Note: Add or delete questions as needed.

15

SELF-STUDY CHECKLIST: PARENT AND COMMUNITY RELATIONSHIPS

Questions	Yes	No	Information/ Action Needed	Source of Information	Person Responsible
1. Does the district encourage active participation of parents of special students in suggesting policy, establishing programs, and instructing the students?					
2. Do we have a parent/community advisory committee for special education programs? Is it active?					
3. Do we provide materials and opportunities for discussion that keep the public well informed about educational opportunities for students with special needs?					
4. Do parents support and feel good about the educational opportunities being offered?					
5. Do we provide information about these programs to the local press?					
6. Are we involving community people in work-study programs and in other ways to acquaint them with the students in positive situations?					

Note: Add or delete questions as needed.

SELF-STUDY CHECKLIST: PERSONNEL QUESTIONS

Questions	Yes	No	Information/ Action Needed	Source of Information	Person Responsible
1. Do we have a full staff of well-trained teachers to work with students in each area of disability?					
2. Are all administrators in our organization sufficiently knowledgeable about special education so they can handle their area of responsibility?					
3. Do we have adequate numbers of support personnel (speech therapists, psychologists, health personnel, career preparation specialists) ?					
4. Do our personnel policies encourage employment *only* of special education personnel who are professionally trained and competent in their field?					
5. Do our personnel and administrative policies contribute to special education personnel being accepted as members of school staffs?					
6. Do our district policies encourage professional growth activities?					
7. Are we making available to other professional personnel (especially regular class teachers) the appropriate in-service training about education of our special needs students?					
8. Are we in compliance with the requirements of the state credential agency?					

Note: Add or delete questions as needed.

17

SELF-STUDY CHECKLIST: RESOURCES

Questions	Yes	No	Information/ Action Needed	Source of Information	Person Responsible
1. Are our overall resources adequate for the operation of a complete special education program or do we need to enter into some type of cooperative arrangement?					
2. Are the facilities in which special programs are housed equal in quality, access, and location to facilities for other programs?					
3. Have buildings been designed or modified to meet student and program needs?					
4. Are special equipment and materials that meet program needs readily available?					
5. Do we have the personnel (numbers, quality) to do the job well?					
6. Are we well informed about all sources of funds (local, state, federal, private)?					
7. Are we actively seeking grants and other funding that would improve and maintain programs?					
8. Do we have an effective process for budget development? Is there opportunity for appropriate input?					
9. Is our system of budget control effective and appropriate?					

Note: Add or delete questions as needed.

SELF-STUDY CHECKLIST: CURRICULUM EMPHASIS

Questions	Yes	No	Information/ Action Needed	Source of Information	Person Responsible
1. Do we have an approved form for development of individualized education programs (IEPs)?					
2. Have IEPs been developed for every handicapped student?					
3. Are teachers using the IEP as a process for improving instruction and assessment?					
4. Does our district have an approved course of study for students whose learning disabilities preclude them from meeting the standards set in the course of study for other students?					
5. Do we provide a proper balance between academic studies and vocational education for these students?					
6. Do we offer a work-study program as part of overall career preparation for secondary students?					
7. Does our curriculum provide a broad spectrum of learning areas to meet the needs of all students? All ages?					
8. Does our curriculum provide a proper sequence?					
9. Is our curriculum sufficiently flexible to meet student needs?					
10. Do we provide for proper transition from one level to another?					

Note: Add or delete questions as needed.

19

SELF-STUDY CHECKLIST: EVALUATION OF PROGRAMS

Questions	Yes	No	Information/ Action Needed	Source of Information	Person Responsible
1. Do we have a local policy that requires some form of systematic, periodic evaluation of our programs for special education students?					
2. Do we have a management system that encourages program changes in response to evaluation data?					
3. Are we "up front" with data that show problems? (Or do we only publish positive findings?)					
4. Are we collecting data that will be needed when we have a "compliance review" by the state education agency?					
5. Do we involve teachers, students, and parents in the total evaluation process?					
6. Do the evaluation data that we have available show that we are basically "OK" in terms of quantity, type, and quality of programs?					

Note: Add or delete questions as needed.

SUMMARY

Chapter 1 has presented an introduction to the material that is covered in more depth in the remaining chapters of this book. It points out some of the special needs of children and youth who require a different or extended type of program or service—one that goes beyond the regular school program. The concept that all educational administrators have a responsibility to this school population is discussed, as are the problems of professional and experiential preparation for this responsibility.

The need to know has been intensified by recent court decisions, legislative action in the various states, and by a federal mandate stating that all handicapped students must receive a free, publicly supported, appropriate education in the least restrictive environment (commonly and sometimes mistakenly called mainstreaming). While this is usually beneficial to children, it sometimes causes problems for teachers and administrators. The California State Board of Education's interpretation of the mainstreaming concept helps give perspective to the benefits and problems of implementing the least restrictive environment mandate.

Finally, Chapter 1 suggests that asking the right questions can serve as a means of self-evaluation for local education agencies. These questions and the responses they generate can be useful in developing, maintaining, and improving school programs. A format for self-study questions and some sample questions compose the final section of the chapter.

NOTES

1. Mainstreaming the handicapped student has been the topic of numerous articles in newspapers, popular magazines and professional journals. This topic has also been featured on such well-known programs as CBS television's "60 Minutes."
2. Court decisions and federal and state legislation are discussed in much greater detail in Chapter 4.
3. Developed as a clarification statement by the California Commission on Special Education and approved by the California State Board of Education in 1978. Reproduced by permission.
4. Chapters 7, 8, 9, and 10 present several approaches to defining administrative models for special education.
5. Federal and state legislation provide a number of specific compliance items that should be included in a list of self-study questions. These are discussed in greater detail in Chapters 4 and 16.

REFERENCES

Burrello, L. C., and Sage, D. D. 1979. *Leadership and change in special education.* Englewood Cliffs, N.J.: Prentice-Hall, Inc.

California State Board of Education. 1978. *The least restrictive environment and mainstreaming: the confusion and a clarification.* Sacramento.

California State Department of Education. 1974. *California master plan for special education.* Sacramento.

Dunn, L. M. 1968. Special education for the mildly retarded—is much of it justifiable? *Exceptional Children* 35:5–22.

Education of the Handicapped Act, P.L. 91–230. Education for All Handicapped Children Act of 1975, P.L. 94–142.

Goldstein, H., Moss, J., and Jordan, L. 1964. *The efficacy of special class training on the development of mentally retarded children.* Cooperative Research Project No. 619. Champaign: University of Illinois.

Johnson, G. O. 1963. Special classes for the mentally handicapped—a paradox. *Exceptional Children* 29:63–69.

Massachusetts Education Code, Chapter 766, 1972.

Pennsylvania Association for Retarded Children v. Commonwealth of Pennsylvania, 334 F. Supp. 1257 (E.D. Pa. 1971).

Rehabilitation Act of 1973, P.L. 93–112.

Reynolds, M. C. 1973. Critical issues in special education leadership. In *Leadership series in special education,* vol. 1, ed. R. A. Johnson et al., pp. 23–33. Minneapolis: University of Minnesota.

Reynolds, M. C., and Birch, J. W. 1977. *Teaching exceptional children in all America's schools.* Reston, Va.: The Council for Exceptional Children.

"60 Minutes," CBS television, January 7, 1979.

Weintraub, F. J., and Abeson, A. 1976. New education policies for the handicapped: The quiet revolution. In *Public policy and the education of exceptional children,* ed. F. J. Weintraub et al., pp. 7–13. Reston, Va.: The Council for Exceptional Children.

ADDITIONAL SUGGESTED READINGS

Administration of Special Education Programs

Gearheart, B. R., and Wright, W. S. 1974. *Organization and administration of educational programs for exceptional children,* 2nd ed. Springfield, Ill.: Charles C Thomas, Publisher.

Johnson, R. A., Gross, J. C., and Weatherman, R. F., eds. 1973. *Leadership series in special education,* vols. 1 and 2. Minneapolis: University of Minnesota.

Meisgeier, C. H., and King, J. D., eds. 1970. *The process of special education administration.* Scranton, Pa.: International Textbook Co.

Mainstreaming

Bookbinder, S. 1978. Mainstreaming: What every child needs to know about disabilities. (Excerpt from the book of the same name.) *The Exceptional Parent* 8,4:48.

Brenton, M. 1974. Mainstreaming the handicapped. *Today's Education* 63,2:20–25.

Chaffin, J. D. 1975. Will the real mainstreaming please stand up! (Or should Dunn have done it?) In *Alternatives for teaching exceptional children,* ed. E. L. Meyen and R. J. Whelan, pp. 173–204. Denver: Love Publishing Co.

Elam, S., ed. 1974. Special issue on special education. *Phi Delta Kappan* 55:513–60.

Eshner, G. L., Winschel, J. F., and Blatt, B. 1976. Mainstreaming: Yes; no; does it matter? *The Exceptional Parent* 6,1:6–12.

Garry, V. V. 1978. Mainstreaming: Children's books about children with disabilities. *The Exceptional Parent* 8,2:F8–12.

Gickling, E. E., and Theobald, J. T. 1975. Mainstreaming: Affect or effect. *The Journal of Special Education* 9,3:317–28.

Jones, R. L., ed. 1976. *Mainstreaming and the minority child.* Reston, Va.: The Council for Exceptional Children.

Mann, P. H., ed. No date. *Mainstream special education: Issues and perspectives in urban centers.* Reston, Va.: The Council for Exceptional Children.

Mann, P. H., ed. 1976. *Shared responsibility for handicapped students: Advocacy and programming.* Coral Gables, Fla.: University of Miami Training and Technical Assistance Center.

Middleton, E. J., Morsink, C., and Cohen, S. 1979. Program graduates' perception of need for training in mainstreaming. *Exceptional Children* 45,4:256–61.

Reger, R. 1974. What does "mainstreaming" mean? *Journal of Learning Disabilities* 7:513–15.

Reynolds, M. C., ed. *Mainstreaming: origins and implications.* Reston, Va.: The Council for Exceptional Children.

Russo, J. R. 1974. Mainstreaming handicapped students: Are your facilities suitable? *American School and University* 47,2:25–32.

Sabatino, D. A. 1972. Resource rooms: The renaissance in special education. *The Journal of Special Education* 6:335–46.

Schmid, R. E., Moneypenny, J., and Johnson, R., eds. 1977. *Contemporary issues in special education.* New York: McGraw-Hill.

Simon, E. P., and Gillman, A. E. 1979. Mainstreaming visually handicapped preschoolers. *Exceptional Children* 45,6:463–64.

Sloan, W. 1963. Four score and seven. *American Journal of Mental Deficiency* 68, 1:6–14.

Thurman, S. K., and Lewis, M. 1979. Children's responses to differences: Some possible implications for mainstreaming. *Exceptional Children* 45,6:468–70.

Tunick, R. H., Platt, J. S., and Bowen, J. 1980. Rural community attitudes toward the handicapped: Implications for mainstreaming. *Exceptional Children* 46,7: 549–50.

Warfield, G., ed. 1974. *Mainstream currents.* Reston, Va.: The Council for Exceptional Children. (*Note:* This reference contains reprints of thirty-eight journal articles published in *Exceptional Children* from 1968 to 1974.)

2

Defining Exceptional Individuals for the Administrator: Physical, Sensory, and Communicative Disabilities

"False barriers established because of real or perceived differences are stripped away when one becomes intimate with the topic of individuals with disabilities."

(Best 1978, p. ix)

INTRODUCTION

Since educational administrators in most positions of leadership have, as a part of their responsibility, the education of special students, it is essential that they develop a better understanding of the characteristics and needs of this segment of the school population. The discussion of characteristics and needs in Chapters 2 and 3 will not deal with the details of the etiology of the exceptionality, since such knowledge is more relevant to professionals in other fields. However, school administrators must be generally informed about the total needs of exceptional individuals[1] if they are to provide leadership for effective school programs. These needs relate to health services, preparation for independent living, preparation for future employment, preparation for family life, social functioning, and citizenship. All of the foregoing, as well as academic achievement, must be considered when planning special education programs.

The quotation (Best 1978) that introduces this chapter expresses a concept that many people fail to grasp. They are aware of such disabilities as blindness, deafness, and retardation, but they don't understand them or really know anyone who is disabled. So we come to such questions as: Who are these students? What are they like? How do they feel? What are their needs and goals? What are the responsibilities of the various professionals who work with the disabled?

Our discussion of individuals with exceptional needs begins with some case reports. This will acquaint the reader with a "real" person and frame the material that follows the case reports in a *people-oriented* context. The presentation is organized on a categorical basis (physical disability, visual impairment, etc.) only to provide a framework for discussion. As differences are discussed, it is important to also remember similarities. Try not to draw rigid categorical lines. The educator's concerns should include: How much is this individual different from the norm? In what ways is he/she different? What programs and services are needed to help this individual? What can the administrator do to provide appropriate programs?

LEARNING ABOUT INDIVIDUALS WITH PHYSICAL DISABILITIES [2]

CASE REPORT ONE

Jim had no physical disabilities until he was nine years old. At that time he was involved in a bicycle-car accident and suffered a serious spinal cord injury. The result was paraplegia (paralysis of the legs) and incontinence (loss of bowel and bladder control). Fortunately, Jim lived in a school district that maintained a good special education program. He spent one year in a special class so that he could have maximum assistance in adjusting to his new situation. After one year, he transferred to an integrated program and attended regular classes. His special services included transportation, physical therapy, adapted physical education, and minor assistance from the special education teacher with toileting needs.

Jim was a highly capable student in academic areas and devoted his full energies toward academic excellence, but he had considerable difficulty with emotional and behavioral adjustment in high school. Inability to participate in sports and lack of social acceptance (i.e., boy-girl relationships, and dating) caused feelings of inferiority and resulted in classroom behavior problems. Fortunately, Jim had teachers who understood his problems and a counselor who helped him develop self-acceptance.

Jim entered college without having determined an educational goal. He talked with counselors in engineering, law, education, and medicine. Each was very encouraging regarding general professional training, but each was careful to point out the difficulty (or impossibility) of succeeding in his/her particular profession. The message Jim received was "Disabled individuals should go to school, but don't expect acceptance or success in *my* professional area."

When he decided on a career in medicine, Jim again got the message "You can't succeed here—too much need for mobility and stamina. People won't accept a cripple as their doctor." Jim, however, refused to accept that discriminatory point of view. He experienced difficulty with admission to medical school, with some course instructors, and with internship assignments, but he also had very strong support from his parents and educational counselors.

Following the completion of his training, Jim entered private practice. As he demonstrated his competence, Jim's coworkers and patients came to realize that his disability did not affect his competence as a doctor and that he was not handicapped in his profession unless others imposed a handicap on him.

Jim lives alone in his own apartment, drives his own car, and is socially and professionally active. His apartment and car are specially equipped. Jim's major problems relate to being able to use public transportation and achieve access to buildings with architectural barriers.

CASE REPORT TWO

Marta B. was a premature baby delivered in the seventh month of pregnancy. Her mother was severely ill during pregnancy, and the delivery was very difficult. The baby's survival was in question for several weeks, and the pediatrician was soon aware of developmental problems. Marta was diagnosed very early as having cerebral palsy, and by four years of age it was evident that she had a variety of associated problems. In addition to having quadriplegic motor involvement, she was also mildly mentally retarded, had a moderate hearing loss, and suffered a serious speech problem. The parents quickly learned that one or more of these associated problems frequently accompany cerebral palsy.

At age three, Marta began attending a special education program for the physically disabled. Her school years (at different times) included the following services:

Special school
Special class in regular school
Physical and occupational therapy
Speech therapy
Preworkshop training
Occupational training in a sheltered workshop.

Through the use of a hearing aid and intensive speech therapy, Marta developed understandable language. This helped a great deal with family acceptance. She greatly enhanced her mobility with an electric (battery) wheelchair, and her arm-hand control was increased by using splints. Her school program emphasized self-help skills, independence (as much as possible) in living, and occupational skills in a sheltered environment.

At the age of twenty-two, Marta is a full-time worker at a sheltered workshop. She has developed a good concept of self, enjoys her work and her coworkers, and participates in many recreational activities. She is unable to live independently, but is an accepted family member in her home. Her parents have worked hard to provide training opportunities and services that would promote maximum development of Marta's abilities, and feel that her development has been remarkable. They attribute much of her success to a good school program.

The purpose for presenting these two case reports is to provide the reader with examples of the diversities of abilities and disabilities that can be found in individuals who are labeled "physically disabled." To help clarify this concept, a few comparisons and contrasts of Jim and Marta may be helpful:

- Marta's disabilities were congenital (present at birth), while Jim's were accidentally acquired.
- Jim has only a physical disability, while Marta is multi-disabled.
- Both are said to be successful adults, but success is measured very differently.
- Marta required numerous special services, while Jim's "special" education mostly consisted of supportive services related to mobility.
- Jim has a physical disability that limits his mobility, but for most of society's expectations he is not handicapped unless other people impose a handicap on him.
- Both Jim and Marta have equal rights under the law to educational opportunities. Each benefited according to his/her abilities and interests.
- Jim and Marta are individuals who face the same problems and joys as nondisabled individuals. They have good and bad days, successes and failures, and dreams of the future. They have adjusted to their own personal abilities and disabilities.

The above case studies and comparisons should assist one in drawing some inferences about individuals with physical disabilities. The disability can be so mild that it presents little or no problem, or so severe that it renders a person basically nonfunctional. Disabilities (or giftedness) can come in many combinations. In all instances, a school program that provides appropriate educational opportunities must be designed or adapted. This requirement often becomes a challenge to persons in leadership roles.

Nature and Extent of the Problem

From the previous discussion, one should readily recognize that there is a relationship between the nature of the disability and the educational needs of the student. An educator is better prepared to understand this relationship if he/she is knowledgeable about the various disabilities that may be found in school populations. To assist the reader in developing that knowledge and understanding, a brief discussion of physically disabling conditions follows. Emphasis is placed on disabilities or functional problems rather than causes of disabilities. For purposes of organization, physically disabling conditions are arbitrarily grouped under five headings:

- Cerebral palsy
- Muscular or skeletal problems
- Fragile and life-threatening conditions
- Serious illness or health impairment
- Disabilities from accident or trauma.

CEREBRAL PALSY Cerebral palsy is the physically disabling condition most commonly found in the schools. Best (1978) compares percentages of students with cerebral palsy in a statewide survey taken in 1965–66 with the percentages of students with this disability found in a large school district in a 1975–76 survey. While there was a difference in the samples and in the results (58 percent in the former study and 40 percent in the latter), the findings do indicate the high incidence of cerebral palsy in the school population designated as physically handicapped. The high incidence is significant to educational administrators because of the diverse and difficult educational problems present among such individuals. They are frequently multi-handicapped and require extensive and varied special services to meet the legal requirements of an educational program that is appropriate to their needs.

The complexity of cerebral palsy is exemplified by the difficulty one finds in arriving at a definition of the condition. However, as one reviews the various attempts at definition, there seems to be consensus on several points. Cerebral palsy:

- is a condition or syndrome or group of syndromes; it is not a disease;
- is caused by a nonprogressive brain injury or lesion;
- includes disability of motor functioning;
- is a congenital (present at birth) condition in about 90 percent of the cases;
- may be evident as a single minor disability (motor functioning), or may be associated with multiple problems that range from mild to profound.

In addition to the above definition, cerebral palsy is sometimes defined or classified according to the different types of motor problems present, or according to the limbs affected by paralysis. This approach to definition/classification is summarized in Table 2–1.

An acquaintance with the information in Table 2–1 should be helpful in gaining understanding of and being able to communicate about disabled youngsters. It may also be helpful to recognize that cerebral palsy is frequently accompanied by other disabilities. More than two decades ago,

TABLE 2–1   CEREBRAL PALSY—DEFINITION BY MOTOR TYPE OR
AREA OF INVOLVEMENT

Type of Involvement	Explanation
Spasticity	The most common type of cerebral palsy, it constitutes some 50 percent to 60 percent of the total. Characterized by muscle interference with voluntary movements which results in jerky, difficult, inaccurate motor control. May include "scissoring" movements of the legs, stiffness, and toe-walking.
Athetosis	The second most common type, it constitutes some 10 percent to 20 percent of the total. Characterized by constant involuntary movements described as irregular, writhing, "worm-like." Motion may affect the hands, arms, legs, mouth, or head.
Ataxia	Occurs infrequently. Characterized by disturbance of equilibrium, loss of balance, and a gait somewhat similar to that of an intoxicated person.
Rigidity	Occurs infrequently. Characterized by high levels of muscle tone and difficulty of voluntary movement.
Tremor	Occurs infrequently. Characterized by shaking or trembling of the limbs. The motion varies in pattern and consistency.
Mixed Types	Perhaps 15 percent or more individuals with cerebral palsy have a combination of types listed above. Characteristics vary.

Area of Involvement	Explanation
Monoplegia	Involvement of one limb.
Paraplegia	Involvement of the legs.
Hemiplegia	Involvement of one side of the body.
Triplegia	Involvement of three limbs—usually both legs and one arm.
Quadriplegia	Involvement of all four limbs.

Cardwell (1956, p. 23) gave some approximate figures for accompanying disabilities: visual defects (about 50 percent); hearing problems (about 25 percent); speech defects (50 percent to 75 percent); convulsive disorders (about 50 percent); moderate to severe mental retardation (about 50 percent). These percentages are basically the same today, and every one of these accompanying problems should affect the type of program that educators provide for these students.

MUSCULAR OR SKELETAL PROBLEMS   Muscular or skeletal problems are frequently referred to as orthopedic disabilities, since they involve the individual's ability to sit or stand in a normal upright position. These disabilities often require more services from health professionals than from educators. Connor (1975, p. 352) indicates that teachers' questions usually are: "Is the condition contagious?" "Can what I'm doing hurt him?" "Am I being too demanding of the child?" Best (1978, p. 46) indicates that educators need to be alert to two primary concerns; "the requirements of the child for safe, comfortable, physical behaviors that are not contradictory to medical treatments or growth and development; and the physical and behavioral concomitants that are necessary for learning and for functioning in school." Meeting those two concerns can require very little or very extensive special education services.

Under the heading of muscular or skeletal problems, one can discuss congenital (present at birth) or adventitious (acquired after birth) conditions, including atypical development of the spinal column as found in spina bifida, birth defects of other skeletal areas, Legg-Perthes disease (disintegration and flattening of the head of the femur), muscular dystrophy, severe childhood (rheumatoid) arthritis, and polio (now virtually eliminated in developed countries). These conditions are the ones most commonly observed in special programs, but are only representative of a long list of medical problems.

FRAGILE AND LIFE-THREATENING CONDITIONS The thought that a child might be seriously injured or die at school strikes terror in the heart of any teacher or administrator. Educators have both a moral and a legal responsibility to avoid such an event at all costs. Thus, it is easy for administrators to find themselves in a position where they must say, "Our school cannot or will not accept a pupil who has a condition that puts us in jeopardy." This position may unnecessarily deny educational opportunities to students whose conditions can be managed by people who have proper training and who are alerted to the students' problems. Examples of conditions, nature of the problems, and precautionary measures to be taken are presented in Table 2–2. Again, the nature of the problems and the extent of danger run the gamut from minor to extensive.

SERIOUS ILLNESS OR HEALTH IMPAIRMENT There are many different conditions that may affect a child's ability to function in school. They may include cardiac problems, hemophilia, rheumatic fever, sickle cell anemia, kidney diseases (nephrosis, nephritis), cystic fibrosis, tuberculosis, epilepsy, gastrointestinal ulcers, and teen-age pregnancy (with or without complications).

Many of these conditions are fully under control. Children with these conditions pursue a normal school program, with only minor precautionary measures being taken by teachers or administrators. However, some conditions and diseases have a contagious period, some require an extended recovery

TABLE 2–2   EXPLANATION OF FRAGILE OR LIFE-THREATENING CONDITIONS
AND PRECAUTIONARY MEASURES

Condition	Nature of Problem	Precautionary Measures
Severe diabetes	Problems in insulin control and diet	• Emergency phone number available • Phone in classroom • Food available as indicated by the physicians
Brittle bones (osteogenesis imperfecta)	Bones fracture very easily	• Limit physical activity
High spinal cord injury	Dependent for breathing on an electrically operated respirator (usually found only in hospital schools)	• Emergency phone number available • Phone in classroom • In-service training on how to operate respirator • Hand pump in case of electrical failure • An aide assigned so that the classroom will never be unattended
Severe asthma	Frequent attacks that make breathing very difficult	• Emergency phone number available • Phone in classroom • Medication available, and proper authorization to administer medication given

Note: In most cases the use of common sense, a small amount of in-service education, and
adequate precautionary measures can remove any excessive concern for the child's
safety. Negligence, however, can never be justified.

period, and some are both serious and chronic. In these cases, special provisions are often necessary if a child's education is to progress.

DISABILITIES FROM ACCIDENT OR TRAUMA   Accident or trauma victims constitute one of the most rapidly growing populations of the physically disabled. Burn victims, individuals with head injuries, persons with spinal cord injuries, drug addicts, and victims of child abuse and neglect are included in this grouping.

It is difficult to determine whether or not more children are suffering serious burns, but improved medical skills ensure a higher survival rate. Recuperation time and the rehabilitation process may be long and painful, and disfigurement is rather common. The educator's concerns must include continuation of school as soon as possible, coordination of therapies as appropriate, and restoration of the child's positive self-image.

Head and spinal cord injuries resulting from diving, automobile, motorcycle, and bicycle accidents seem to be rising dramatically. These problems, and those of drug abuse, are more prevalent among secondary school students. Paralysis, loss of sensation, impaired learning abilities, and serious emotional problems are all factors that may have an effect on the individual's ability to function in school.

Child abuse and neglect, though not limited to younger children, are more in evidence at younger age levels. Occasionally, one sees a child who has been battered to the point of having permanent physical disabilities, but more frequently the long-term effects are emotional and behavioral. While not as visible, these problems can be very serious. Problems such as social and emotional withdrawal, lack of attention, low motivation, and "acting out" are frequently the outcome of physical or emotional abuse or neglect of children and may result in referral for special education services.

Program Needs and Tips for Administrators

When evaluating and determining the program needs of the physically disabled student, the educator must first think about the individual and his/her current condition.

Obviously individual needs differ greatly. Some conditions may be temporary if properly treated (Legg-Perthes disease), some are permanent but the effects can be partially alleviated (spina bifida), some are chronic but transitory (rheumatoid arthritis), and some are progressive (muscular dystrophy). While many of these conditions do not have an intrinsic relationship to learning and to school performance, they certainly do affect the child's ability to participate in learning experiences. This becomes the educator's challenge— to enhance the child's ability to participate in as many as possible of the school's opportunities for learning. Also, the alert teacher and program administrator may provide invaluable assistance to parents and to the child's doctor by observing and reporting changes in functional abilities. For example, "I've noticed that Suzy has been limping a great deal more during the last month. Is it possible that her brace needs to be adjusted?" This type of concern is usually well received, and is certainly appropriate in terms of the child's overall development.

The concern for individual needs leads educators to ask questions. A general question might be "What is this child like?" And general questions can lead to specifics such as:

- Does he/she have problems with mobility? Is it difficult to walk or climb the stairs? Does the child need braces, crutches, a wheelchair, or transportation to school?
- What about his/her written communication abilities? Can the child hold a pencil? Does he/she have adequate hand and finger control, or is there need for a typewriter?
- Can he/she handle school materials such as paper and books? Are normal daily routines—lunchtime, toileting, a full school-day schedule— too much for the child to handle?

This type of query should lead to providing the services that will enhance the student's functional abilities.

The school administrator must also ask questions about programs. Some pupils with physical disabilities can function in regular programs without special assistance, but others cannot. They must be served by some other model that may provide (1) a regular class placement with modifications, (2) a supplementary service such as speech therapy, (3) an instructor in a special class, (4) an instructor in a hospital, or (5) an instructor at home.

Another administrative function is to delegate responsibility to others in order to assure that all of a pupil's educational needs will be met. Special education programs are most successful when it is recognized that many people in the administrative structure must be involved. Table 2–3 summarizes some of the characteristics and program needs of pupils with physical disabilities. It also shows how the responsibility for meeting the program needs may be distributed throughout the staff of the schools.

LEARNING ABOUT SENSORY DISABILITIES: VISUAL PROBLEMS

People frequently emphasize their knowledge that a certain event happened by saying, "I saw it happen" or "I was there and heard it myself." Pondering this type of statement confirms the well-known fact that we get a majority of our information through two of our five senses—vision and hearing. If a person loses one or both of these channels of sensory input, he/she faces major learning problems. The school must work to resolve or circumvent these problems. Its challenge is to provide a learning environment that will allow visually or hearing impaired students to reach their optimal level of development.

CASE REPORT

Henry, a senior in college, is majoring in special education and intends to become a teacher of blind children. He is not handicapped, but he received an assignment to simulate blindness in himself in order to experience the difficulties that a congenitally blind young adult would have in mobility, communication, concept formation, and relationships with other people. Here are excerpts from Henry's report:

"I secured the necessary materials for the assignment: blackout blindfold, long white cane, cassette recorder, and an assistant to help me with reading, driving, etc. My lack of experience contributed to relatively poor performance, but in many areas I felt I could simulate the problems and work out the solutions. . . . I couldn't drive so I took the bus or rode with someone else. I could learn the necessary mobility skills for independent travel. I could not take class notes so I recorded them and studied through listening—no problem. I began to understand my in-

TABLE 2–3   RELATIONSHIP OF PROGRAM NEEDS AND
ADMINISTRATIVE RESPONSIBILITIES

Characteristics/Needs of Physically Disabled Individuals	Persons with Primary Responsibility
Individuals with physical disabilities cover a full spectrum of scholastic abilities, ranging from the profoundly retarded to the highly gifted. Administrative arrangements, curricular offerings, and teaching strategies must provide for this range of different needs.	teacher, principal, director of special education, superintendent
Some individuals are not ambulatory, so facilities that allow access to school programs must be available (required by Section 504 of the Vocational Rehabilitation Act).	supervisor of buildings and grounds, superintendent, board of education
The scheduling of students and classes requires special attention to allow for the inclusion of needed therapies (physical, occupational, speech).	principal, school counselors, teachers, supervisor of various therapy programs
Some students have special toileting needs. Bathrooms must be properly constructed and equipped with wide entry ways, wide stalls, wall bars, special sinks.	maintenance supervisor, supervisor of buildings and grounds, principal
Special emergency procedures are needed as life-protecting measures. The youngster who is dependent on a mechanical respirator, the severe diabetic who frequently has problems of insulin control, the uncontrolled epileptic, and others depend on special devices and aids.	teacher, teacher aide, principal, school nurse
Special consideration must be given to the fact that many of these students "spend less time in school." Illness, surgery, corrective rehabilitation procedures, and therapies often cause absence for extended periods of time and shortened or interrupted school days.	teacher, principal, director of special education
Counseling needs are often much more extensive than for the nondisabled. Problems are particularly acute for individuals who have recently been disabled, as they psychologically and physically adjust to altered abilities and life styles.	coordinator of pupil personnel services, counselors, principal
Transportation of the physically disabled requires special equipment and specially trained drivers. When planning the bus routes, attention must be given to distances, time on the bus, and safety features unique to this population.	director of transportation, coordinator of staff training, maintenance supervisor
Lower student/teacher ratios, special transportation, special equipment needs, therapies, and other services all contribute to costs. Since expenses are much higher than for nondisabled students, proper budget planning is essential for program success.	associate superintendent for business, director of special education

ability to simulate certain problems when someone remarked about what a clear day it was and how near the mountains looked. I could visualize that because I have seen it hundreds of times. How could I understand what it would be like to respond to my friend's comment if I had never seen a mountain? I began to wonder how a congenitally blind individual learns about mountains, mosquitoes, colors, cells, freeways. I could find no technique to take away the concept development that I have as a result of years of seeing, and I began to understand the ways in which visual handicaps impose learning problems."

Nature and Extent of the Problem

Visual handicaps are described in different ways for different purposes. For example, one frequently hears the term legal blindness. This refers to a person who (1) has visual acuity of 20/200 (sees at a distance of 20 feet what the normal eye sees at 200 feet) in the best eye after correction, or (2) has *tunnel vision* (sees in an arc of no more than 20 degrees). While this type of definition may serve some purposes well, it has little to offer the educator. For school purposes, we must be concerned with the manner in which sensory input can be utilized in the learning process. Following are appropriate questions for educators to ask:

- What are the unique needs of a blind or partially seeing learner?
- Does he/she have enough vision to use print as the primary learning tool when combined with the use of low vision aids, large-print books, etc., or is Braille needed?
- Did the individual lose his/her vision prior to age five? (This will affect visual imagery and spatial concept development.)
- Are any additional learning disabilities present?
- Does he/she have *"travel* vision" (enough sight to move from place to place without assistance)?
- How are both near-point and far-point vision affected? How must the learning environment or materials used by modified to help the individual?
- What about functional use? Can he/she really use his/her residual vision, or is the test information misleading?
- How does the visual loss affect the learning situation?

For the child who has no vision, the answers to the above questions may be more obvious. For those who have low vision and for partially sighted individuals, answers to these kinds of questions will help determine the special services, adaptations, and devices needed to advance learning. It is important to remember that the maximum utilization of all residual vision reduces the degree of disability and enhances the learning process.

TYPES AND DEGREE OF VISUAL LOSS The determination of cause, type, and degree of visual loss is the responsibility of an oculist or ophthalmologist (a physician who specializes in diagnosis and treatment of defects and diseases of the eye) or an optometrist (a licensed, nonmedical practitioner who measures refractive errors and eye muscle disturbances and prescribes glasses, prisms, and exercises).[3] Applying this information to the individual's school program should be a cooperative effort between these professionals and educators. The main types of visual problems are listed and explained in Table 2–4.

While educators do not diagnose types of visual problems, they are responsible for observing that a child may have a visual problem and recommending that professional testing be conducted. Many local education agencies (LEAs) have regular screening programs, usually conducted by the school nurse, and teachers are responsible for watching for the signs of any visual difficulties in their students. A general understanding of the terms defined in Table 2–4 should be helpful in this process.

PREVALENCE Hallahan and Kauffman (1978, p. 338) discuss the problems involved in trying to accurately assess the number of individuals with a given

TABLE 2–4 TYPES OF VISUAL IMPAIRMENTS

Name	Description
myopia (nearsightedness) hyperopia (farsightedness) astigmatism (blurred vision)	Errors of refraction that usually relate to shape of the cornea, lens, or eyeball. Usually correctable by glasses, but may cause serious difficulties in learning if uncorrected.
strabismus (crossed eyes) nystagmus (rapid, involuntary movement)	Caused by loss of vision in one eye or improper muscle functioning. May be very minor or so severe as to seriously limit functional use of vision.
cataracts	A clouding of the lens that causes severe problems of distance vision, clarity of objects, color vision. May or may not be correctable by surgery.
glaucoma	A progressive disease that results in damage to the optic nerve and subsequent blindness.
diabetic retinopathy colomboma retinitis pigmentosa retrolental fibroplasia	Various diseases resulting in noncorrectable damage to the retina of the eye. Loss of vision can be partial or complete.

handicap. Those who are legally blind are not always functionally blind or educationally blind. In 1975, the U.S. Office of Education indicated that .1 percent of children were visually handicapped. This would mean approximately 66,000 school-age children in the United States. However, the most recent reports show that some 36,000 pupils are receiving special education services. This may indicate that many children are not receiving the services they need, or that some who have visual disabilities are able to function acceptably without special services.

Program Needs and Tips for Administrators

Once one recognizes and accepts the fact that visually impaired students can and do have very good potential for success in school, one is ready to become more specific about the information and educational decisions that facilitate successful learning. The topics of greatest significance for administrators include:

- Types and degree of visual loss (as related to functional abilities)
- Prevalence (how many can we expect?)
- Teaching materials and other resources needed
- Administrative arrangements and management
- Mobility training
- Developing daily living skills
- Overcoming common misconceptions
- Organizations that can help
- Suggestions for principals and teachers.

For the child who is educationally blind, the use of Braille textbooks, Braille writers, recorders, talking calculators, travel aids, and readers (people who read for the blind student) will be invaluable.

In planning for the needs of the visually handicapped students, it is important for the educational leader to remember what sort of learning and behavioral problems these students encounter. Severe vision loss results in (1) limitation in the child's range of experiences, and thus, greater problems of concept development, (2) limitations in one's ability to move from place to place, (3) limitations in one's ability to manipulate the environment and to locate one's self in that environment. To deal with these problems at the various grade levels and for youngsters with differing needs, a range of special programs should be available, including special classes, resource room teachers, itinerant teacher-specialists, braillists (people to convert printed materials to Braille), and special materials and equipment. Providing these resources is an essential administrative responsibility.

The child who is visually impaired but not educationally blind has some unique needs. The range of special programs is about the same as for the blind, but the ability to use the visual channel as a primary means of gathering information makes a significant difference, for many learning problems may be alleviated by utilization of proper materials and equipment. Optical aids, nonoptical aids (e.g., large print books), tactual aids, auditory aids, and mobility aids should be utilized.

MOBILITY TRAINING   For the person who is totally blind or who has very poor travel vision, the ability to move about is crucial to success in the home, at school, in the community, and at work.

The ability to orient one's self in space and to travel from one point to another—a normal part of the sighted person's development—can be learned by the blind person only through special training. Such training *must* be a part of the school's program. The blind individual can learn orientation and protective techniques for familiar environments (home, school) and travel techniques for larger, less familiar environments.

The ability to use public transportation gives the individual the greatest range of independent travel. For short distances, the greatest independence is probably gained by use of the long cane (sometimes called the Hoover cane). Other methods of local travel include the use of a sighted guide (a person who assists) or use of a guide dog. Skill and confidence in travel can be learned. Mobility training is one of the most important areas of the school curriculum.

DAILY LIVING SKILLS   Scholl (1975) defines "daily living skills" as activities of daily living or life adjustment skills. Instruction in these activities should begin in infancy (as it does for nonhandicapped children), and development should continue indefinitely (as it does for us all). Again, however, the educator must remember that many skills that are incidentally learned by other children must be purposefully and sequentially taught to handicapped children. Examples of daily living skills include:

- Eating with appropriate manners
- Personal cleanliness and good hygiene practices
- Social graces and skills
- Cooking for one's self and others
- Cleaning one's own room or house
- Care and wearing of clothing
- Handling of money (bills as well as coins)
- Dating and sexual relationships
- Budgeting—time, money
- Work attitudes, habits, courtesies, skills
- Use of free time, recreation.

There is solid evidence that appropriate training can lead to total or partial independence and mastery of the skills of daily living. Surely no educator would assign this area of the curriculum a lower priority than other areas, such as academics. Implementing this expanded curriculum within available time slots or providing extra time for learning essential skills and academic material is an administrative challenge.

ATTITUDES, FEARS, COMMON MISCONCEPTIONS It is to be hoped that we have passed the time when we feel only pity for the"poor little blind kid" and recognize that this disability is minimized by and responds well to proper educational techniques. To quote Early (p. 1):

> Loss of vision does not mean loss of ability. Visually handicapped teen-agers can do geometry, apply make-up, enjoy movies and sporting events, and go out on dates—through a variety of non-visual adaptations. Visually handicapped adults can manage a business, teach a class, mend a dress, and argue a legal case. All of these things can be accomplished without sight. Sometimes, the non-visual methods require equal or even less effort; often they demand extra time, extra concentration, extra exertion, or extra tension. But the important facts are that the methods exist and that they work, that they make of vision handicaps at worst a physical nuisance, but not a physical deterrent.

Many of the problems experienced by visually impaired individuals are problems that are imposed on them by well-meaning but uninformed peers, parents, teachers, and school administrators. Some factual information about common misconceptions may help overcome socially imposed problems. Table 2–5 presents this information. It includes information on the topic from Corn and Martinez (1977) and from Hallahan and Kauffman (1978) as well as the observations of this writer.

Since school principals are responsible for the instructional programs in their schools, they should be prepared to assist teachers and to make suggestions for working with different types of youngsters. The building administrator may expect any of three different types of situations in his/her school that involve teachers and students with visual problems.

Some schools do not have a program for students with vision problems, but send the students to another school. In this type of school, teachers need to know how to look for children who exhibit problems. They also must know how to refer children for assessment and how to utilize assessment information if the problems are minor and the child remains in a regular class.

A second type of situation exists when a special program for the visually handicapped is located at a school site. It is assumed that a teacher-specialist who is knowledgeable in the field will be assigned to the program. The principal may then adopt a supporting role, and the special teacher can work with regular classroom teachers as well as with pupils and their parents.

A third type of situation exists when visually handicapped students are

TABLE 2-5   MISCONCEPTIONS AND FACTS ABOUT THE VISUALLY IMPAIRED

Misconceptions	Facts
A Snellen Chart test is a good measure of all types of visual problems.	The Snellen Chart measures only far-point vision; it is not a test for near-point vision.
Wearing glasses always helps correct problems of vision.	Glasses will totally correct some problems, partially correct others, and provide no help for some conditions.
A person with weak eyes should use them sparingly to "conserve" vision.	Unless a medical specialist indicates to the contrary, using one's vision will *not* cause deterioration.
Legal blindness means nonusable vision.	Most legally blind people have some functional vision. Only a small percentage are totally blind.
A person should never study in dim light.	Individuals with some conditions, such as cataracts and albinism, can see better in dim light.
Holding a book very close to the eyes or sitting close to a TV set is harmful to vision.	This is a compensating technique for some types of problems. It is not harmful to the eyes if closeness brings proper focus.
A person who loses the visual sense develops superior abilities in hearing, smell, touch, and taste.	A person may learn to use his/her other senses more effectively, but does not develop better sensory acuity.
Loss of vision in one eye is always a serious handicap.	This causes a general loss of depth perception (which requires bifocal vision), but it does not represent a 50 percent loss of visual ability.
Guide dogs will take a person wherever he/she wants to go.	A guide dog is primarily a safeguard against traffic and obstacles. The person must know where he/she wants to go and maintain control of his/her travel.

assigned for part or all of the school day to a regular class. This should not be, but often is, a frightening situation for the regular classroom teacher. However, some suggestions made by Corn and Martinez (1977, pp. 5–6) may be helpful in alleviating a teacher's concerns.[4]

1. Feel comfortable using words such as *see* and *look*. These words are as much a part of the vocabulary of the child with visual handicap as they are of anyone else's. He uses them to connote his methods of seeing, either touching or looking very closely, and in expressions used in daily conversation, such as, "See you soon."
2. Introduce him as you would any student. Questions will arise from

other children and adults. Encourage the visually handicapped child to answer these questions for himself.

3. Include the visually handicapped student in all activities (physical education, home economics, industrial arts, etc.). The resource or itinerant teacher can offer suggestions as to methods and special equipment or aids which may be helpful in some activities.

4. At times all children like to be the center of attention (team captain, program announcer, etc.). Encourage the visually handicapped child to take leadership positions just as other children do.

5. The same disciplinary rules that apply to the rest of the class should apply to the visually handicapped child.

6. Encourage the visually handicapped student to move about the classroom to obtain his materials or visual information. He will know his own needs and his method of compensating will soon become part of classroom routine.

7. The visually limited child may not be aware of and therefore may not become interested in events occurring at a distance from him. He may not notice, for example, a facial expression, nod, or arm movement suggesting that he come over to you or respond to a question. Verbal cues may be necessary.

8. Provide additional work, desk, or locker space as needed to accommodate special materials (bulky Braille or large print books, reading stands, etc.).

9. As a result of getting to know their classmate with a visual handicap, students may become interested in topics related to vision impairment. You may wish to incorporate this into class lessons: in science, light and optics may be a topic for discussion; in health, attitudes towards disabilities; social studies lessons may include information about service agencies in the community. If the visually handicapped child feels comfortable about this information, he may want to participate in the presentation of the lesson.

10. All children are sensitive to peer criticism. Your own acceptance of the visually handicapped child will serve as a positive example for the class.

11. The visually handicapped student may bring adaptive aids into the classroom. Encourage him to use the aids as needed and to answer any questions that others have about the aids as they arise.

12. Because some visually handicapped children prefer not to bring attention to their handicap, they will use special aids and assistance from others only when absolutely necessary. In general, you should respect the child's wishes, but if you suspect he really needs more aids or assistance than he is using, you may wish to discuss this problem with the resource teachers.

13. When approaching a blind student, unless he knows you well, always

state your name. Voices are not always easy to identify, particularly in crowds or stress situations.

14. A totally blind child or a child with severe visual impairment may exhibit certain mannerisms (fingers in the eyes or eye poking, rocking, extra movements). Encourage good posture and consult with the resource or itinerant teacher for dealing with this behavior.

LEARNING ABOUT SENSORY DISABILITIES: HEARING IMPAIRMENTS

"It would be a mistake to argue that hearing impaired children are just like all other children. They are not. By virtue of their exceptionalities they are different. The personal and social success of hearing impaired children depends upon the degree to which we as individuals and as a society will accept their differences and upon the quality of methods, techniques, and devices developed to ameliorate their handicapping condition."

(Payne et al. 1979, p. 116)

Hearing impairments can be defined and discussed in many ways. The audiologist discusses the problem in terms of degree of hearing loss (hearing sensitivity, measured in decibels) and in terms of area of loss (which sound frequencies cannot be heard). The otologist is concerned not only with the above, but also with cause, prevention, and treatment. The educator is concerned with the individual's ability to learn (through hearing or an alternative method of sensory input) and to develop a language that will facilitate communication with other people. Thus, the definition of hearing impairment reflects one's orientation to the problem. This discussion, of course, will emphasize the educator's perspective and the educational programs that serve pupils with hearing disabilities.

CASE REPORT ONE

Bill is twelve years old and in the sixth grade. He had normal hearing until age six, when he became very ill with a viral infection and high fever. From this illness he developed a severe hearing loss, and he now wears a hearing aid in each ear. The hearing aids are of some help, but Bill does not hear many of the sounds of normal conversation. He does, however, have well-developed communication skills. Through good programs of therapy and education, Bill has maintained the speech patterns that had been developed prior to the loss of hearing. His school program has emphasized language development, learning to use his residual hearing abilities, and the development of skills in speechreading (lipreading).

For two years following his illness, Bill's school program was in a special class for the hearing impaired. He then was placed in a regular class, but attended the special class resource room for part of the school day. He currently attends a regular class but has periodic services from the school audiologist and a weekly language development session with the speech therapist. Bill is able to function well in school and at home. He is well accepted by his peers and by family members.

CASE REPORT TWO

Shawn is fourteen years old. His hearing problem was identified at about six months of age and later confirmed as a profound loss. The probable cause of the problem was identified as maternal rubella (German measles). His mother had a very light case of rubella during her second month of pregnancy.

In spite of extensive speech and language training, Shawn has not developed good oral language skills. He speaks in the monotone voice that often characterizes a deaf individual's speech and is not easily understood by other people. He does not hear most of the speech sounds and is not skilled at speechreading. He is skilled at sign language and fingerspelling and uses this method of communication whenever possible.

Shawn is a member of a special class, but attends regular classes for physical education and shop. The nonhandicapped kids accept him, but his only close friends are other hearing impaired students.

Like many of the other pupils in his class, Shawn does fairly well in mathematics, shop, and physical education classes, but his reading, language, and spelling skills are at about the third grade level. Conceptual development is also at the third to fourth grade level, even though testing shows normal intellectual ability.

The reader of these case reports can compare and contrast the characteristics and functional abilities of these two individuals with hearing impairments. They both have severe to profound hearing loss, but their adaptation to that loss is quite different. Bill lost his hearing after developing speech and language abilities, while Shawn was prelingually deaf. Also, Shawn has a greater degree of hearing loss which has caused more difficulty in developing both langauge concepts and the ability to communicate with other people. Bill's ability to communicate has contributed to both his academic and his social success, while Shawn's difficulty with communication has caused serious learning problems and difficulty in making close friends with his nonhandicapped peers.

Nature and Extent of the Problem

DEFINITIONS As previously mentioned, hearing impairments are defined in several different ways. These definitions may include (1) degree and type of hearing loss, (2) time of onset, (3) physiological location of the problem, and (4) ability to process language through the auditory channel. Each of these definitional approaches requires some further explanation.

The most general way to utilize degree of loss in a definition is to use the term (1) deaf and (2) hard of hearing. By this definition, the individual who is hard of hearing probably has a loss of 30 to 70 decibels, but his/her hearing (with amplification) is functional for learning language. The individual who is deaf has a loss of more than 70 decibels and has great difficulty in processing speech sounds and in learning language through the auditory channel. More specific definitions may use the terms slight, mild, marked, severe, or extreme hearing loss.

The time of onset of hearing loss is referred to as *prelingual* or *postlingual* deafness. The case studies demonstrated the effect this factor can have on the individual's ability to function in the school program and his/her learning and social status. Knowing the time of onset plus the degree of loss can greatly assist the educator in planning the school program.

When the discussion of hearing impairments is conducted from a physiological viewpoint, the focus is (1) the outer ear, (2) the middle ear, or (3) the inner ear. The outer ear consists of the auricle and the auditory canal. It is connected to the middle ear by the tympanic membrane (ear drum). The outer ear's function is to gather sound waves and funnel them to the eardrum which, in turn, conducts vibrations to the middle ear.

The middle ear consists of the internal side of the eardrum and three tiny bones called ossicles. These small bones, through a complicated leverage system, conduct the vibrations from the eardrum to the oval window of the cochlea. When there is a malfunction of the outer or middle ear, the sound vibrations are not passed along properly and the person is said to have a conductive hearing loss.

The inner ear is very small and extremely intricate. It contains the vestibular mechanism (which is responsible for the sense of balance) and the cochlea, which converts the sound vibrations of the middle ear to electrical signals. These signals are then conducted by the auditory nerve to the brain. When this part of the hearing mechanism functions improperly, the person is said to have a sensorineural hearing loss. The significance of this will be discussed as part of the explanation of what different people actually hear.

The fourth way in which hearing loss is defined is in terms of the ability to process speech via the auditory channel. It seems obvious that the degree of hearing loss would be a determining factor in this ability. Perhaps less obvious is the fact that the nature of the loss is also highly important. An individual may hear low frequency sounds quite well, but having a high frequency loss may prevent the person from hearing many of the speech sounds.

WHAT DOES THE HEARING IMPAIRED PERSON HEAR? A hearing impairment results in (1) a loss of sensitivity to sound, or (2) a loss of clarity, or (3) a combination of both. It is fairly easy for us to know how an individual hears when he/she has a loss of sensitivity. One can simulate this by using a set of ear plugs or by turning down the volume on a TV set. When the loss of volume is slight, one can compensate by using greater concentration. But with a 40 to 50 decibel loss it becomes very difficult to understand spoken language. Wearing hearing aids may be compared to turning up the volume on the TV set.

A hearing impairment that results in loss of hearing at the high frequencies causes a loss of speech clarity. The individual hears some sounds, but misses sounds like *ss, sh, p, f, t, th,* and *ch.* Thus, the person misses key sounds in a word or key words in a sentence. For example, the sentence

"I shot the basketball from the top of the key as the forward charged in to block the shot attempt"

may sound like:

"I   o   e ba ke ball rom   e op of   e key as   e orward   arged in o block   e   o a em."

If a person hears all sounds below 2,000 cycles per second (CPS), he/she will be able to interpret spoken language quite well. If the sounds above 1,000 CPS are lost, speech sounds are very garbled, and if the hearing range drops to 250 CPS, speech is unintelligible. Any of these frequency losses can be accompanied by a loss in sensitivity.

PREVALENCE While as many as 5 percent of school-age children have some loss of hearing, U.S. Office of Education estimates indicate that only .5 percent have sufficient loss to be classified as hard of hearing and .075 percent are estimated to be deaf. Even these numbers are considerably higher than the most recent count of pupils receiving special education services. This count shows more than 51 million school-age children in the United States, with approximately 87 thousand who are receiving special services as deaf and hard of hearing pupils (approximately .17 percent). The actual numbers range from

7,267 in California and 7,262 in New York down to 185 in Nevada and 122 in Vermont.

Program Needs and Tips for Administrators

There are many program needs that must be considered by administrators as they plan and implement services for children with hearing impairments. One of the first of these relates to the identification of those individuals who have problems.

SCREENING Severely hard of hearing or deaf children will usually have been identified long before they enter school, but youngsters with a mild hearing loss may not have been noticed by their parents as having this type of problem—though usually the indicators of some problem are evident. The school should have a school nurse or other person who has had audiometric training test each child's hearing ability. Those pupils who are identified by the screening procedures should be referred for professional evaluation. The results of that evaluation can be useful in planning an appropriate educational program.

ATTITUDES, FEARS, MISCONCEPTIONS It is often said that the greatest handicap one can have is the one imposed on him/her by other people. Imposing a handicap on others is not usually done intentionally. It is done because of a lack of information and an improper attitude. School administrators should develop an understanding of the hearing impaired individual so that they can enhance rather than impede the educational program. Table 2-6 presents a few misconceptions and facts that are highly relevant for educators.

Administrators and teachers who have developed an understanding of hearing impairments and positive attitudes toward these pupils can help plan a school program that provides the best possible opportunities. A few general statements or suggestions may be helpful:

- Hearing impaired children need to be accepted by others and to have friends. Help the process along.
- Most of these pupils are significantly below grade level in reading. Instruct appropriately.
- Development of language concepts and speech skills is the area of greatest difficulty. Teachers and speech therapists must devote much effort to this curricular area.
- Deafness is a *hidden* handicap. The deaf do not receive the same type of understanding from other people as is given to the blind or physically disabled.

TABLE 2-6   COMMON MISCONCEPTIONS AND FACTS ABOUT THE
HEARING IMPAIRED

Misconceptions	Facts
All hearing impairments are hereditary.	Some are hereditary; some are acquired.
A deaf person cannot hear at all.	The degree of impairment may be at any level, but very few are totally deaf.
Individuals who have a severe hearing loss do not learn to speak.	Given proper training at the right time, most children do learn to speak, but there is great variance in speech quality and in use of language.
Many deaf pupils are also retarded.	The number who are retarded is small. Academic retardation frequently leads educators to this erroneous conclusion.
Hearing aids can compensate for most problems.	Hearing aids work well with conductive losses but less well with sensorineural losses in which the individual hears different frequency sounds at different intensities. However, hearing aids do help most people.
Speechreading is a highly effective means of receptive communication.	Speechreading supplements other observations and the sounds that are heard, but used alone it is not highly effective.
Learning manual communication is a negative influence in the development of oral language.	This is controversial, but a majority of educators now favor a combined approach that uses both oral and manual methods.
Learning manual communication is the "best way to go" for the deaf.	This is okay for communicating with other deaf individuals, but does not allow one to communicate with the majority of people—who do not sign and fingerspell.

- Parents frequently need help. Direct them to the local parents' group.
- Hearing loss can be a serious handicap. As educators, try to be a part of the solution rather than a part of the problem.
- Remember that hearing loss can relate to either sensitivity (loudness) or frequency (pitch) or both. Children with hearing problems *do not all hear alike*.
- A hard of hearing person can use the auditory channel to learn and understand speech, but special adaptations are needed; a person who is deaf cannot use his/her hearing (even when using a hearing aid) to understand speech.
- With improved electronics and improved teaching techniques, more deaf individuals can learn to speak. Educators must provide the school services that make this possible.

LEARNING ABOUT OTHER COMMUNICATIVE DISABILITIES

> "A lisp is cute in a toddler or tem-
> porarily toothless 6-year old, and
> the stammer of a young child for
> a word is understandable, but the
> persistence of these speech char-
> acteristics in older children and
> adults is neither cute nor generally
> acceptable."
>
> (Swartz 1975, p. 70)

The other communicative disabilities discussed here may be broadly described as (1) problems of language development, or (2) problems of speech.
Language is defined by Hallahan and Kauffman (1978, p. 224) as "the communication of ideas through symbols that are used according to semantic and
grammatical rules." Speech is the oral presentation of language (words,
phrases, sentences) in a manner that is intelligible to other people. Thus, language is closely related to cognition and developing and expressing concepts,
while speech is the vehicle by which language is orally expressed.

CASE REPORT ONE

Mary C. is five years old and has been in kindergarten for two months.
The teacher has informed the principal that Mary is seriously retarded in
her language development and probably needs special help. Observation indicates that she is at the one and a half to two year level in language development—using only two or three word utterances such as
"Mary hurt" or "want more milk."

Teacher observation and psychological testing indicate that Mary functions well in nonlanguage areas. She is not judged to be mentally retarded. Further testing by the speech and language specialist indicates
normal hearing, but a significant problem in the ability to understand
and formulate language. There seem to be problems of auditory perception, comprehension of language, auditory memory, and verbal expression.

Since many of the characteristics of childhood aphasia are present, a
neurological examination is conducted, but there is no proof of brain
damage. Mary is identified as a child with severe language disabilities
and referred for special education services.

CASE REPORT TWO

Billy B. is a twelve-year-old boy of above average academic ability. A
handsome boy, he demonstrates good athletic ability and outstanding
musical talent. Billy sings in the school chorus and in the church youth

choir without any difficulty, but when he is called on in class or answers a telephone he has tremendous difficulty in responding. Billy is a stutterer.

When he was only four or five years old, Billy's parents thought the problem would resolve itself as he grew older, but it has not gone away and seems to be getting worse. Billy is very self-conscious about his problem and has devised many avoidance techniques. He always selects a position in any crowd where he can be inconspicuous and avoids, whenever possible, the need to speak. He is particularly sensitive about group situations.

Billy not only has a speech problem, but is also developing emotional problems as a result of his low self-esteem and withdrawal from situations that require oral expression.

These case studies present only two of the various types of communication problems that arise in the schools. Many other language and speech development problems are found in every school. Children with communicative disorders account for most of the disabled children in the schools. Over the years, every teacher and school administrator will confront many pupils with some type of communicative problem. It is essential for the administration to know how to identify these problems, when to refer children for special services, and how to help alleviate these problems.

Nature and Extent of the Problem

As with other disabilities, an assessment of prevalence depends on the definition used and the cutoff point at which deviance and normalcy are established. A commonly used prevalence figure for speech and language problems is about 5 percent of the school population. The most recent figures available from the Bureau of Education for the Handicapped (1980) indicate that nationally nearly 1.2 million school-age children were receiving special education services for speech and language impairments. A majority of these pupils attend regular classes and receive individual or small group instruction from a speech and language specialist one to three times per week. Usually, only pupils with severe language disorders are served in a special class.

LANGUAGE DEVELOPMENT　Developing language is one of the most complex learning processes in which human beings are involved. It seems nothing short of a miracle that, within three or four years, a child can progress through the stages of babbling, vocal play, and echolatic reproduction of words, to mastering the use of words in complex sentences so that receiving and expressing ideas and concepts becomes possible.

But just as language development can seem like a miracle, the absence of proper development can present a great mystery. Most of us have observed the developmental sequence of language in children and are familiar with that sequence. When language does not develop in this sequence (or does not develop at all), special concern must be directed to discovering the cause and establishing methods of intervention.

One of the most prevalent causes of delayed language is intellectual retardation. It is generally recognized that retardation and delayed language are closely related. School programs for the mentally retarded usually place heavy emphasis on language development as an important area of the curriculum. But educators must recognize that intellectual retardation is only one of the causes for delayed language development.

Another known cause of delayed language development is environmental deprivation. Since language is learned from listening to others, the child who gets very little opportunity to listen to and converse with other people will frequently exhibit delay in language development. A child's language environment will also determine the structure of language that is developed. There may be many grammatical and syntactical problems in a child's language, simply because he/she is following the model provided by parents with the same problems.

When an adult suffers brain injury in a particular area of the brain and loses part or all of his/her expressive or receptive language abilities, he/she is described as having aphasia. These same symptoms are sometimes seen in children—some of whom have sustained injury to the brain and some whose possible brain injury cannot be documented. This discussion will not be concerned with cause, but rather with the characteristics of this type of language disability.

It is possible for a person to have normal hearing ability but to have no ability to attach meaning to any verbal symbols. To this individual, all language sounds much as a foreign language sounds to other people. A person with this kind of problem may be described as having a *receptive language disability*. Other individuals can hear and understand language and can conceptualize thoughts for verbal or written expression, but have difficulty in finding the words to express their ideas. This is described as an *expressive language disability*. Thus, an individual who has aphasic language problems may have either a receptive or an expressive disability, or both, and may experience any degree of difficulty from very mild to a complete inability to use language symbols for the coding or decoding of ideas.

SPEECH DISORDERS   The expectations we have for normal speech are dependent on a number of factors, including geographic origin, national background, and age of the speaker. We do not think of the person who has a southern or western or foreign accent as having a speech disability. And when a three-year-old child says, "I wan awound the wocket" for "I ran around the rocket," no one advocates immediate speech therapy. But when one has speech patterns that are not geographically based or age appropriate, or interfere with the ability to communicate, or cause difficulty for the listener or the speaker, the individual may be classified as having a speech disorder.

Speech disorders may be discussed in terms of organic or functional etiology (cause), or from the perspective of type of disability (articulation problems, voice disorders, problems of fluency). The school site administrator should at least be aware of both orientations (etiology and type) so that he/she may act appropriately in obtaining special services for the child.

From the etiological perspective, functional problems are the most prevalent. In pupils with functional problems there is no identifiable physical pathology; the speech mechanism (e.g., lips, palate, tongue, vocal cords) is normal and there is no identifiable brain damage. Usually the exact cause cannot be pinpointed, but most experts theorize that the speech problem is a learned behavior. Since the individual has learned to use the speech-producing parts of his/her body improperly, he/she produces the sounds of speech inaccurately. The approach to remediation is appropriate instruction and modeling by parents and teachers or speech therapy by a qualified therapist. Both approaches may be required.

The organic origins of speech problems include hearing impairments, central nervous system damage (e.g., cerebral palsy), and damage to the speech mechanism (e.g., cleft palate). Many organic problems make it difficult or impossible for the individual to produce certain sounds. Some conditions can be medically corrected or alleviated but others cannot, and the challenge is to develop understandable speech by the use of compensating techniques or to learn an alternative method of communication.

Damage to the speech mechanism relates to deformities of the mouth, throat, or larynx. Other organic problems affect the muscles and nerves that control movements of the tongue, lips, and soft palate. In either case, the body parts relating to articulation do not function properly and the result is an articulatory disability.

Speech disorders, whether of functional or organic etiology, may also be classified according to the type of speech problem. The problems are usually discussed under three major classifications: (1) problems of articulation; (2) voice disorders; and (3) disorders of rhythm. The three, however, are not mutually exclusive.

Problems of Articulation. Articulatory disorders run the gamut of severity from the hardly noticeable lisp to unintelligible speech. An easy way to remember the types of articulatory disorders is to think of the word "SODA." The letters stand for (1) substitutions, (2) omissions, (3) distortions, and (4) additions. All four can be demonstrated by using the word *like* in a sentence:

- I wike you. (substitution)
- I ike you. (omission)

• I lak you. (distortion)
• I liket you. (addition)

Articulation problems are the most common speech disorder and (unless there is an organic basis) the most easily corrected.

Voice Disorders. Voice disorders relate to one or more voice characteristics, such as pitch, loudness, or quality. While the terms pitch and loudness need no definition, quality is not so easily defined. We might think of descriptors such as hoarse, nasal, piercing, or unpleasant. While voice disorders *may* impede communication, it is more likely that communication is merely made less desirable or pleasing. One may not enjoy listening to a person with voice disorders. These conditions most definitely should have the attention of a speech pathologist. Children should also be examined by a physician who has special training in this field.

Rhythmic Disorders. In order to be intelligible and pleasing to the listener, speech sounds must follow certain rhythmic patterns. The rate at which the different sounds are produced, the duration of sounds and the pauses between sounds, the sequence or order in which the sounds are produced, the rhythm, and the fluency of speech are each dimensions of human speech flow. These are some of the speech characteristics that make each speaker unique. Differences in these characteristics become disorders when they cause problems for the speaker or the listener.

The most common rhythmic disorder is stuttering. Stuttering is defined as "abnormal repetitions, hesitations, or prolongations of speech sounds, syllables, or movements required for articulation." (Hallahan and Kauffman 1978, p. 237). There are several theories regarding etiology, but for most stutterers the cause is unknown. However, most stutterers can gain better control of their speech through therapy.

Program Needs and Tips for Administrators

Unless the child has a severe language disorder, he/she is usually a member of a regular class. The special services provided usually take the form of individual or small group instruction from a speech and hearing specialist. Since this specialist typically has a pupil load of fifty to sixty children, the time with each child is limited to one to three sessions per week. And, while these therapy sessions are necessary and very helpful, successful remediation is much more likely to occur if the classroom teacher and the parents also become involved in speech training. The school principal should provide leadership in planning for this type of cooperative effort.

Weiss and Lillywhite (1976) provide a list of "101 ways to help children learn to talk." This list includes suggestions such as "spend more time talking to the child," "make certain that speech and language learning are fun," and "provide the child with many experiences in listening." The suggested activities are appropriate for teachers' and parents' participation. The speech specialist should help as needed, but much can be accomplished by those who spend more time with the youngster. This will also allow the specialist to spend more time with pupils who have more serious disorders.

SUMMARY

Chapter 2 discusses exceptional individuals in the schools who have physical, sensory, and communicative disabilities. The material attempts to acquaint the reader with characteristics common to various groups of disabled people and to encourage him/her to get to know and understand these individuals. Positive attitudes are as important as appropriate services when providing school programs for disabled students. As educational leaders, administrators can influence attitudes and are required by law to provide appropriate services.

Each type of disability is introduced by one or more case studies to give the discussion a personal orientation. Case studies are followed by information regarding a disability's prevalence and a discussion of its characteristics. Finally, for each disability, the chapter contains information on program needs and tips for administrators. Chapter 3 will follow the same format in discussing mental, emotional, and behavioral disabilities.

NOTES

1. The term "individuals" rather than "children" is currently in popular use in the literature and educational legislation due to the expanding age range of people being served by the schools.
2. All case reports are composites that provide realistic examples, but they do not refer to actual persons.
3. Definitions are from the "Vocabulary of Terms Relating to the Eye," Pub. no. P–607, New York: National Society for the Prevention of Blindness, Inc., 1964.
4. Suggestions are quoted by permission of the authors and the American Foundation for the Blind.

REFERENCES

Best, G. A. 1978. *Individuals with physical disabilities*. St. Louis: C. V. Mosby Co.
Bureau of Education for the Handicapped. 1980. *Number of handicapped children reported served under P.L. 94–142 and P.L. 89–313 for school year 1979–80.* May 14.

California State Department of Education. 1978. *Fingertip facts on special education in California.* Sacramento.

Cardwell, V. 1956. *Cerebral palsy—advances in understanding and care.* New York: Association for Aid of Crippled Children.

Connor, F. P. 1975. The education of children with crippling and chronic medical conditions. In *Education of exceptional children and youth,* 3rd ed., ed. W. M. Cruickshank and G. O. Johnson, pp. 352–465. Englewood Cliffs, N.J.: Prentice-Hall, Inc.

Corn, A .L., and Martinez, I. 1977. *When you have a visually handicapped child in your classroom: Suggestions for teachers.* New York: American Foundation for the Blind.

Early, G. L. No date. *The resource/itinerant program for visually handicapped students.* Bute County, Ca.: Superintendent of Schools Office.

Hallahan, D. P., and Kauffman, J. M. 1978. *Exceptional children: Introduction to special education.* Englewood Cliffs, N.J.: Prentice-Hall, Inc.

National Society for the Prevention of Blindness, Inc. 1964. *Vocabulary of terms relating to the eye.* New York. Pub. no. P–607.

Payne, J. S., Kaufmann, J. M., Patton, J. R., Brown, G. B., and DeMott, R. M. 1979. *Exceptional children in focus: Incidents, concepts, and issues in special education,* 2nd ed. Columbus, Ohio: Charles E. Merrill Publishing Co.

Scholl, G. T. 1975. The education of children with visual impairments. In *Education of exceptional children and Youth,* 3rd ed., ed. W. M. Cruickshank and G. O. Johnson, pp. 293–351. Englewood Cliffs, N.J.: Prentice-Hall, Inc.

Swartz, L. L. 1975. *The exceptional child: A primer.* Belmont, Ca.: Wadsworth Publishing Co., Inc.

Weiss, C. E., and Lillywhite, H. S. 1976. *A handbook for prevention and early intervention: Communicative disorders.* St. Louis: C. V. Mosby Co.

3

Defining Exceptional Individuals for the Administrator: Mental, Emotional, and Behavioral Differences

"The mentally retarded are, as a group, inefficient learners, this characteristic more than any other differentiates them from their nonretarded peers."

(MacMillan 1977, p. 336)

INTRODUCTION

We all recognize that each person is an individual and has characteristics that are unlike those of anyone else. We even take pride in and emphasize many of the different characteristics that we personally possess, unless those characteristics have a negative connotation. Then we use a complex set of behaviors to circumvent, minimize, or even hide the fact that *we are different*. If we are not well informed on a topic, we avoid discussions regarding it; if we have poor coordination, we avoid sports. We can do these things because we have good coping skills and because we do not differ from the norm to a very significant degree. It is the inability to cope with life's situations and the degree to which one is different that sets apart individuals with mental, emotional, and behavioral disabilities.

All of us have learning problems with certain topics; all of us have emotional problems at some time; all of us have behaved inappropriately on occasion. But it is the *degree* to which we differ from the norm and the *frequency* with which inappropriate behavior occurs that make us say that one person is normal and another is not.

Many of the disabilities discussed in Chapter 2 have characteristics that are easy to see and to understand; the problems discussed in this chapter are less visible. Parents and teachers tend to see a learning disabled child as lazy or to believe that a child with a behavioral disorder can control the unacceptable behavior if he or she wants to. This is why it is so important for teachers and educational leaders to develop a better understanding of these children's characteristics.

Just as some pupils are significantly below the norm in their abilities to learn, others are significantly above the norm. Most of us do not consider it a problem to be gifted, but these children also have special needs. It is to be hoped that an understanding of their needs will result in school programs that challenge these pupils and enhance the development of their full potential.

LEARNING ABOUT INDIVIDUALS WITH MENTAL RETARDATION

From the educator's perspective, mental retardation is a condition that affects an individual's general ability to learn school materials, to adapt to the social demands characteristic of a given age level, and to maintain appropriate interpersonal relationships with other people. This approach to mental retardation is far more productive for educators than talking about intelligence in terms of standard deviations below the mean or discussing chromosomal defects or genetic factors or cultural problems. The latter approaches provide information that supplements that received from the primary approach, and they will be briefly discussed in this chapter. However, emphasis will be placed on the way the individual functions and what that means for school programs.

CASE REPORT ONE
_____

Suzy B. is eighteen years old and a senior in high school. She has been in a school program for the educable mentally retarded (EMR) since she was in the second grade. Her psychological test scores have consistently been in the high 60s, with higher scores in the performance areas and lower scores in the verbal areas. Suzy is an attractive girl with no visible handicaps. There is no known cause of her problem, but she has a younger brother who is also in a special class.

As a young child, Suzy was very shy. She was not well accepted by her peers in first or second grade and had no close friends. After being placed in a special class, this situation changed. Suzy was now one of the "top group" in the academic subjects. She demonstrated good athletic skills and took physical education with the regular class.

In high school, Suzy was counseled by the special education teacher to enroll in the work-study program. This program emphasized the importance of functioning as a well-rounded young adult. Suzy completed driver education classes and received her driver's license; she learned to handle money and a checking account; she learned about cooking, washing clothes, and housekeeping; and she learned about the world of work.

Suzy is currently enrolled in three on-campus classes and has three periods of off-campus work experience. She is paid the minimum wage for her job as a waitress in a fast-food restaurant, and is well liked by her employer.

By some standards Suzy has not succeeded in school. She scores at the fifth grade level on standardized tests of achievement and has not been able to be mainstreamed for any academic classes. But by other standards, Suzy is very successful. She has good functional use of her reading and arithmetic skills, is well accepted by her family and peers, works successfully, and is generally well adjusted.

Stanley O. is fourteen years old and a member of a special class for the trainable mentally retarded (TMR). His problem was identified by a pediatrician a few days after birth as Down's Syndrome (formerly called mongolism). While Stanley's parents were devastated by this news, they eventually accepted the situation and determined that they would do everything in their power to help Stanley develop his abilities to their fullest potential.

Stanley's development was slow. He sat alone at twelve months and walked at twenty months. His conceptual development and language skills also developed very slowly. While he did not have serious physical defects, Stanley did have a great deal of illness related to respiratory infections.

When he was five years old, Stanley entered a special class for TMR pupils. The class focused on concept and language development and on basic self-help skills, such as toileting, dressing, and personal care. Stanley's self-help curriculum has now progressed to cover areas such as care of clothes, food preparation (making sandwiches, fixing frozen foods), and prevocational skills. In all likelihood Stanley will not be employable in competitive industry, but he will be able to work in a sheltered workshop.

Stanley's home atmosphere is supportive. His parents and older siblings accept him, and he is a contributing member of the family. There are times of stress, but the family has learned to cope. There are also some concerns for the future. His parents are fifty-five and fifty-four years old, and they are beginning to be concerned about Stanley's well being when they can no longer care for him. They are certain that he will never be able to live independently.

The case reports give examples from the groups most commonly seen in the school. However, school administrators should recognize that the schools also operate programs for the more severely retarded individual. These programs may be referred to as development centers for the handicapped or day care centers. In the example case studies, the degree of mental retardation and the potential for development are the most critical factors. The ability to handle academic learning and the ability to develop skills leading to independent living are two of the most important characteristics separating the EMR group from the TMR group.

Suzy was not able to function well in a regular class on a full-time basis, but was able to take physical education, driver education, and a few other classes in the regular program. Her least restrictive environment was special class placement with part-time assignment to regular classes. Suzy has very good potential for living successfully as an independent adult. This is due, at least in part, to a good school program.

Stanley's training has had different goals. He has learned to read signs that warn of danger and that relate to social requirements ("Men," "Women," "Keep Out"), but cannot read as reading is usually defined. Stanley's educational placement has been in a special center located on a regular school campus, but separate for the instructional program.

Nature and Extent of the Problem

The most widely used definition of mental retardation is the one proposed by the American Association on Mental Deficiency (AAMD): (ed. Grossman 1973, p. 5)

> Mental retardation refers to significantly subaverage general intellectual functioning existing concurrently with deficits in adaptive behavior, and manifested during the developmental period.

The regulations for P.L. 94–142 (45 CFR, § 121a.5) add to the above definition by indicating that mental retardation is a condition. ". . . which adversely affects a child's educational performance."

For educators, the key to understanding the definition previously given is to know what is meant by adaptive behavior. This is explained in the AAMD Manual (ed. Grossman 1973 p. 12) as follows:

During infancy and childhood in:

1. sensory-motor skills development
2. communication skills (including speech and language)
3. self help skills
4. socialization (development of ability to interact with others).

During childhood and early adolescence in:

5. application of basic academic skills in daily life activities
6. application of appropriate reasoning and judgment in mastery of the environment
7. social skills (participation in group activities and interpersonal relationships.

During late adolescence and adult life in:

8. vocational and social responsibilities and performances.

To this point, the discussion of mental retardation has focused on intellectual functioning, ability to learn academic and nonacademic materials, and ability to adapt to social expectations or demands placed on an individual at a given age and in a particular situation. These criteria for discussing and classifying the functional abilities of the retarded are often related to or replaced by a classification system based on tests of intelligence as reported by an intelligence quotient (I.Q.). Even though many educators no longer consider the I.Q. score to be a highly significant item of information, it is important to understand how professional persons use this information for purposes of classification. This information is summarized in Figure 3–1.

Comparisons are based on respective levels of retardation. While severity of retardation is a critical factor, it does not account for such variables as motivation, training, and opportunity, which are also important in determining how the individual functions.

The reader should also realize that other professionals may approach mental retardation very differently. An attorney or a judge is not so interested in terms such as EMR, TMR, mild or severe retardation as he/she is in the ability to distinguish between right and wrong or the ability to be responsible for obeying the law. The physician is concerned with causes of the problem and various methods of prevention or treatment.

CAUSES AND RELATED FACTORS Definitive causes of mental retardation are known in only a small percentage of the cases. MacMillan (1977) estimates that cause is known in less than 25 percent of the cases, and Heward and Orlansky (1980) estimate between 6 and 15 percent. Most educators are aware of chromosomal disorders such as Down's Syndrome or metabolic problems such as phenylketonuria. These are pathological disorders that can be identified and sometimes prevented or treated. But in a majority of cases, there is no known pathology.

A discussion of causative factors usually leads to the nature-nurture or heredity-environment debate. While this issue may never be fully resolved, definitive research studies indicate that a child's measured I.Q. can frequently be increased and that good educational programs can improve adaptive behavior. This information is very significant. It provides educators with a rationale for operating educational programs for retarded individuals since they too can improve their abilities and most can learn daily living skills.

PREVALENCE The numbers of school-age children classified as mentally retarded vary greatly in different school districts. This variation is due to socioeconomic differences (there seems to be a higher percentage in lower socioeconomic groups), to the definition used (I.Q. cutoffs range from 70 to 80), and to methods of identification (which tests are used).

If assumptions about distribution of intelligence are correct, about 2.14 percent of the population would score between 0 and 70 on an I.Q. test. When

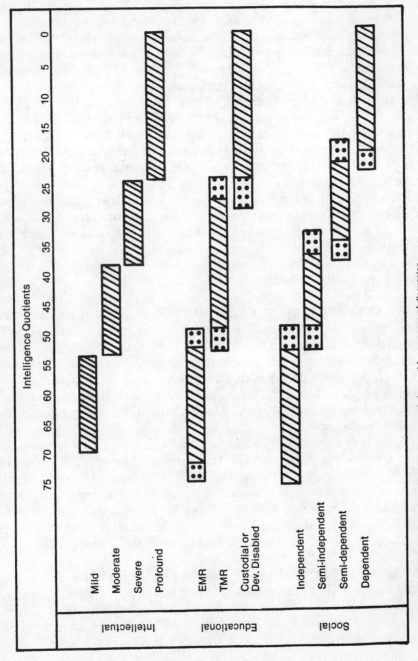

FIGURE 3–1 COMPARATIVE CLASSIFICATIONS OF MENTAL RETARDATION

Note: The terms used in classification may properly be used for purposes of discussion, but they are imprecise and overlapping (:::::::). A score on an I.Q. test is only one way of describing how the individual functions.

those who have pathological conditions are added to the previous figure, the projection is for about 3 percent to be classified as mentally retarded. The 3 percent figure has been widely used and was the basis for estimating the population by the President's Committee on Mental Retardation. However, compared to the number of children that the schools are identifying as mentally retarded, these figures seem too high. Many professionals are now using a 1 percent prevalence figure, but this appears to be too low. Based on the most recent counts reported to the Bureau of Education for the Handicapped, there are 944,909 mentally retarded pupils in special programs, out of a total school population of 51,317,000. These figures indicate a prevalence of 1.8 percent.

Program Needs and Tips for Administrators

Schools usually place the retarded pupils they serve within three groups: the educable mentally retarded (EMR), the trainable mentally retarded (TMR), and the severely to profoundly retarded (referred to as developmentally disabled, severely retarded, or multihandicapped). The individuals in these groups are served through a wide array of programs. The most frequently used are (1) regular class with special assistance, (2) resource room or special-help groups, (3) special class, (4) special school, and (5) residential institution. Appropriate placement is crucial if the individual is to develop potential skills.

School administrators can significantly contribute to the success of retarded students in numerous ways, but perhaps the most important of these is positively affecting the attitudes of other people toward retarded individuals and to the curriculum offerings of the schools.

Administrators, as educational leaders, can have a great deal of influence on the attitudes of teachers, students, and the community at large. They can begin by becoming fully informed about mental retardation and then helping others to do so. Consider the following facts:

- Most children classified as mentally retarded are *mildly* retarded.
- The mildly retarded usually do not differ from other children in physical appearance or physical abilities.
- The mildly retarded can learn academic materials and usually gain a functional level of reading, writing, and arithmetic skills.
- The majority of mildly retarded individuals work for a living and live independently as adults.
- Many who are classified as EMR at one stage of their life improve their abilities so that they no longer receive that classification.
- Most TMR students do not achieve well in academic subjects, but they can develop a reading ability that enables them to understand informational signs, food labels, and other necessary material.

· TMR individuals usually develop the skills of daily living, allowing them to live in a family as a contributing member.
· Given proper training and the opportunity, most TMR individuals can work productively in a sheltered environment.
· The severely and profoundly retarded constitute a very small proportion of the population.
· While the severely and profoundly retarded need a great deal of care, they also have potential for learning and should be given the opportunity to develop their abilities and skills.

Administrators, in various roles, have extensive influence over students' curriculum. Just as it is for any other student, the curriculum for retarded students is a determining factor in their development. Since these individuals learn more slowly than other pupils and may be less able to handle certain curricular areas, their curriculum needs to be modified. The individualized education program (IEP) is the vehicle for developing an appropriate school program (see Chapter 14).

While there is no prescribed curriculum that can meet the needs of all, mentally retarded students need a curriculum including specific instruction to develop (1) self-help skills, (2) skills of independent living, (3) physical/motor skills, (4) language/communication skills, (5) personal/social skills, (6) vocational work skills, and (7) basic subject skills relating to the previous items. Providing leadership for developing and implementing a curriculum appropriate for the mentally retarded student is an administrative responsibility. School principals can play a key role in implementing a special education curriculum that is appropriate to the development of these students.

LEARNING ABOUT INDIVIDUALS WITH LEARNING DISABILITIES

In contrast to mental retardation, which affects learning abilities across all areas of intellectual functioning, learning disabilities occur when a specific area or areas of the psychological processes are deficient. The term *excludes* learning problems that are primarily the result of visual, hearing, or motor handicaps; mental retardation; emotional disturbance; or environmental, cultural, or economic disadvantage (Davis 1980). Also, as defined in the Dec. 29, 1979 *Federal Register*, the individual classified as having a specific learning disability must have a severe discrepancy between achievement and intellectual ability in one or more of the following areas: (1) oral expression; (2) listening comprehension; (3) written expression; (4) basic reading skill; (5) reading comprehension; (6) mathematics calculation; or (7) mathematics reasoning.

Trying to define what learning disabilities are is one way to develop an understanding of the problems involved when an individual is learning disabled. Another approach is to list characteristics and explain the implications of each one (Mercer 1979). These definitions and listings of characteristics help one develop an image of individuals with specific learning disabilities. The following case report should also contribute to the reader's understanding of this condition.

CASE REPORT
_____

Omar is the younger of two children in his family. His father is a very successful salesman and his mother is a teacher. Both are ambitious, busy people who work hard at their jobs and take their family responsibilities seriously. Both are perplexed and frustrated about Omar's progress in school.

A developmental history indicates that Omar was an "irritable" baby who did not sleep well and cried a great deal. The history indicates that his development in gross motor skills (e.g., sitting, crawling, walking) was within the normal range, but his visual/fine motor skills have been developing very slowly. At age nine, Omar still has difficulty tying his shoes, zipping his coat, and buttoning his pants and shirts.

His first and second grade report cards indicated that "Omar is an intelligent boy, but is having great difficulty with recognizing letters and words. He also has difficulty with numbers and does not seem to have the fine motor control that is needed for writing."

Omar is now in the third grade, and his teacher recommended him for testing and possible placement in the learning disabilities (LD) program. The teacher has kept detailed anecdotal records that include entries such as the following:

"Runs around room knocking over desks, etc., very difficult to keep him in his seat."

"Unable to read, but fakes it by memorizing stories."

"Withdraws from failure-situations; compensates by fantasizing about accomplishments."

"Very moody today."

"Has a surprising amount of information about cars, current events, animals, etc."

"Very impulsive; intentionally tore a book in pieces today."

_____

Omar is a classic example of the type of youngster who is referred by a teacher for possible placement in an LD program. The content of the case report emphasizes observable behaviors rather than descriptive terms such as brain damage, hyperactivity, neurological impairment, incorrigibility, or dyslexia. A description of observable behaviors is more objective, more accurate, and more useful in evaluation or teaching.

The reader should note the differences in the characteristics of the LD child and the MR child. These different characteristics are important factors in developing an educational program that meets the needs of each individual.

Nature and Extent of the Problem

The case report and the preceding discussion identify many of the characteristics of LD children. The divergence of professional points of view has narrowed as the legal definition for P.L. 94–142 has become operational. This definition, by its very nature, has made discrepancy between ability and achievement the most important factor in defining the nature of the problem. As Heward and Orlansky (1980, p. 83) indicate: "... the single common characteristic of children with learning disabilities is a specific and significant achievement deficiency in the presence of adequate, overall intelligence." A broader perspective is given by Hallahan and Kauffman (1978, p. 122). They indicate that five major ideas are included in most definitions:

1. There is academic retardation.
2. An uneven pattern of development exists.
3. The individual may or may not have central nervous system dysfunction.
4. Learning problems are not due to environmental disadvantage.
5. Learning problems are not due to mental retardation.

An even broader description of characteristics than that provided by Hallahan and Kauffman (1978) is given by Tarver and Hallahan (1976) in a summary of the ten characteristics most commonly cited in the literature, including (1) hyperactivity, (2) perceptual motor impairments, (3) emotional lability (ups, downs, moodiness, anxiety), (4) general coordination deficits, (5) disorders of attention, (6) impulsivity, (7) disorders of memory and thinking, (8) specific academic problems in reading, writing, spelling, and/or arithmetic, (9) disorders of speech and hearing (language problems), and (10) equivocal neurological signs.

Another way to describe the nature of children with learning disabilities is given by Hewett and Forness (1977, p. 101):

These children may have great difficulty learning to read, write, spell, or master basic arithmetic skills, yet they are not mentally retarded. They may visually perceive symbols and letters in a distorted fashion; given the word *girl* to copy, they may write *gril,* unable to see the difference between the two. Yet they have normal vision. Or they may distort words they hear; when asked if *cope* and *coke* are the same or different words, they may nod and say they hear the words as identical. Yet their hearing is unimpaired. The child with a learning disability may also exhibit a high activity level and be impulsive and easily distracted.

From the definitions given, the case study, and the many listings of characteristics, the reader can readily see how complex learning disabilities are. They are more difficult to define than deafness and less visible than a crippling condition, but the problems are there and the functional disability is just as real.

CAUSES AND RELATED FACTORS Very little is known about what causes learning disabilities. Heward and Orlansky (1980, p. 83) state it well:

> In almost every case, exactly how a child comes to have a learning problem is unknown. However, a variety of causes for learning disabilities have been proposed. These etiological factors generally fall into three categories—brain damage, biological imbalance, and environmental factors.

Hallahan and Kauffman (1978) combine the first two of these categories as organic problems. They also discuss environmental factors and add another entitled genetic factors.

The attempts to verify that organic problems are a major cause of learning disabilities have not been very fruitful. While an organic pathology can be identified in some cases, many other children with similar characteristics give no evidence of pathology. Also, this type of explanation sounds final and not conducive to remediation. It would not be in the best interests of children to use a crutch that implies, "This child is brain damaged, and cannot be expected to learn."

Some medical researchers and practitioners believe that learning disabilities are caused by biological disturbances and biochemical imbalances in the body. The problems could be caused by diet, allergies, inherited causes of biochemical problems, or related factors. The proponents of this type of explanation of cause are experimenting with diet control and with the prescription of certain drugs. And for some children, these approaches appear to help.

Lovitt (1978) discusses environmental influences that may relate to learning problems in children. Included are emotional disturbance, lack of motivation, and poor instruction. Many educators feel that poor instruction (at home or at school) is a major contributing factor. If it is, the problems of many children may be alleviated by providing appropriate educational programs.

PREVALENCE The percentage of the population with specific learning disabilities is dependent on the definition used. Various authors discuss figures ranging from 1 percent to 30 percent. The first is too low; the latter is obviously too high. The most realistic and practical figures are those defined by law. Various state statutes usually put a cap on the prevalence figures for learning disabilities at 2 to 3 percent of the school-age population. The most recent national figures from the unduplicated pupil counts show that 1,281,406 children are being served in programs for the learning disabled from a total school population of some 51,317,000. That indicates a percentage figure of 2.5 percent.

Program Needs and Tips for Administrators

The most common administrative arrangement for serving the learning disabled is to assign a pupil to the regular classroom teacher for a large part of the school day and to a learning disabilities group, resource room, or itinerant teacher for other class periods. But even though this type of administrative arrangement is the most common, some individuals with learning disabilities need the more intensive services available in a special class. They would not usually be served in the more restrictive environment of a special school or residential center unless there are accompanying emotional/behavioral disorders. Since reading disabilities are so common, they are usually treated within the special education part of the program.

For several years, educators and researchers have experimented with different instructional techniques or program models in attempts to find the best approaches to meeting the needs of learning disabled children. Table 3–1 summarizes some of these techniques and models.

In addition to knowing about the various administrative arrangements and the instructional techniques and models that are most commonly used in serving LD children, administrators may benefit from consideration of the following statements:

- Learning disabled individuals are the source of many frustrations for teachers, but their condition is also very frustrating to the LD student.
- A learning disability is a bona fide handicap. It is not the same as being slow or lazy or retarded.
- Hyperactivity, distractibility, inability to concentrate, and other characteristics are usually not under the conscious control of the LD individual. However, control can be developed to some extent.
- Such descriptive terms as "brain damaged" and "perceptually disabled" are far less useful to educators than functional descriptions of behavior.
- A learning disability may be specific to one area of cognitive functioning or may encompass many areas.
- A learning disability frequently is a related or causative factor in emotional and adjustment problems.
- Career preparation and daily living skills are frequently neglected curricular areas for LD individuals. At some point in the pupil's educational program it may be appropriate to shift the major emphasis from academic remediation to functional life situations.

TABLE 3–1 INSTRUCTIONAL TECHNIQUES/MODELS FOR LD CHILDREN

Descriptive Term	Explanation
1. Diagnostic-Prescriptive Approach	In this model the child is assessed in various learning areas (diagnosis) and an educational plan is developed (prescription). The educational plan and teaching techniques are directed specifically to remediation of the diagnosed problem(s).
2. Structure/Stimulus Reduction	This model is based on the concept that some children's learning disabilities are closely related to distractability or to hyperactivity. Thus, irrelevant stimuli are reduced and structured activities are increased.
3. Ability or Process or Skill Training	This model assumes that a child fails to learn because (1) he/she lacks certain abilities or processes related to learning a task; or (2) he/she lacks certain skills related to learning the task. Thus, remedying a defective process (e.g., improving visual perception) or teaching certain skills (e.g., word analysis techniques) may result in amelioration of a learning problem in the area of reading.
4. Cognitive Training	This approach assumes that many learning disabilities are related to deficient problem-solving skills. Teaching the child problem-solving skills will enable the child to utilize these skills in the learning process.
5. Reinforcement/Behavior Modification	Reinforcement of appropriate behavior is a technique that is widely used in school programs. When carefully planned, as in Hewett's engineered classroom (Hewett 1968), the reinforcement is part of the process of behavior modification. In this type of program, appropriate behaviors are identified and reinforced according to a preplanned schedule.
6. Task Analysis and Precision Teaching	In this approach to teaching, very specific objectives are adopted and the steps that lead to accomplishment of the objectives are identified. As learning progresses, accomplishment of each step is recorded and instruction is directed to the next step. The concept of learning by very small increments is the basis of this technique.
7. Multisensory Approach	This approach involves more than one channel of sensory input in the learning process, rather than directing instruction to a single sense. The teaching materials and techniques are aimed at two or more channels of sensory input. The Fernald method is an example of a multisensory approach.

Note: These techniques/models are not mutually exclusive, and most educators use the combination that seems to work for them.

LEARNING ABOUT INDIVIDUALS WITH BEHAVIORAL DISORDERS

The term behavior disorders has many synonyms and a variety of meanings, depending on the agency or person giving the definition. It encompasses such terms as emotional disturbance, maladaptive behavior, psychological disorders, socially maladjusted, abnormal or bizarre behavior, delinquent, psychotic, and autistic. Different terms are applied in order to establish appropriate remedial programs in different states, and there are many different ways of combining these terms or conditions in order to structure a categorical program.

Subsequent pages will give more detailed definitions and discussion of characteristics, but the following description by Heward and Orlansky (1980, p. 113), even though harsh, helps the reader gain understanding:

> Behavior disordered children are seldom really liked by anyone—peers, teachers, brothers or sisters, their parents. Even sadder, they often don't even like themselves. They are difficult to be around, and attempts to befriend them may get you nothing but rejection, verbal abuse, or even physical attack. With some emotionally withdrawn children, any overtures seem to fall on deaf ears; and yet these children are not deaf.

The preceding description of children with behavioral disorders emphasizes the problems and the difficulties encountered when working with these individuals. And while the description is, in many cases, accurate, it is a description of current status. Educators must adopt the belief that this condition, like other handicaps, is subject to improvement, remediation, amelioration, and even elimination, depending on the individual and the appropriateness of the services he/she receives.

CASE REPORT ONE

Brett is eleven years old and is in a special class for the EMR, but his teacher has indicated that she believes the placement is inappropriate. Her other students are all retarded in academic abilities, but they have learned good social skills and *behave* like other children their age. By contrast, Brett sometimes seems to have better academic skills, but his behavior is out of control. He demands an inordinate amount of attention and will misbehave until he receives it. He has also become very abusive of his peers by hitting, kicking, spitting, and pulling hair.

Miss Sime, the teacher, is an experienced and qualified professional. She is not shocked by deviant behavior, but she says that Brett is destroying her class. She is concerned about the safety of the other children, and has received numerous complaints from parents. Miss Sime has requested an immediate meeting of the individualized education plan (IEP) committee to consider a change in Brett's educational placement.

CASE REPORT TWO

Jimmy is seven years old and has never attended school. The schools first became aware of him when a neighbor called. She had seen one of the "child find" announcements on TV [brief public service announcements that encourage viewers to report to their local school any handicapped child who may need special education services]. Jimmy's parents recognized that he was seriously handicapped and didn't think the schools would have a program for him.

At the request of the Director of Special Education, Jimmy's parents brough Jimmy to the school for a meeting with Dr. Benz, the school psychologist. Dr. Benz did not attempt to conduct formal testing, but did try to get Jimmy involved in playing with him. Jimmy completely ignored Dr. Benz. He would not maintain eye contact, accept toys, or respond to any attempts at conversation. Instead, he rocked back and forth—often with his eyes closed and while flipping his hands up and down. The parents said that Jimmy was sometimes more responsive, but that today's behavior was not uncommon.

After a great deal more observation and collection of information, Jimmy was diagnosed as being autistic. The IEP committee decided on a placement in a special class for the seriously emotionally disturbed (SED). He has been in the class for six months and has reduced his rocking and hand flipping, but still has minimal eye contact and very limited expressive language abilities.

These two case reports present children with very different behavioral characteristics. Brett is aggressive, demanding, and acting out. He makes unprovoked attacks on others and is highly disruptive of the classroom environment. Jimmy, on the other hand, is withdrawn and out of touch with reality. He does not usually bother other people, and does not seem to want their attention. He frequently withdraws into his own world and rejects any attention or affection from others.

Brett and Jimmy are both severely handicapped, but individuals with behavioral disorders can have any degree of disability, ranging from very mild to a level of severity that makes them essentially nonfunctional. As in other areas of disability, the greater numbers of people involved are in the mild range.

The characteristics described in the case reports are mostly those which are *observable*; they are the symptoms rather than the cause. They represent descriptions of *current* behavior rather than characteristics that are permanent in nature. Describing a behavioral characteristic is not comparable to describing the color of a person's eyes; it is more like telling his/her age.

Nature and Extent of the Problem

The nature of individuals with behavioral and emotional problems is discussed by Kirk and Gallagher (1979, p. 389) as follows:

> A child who is extremely withdrawn and fearful, who does not relate to other people, and who does not seem to respond to the environment (notwithstanding average intelligence) is one whose behavior is interfering with his or her own development. Such children have been termed *withdrawn, neurotic, autistic,* and *schizophrenic.*
>
> Children of another type behave in ways that create repeated conflict with siblings, parents, classmates, teachers, and community. They disturb by directly interfering with the lives of other people. Neighbors call them *bad boys* or *bad girls.* Teachers call them *conduct problems.* Social workers say they are *socially maladjusted.* Psychiatrists and psychologists say they are *emotionally disturbed.* If they come in conflict with the law, the judge may call them *delinquent.*

The descriptive terms used by the different professions help us to know what these children are like, how they are perceived by others, and some of the problems they may face. A description by Lovass and Newsom (1976) of autistic children also helps one gain perspective. They list six common characteristics of autism:

- Apparent sensory deficit
- Severe affect isolation
- Self-stimulation
- Tantrums and self-mutilatory behavior
- Echolalic and psychotic speech
- Behavior deficiencies.

A review of the codes and state plans of a number of states reveals many similarities and a few differences in definition. The regulations for the state of New York (Office for Education, § 200.1(d)(3)) say, "An emotional reason means a condition of psycho-social origin leading to behavior which interferes with the child's ability to adjust to, and benefit from, existing regular class programs."

Florida has one definition for emotionally disturbed children and a different one for socially maladjusted students. Section 6 A–6.3016 cites criteria for eligibility for emotionally handicapped programs. These criteria include: evidence of severe emotional handicaps; the problems exist over an extended period of time; the behavior disrupts the student's own learning; and the problem is not due to sensory, physical, or intellectual handicaps. By contrast, Section 6 A–6.3017 defines socially maladjusted students as those who are adjudicated by a court; or placed in a community facility for drug abuse; or have frequent conflicts of a disruptive nature with other students and staff;

exhibit negative behavior that is general rather than isolated; "act out" in a way that interferes with their own learning; show unsatisfactory academic progress; and reject or do not respond to efforts to provide help. It is interesting to note that programs for the emotionally disturbed receive funds for exceptional pupil programs, but programs for the socially maladjusted have been placed in basic education.

CAUSES AND RELATED FACTORS   In trying to deal with causes, prevention, and treatment of behavioral disorders, one must first recognize that the "state of the art" is such that our knowledge and practice do not resemble those of an exact science. It is generally accepted that both physiological and psychological factors may be involved, but knowledge of specific factors is limited. Many theorists agree that there is a certain amount of biological predetermination of the individual's personality or temperament, and almost everyone would agree that psychological/environmental factors are highly relevant.

The causes of behavioral disabilities may be very important to educators, and definite action can be taken to try and determine causation. First, the handicapped individual should have a thorough medical evaluation. Some children who apparently have a biochemical imbalance respond well to prescribed drugs. Teachers and administrators can provide invaluable information regarding behavior and learning at school when the M.D. is trying to find the right prescription and the correct dosage.

A second way in which the educator may assist is in psychological evaluation and counseling. The psychologist must rely on teachers, administrators, and parents for information related to assessment and for cooperation in a counseling program. Parents and educators must constantly seek to be a part of the solution rather than a part of the problem.

Obviously, the most direct access that educators have to behaviorally disordered children is through their opportunity to work with the individuals at the school—in class, on the playground, or in other school situations. An appropriate school experience can be highly effective in helping some children to cope with their environment and develop a state of good mental health.

PREVALENCE   In reporting on numbers of children served, the Bureau of Education for the Handicapped (now the Office of Special Education) reports numbers of emotionally disturbed (perhaps a narrower term than behavioral disorders) children as being 331,069 for the nation as a whole. This gives a prevalence figure of approximately .65 percent of the school-age population. It is much lower than might be estimated by teachers and school principals, who indicate that an average of two to three children per classroom show signs of emotional or behavioral problems. That would indicate a prevalence of about 6 percent to 10 percent—some twenty times as high as the number receiving special services. The difference is undoubtedly explained by the fact that a majority of the children's problems are of a mild nature and are handled in the regular classroom rather than in special programs.

Program Needs and Tips for Administrators

Perhaps the most pressing need of individuals with behavioral disorders is for better understanding of their problems. Other people have more difficulty accepting these children's problems than those of any other group of handicapped children. Parents, teachers, administrators, and others are frequently greatly frustrated in trying to work with these children. They often have the feeling (consciously or unconsciously) that the disturbed child could control the unacceptable behavior if he/she wanted to. A comparison of attitudes may explain this point.

Picture three children. One is a paraplegic, one is blind, and one is deaf. Now imagine saying to the paraplegic, "Get up and walk, you are just lazy"; to the blind child, "Pay attention to what I am doing; you can see if you want to"; and to the deaf child, "Listen to me, I know you can hear." Everyone would agree that the preceding statements are ridiculous. But, in essence, we frequently make similarly unrealistic demands of children with behavioral disorders. "Sit still, pay attention, maintain eye contact, be nice to other people, remember what I am telling you" may, for different children with behavioral disorders, be quite as impossible as the commands listed for the children with other handicaps. Yet, as educators, we fail to recognize this type of inability to perform. There is one major difference, however, and that is the potential for success. While the totally blind child cannot learn to see, the aggressive child may learn to control his or her behavior, and the withdrawn child may learn to attend to stimuli and to relate to other people. The point to remember is that they may learn these skills, but they do not necessarily have them as a part of their repertoire of current abilities.

Individuals with behavioral disorders obviously need appropriate services. To the medical profession this means treatment; to psychologists it means therapy; to educators it means special education. There has been a significant shift, in recent years, to naming the school as the agency with primary responsibility for the habilitation program. Medical treatment, psychological therapy, and social work services are often seen as ancillary to the educational program. This places a tremendous responsibility on school personnel.

The administrative models by which children with behavioral disorders are served include the full range of special education possibilities. The child with mild problems should be a member of a regular class, with supportive services as appropriate; the child with moderate problems may need a special class at a regular school; and the child with severe problems may need to be in a residential program. As with other children, these pupils should be in programs with nonhandicapped peers whenever feasible, and should move toward the least restrictive environment that their functional abilities will allow.

Within these different administrative models, an appropriate educational program for each child must be developed.

When teachers and administrators think of goals and objectives for their pupils, they usually think in terms of academic areas such as reading and arithmetic. Working with children with behavioral disorders requires a reorientation of goal areas. Sometimes academic learning cannot happen until the emotional/behavioral characteristics are under control. These become the primary goal areas, and the academic activities are often a means to accomplishment of the goals for improved mental health.

Due to the nature of the problems of these children, school personnel (administrators, teachers, bus drivers) must learn to cope with their own feelings and plan programs that not only meet the child's need but also allow them as professionals to control the frustration or even anger that they may feel when working with aggressive or withdrawn pupils. Long and Newman (1976) suggest four alternative behaviors that may be used by teachers. Planning in advance for the handling of different situations can be very helpful. The suggestions made by Long and Newman (1976) and further explained by Kirk and Gallagher (1979, pp. 408–9) include:

1. *Preventive planning.* The creation of a hygenic environment will allow the child to bring his or her behavior under control.
2. *Permitting.* Certain types of behavior should be sanctioned by the teacher at times, such as running and shouting on the playground.
3. *Tolerating.* The teacher should tolerate the behavior because it is temporarily beyond the child's ability to control; but it is explained to the child that improvement is expected.
4. *Interrupting.* The teacher should interfere with a behavior sequence for the protection of the child, for the protection of others in the class, or for the protection of ongoing classroom activities.

Whenever or wherever (in the classroom, on the bus, in the cafeteria) there are problems of a behavioral nature, they may become problems for the administrator. If the problems persist or if they are very serious in nature, the teacher, bus driver, or cafeteria supervisor will expect (and should receive) help from the administrator. The following suggestions may be helpful to administrators as they try to assist school personnel or parents who are working with behaviorally disordered children.

- Parents, teachers, and others are often the targets of children's aggressive behavior. Each is probably frustrated, but trying to help with the solution. Avoid situations that place the blame on others. Work as a team to deal with the child's problems.
- Recognize that hostility and aggression are directed toward authority figures or whoever happens to be there. Don't take it personally.

- Remember that understanding why a person acts as he or she does is not the same as condoning or accepting that behavior.
- It is important to work closely with the child's doctor. Prescribed drugs are sometimes very effective in helping a child control unacceptable behavior.
- Work cooperatively with psychologists and psychiatrists. Counseling or therapy is very helpful for some children.
- Help the child to succeed at school work. This can be very therapeutic.
- Even though withdrawal does not tend to cause problems for others, it is a serious problem for the individual. Be as concerned about the needs of the withdrawn child as you are about the needs of the acting-out child.
- Probably the number one curriculum goal must relate to development of social skills and interactions with other people.
- When placing children with behavior problems with a regular classroom teacher, choose carefully.
- Establish (on an individual basis) the standards of behavior that are desirable and those that will be tolerated. Be understanding, provide good models, use appropriate educational interventions, but maintain the established standards.

LEARNING ABOUT INDIVIDUALS WHO ARE GIFTED

"The learners in the upper 2 percent of the intelligence scale need as much special instruction to continue their growth as the students at the lower end. Yet seldom are special classes provided, or resource personnel made available. Since all students must adjust to the average classroom program, the gifted student loses the most."

(Clark 1979, p. 135)

Some state and local administrative structures include the gifted within the special education program, while in other areas these students are not placed within the special education framework. But regardless of administrative location, gifted learners have certain needs that frequently are not met by regular school programs. The concept that "bright children will make it on their own" may be true for some, but if these bright children are to be challenged by their school experiences and encouraged to fully develop their abilities, some modification of the regular school program may be necessary.

Gifted children, when considered within the framework of special education, are in a unique position. Other groups are discussed in terms of the conditions that prevent or make it difficult to function normally. Giftedness places the individual at the opposite end of the continuum of human abilities. Kirk and Gallagher (1979, p. 59) explain this different situation:

Children of all of the other groups described under the label *exceptional* are children with a deficit in one or more parts of the information-processing system. The gifted are the only group that has a surplus of abilities or talent. In the gifted child the central processing functions . . . of memory, association, reasoning, extrapolation, and evaluation are enhanced and such advanced development influences positively the other major components of information processing.

The surplus of abilities and talents and the advanced central processing functions that Kirk and Gallagher identify are the very reasons why gifted individuals need special consideration in their educational programs. If this special consideration is not provided, the surplus may not be utilized and the greater abilities not challenged or expanded. The individual who is gifted may then function at a nongifted level.

CASE REPORT ONE

Monique B. is five years old and has recently entered kindergarten. She is the only child of parents who are well educated and have high goals for her future. Mr. B. is an engineer and Mrs. B. is the assistant librarian at the university. Both parents spend a lot of time with their daughter and encourage her to learn new things and to pursue her learning interests.

Monique began reading at three years of age and can now read third grade books easily and with good comprehension. She can tell time, can add and subtract single column numbers, and can explain the calendar. Obviously, recognizing colors, identifying shapes, and discussing the concepts of big versus little and over versus under are baby stuff to her.

The kindergarten teacher, Mrs. C., is somewhat overwhelmed. She has Monique help her with the other kids, but Monique wants to answer all of the questions and dominates all of the discussions. She shares things about telescopes, rockets, sports, etc. that even the teacher doesn't know about—and she wants to learn more about reading and arithmetic. Mrs. C. knows she should be pleased to have a student of this caliber, but she is beginning to see Monique as a discipline problem and says she can't teach second grade arithmetic, third grade reading, and "who knows what level" science while also teaching twenty-eight other children at the kindergarten level.

CASE REPORT TWO

Patrick L. is the youngest child in a family of eight children. His father was a high school dropout. His mother finished high school with honors, but did not go on to college. She likes to read and does so as her main type of recreation. She reads to her children when there is time, but having a large family does not leave much time for this.

Patrick was very shy his first year in school and did not make any special impression on the kindergarten teacher. Her entry on the *cumulative record* said, "Patrick is a handsome boy who is about average in height and weight. He has good coordination and likes sports. He is also interested in music and art. He is shy, but will participate when called on. He is a good student and a rapid learner."

Patrick's first and second grade reports were very similar, but group testing at the end of second grade showed that he was reading at the 4.8 grade level and had arithmetic concepts at the 4.2 grade level. The teachers had Patrick in the top group in the class, but had no idea that he would score so high on the tests.

In the third grade, Mr. M. saw Patrick's test scores and recognized him as a highly capable, but not highly motivated student, and he decided to try to interest Patrick in science activities. As Mr. M. described it, "It was like a duck finding water." Patrick was highly motivated by the science projects, and this motivation, fanned under the continuing encouragement of Mr. M., soon spread to other areas.

In the fourth grade, Patrick was tested by the school psychologist and identified as mentally gifted. Since that time his school program has included special provisions for cluster grouping and enrichment classes. Patrick is now a junior in high school and is registered in four classes in the honors program. He is active in sports, plays in the school band, is a member of the student council, and is a candidate for outstanding student of the year. He is popular with his peers and liked by all of his teachers. They say, "His giftedness has not gone to his head."

These case studies again allow us to make some comparisons of individuals and to draw some inferences about them. In Monique's case, the intellectual superiority was evident as soon as she entered school. In Patrick's case, it was discovered later by an alert teacher who helped identify and nurture the giftedness. Patrick, who probably was not as highly gifted as Monique, was more of a conformer, while Monique started school as one who always rocks the boat. One student needed a modified school program; the other almost demanded it. One teacher was overwhelmed (and understandably so), while another saw a gifted student as an opportunity and a challenge. In both cases there was an individual who had needs that were different from those of his/her classmates. That is the challenge of giftedness: to provide school programs that meet the unique needs of these children, foster and encourage learning, and make it possible for them to achieve their full potential.

Nature of and Nurturing of Giftedness

Clark (1979, p. 5) gives this definition:

> ... the word gifted refers to people who have developed high levels of intellectual ability or who show promise of such development. Let us distinguish these individuals from those of more average mental accomplishments by the former's ability to think in abstracts, to generalize, to solve complex problems, and to see unusual and diverse relationships.

The reader should note that the definition does not use the term I.Q., but utilizes terms that describe superior intellectual functioning in a broader orientation. This writer also believes in this type of definition, but the use of I.Q. scores to identify giftedness is still very much a part of the thinking of many professionals. Many states use I.Q. scores to identify the lower limit for those who will be classified as gifted. In spite of its problems, the I.Q. test is one way to get an objective measurement of intellectual functioning, and I.Q. scores can be used to limit the population that is identified.

Definitions give us some assistance in understanding the nature of giftedness, but perhaps a better approach is to review the characteristics of individuals who are classified as gifted. A review of the writings of several authors, Clark (1979), Gallagher (1976), Kirk and Gallagher (1979), Hallahan and Kauffman (1978), and Heward and Orlansky (1980), provides an extensive listing of characteristics, many of which are included in Table 3-2.

TABLE 3-2 CHARACTERISTICS OF GIFTED INDIVIDUALS

Area of Uniqueness	Explanation
1. Background	1.1 Frequently (but not always) the gifted come from a better than average socioeconomic background and from a solid family. 1.2 Parents are often high achievers who expect a lot from their children and provide many enriching experiences.
2. Health and Physical Characteristics	2.1 Contrary to popular belief, gifted individuals have slightly better health, on the average, than their peers. They often are well coordinated, like sports, and excel at competitive games. 2.2 Individuals do not have better sensory abilities but often utilize them more effectively. There are fewer sensory defects in the gifted.

TABLE 3–2   (*Cont'd*)

Area of Uniqueness	Explanation
	2.3 On the average, gifted children are slightly taller and stronger. They learn to walk earlier, and development is generally more rapid.
3. Intellectual and Educational Characteristics	3.1 By definition, the gifted excel in intellectual functions.
	3.2 The gifted have high verbal ability, varied interests, and an increased capacity for processing information.
	3.3 Achievement in school is frequently two or more grades above the normal level.
	3.4 A high percentage attend college.
4. Emotional Characteristics	4.1 The gifted tend to be more emotionally stable.
	4.2 There is a greater ability to handle personal problems.
	4.3 There is a heightened sensitivity to the feelings of other people.
	4.4 Idealism, a sense of justice, and emotional depth are common in the gifted.
5. Social Characteristics	5.1 The gifted are motivated by social expectations.
	5.2 There is a high level of understanding of social problems.
	5.3 The gifted are usually popular with peers and adults and are socially accepted.
	5.4 There is a high level of self-acceptance.
	5.5 There is a tendency toward happier marriages and fewer divorces.
6. Moral and Ethical Characteristics	6.1 Gifted children are less prone to cheat or be dishonest.
	6.2 They are more concerned with moral values.
	6.3 The gifted tend to be concerned with social problems and solutions.
7. Occupational Characteristics	7.1 The gifted choose occupations that demand high levels of ability.
	7.2 A high percentage enter the professions and management.
	7.3 Several follow-up studies indicate that gifted children become gifted adults and that occupationally they are winners.

Note: The characteristics listed are generalizations describing a group of people. Individual gifted children may possess any combination of these characteristics, but certainly not all of them.

Giftedness cannot be created by the schools, but it can be nurtured. What is frightening is that it can also be suppressed and potential can be wasted. The process of nurturing abilities, of course, should be emphasized for all children. In this need, the gifted are not unique. But the methods by which this is done may be. It is very natural for teachers to direct instruction to the average or middle range of the class. For gifted students, this may mean day after day of instruction about something they already know. In terms of motivation for learning, this can be devastating.

To provide for the educational needs of gifted individuals, schools must offer some means that allow individuals to pursue their interests and must make instruction challenging and exciting. Several approaches to meeting these needs are used, and some of them are administrative arrangements. It is to these administrative arrangements that this discussion is directed. Three terms describe the traditional administrative structures for education of the gifted: (1) ability grouping; (2) acceleration; and (3) enrichment. These approaches have a close relationship to the regular school program and should not be perceived as independent programs. Each is described in the following material.

Ability grouping is partially explained by its name—children are grouped according to their abilities so that a teacher can more effectively work with them. Different methods of ability grouping are used. One approach is to place a cluster of gifted children in a selected regular classroom. Thus, one of the groups within that class will be working at advanced levels. This has the advantage of keeping students with their age group while they receive advanced instruction. It also provides gifted students with many opportunities to assume leadership roles.

Another method of ability grouping is the special class. In this structure, all class members are gifted. And while this may have instructional advantages, it also has disadvantages, particularly at the elementary school level. The special class does not provide adequate opportunities for everyone to exercise leadership abilities. It may also inhibit socialization with peers who are not gifted and decrease exposure to different types of children. The special class seems to work better in a departmentalized situation (usually in the secondary schools) where students in honors programs are in a type of special class for some periods of the day but not for all classes.

Acceleration can take many forms (Clark 1979). Included are early entrance to formal schooling, moving through grades more rapidly (e.g., three grades in two years), skipping grades, advanced placement, and moving through material at an accelerated rate. Clark summarizes the research and indicates that it is almost uniformly positive regarding acceleration. A concern is expressed by some practitioners about social factors in some accelerated situations. For example, a fourteen-year-old adolescent who is a senior in high school may have some social problems.

The remaining administrative arrangement is called enrichment. Heward and Orlansky (1980, p. 314) define enrichment experiences as ". . . those that let each youngster investigate topics of interest in much greater detail than is ordinarily possible with the standard school curriculum." Clark (1979, p. 114) says, "Enrichment is usually the addition of disciplines or areas of learning not normally found in the regular curriculum." These additions to the curriculum can be made in the regular classroom or in a variety of special programs. Enrichment can work very well, but Kirk and Gallagher (1979, p. 83) express one highly important caution:

> . . . unless the administrators and teachers have a clear vision of what their objectives are, enrichment turns out to be merely a piling on of more and more facts, rather than more and more organization and unification of complex ideas.

State codes seldom, if ever, prescribe that any particular administrative arrangement must be used, so these decisions are made at the local level. They are usually made by administrators who work in conjunction with teachers and parents. The most effective program should be determined by considering a number of factors, including ages of pupils, numbers of pupils involved, level of giftedness of the individuals involved, resources available, and teachers' and parents' preferences. Whatever model is utilized, the objective must be to provide appropriate programs for the individual student. Giftedness can be nurtured and developed if the schools do their job well.

Program Needs and Tips for Administrators

In previous sections of this chapter and in Chapter 2, the author has discussed the need for development of knowledge, understanding, and positive attitudes toward individuals with a variety of disabilities. It may seem to some readers that these factors are not problems when dealing with the gifted. However, such is not the case. Gifted pupils have special characteristics and needs that are often not met. They frequently work below their ability level because that is where the class is working; they sometimes get more of the same because that keeps them busy; and their enthusiasm and creativity are sometimes stifled because they are seen as being overly aggressive. Teachers often understand the needs of the gifted pupil, but are unable to provide for those needs because of lack of resources, too many children in their class, lack of expertise in the gifted pupil's area of interest, or any of a number of other reasons. Given the proper support system, many teachers can and do provide challenging, appropriate instruction.

Providing high-quality programs for the gifted is no less challenging than doing so for the handicapped. These children also must be considered as individuals who may need different programs. Any attempt to educate them by use of only one model (e.g., regular class, enrichment, acceleration) may work for some children, but will be inappropriate for others. While program decisions will have to be made according to each local area's capability, some suggestions may be helpful:

• Encourage administrators, teachers, and other staff personnel to learn more about the characteristics of gifted individuals.
• Provide in-service education.
• Develop a workable process for screening and identification.
• Identify available and obtainable resources.
• Carefully select teachers who will work with gifted students.
• Involve teachers and parents in planning the program.
• Utilize the services of museums, colleges, theaters, and laboratories to enhance the programs.
• Involve people from the community as models, guest lecturers, and mentors.
• Develop alternative program models so all pupils may be appropriately served.
• Help teachers accept children who ask diverse questions, have a variety of interests, demonstrate drive and aggressiveness, and challenge the thinking of the teacher.
• Involve gifted students in a variety of leadership roles.

As a group, gifted individuals have all of the other positive and negative characteristics found in the general population. As individuals, they also possess a high level of motivation, broad interests, and a special capacity for learning. These characteristics can be nurtured and expanded by appropriate school programs. This is the challenge to administrators of school programs everywhere.

SUMMARY

Chapter 3 discusses exceptional individuals in the schools who have mental, emotional, and behavioral differences. As in Chapter 2, the goal of this material is to acquaint the reader with the characteristics of these individuals and to encourage him or her to develop a greater understanding of their educational needs.

Each exceptional area is introduced by case reports in order to orient the reader to individual problems and advantages. The emphasis is on people rather than things, and people are different. How they are different is one of the thrusts of the chapter; what the schools should do about their differences is another.

Chapters 2 and 3 emphasize what school administrators need to know about exceptional individuals. The material presented on each exceptional area is brief, and the person who seeks more detailed information will find it in the cited references.

REFERENCES

45 C.F.R. § 121a.5.

Clark, B. 1979. *Growing up gifted.* Columbus, Ohio: Charles E. Merrill Publishing Co.

Davis, W. E. 1980. *Educator's resource guide to special education:* Terms—laws— organizations. Boston: Allyn and Bacon, Inc.

Florida Statutes and State Board of Education Rules. 1979. In *A resource manual for the development and evaluation of special programs for exceptional students.* Tallahassee: State Department of Education.

Gallagher, J. J. 1976. The gifted child in the elementary school. In *The intellectually gifted: An overview,* ed. W. Dennis. New York: Grune and Stratton.

Grossman, H. J., ed. 1973. *Manual on terminology and classification in mental retardation.* Washington, D.C.: American Association On Mental Deficiency.

Hallahan, D. P., and Kauffman, J. M. 1978. *Exceptional children: An introduction to special education.* Englewood Cliffs, N.J.: Prentice-Hall, Inc.

Heward, W. L., and Orlansky, M. D. 1980. *Exceptional children: An introductory survey to special education.* Columbus, Ohio: Charles E. Merrill Publishing Co.

Hewett, F. M., Forness, S. R. 1977. *Education of exceptional learners,* 2nd ed. Boston: Allyn and Bacon, Inc.

Kirk, S. A., and Gallagher, J. J. 1979. *Educating exceptional children,* 3rd ed. Boston: Houghton Mifflin Co.

Long, N. J., and Newman, R. C. 1976. The teacher and his mental health. In *Conflict in the classroom,* 3rd ed., ed. N. J. Long, W. C. Morse, and R. C. Newman, pp. 399–413. Belmont, Ca.: Wadsworth Publishing Co.

Lovass, O. J., and Newsom, C. D. 1976. Behavior modification with psychotic children. In *Handbook of behavior modification and behavior therapy,* ed. H. Leitenberg, pp. 303–60. Englewood Cliffs, N.J.: Prentice-Hall, Inc.

Lovitt, T. C. 1978. The learning disabled child. In *Behavior of exceptional children,* 2nd ed., ed. N. G. Haring. Columbus, Ohio: Charles E. Merrill Publishing Co.

MacMillan, D. L. 1977. *Mental retardation in school and society.* Boston: Little, Brown, and Co., Inc.

Mercer, C. D. 1979. *Children and adolescents with learning disabilities.* Columbus, Ohio: Charles E. Merrill Publishing Co.

Office for Education of Children with Handicapping Conditions. Part 200 of the Regulations of the Commissioner of Education. Albany, N.Y.: State Education Department.

Tarver, S., and Hallahan, D. P. 1976. Children with learning disabilities: An overview. In *Teaching children with learning disabilities: Personal perspective,* ed. J. M. Kauffman and D. P. Hallahan, pp. 2–57. Columbus, Ohio: Charles E. Merrill Publishing Co.

II

Knowing the Framework for Development and Operation of Special Education Programs

4

Laws, Regulations, Policies, Hearings, and Court Decisions

"As a general rule, the nation's public schools were highly ingenious and very successful in denying educational opportunities, equal or otherwise, to handicapped children."

(Turnbull and Turnbull 1978, p. 19)

INTRODUCTION

School administrators who look at the "big picture" of what is occurring on a district, state, or national basis soon come to realize that educational programs have their roots in the laws and regulations that mandate their existence and provide the funds for their continuance. The general public, parent groups, and professional educators also realize that many of the special interests they champion will only be aided if they can influence legislative bodies to adopt favorable laws and regulations.

Parents of handicapped children and handicapped individuals speaking on their own behalf have for decades presented the philosophical point of view that laws regarding compulsory attendance, equal educational opportunity, obligation of school districts to provide programs, etc., should apply to *all* children. On a philosophical level, state governments, local school boards, and educational leaders have expressed agreement. In practice, however, there have been tremendous discrepancies between the educational opportunities available to the handicapped student and those available to the nonhandicapped student. This situation has led to increased activity by proponents of special education programs. Through the legislative and judicial processes, they hope to establish requirements stating that local education agencies must provide for their handicapped students.

La Vor (1976), in writing a history of federal legislation for exceptional persons, indicates that laws providing for the education and training of the handicapped can be traced back to the early 1800s, when the federal government set aside land for a "seminary of learning" for the deaf. And, while not specifically mentioned, the rights of the handicapped are protected by certain provisions of the Constitution. Since these early beginnings there have been hundreds of statutes and regulations passed at national and state levels. For a review of historical development and detailed discussion of these laws, regulations, and court decisions, the reader is referred to the suggested readings at the end of this chapter. The material presented here will focus on six items essential to the day-to-day decision making of the practicing administrator: (1) knowledge of the framework of laws, regulations, policies, and legal decisions that govern programs; (2) a review of the constitutional provisions and major laws at the national level; (3) a review of the process and function of state laws; (4) the importance of local policies; (5) an overview of significant court decisions; and (6) an introduction to due process hearings. Items of compliance and enabling features of the codes will receive particular attention in this chapter.

THE LEGAL FRAMEWORK FOR SPECIAL EDUCATION PROGRAMS

Educational programs for exceptional individuals are not unique in finding their roots in the legislative/judicial process. Much of what is said about them could apply to the educational program of any pupil, but emphasis will be given to special education provisions. The legal framework for educational programs includes:

- Constitutional provisions for certain guaranteed rights
- Federal laws covering educational programs for the handicapped and gifted
- Federal regulations that provide implementation details for the federal laws
- State laws—the major vehicles through which educational programs are described, authorized, and implemented
- State regulations that provide procedures for implementing state and federal laws
- Policies of local education agencies
- Legal opinions and court decisions (relating to all of the above—they may range from a county counsel's opinion regarding the meaning of a law to a decision by either a state or the U.S. Supreme Court)
- Decisions of due process hearing panels established by certain federal and state laws to deal with individual cases.

To reduce the scope of the legal framework for special education programs, one might group the above eight topics under the headings (1) national level, (2) state level, (3) local level. One might also generalize by purpose, as shown in Table 4–1. This is an oversimplification, but helps demonstrate relationships.

It should be noted that federal law has precedence over state law and state law over local law. However, the laws at one level are sometimes purposefully written in a way that allows the lower level of government to establish the

TABLE 4–1   COMPARISON OF PURPOSE

Level of Law, Regulation, Policy	Purpose or Function
National Level	Tells what must be done (mandatory) or what may be done (permissive). Permissive action is encouraged by granting of funds. Provides funds for states and LEAs.
State Level	Tells what must be done (mandatory) and what may be done (permissive) within the schools of the state. Also provides the framework for how school programs are to be offered and for state and local funding. School programs are a basic responsibility of each state, and most of the "what and how" questions are resolved at this level.
Local Level	Determines what the LEA's school programs will be and how they will be conducted (within the provisions of state and national codes). Contains the policies and regulations for day-to-day operation and for the utilization of all LEA funds.

standards. For example, federal law specifically gives precedence to the states when it comes to determining the age of mandatory school attendance.

A more accurate way to view the legal framework for special education programs is to group programs according to precedence. This method also recognizes the branches of government with primary responsibility. Precedence grouping is illustrated in Table 4–2.

FEDERAL LAWS AND REGULATIONS

It is only within the past two decades that federal laws and regulations have attained a significant role in public school education. Prior to that time, it was said that since the Constitution was silent regarding education it was the province of the states. The federal role was mostly limited to assisting states and LEAs with monetary grants, research, and information gathering. The change began when court decisions regarding due process requirements and guarantees of equal protection under the law (the Fifth and Fourteenth Amendments) were applied to educational programs by the courts. The influence of the federal government on education also increased dramatically as it began to provide more funds for local schools. The Elementary and Secondary Education Act of 1965 is a good example of how increased federal funding brought an increase in federal influence. Most recently, Congress has enacted the "rights to education" laws prescribing compliance items for many of the educational services that states and LEAs *must* provide. Three of these

TABLE 4-2   LAWS AND REGULATIONS BY PRIORITY OF IMPORTANCE

Laws and Regulations	Source	Judicial Review
Constitutional law • Federal Constitution (Fifth and Fourteenth Amendments) • State constitution (sections relating to education) • Local charters (in some states)	Basic documents for the operation of national, state, and local government	
Statutory law • Federal laws relating to education of exceptional individuals (P.L. 94–142, P.L. 93–112, P.L. 93–380)	Congress	Challenges of the validity of laws and regulations, substantive challenges, and those relative to
• State laws relating to education of exceptional individuals (often called the state education code)	Various state legislatures	proper implementation are handled through the judicial process. This may include legal opin-
• Policies of local education agencies relating to special education programs	Governing boards of the LEAs	ions by the attorney general or by county counsels, due process hearing panel actions, and court cases in federal or state courts.
Regulatory codes • Title 45 of the Code of Federal Regulations (sections relating to education of the handicapped and gifted)	Executive branch (Secretary, Department of Education)	
• State administrative codes	State boards of Education, state superintendents of instruction, and/or state departments of education	
• Local administrative regulations	LEA superintendent and/or local governing board	

laws, and their accompanying regulatory codes, constitute the major provisions for special education programs.

The Rehabilitation Act of 1973 (P.L. 93–112) as Amended

The movement to guarantee the rights of handicapped individuals has, in many ways, paralleled the movement to assure civil rights for all people. Antidiscriminatory legislation emphasizes the importance of treating all groups and individuals fairly. The prohibition of discrimination against the handicapped that carries the greatest legal weight is found in the Rehabilitation Act of 1973 (P.L. 93–112).

Three sections of P.L. 93–112 are of significance as "civil rights" legislation. Section 502 mandates the elimination of architectural barriers that make buildings inaccessible to the handicapped, and Section 503 states that federal contractors (with contracts of $2,500 or more) must take affirmative action to employ the handicapped. These sections of the law are of great importance, but it is Section 504[1] that has the greatest relevance to educational programs. Section 504 states:

> No otherwise qualified handicapped individual—shall, solely by reason of his/her handicap, be excluded from the participation in, be denied the benefits of, or be subject to discrimination under any program or activity receiving federal financial assistance.

Since local education agencies almost invariably receive federal assistance, they are subject to the provisions of Section 504. Thus, school administrators must assume responsibility for implementation of the necessary local policies and procedures.

The general meaning and significance of Section 504 and the implementing federal regulations (45 C.F.R. § 84.1, et seq.) were summarized in remarks made by former HEW Secretary Joseph Califano on April 29, 1977:

> For decades, handicapped Americans have been an oppressed and, all too often, a hidden minority, subjected to unconscionable discrimination, beset by demoralizing indignities, detoured out of the mainstream of American life and unable to secure their rightful role as full and independent citizens.
> Today I am issuing a regulation, pursuant to Section 504 of the Rehabilitation Act of 1973, that will open a new world of equal opportunity for more than 35 million handicapped Americans—the blind, the deaf, persons confined to wheelchairs, the mentally ill, or retarded, and those with other handicaps.
> The 504 regulation attacks the discrimination, the demeaning practices, and the injustices that have afflicted the nation's handicapped citizens. It reflects the recognition of the Congress that most handicapped persons can lead proud and productive lives, despite their disabilities. It will usher in a new era of equality for the handicapped individuals in which unfair barriers to self-sufficiency and decent treatment will begin to fall before the force of the law.

The federal regulations for Section 504 are divided into seven subparts[2]: (1) general provisions, (2) employment practices, (3) program accessibility, (4) preschool, elementary, secondary education, (5) post-secondary education, (6) health, welfare, and social services, and (7) procedures. While a detailed discussion of all subparts is not appropriate on these pages, certain major points of great significance to school administrators should be noted:

- A free appropriate education must be provided to all individuals (within prescribed age levels) and no otherwise qualified individual—preschool through adult age—may be excluded from a school program on the basis of a handicap.
- Programs and services must provide opportunities to achieve equal results. They may be separate if necessary, but must be equivalent and must give qualified, handicapped individuals the option of participating in regular programs.
- LEAs (and other agencies) may not support any person or entity that discriminates against handicapped persons.
- Programs (for purposes of this discussion, school programs) must be placed in sites and physical facilities that allow access to handicapped individuals.
- In determining services agencies may not utilize any criteria that will be discriminatory or impair the handicapped individual's opportunity to accomplish objectives.
- Testing/evaluation must be nondiscriminatory.
- Parents are guaranteed certain procedural safeguards and due process procedures.

As can be seen from this partial listing of 504 requirements, this law and the accompanying regulations are designed to protect the civil rights of the handicapped. Education is one of those civil rights. The nature of the guaranteed educational programs are more fully defined in other legislation, such as P.L. 94–142. A detailed discussion of P.L. 94–142 follows. The reader should note how similar several major provisions of P.L. 93–112 and P.L. 94–142 are, even though the former is a civil rights law and the latter is an education law.

The Education for All Handicapped Children Act of 1975 (P.L. 94–142)

While numerous other laws relating to education of the handicapped have been adopted, the one of greatest importance to handicapped children, to their parents, and to school personnel is P.L. 94–142. It is of such significance that it is often referred to as "The Bill of Rights for the Handicapped." It incorporates many of the concepts and provisions of previous legislation and provides a long-term vehicle for educational programs and for monitoring states and LEAs for compliance with the law. The need for sweeping legislation at the federal level is explained by the findings of Congress (Section 601 (b)). The Congress finds that:

1. there are more than eight million handicapped children in the United States today;
2. the special education needs of such children are not being met;
3. more than half of the handicapped children in the United States do not receive appropriate educational services which would enable them to have full equality of opportunity;
4. one million of the handicapped children in the United States are excluded entirely from the public school system and will not go through the educational process with their peers;
5. there are many handicapped children throughout the United States participating in regular school programs whose handicaps prevent them from having a successful educational experience because their handicaps are undetected;
6. because of the lack of adequate services within the public school system, families are often forced to find services outside the public school system, often at great distance from their residence and at their own expense;
7. developments in the training of teachers and in diagnostic and instructional procedures and methods have advanced to the point that, given appropriate funding, state and local educational agencies can and will provide effective special education and related services to meet the needs of handicapped children;
8. State and local education agencies have a responsibility to provide education for all handicapped children, but present financial resources are inadequate to meet the special educational needs of handicapped children; and
9. it is in the national interest that the Federal Government assist State and local efforts to provide programs to meet the educational needs of handicapped children in order to assure equal protection of the law.

Congress declared its intent in Section 601(c) and set the tone for vast changes in public school programs to provide full educational services to the handicapped:

It is the purpose of this act to assure that all handicapped children have available to them within the time periods specified—, a free appropriate public education which emphasizes special education and related services designed to meet their unique needs, to assure that the rights of handicapped children and their parents or guardians are protected, to assist States and localities to provide for the education of all handicapped children, and to assess and assure the effectiveness of efforts to educate handicapped children.

A careful review of P.L. 94–142 and the implementing regulations (45 C.F.R. § 121a.1 et seq., published in the *Federal Register*, August 23, 1977) indicates at least ten major topics that are significant to the practicing school administrator. These topics and their implications are presented below:

MAJOR PROVISION 1: CONGRESSIONAL INTENT   It is the intent of congress that a free and appropriate education and related services be provided to *all* handicapped children.

Focal Points:

Some children have been excluded from school; some have their needs only partially met; many have not received appropriate educational services.

Parents were often left to find and pay for all needed services for their children.

Implications for Educational Administrators:

As of September 1, 1980, all handicapped individuals ages three to twenty-one (unless the preschool age is in conflict with existing state law and practice), regardless of the nature of severity of handicap, must be provided an appropriate educational program.

Related services such as transportation, speech pathology, and psychological services must be provided.

Priorities for implementation are first the unserved, and second the inappropriately served.

The programs are to be provided at no cost to parents (these costs may be major problems for local school budgets).

Districts (LEAs) must "seek out" the handicapped and provide the needed assessments and educational programs.

MAJOR PROVISION 2: ENTITLEMENTS AND ALLOCATIONS   Section 611 authorizes grants to states to assist in providing the mandated programs. LEAs may also apply for preschool incentive grants, grants for the removal of architectural barriers, and grants for educational media.

Focal Points:

The authorization for funds (not necessarily the appropriation) increases from 5 percent of the average per pupil expenditure (1978) to 40 percent by 1982.

Twenty-five percent of the appropriation may be retained by the state education agency to carry out its mandate; the remaining 75 percent must "flow through" to the LEAs.

Incentive grants may be available to states who are in compliance with other provisions and who provide preschool-age (three to five) programs. States or LEAs may apply for funds to remove barriers as provided in P.L. 90–480.

Funds are authorized to operate media and materials centers to facilitate the use of new educational technology.

Implications for Educational Administrators:

If appropriations reach the level of authorization, this would be a significant increase in available money for special programs. History, however, would indicate that appropriations will be much lower than authorizations and that the fiscal problems of implementation will fall mostly to states and to local education agencies.

With the funds received by state education agencies (SEAs), they can be expected to provide greater technical assistance.

Preschool incentive grants (if adequately funded) can be very helpful where state and local funds have been difficult to obtain. However, they must be thought of as "seed money."

Removal of architectural barriers must be a long-term project where there are existing buildings. Federal grants will be helpful, but properly locating programs must be used as a short-term solution.

MAJOR PROVISION 3: STATE PLANS AND LOCAL APPLICATIONS
To qualify for federal assistance, each state must develop and submit to the commissioner of education a plan for the education of handicapped children of the state. The plan must be updated annually. LEAs that want to receive funding must submit an application to the state education agency.

Focal Points:

Eligibility for funding is dependent upon a plan that implements the provisions of the law and upon demonstrated compliance with the law. It must include the following (a partial listing):

A policy assuring a free appropriate public education for all handicapped children.

Procedures for establishing procedural safeguards and due process.

Procedures for nondiscriminatory testing.

Programs emphasizing least restrictive environment.

An individualized education program (IEP) for every handicapped child.

A comprehensive plan for personal development.

Local applications must include assurances of compliance and appropriate procedures at the local level to implement the provisions of the state plan.

Implications for Educational Administrators:

Each item in the law and in the state plan is passed on to LEAs as a compliance item.

State eligibility is dependent on compliance by all LEAs. As such, LEAs will be monitored for compliance.

The compliance items are numerous and complex. The requirements of the federal law and of the state plans have greatly increased the workload of local administrators. Child counts, recordkeeping, correspondence with parents, due process panels, etc., all add to the administrative load.

MAJOR PROVISION 4: PROCEDURAL SAFEGUARDS (RIGHTS OF STUDENTS AND THEIR PARENTS) AND DUE PROCESS PROCEDURES   Section 615 requires that states and LEAs provide procedural safeguards and due process procedures for students and their parents or guardians.

Focal Points:

Certain rights are guaranteed. Included are:

The right to examine all relevant student records.

The right to confidentiality of records and procedures.

A surrogate to act in place of the parent or guardian when necessary.

No assessment or change of placement without informed parental consent (information must be in the parent's native language, if possible).

The opportunity to give input and to assist in developing the IEP.

The right to challenge a decision by school personnel and to have an impartial panel or hearing officer decide issues that are unresolved.

The right to present information to a due process panel or officer or to have information presented by someone representing the parent.

The right to appeal the decision of a due process panel or officer.

The right to an outside assessment.

The right to private school placement—at no cost to the parent—if the LEA does not provide an appropriate program.

Implications for Educational Administrators:

Providing the procedural safeguards and due process procedures can be very time consuming. Good management procedures are needed to meet this requirement and to prevent unnecessary differences with parents.

The LEA has a responsibility to help parents become informed and to involve them in the educational process.

Properly developed procedures will help avoid adversary relationships and unnecessary hearings.

When requested by parents, due process hearings must be convened. The law does not give parents a choice between public and private schools, but does provide for private school placement when the LEA does not or cannot provide an appropriate educational program. The LEA must decide how the appropriate programs are to be provided.

MAJOR PROVISION 5: LEAST RESTRICTIVE ENVIRONMENT To the maximum extent appropriate, handicapped children must be educated with children who are not handicapped. Removal of handicapped children from the regular educational environment may occur only when the handicap is such that education in regular classes cannot be satisfactorily achieved.

Focal Points:

The intent is to prevent unnecessary categorization, labeling, and segregation of handicapped students.

Children should be assigned to programs on the basis of individual need rather than on the basis of a category.

A major part of the responsibility for education of the mildly handicapped remains with the regular educator.

The requirements for the least restrictive environment *do:*
1. Make necessary a full range of educational alternatives;
2. Prevent the "dumping" of children with behavior problems into special education programs; and
3. Indicate the need for special education training for regular education personnel.

The requirements *do not:*
1. Alleviate the need for special education programs or special class placement for some children.
2. Mandate regular class placement for everyone.
3. Make regular and special education programs an either/or situation.

Implications for Educational Administrators:

LEAs must provide for the availability of a full continuum of programs and related services.

No child may be placed without having been properly assessed. The nature and degree of the handicap are the critical factors.

If this practice is to be effective, children, parents, and regular education personnel must be properly oriented and prepared. The school principal is the primary implementer.

The terms "least restrictive environment" and "mainstreaming" are *not* synonymous. Not every child can be mainstreamed, but each one can be served in the least restrictive environment.

MAJOR PROVISION 6: PUPIL ASSESSMENT/EVALUATION The states must establish (and the LEAs must utilize) evaluation and assessment procedures and materials that are not racially or culturally discriminatory. No single procedure shall be the sole criterion for determining the appropriate educational program for the child.

Focal Points:

All handicapped children must be identified, located, and evaluated.

A method must be developed to determine which children are receiving the needed special education and related services.

Prior notice must be given and written parental permission received before there can be an assessment or a change of program.

Parents have the right to an independent evaluation. In some instances this is at public expense.

Assessment must be conducted in the child's native language, if appropriate.

Implications for Educational Administrators:

The LEAs must be involved in a program to find or "seek out" all handicapped individuals who need special education services.

Procedures for appropriate notice to parents must be developed.

The notice to parents must contain certain prescribed content.

Testing must be carefully conducted so as not to involve cultural or language discrimination.

Testing personnel who are fluent in languages other than English will be needed in many geographic areas where another language is the native language of many children.

MAJOR PROVISION 7: THE INDIVIDUALIZED EDUCATION PROGRAM Each local education agency shall develop, implement, maintain records of, and periodically review and revise an individualized education program for every handicapped child.

Focal Points:

An IEP is required for every student.

The IEP is a *written* document that includes (1) a statement of the present levels of performance, (2) annual goals and short-term objectives, (3) specific services to be provided and the extent of integration in regular programs, (4) dates for the initiation of services, and (5) criteria and evaluation procedures.

The IEP must be developed by a team of people, including the parent.

The IEP must be reviewed at least annually to determine its success.

Implications for Educational Administrators:

Parents must be involved in the educational process to an extent seldom seen prior to this law.

School personnel must develop skills in writing and implementing IEPs.

Curriculum and teaching procedures must be modified to meet this new requirement.

There is *not* an accountability factor to ensure student progress, but LEAs are accountable for developing, implementing, and evaluating the IEP of every handicapped student.

MAJOR PROVISION 8: COMPREHENSIVE SYSTEM OF PERSONNEL DEVELOPMENT   Each annual program submitted by the states must include a description of programs and procedures for the development and implementation of a comprehensive system of personnel development. Each application by a local education agency must include procedures for the implementation and use of the comprehensive system of personnel development established by the state education agency.

Focal Points:

All personnel necessary to carry out the purposes of the Act must be properly trained.

In-service training of general and special education instructional staff is required.

In-service training of support staff and those providing related services is required.

The plan must include procedures for disseminating information about handicapped children and about promising educational materials and procedures.

Implications for Educational Administrators:

Most general education teachers and administrators have had little or no training in working with handicapped children. Providing training (even at the awareness level) to this large number of professionals is a monumental task.

One of the greatest in-service needs involves attitudes. Attitude change is much more difficult to accomplish than the giving of information.

In-service education programs can be very expensive. LEAs usually have little or no budget for this purpose.

Freeing teachers from teaching responsibilities so that they can participate in in-service training experiences is difficult.

In-service programs for special education can measurably benefit the general instructional program.

MAJOR PROVISION 9: COOPERATION WITH OTHER AGENCIES   To fully implement programs that are in keeping with congressional intent that all handicapped children have a free appropriate education and related services, it is necessary for state education agencies and local education agencies to cooperate fully with one another and with numerous other public and private agencies (e.g., private schools, rehabilitative service agencies, and health agencies).

Focal Points:

Handicapped children may be placed in private schools for their educational program, but responsibility for the education of that child remains with the LEA.

Providing many of the required related services (e.g., audiological testing, medical services, occupational therapy) requires close cooperation and (usually) formal contractual agreements.

Frequently, LEAs do not have an adequate population base to provide all of the necessary school programs. They must develop cooperative agreements with other districts or intermediate agencies.

Many other agencies, such as departments of vocational rehabilitation, have, provided services to the handicapped for many years. This Act now requires greater coordination of services.

Implications for Educational Administrators:

More resources are now available for carrying out the mandate to educate all handicapped children.

Private schools can often provide services that LEAs are unable to provide. LEAs elect to utilize these services. However, parents and school personnel sometimes disagree on the need for private school placement. Procedures must be worked out to resolve these differences.

School administrators have a greater need to be well informed about services available from other agencies.

Procedures for cooperative agreements must be developed in advance of need. Sometimes the process takes considerable time.

MAJOR PROVISION 10: WORKING WITH PARENTS   Parents of handicapped children must be involved in approving assessment procedures and in determining how and where the child will be educated. They have the right of dissent, and due process procedures must be available in the event the parent(s) feels that the child is not being appropriately educated.

Focal Points:

Parents must be notified and have the opportunity to give informed consent regarding assessment.

Parents must be notified of a planned change in their child's educational placement.

Parents must have access to all relevant school records.

Parents have the right to an independent assessment of their child.

Parents may request an *impartial due process hearing* to resolve differences with the LEA.

Parents (or the LEA) may appeal the findings of the local due process hearing to the state education agency and even to the federal courts if they feel a need to do so.

Implications for Education Administrators:

The provisions of this Act have increased parental participation with the schools in a very positive way.

Parents feel more involved in the educational process and many become more involved in teaching their children.

Parents have become much more aggressive in seeking their rights.

Administrators are spending increasing amounts of time in dealing with parents' requests or demands. Fair hearing procedures are extremely time consuming.

COMPLIANCE WITH PROVISIONS OF THE LAW   Both P.L. 93–112 and P.L. 94–142 may be described as compliance laws. In essence, they describe many provisions (as discussed above) and then prescribe the ways in which the states and LEAs will be monitored for compliance. They also provide penalties for noncompliance (possible loss of all federal funds) and ways in which compliance can be forced (orders from state agencies or from the courts). The Office of Special Education is responsible for monitoring compliance of the state education agencies (SEAs), and the SEAs are responsible for providing educational services. In preparation for this type of review, administrators should conduct regular self-studies to determine their status. In conducting a self-study, LEAs can utilize checklists such as those proposed in Chapter 1 of this book and should also check with their SEA regarding guidelines for compliance reviews, such as the sample compliance checklist found in Appendix 1.

HOW IS IT WORKING?   One of the provisions of P.L. 94–142 is that there be an annual progress report to Congress. The report of the Department of Health, Education, and Welfare (1979) included the following information:

- Special and regular education personnel and parents have devoted more time to identifying children's needs, developing individualized education programs, and determining optimal placements.
- About 3.8 million handicapped children were served during the 1977–78 year (the first year of implementation) under P.L. 94–142 and related legislation. That was about 7.4 percent of the nation's school-aged (five to eighteen) children and represents an increase of some 55,000 children from the previous year.
- There is a requirement in the Act regarding placement in the least restrictive environment. The predominant placement for handicapped pupils was the regular classroom, with auxiliary services provided.
- There is still a need to develop more options for the placement of children and to alert school staffs about the options.
- There is increasing support for in-service education and an anticipated need for 85,000 new special education teachers over the next two years.
- State activities have been enormous, but there are problems with establishing adequate monitoring procedures and needed cooperative agreements.
- There has been an increase in funding from $315 million to $804 million, and the allocation formula provides greater flexibility for local agencies.
- Given that the Act has been in effect for a very short period of time, a great deal of activity has occurred.

Gifted and Talented Children's Act of 1978

The Gifted and Talented Children's Act provides financial assistance rather than being a compliance act. Through the adoption of H.R. Res. 15 in October 1978, the 95th Congress declared its intent:

It is the purpose of this part to provide financial assistance to state and local education agencies, institutions of higher education, and other public and private agencies and organizations, to plan, develop, operate, and improve programs designed to meet the special educational needs of gifted and talented children. [Section 901(c)]

This Act provides funds for grants to states, but they may be used solely to plan, develop, operate, and improve programs and projects that:

- are designed to identify the educational needs of gifted and talented children;
- are of sufficient size, scope, and quality to hold reasonable promise of making substantial progress toward meeting such needs;
- give appropriate consideration to the particular educational needs of disadvantaged gifted and talented children.

Programs funded under state grants may include in-service training of personnel to teach such children.

In addition to the state grant program, the Commissioner of Education has discretionary funds for in-service education projects, model projects for identification and education, a dissemination clearinghouse, statewide planning, and research and demonstration.

While appropriations for this Act have so far been comparatively small, a precedent has been established for using federal funds for programs for the gifted and talented. Administrators should study the ways in which their agency can obtain and utilize these funds to educate the gifted and talented.

STATE LAWS AND REGULATIONS [3]

As was indicated in Tables 4–1 and 4–2, the basic responsibility for the education of children rests with the state. To provide the means for meeting this responsibility, states have at least two levels within their legal framework. Laws passed by the state legislature form the framework's first level. These laws are often referred to as "the education code." They tend to be general in nature but cover the total program of education for children. They can be repealed or modified only by the legislature. The framework's second level consists of administrative regulations that provide the details for more general laws. These regulations are adopted by the state board of education, the state department of education, and/or the state's chief education officer.

In addition to the laws and regulations described above, each state develops an annual program plan as required by P.L. 94–142. This plan does not make new policy for the state, but explains the framework of state laws and regulations and reports the state's and its LEAs' activities and planned activities with regard to federal compliance.

A review of education codes from different states shows many similarities and a few differences that are of interest to school administrators. In some states, the provisions of the law are detailed and voluminous and all activities that LEAs may or must engage in are prescribed. This approach says, "If it's not in the code, you can't do it." Education codes from other states tend to be very brief by comparison. They provide direction and standards, but do not prescribe every detail on how the code's requirements are to be met.

In the era prior to P.L. 94–142, different states' laws and regulations varied considerably. These laws have become more similar as they have been revised to come into compliance with federal requirements. Topics that are generally found in state codes and regulations are discussed below. References to other chapters and brief examples from several state codes are provided to help the reader understand the nature of state legal frameworks.

LEGISLATIVE INTENT   The following example is from the Missouri Department of Education (1975, foreword):

> The 77th General Assembly, First Regular Session, by enactment of House Bill 474 has declared it to be the policy of the State of Missouri to provide to all handicapped and severely handicapped students special services sufficient to meet their needs and maximize their educational capabilities. The needs of such students for early recognition, diagnosis and intensive educational services leading to more successful participation in home, employment, and community life are recognized.

DEFINITION OF TERMS   This section defines the major terms used in each document.

FINANCIAL PROVISIONS   These sections explain how the state and the LEAs obtain tax money, how these funds are allocated to the different special education programs, and how LEAs may utilize the funds. (See Chapter 15.)

Description of the Categorical (or Noncategorical) System under Which Exceptional Children Are Served. The following example is from Florida Department of Education (1979, § 6A–6.301). Note that these sections describe ten categorical programs.

ELIGIBLE EXCEPTIONAL STUDENTS

An exceptional student shall mean any child or youth enrolled in or eligible for enrollment in the public schools of a district who requires special instruction or special education services to take full advantage of or respond to educational programs and opportunities because of a physical, mental, emotional, social or learning exceptionality as defined in rule 6A–6.3011 through 6A–6.3020, FAC.

DEFINITION OF VARIOUS FRAMEWORKS OR MODELS THAT SCHOOLS MAY USE TO PROVIDE SERVICES   Examples are given in Chapter 7.

CHILD WELFARE AND ATTENDANCE   The following example is from the New York State Education Department (1978, § 200.12):

The board of education or trustees of each school district shall locate and identify all handicapped children from birth to 21 years of age who reside in the district. A register of such children shall be maintained and revised annually by the district committee on the handicapped. Procedures shall be implemented to assure the availability of statistical data to readily determine the status of each handicapped child in the identification, location, evaluation, placement and program review process. Data shall be reported by September 15 to the committee on the handicapped.

RESPONSIBILITIES OF THE STATE EDUCATION AGENCY   This section explains what the SEA will do to meet the requirements of federal and state laws.

RESPONSIBILITIES OF THE LOCAL EDUCATION AGENCY   See Chapter 7.

CERTIFICATION REQUIREMENTS   The following example is from the California State Board of Education (1979, § 3113):

SPECIAL CLASSES AND CENTERS

A special class or center shall meet these standards:
   (a) A special class teacher shall: (1) Hold a special education teaching credential or an appropriate specialist credential. Teachers of classes for pregnant individuals and drug-dependent individuals need hold only a teaching credential for elementary or secondary grades, as appropriate, AND (2) Possess the necessary competencies to teach the individuals assigned to that class, as verified annually by the superintendent of the local education agency and approved by the local board of education.

ASSESSMENT AND PLACEMENT PROCEDURES   See Chapter 11.

COURSES OF STUDY   See Chapter 14.

FACILITIES, TRANSPORTATION, AND OTHER RELATED SERVICES   The following example is from the Texas Education Agency (1973 § 2.10):

Each school district operating an approved special education program shall be allotted a transportation allowance for transporting children in special programs who are unable to attend the special education program in the public school unless such transportation is provided.

PARENTAL RIGHTS, PROCEDURAL SAFEGUARDS, AND DUE PROCESS PROCEDURES   The following example is from the Illinois State Board of Education (1979, Article X, 10.01):

After informal procedures consistent with these rules and regulations have been exhausted, and there remain differences between the local school district and the parents or other persons having primary care and custody of the child, or the child, an impartial due process hearing may be requested.

The above material provides only a few examples of the types of information found in state codes and regulations. School administrators must realize that these documents provide the authorizations, the resources, and the guidelines for the operation of all school programs. It is essential that they become acquainted with the provisions on education of exceptional children that apply to their particular state.

LOCAL POLICIES AND REGULATIONS

If laws and regulations at the federal and state levels could be described as serving the purpose of policy making and enabling, then policies and procedures at the local level might be thought of as implementing the total legal framework. While some school districts proceed on an informal basis without written procedures (depending mostly on the state codes for direction), many others develop extensive rules for use at the local level. These local rules can serve several purposes. They can (1) summarize what must be done to comply with federal and state laws, (2) formalize how to achieve compliance, and (3) be used as a source of information for school board members, administrators, teachers, and parents.

Local rules follow many different formats, but can often be described as follows:

- Board Policies: philosophy and general rules adopted by the local board of education to govern actions of the board and of the board's employees.
- Administrative Regulations: rules adopted by the superintendent and his/her staff to provide details on how to implement board policies.
- Procedural Guides: handbooks mostly used by principals and teachers at the individual school sites, such as "A Teacher's Handbook for the Development of IEPs," or "A Guide for School Personnel: Referring Students to Special Programs."

To assist the reader in understanding the nature of local policies and regulations, some examples of local materials are provided in Appendix 2.

LEGAL OPINIONS AND COURT DECISIONS

While the process of making laws is traditionally seen as the responsibility of the legislative branch of government, legal opinions by state attorney generals and by county counsels also serve to change the policies and actions of the various education agencies. This is accomplished through the process of reviewing and interpreting the law and administrative policies for the education agencies. De Young (1976) indicates that an attorney general's opinion is legally binding on the commissioner of education in only one state; in three states immunity is provided for those who follow the opinion. However, in most states these legal opinions are highly respected and usually followed. This is another way in which the educational rights of the handicapped have been enhanced.

Turnbull and Turnbull (1978) discuss case law and label the courts as "lawmakers" through the case law process. They say, "It is their unique function to say what the Constitution or a federal statute or regulation means in a given case, to issue a decision setting forth the facts that underlie their interpretation, and to enter an order commanding the parties in the case . . . to take certain action." (1978, p. 11)

Even though educational opportunities have been provided for many individuals since the beginning of our nation's history, these opportunities have not always been available to all who desire them. And even though compulsory education laws have been in effect in most states for decades, local districts did not apply these laws to handicapped children. Many did not even provide the opportunity for these children to attend school. Laws and practices in the various states have changed gradually over the past thirty to forty years, but have fully developed only in very recent times. Martin (1979) points out that federal statutes on the handicapped child's right to education began to be written about a decade ago because many handicapped children continued to be excluded from school. Two reasons are cited for this exclusion: "The first was that the persons being injured were not recognized as having rights that they could complain about. The second was a rigid definition of education." (Martin 1979, p. 11) These reasons have become the focus of numerous court cases.

The U.S. Constitution makes no direct reference to public education or education of exceptional individuals. Yet it has been the basis of many "right to education" laws and court decisions. These laws and decisions usually relate to the Fifth and Fourteenth Amendments, which guarantee due process of law and equal protection under the law. In terms of educational opportunities, the best known of all court decisions regarding due process and equal protection was the 1954 case *Brown v. Board of Education*. This was a civil rights case regarding black students rather than a case regarding handicapped students, but it caused a fundamental change in legislation and it established certain principles that were later applied to cases regarding the rights of exceptional pupils.

Since the Brown decision, many cases have been brought to establish the concept of equal protection for the handicapped and to further the argument that any process that limits or denies educational opportunities violates the individual's constitutional rights to equal protection as guaranteed by the Fourteenth Amendment.

Abeson (1976) provides excerpts from four of the major court cases that have established equal protection rights for the handicapped (as *Brown v. Board of Education* did for racial minorities). They include:

- *Pennsylvania Association for Retarded Children v. Commonwealth of Pennsylvania*
- *Mills v. Board of Education of the District of Columbia*
- *Maryland Association for Retarded Children v. State of Maryland*
- *In the Interest of G. H., a Child.*

The above cases, as well as others that are less well known, have helped to firmly establish the principles that handicapped students have a right to an education and it is unconstitutional to deny that right, that public funds must provide for educational opportunities, and that handicapped individuals or their parents or guardians have legal redress in the courts if these rights are denied.

The courts have dealt with concepts other than equal protection or the right to education. Cases such as *Diana v. California State Board of Education* and *Larry P. v. Riles* dealt with discrimination in testing and in program standards. *Allen v. McDonough, Frederick L. v. Thomas,* and other court cases have dealt with the need to provide an education that is appropriate to a student's needs, while still other cases apply to transportation, free education, program access, zero reject, roles of parents in the educational process, and various civil rights issues.

The court cases have stimulated the adoption of federal and state laws that are aimed at bringing educational agencies into compliance. Because of time constraints, school administrators seldom read court decisions, but they do study their implications and find it necessary to read laws and regulations. Many of these laws and regulations are written in reaction to court decisions. Thus, when schools gear up to comply with the new laws, they are also preparing to comply with the decisions of the courts.

THE IMPARTIAL DUE PROCESS HEARING

The term "due process" has its roots in the Fourteenth Amendment to the Constitution. It states that: "... no state shall make or enforce any law which shall abridge the privileges or immunities of citizens of the United States; nor shall any state deprive any persons of life, liberty, or property without due process of law...." Krotin (1977) discusses the evolution of the application of the due process clause to special education. The court cases and new laws discussed in previous pages apply the constitutional provisions to specific school requirements. Whenever parents feel that they or their children are being denied due process rights, they can request a hearing in which a ruling is made regarding the alleged denial of rights and how the issue is to be resolved.

The impartial due process hearing is an entirely new concept for many school administrators. It has long been a "fact" that the school had authority to make certain kinds of decisions. Students and parents could protest and negotiate, but the responsible school official made the final decision and students and parents had little or no recourse. Schools have lost this autonomy in relation to certain types of decisions. P.L. 94–142, Section 615(b)(2), gives parents the right to have an impartial due process hearing to resolve differences with the schools. This parental right applies whenever the schools (1) propose to initiate or change the identification, evaluation, or educational placement of the child or the provision of a free appropriate public education, or (2) refuse to initiate or change the identification, evaluation, or educational placement of the child or the provision of a free appropriate public education to the child.

The right to an impartial due process hearing is being exercised by increasing numbers of parents when they feel that their children are not being appropriately served. This has significant implications for school administrators in terms of time commitments, costs, non–public school placements, purchase of related services, and a number of additional items. It is absolutely vital that administrators establish and maintain procedures for meeting the needs of children. In this way, they can negate the need for parents to assume an adversary role and the need for involvement in the hearing process. In the event that hearings become necessary, the local education agency should have an established set of procedures to rely on. While procedures may vary in different agencies, there are certain procedural safeguards that must be included. The parents have the right to:

- present evidence and call witnesses;
- be represented by person(s) of their choice;
- have an impartial panel or hearing officer;
- expect action within a reasonable time period;
- have the hearing at a time and place that is convenient and with notice well in advance;
- have access to all relevant records concerning the child;
- be provided with a translation of notices and proceedings as needed; and
- appeal to a higher level.

Since the LEA bears the responsibility of responding to requests for due process hearings and is often responsible for establishing the panel, there should be written local policies to serve as procedural guidelines. Examples of a local board policy and administrative regulations for this purpose may be found in Appendix 2.

COMPLIANCE REVIEW PROCEDURES

The information on the previous pages concerning the laws and court decisions at both state and federal levels indicates the "teeth" that have been included by jurists and legislators to ensure that handicapped individuals are provided with equal protection under the law and the right of due process. Each state agency is required to conduct compliance studies to make certain that the LEAs meet the provisions of the law. State education agencies usually have available a "checklist" or "list of review questions" that is used in program reviews of the LEAs. LEA administrators should obtain copies of this material to assist them in self-study and in preparing for the visit of compliance review teams. Examples of questions may be found in Appendix 1. Individual parents and formal parent organizations are very active in seeing that their children are appropriately served. School programs for handicapped students are no longer merely permissive. They are mandatory, as they should be.

These new requirements should be looked upon as an opportunity rather than a burden. They provide administrators with the resources needed to meet the needs of all children. That is what school is all about; it corresponds with the personal philosophy of most educators.

SUMMARY

Chapter 4 has presented an overview of the structure of laws, regulations, and court decisions that constitute the legal framework for education of individuals with exceptional needs. It compares the purpose of different levels of codes and the areas of legal priority.

Three major federal laws (and their accompanying regulations) are discussed. These laws and regulations are of primary importance in administration of school programs for the handicapped and the gifted. P.L. 94–142 is discussed in detail, with attention to ten major provisions of the law, the focal points within each major provision, and the implications for educational administrators.

State laws and regulations are the foundation of school programs. The material typically found in state laws and regulations is discussed, and examples from the codes of several states are included.

Local school board policies and administrative regulations define the "how to" requirements for implementation of programs. The structure of local policies and regulations is briefly discussed, and a suggested outline for local policies and regulations is presented. Examples of local policies and regulations may be found in Appendix 2.

The influence of official legal opinions and various court decisions is discussed, and specific information from landmark cases is included. The impartial due process hearing, a quasi-judicial approach to resolving differences between parents and the schools, is having a significant impact on school operations and on administrative decisions.

Finally, Chapter 4 discusses compliance issues and procedures. The laws, regulations, legal opinions, and court decisions of recent years have totally changed the compliance issues and procedures. Appropriate special education programs and services can no longer be seen as a gift from the schools. They are mandatory and they are the legal right of the student.

NOTES

1. A detailed analysis and review of the provisions of Section 504 and the accompanying federal regulations may be found in the pamphlet *The Rehabilitation Act: An Analysis of Section 504 Regulations and Its Implications for State and Local Education Agencies,* prepared by the National Association of State Directors of Special Education, Inc., 1201 16th Street, Suite 610E, Washington, D.C. 20036; and Pottinger and Company Consultants, 1730 Pennsylvania Avenue, N.W., Suite 900, Washington, D.C. 20006.
2. For a detailed discussion of the Regulations the reader is referred to: "Section 504 and the New Civil Rights Mandate," *Amicus,* September 1977, pp. 21–33.
3. Information concerning state laws and regulations for special education programs can usually be obtained from the special education division of an individual state's department of education.

REFERENCES

California State Board of Education. 1979. *Title 5, Administrative regulations, education.* Sacramento.

45 C.F.R. § 84.1–84.61, 121a.1–121a.745.

Department of Health, Education, and Welfare, Office of Education. 1979. *Progress towards a free appropriate public education: A report to congress on the implementation of Public Law 94–142: The Education for All Handicapped Children Act.* Washington, D.C.

DeYoung, H. 1976. Opinions of the attorney generals. In *Public policy and the education of exceptional children,* ed. F. J. Weintraub et al., pp. 230–39. Reston, Va.: The Council for Exceptional Children.

Education for All Handicapped Children Act of 1975, P.L. 94–142.

Florida Department of Education. 1979. *A resource manual for the development and evaluation of special programs for exceptional students,* vol. 1–B. Tallahassee.

Gifted and Talented Children's Act of 1978, House Resolution 15.

Illinois State Board of Education. 1979. *Rules and regulations to govern the administration and operation of special education.* Springfield.

Krotin, L. 1977. Due process in special education: Legal perspectives. In *Due process in special education: A legal analysis,* ed. L. Krotin and N. B. Eager. Cambridge: Research Institute for Educational Problems.

LaVor, M. L. 1976. Federal legislation for exceptional children: A history. In *Public policy and the education of exceptional children,* ed. F. J. Weintraub et al. pp. 96–112. Reston, Va. The Council for Exceptional Children.

Martin, R. 1979. *Educating handicapped children: The legal mandate.* Champaign, Ill.: Research Press Co.

Missouri Department of Education. 1975. Special education services: Regulations, standards, and procedural guidelines. (mimeograph). Jefferson City.

The National Association of State Directors of Special Education, Inc. 1977. *The rehabilitation act: An analysis of the section 504 and its implications for state and local agencies.* Washington, D.C.: Pottinger and Company Consultants.

New York State Education Department. 1978. *Amendment to the regulations of the commissioner of education.* Albany.

Texas Education Agency. 1973. *Administrative guide and handbook for special education.* Austin.

Turnbull, H. R., and Turnbull, A. 1978. *Free appropriate public education: Law and implementation.* Denver: Love Publishing Co.

———. 1977. Section 504 and the new civil rights mandates. *Amicus,* Sept.: 23–33. South Bend, Ind.: National Center for Law and the Handicapped, newsletter.

Vocational Rehabilitation Act of 1973, P.L. 93–112.

COURT CASES

Allen v. McDonough, No. 14,948 Super. Court (Mass., June 23, 1976).

Brown v. Board of Education, 347 U.S. 483 (1954).

Diana v. California State Board of Education, No. 70–37 RFP (N.D. Cal., 1970 and 1973).

Frederick L. v. Thomas, 408 F. Supp. 832 (E.D. Pa. 1976).

In the Interest of G. H. 218 N.W. 2d 441 (N.D. 1974).

Larry P. v. Riles, Preliminary injunction 343 F. Supp. 1306 (N.D. Cal. 1972). Permanent injunction 495 F. Supp. 926 (N.D. Cal. 1979).

Maryland Association for Retarded Children v. State of Maryland, Equity No. 100/182/77676 (Cir. Ct. Balt. April 9, 1974).

Mills v. Board of Education of the District of Columbia, 348 F. Supp. 866 (D.D.C. 1972).

Pennsylvania Association for Retarded Children v. Commonwealth of Pennsylvania, 334 F. Supp. 1257 (E.D. Pa. 1971).

ADDITIONAL SUGGESTED READINGS

Johnson, R. A., Gross, J. C., and Weatherman, R. F., eds. 1973. *Special education in court. Leadership series in special education,* vol. 2. Minneapolis: The University of Minnesota.

National Association of State Directors of Special Education. 1978. *Legal considerations in the education of the handicapped: An annotated bibliography for school administrators.* Washington, D.C.: February.

Riley, D. P., Nash, H. D., and Hunt, J. T. 1978. *National incentives in special edu-*

cation: A history of legislative and court action. Washington, D.C.: National Association of Directors of Special Education.

Weintraub, F. J., Abeson, A., Ballard, J., and LaVor, M. L. 1976. *Public policy and the education of exceptional children.* Reston, Va.: The Council for Exceptional Children. (Note: In addition to the articles cited above, this book contains numerous other articles and chapters that deal in detail with laws, regulations, policies, and court cases.)

5

Administrative Roles in the Local Education Agency

"When a board member or a superintendent is called upon to define the responsibility of the school district to serve all children equally and appropriately, does he/she include handicapped children, too?"

(Burrello and Sage 1979, p. 218)

INTRODUCTION

The persons who have responsibility for any given program must answer four basic questions if they are to have success in managing their stewardship. Stated very simply, these four questions are (1) What must be done? (2) Who will do it? (3) How and when will they do it? (4) What is our current status? In more sophisticated terminology, these concerns become functions, roles, procedures, and evaluation. If these items can be clearly delineated, the organization can be more efficiently managed and the answers to the four basic questions become available.

If the four questions are applied to special education programs, the answers, in extreme generalities, look like this:

1. *What must be done?*
   The district must provide a free appropriate public education for *all* children with exceptional needs.
2. *Who will do it?*
   All district personnel have some role to perform that relates to the education of children. The role that each has regarding education of these children shall be defined in the various job descriptions. For many employees, their responsibility for handicapped students is the same as it is for any other student.
3. *How and when will it be done?*
   It will be done in accordance with the law and the district's policies, will provide a range of alternatives, and will assure placement in the least restrictive environment. It will be done according to a pre-planned timeline.
4. *What is our current status?*
   Our current status is determined by our ongoing evaluation plan

which provides descriptive material about each special education program. (See Chapter 16.)

While each of the above highly general answers would appear to be obvious, such is not the case. For example, it is not uncommon to hear a school principal say, "The special education kids are not really my responsibility; that program belongs to the director of special programs." Or, a teacher might say, "I have in my room twenty-nine of *my own* children, and two *who are really special education students*." While the foregoing statements might previously have been appropriate, they do not coincide with the new philosophical and legal views on providing the least restrictive environment and equivalent opportunities for *all* students.

A review of the professional literature regarding roles, functions, and tasks does not provide the reader with a consensus on the topic. A much-quoted article by Newman (1970) gives seven major headings for administrative functions in special education: (1) planning, (2) organizing, (3) directing, (4) coordinating, (5) staffing, (6) budgeting, and (7) reporting. Within each of these functions are numerous administrative tasks, such as developing policies, placing classes at school sites, and directing in-service meetings.

Raske (1979) indicates that when it comes to directing special education programs, the duties of general administrators and special education administrators seem to be similar in nature. The major difference is the amount of time allocated to various tasks. In Raske's study, general administrators indicated that they allotted 14.6 percent of their time to special education. They identified fifteen administrative tasks that they perform. These tasks range from participation in IEP meetings to arranging transportation and in-service programs.

In *Profiles of the Administrative Team*, produced by the American Association of School Administrators (1971), the chapter titles identify another approach to categorizing roles. Categories include (1) general administration, (2) instruction, (3) business affairs, (4) personnel services, (5) pupil services, (6) school-community relations, and (7) human relations. Within each of these areas the authors discuss those individuals who have primary responsibility, the specific tasks involved, working with other professionals, etc.

This chapter emphasizes an operational approach, wherein the administration of an LEA says, "We know what needs to be done; now let's identify who has primary responsibility and who has a supportive assignment for the identified functions and tasks. Only then are we organized for planning, implementing, and maintaining programs."

While there is no generally accepted definition and differentiation of the terms "role, function, and task," they will be used in this chapter as follows:

- Role is a general term that defines an area of responsibility. For example, an individual functions in a leadership *role*.

- Functions are action-oriented responsibilities that relate to the more general role. For example, it is a *function* of the principal's leadership role to involve staff and students in the process of new program development. Functions are subsets of roles.
- Tasks are the operational, day-to-day actions that contribute to accomplishment of one's assigned functions. For example, it is an administrator's task to meet with the faculty to discuss implementation of a new special education class. Tasks are subsets of functions.

Our discussion of the board of education, superintendent, and central office staff will emphasize their respective roles and functions. A more detailed discussion, including tasks, is presented only for those at the operational level, such as the special education administrator and the building principal.

DEVELOPING POLICY AND COMMITMENT: WORKING WITH THE BOARD OF EDUCATION

A local school district's board of education is in essence like the board of directors of a corporation. The board has the legal responsibility to provide school programs for students within its prescribed boundaries. To do so, it must operate an extensive instructional program along with personnel services (employment, employee benefits, employee relations), a business division (budgeting, accounting, disbursement, purchasing), and maintaining extensive ties with the community. School board members come from all walks of life and have a wide range of personal school experiences. They have a variety of motivations for service, and their knowledge about school programs extends from near zero to 100 percent. Except in very large school systems, board members usually serve without pay and donate hundreds of hours per year to fulfill their responsibility.

Obviously, the philosophy of the local school board is a major factor in whether or not the district provides a high-quality special education program. The board establishes its own philosophy, directly or indirectly expresses the commitment of the district, and establishes general program policies. Administrators should pursue certain objectives that will help board members develop policies and provide programs.

- Be certain that individual board members are "educated" concerning the characteristics and needs of exceptional children.
- Give board members information on requirements of federal and state laws and regulations.
- Inform board members of parental support for special education programs.

- Assist the board in developing and implementing formal, written policies and regulations covering the operation of special education programs.
- Involve the board in the planning process rather than presenting a finished plan for their approval or rejection.
- Keep board members informed about programs—about things that are going well and also about problem areas.

If the above objectives are accomplished, board of education members can more effectively perform their roles. They will be able to commit the district to a positive plan of action, develop district policy, and provide the necessary resources for the program.

ACTION AT THE TOP: THE SUPERINTENDENT AND HIS/HER STAFF

> "Responsibilities of chief school executives have become so complex and extensive that a corps of top-level assistants, to provide a wide variety of specialized functions, is absolutely essential."
>
> (Conner 1971, p. 6)

The superintendent is usually secretary to the board of education and is the school district's chief executive officer. All communication between the school board and the district employees is transmitted through the superintendent or with his/her approval. Thus, the superintendent must be knowledgeable about special education legislation and the needs of children. Appropriate action at the top requires an active leadership role and includes the following functions:

- informing the board of education about district programs and program requirements;
- selecting administrator(s) who are qualified to give leadership to programs, and employing teachers and support personnel who can implement programs;
- developing administrative lines, rules, and procedures that will enhance the program;
- providing leadership through the activities of planning, implementing, maintaining, and managing programs; and
- demonstrating a commitment to programs that sets a positive tone for others to emulate.

In school districts that are large enough to have several persons on the administrative staff, there is usually a superintendent's cabinet, or a group by another name, that serves as the administrative policy making group. If special education programs are to function well within a district, there must be at least one person on the administrative cabinet who will serve as the program advocate and technical expert.

The superintendent's role should basically deal with planning and organizing of programs, working with the board of education and the public, and directing his/her staff of central office administrators and site administrators in their roles. One critical area of administration is strategic planning for the future. The superintendent should encourage others and participate in creative planning that will lead to continued improvement of programs.

The superintendent's cabinet usually includes associate and assistant superintendents as well as directors of divisions of instruction, business, and personnel. All these persons and their subordinates have specific functions that relate to special education programs. Table 5–1 lists examples of roles and functions in top-level administrative positions.

In the organizational structure outlined in Table 5–1, the assistant superintendent for special services is the technical expert for special education programs and should be the cabinet-level administrator who serves as the advocate for these programs. The individuals responsible for the day-to-day management of identification, placement, planning, and program maintenance (directors of special education, pupil personnel staff, and other middle management personnel) will be members of his/her staff. But while this administrative line may appear the most visible, special education programs will not function well unless there is planning, organization, and commitment in other administrative lines (such as instruction, business, and personnel). When good programs are in effect, one invariably finds a philosophically committed board of education and an informed, action-oriented group of individuals at the top level of administration.

PROGRAM LEADERSHIP: THE SPECIAL EDUCATION ADMINISTRATOR

The special education administrator may be called a director, coordinator, or supervisor. This is usually a middle management administrative position, but in a large system the administrator might be an assistant superintendent. This position may include both line and staff administrative responsibilities. For example, a special education administrator might be directly responsible for the speech therapy program and for a school in a hospital setting (line responsibilities), but also provide assistance and support services to the principal and special education teachers at a regular school site (staff responsibilities).

TABLE 5–1 SUPERINTENDENT'S STAFF AND EXAMPLES OF FUNCTIONS
REGARDING SPECIAL EDUCATION

Position	Administrative Functions Regarding Special Education Programs
Superintendent	• Has overall responsibility for program operation • Is responsible for compliance with federal and state laws • Develops local policies and regulations • Supplies the board of education with information • Provides leadership for all personnel by giving commitment to the programs • Acts as community liaison • Acts as advocate for special education programs • Establishes channels of communication and responsibility
Assistant Superintendent, Business Affairs	• Identifies all sources of income • Prepares the programmed budget for special education • Maintains budget control • Selects and develops appropriate sites for various programs • Purchases special education equipment and materials • Arranges special transportation • Conducts staff negotiations • Contracts for services from other agencies
Assistant Superintendent, Personnel	• Identifies training and certification needs for special education teachers and other personnel • Recruits qualified staff • Prevents the assignment of nonqualified staff • Handles employee benefits
Assistant Superintendent, Special Services	• Has line responsibility for directors of special education and pupil services • Plans and develops programs • Provides technical assistance in budget development • Provides technical assistance for instructional programs • Is the district's designated representative for due process hearings • Initiates procedures to "seek out" and identify all handicapped pupils • Assesses pupils • Provides parents with information • Assigns pupils to special programs • Conducts annual reviews and periodic reassessment of pupils • Has general responsibility for parent advisory committee

TABLE 5-1 *(Cont'd)*

Position	Administrative Functions Regarding Special Education Programs
Assistant Superintendent, Special Services	• Maintains pupils' central office records • Does all reporting • Provides in-service training programs for regular and special education personnel • Prepares for compliance reviews
Assistant Superintendent, Instruction	• Has line responsibility for principals and teachers • Is responsible for curriculum and materials development • Prepares IEPs • Implements alternative program models and least restrictive environment policies • Provides related services (e.g., physical therapy) • Establishes and maintains special education instructional programs

The school principal is directly responsible for programs at the school site.

The special education administrator should have an extensive background in his or her field in order to be prepared for the responsibilities inherent in this position. In medium-sized or larger school districts, the special education administrator devotes 100 percent of his/her time to this assignment. This administrator is the technical expert upon whom others depend for assistance. By combining personal experience and observation with information from studies and writings by Newman (1970), Raske (1979), Nevin (1979), Marro and Kohl (1972), and Burrelo and Sage (1979), we arrive at a definitive profile of the special education administrator that may best be described in terms of the following roles and functions.

Role No. 1: *Program Advocate*
- Provide information for top-level administration and the board of education
- Represent special education to others in the educational system
- Initiate program development activities
- Serve as liaison to communicate parents' requests

Role No. 2: *Compliance Monitoring*
- Provide services for all children
- Give procedural guarantees to children and parents
- Provide building site personnel with information on laws and regulations

· Give awareness training on compliance
· Maintain records and do reporting
· Prepare district personnel and all materials for monitoring by compliance review teams

Role No. 3: *Program Planning*
· Assess needs of individuals and of the system
· Develop plans for local use and to meet state and federal requirements
· Develop policies, regulations, and guidelines
· Present plans to those in policy making positions
· Involve appropriate individuals in the planning process
· Interpret the laws and planning for compliance
· Plan for adequate resources (budgeting)

Role No. 4: *Program Implementation (for the System and for Individual Pupils)*
· Select sites
· Schedule programs
· Establish lines of communication and responsibility
· Identify, assess, and place pupils
· Arrange support services (e.g., transportation, counseling)
· Develop IEPs

Role No. 5: *Program Operation or Maintenance*
· Coordinate the entire special education program
· Provide support services to site administrators and teachers
· Provide budget control
· Maintain pupil counts and other records
· Keep superiors and others informed
· Assist in staffing
· Review IEPs
· Reevaluate placement of each pupil periodically (at least every three years)
· Administer certain programs directly
· Monitor services from other agencies

Role No. 6: *Consulting*
· Research items and answer questions
· Provide technical knowledge regarding handicapping conditions and resultant pupil needs
· Assist principals
· Assist teachers
· Advise district personnel on preparation for due process hearings

Role No. 7: *Working with Parents*
· Provide information
· Ensure procedural safeguards and due process procedures

- Obtain parental permissions
- Counsel

Role No. 8: *Legislation*
- Provide information for other school personnel
- Translate legislative requirements into programs
- Suggest legislative changes to appropriate persons
- Advocate adoption of needed legislation

Role No. 9: *Personnel*
- Provide in-service education on special education techniques for general and special education personnel
- Work cooperatively with training institutions
- Describe personnel needs
- Assist in the selection process

In a lighter approach to the competencies required of the special education administrator, this writer has proposed ten tongue-in-cheek "Thou shalts."

1. Thou shalt be a whiz at program development so that a free and appropriate education and related services will be provided to all handicapped children.
2. Thou shalt be a financial wizard, develop budgets, apply for grants, find money to remove architectural barriers in fifty-year-old buildings, conduct preschool programs, fund private school placements, etc. *All of this thou must do* without angering the superintendent.
3. Thou shalt be a skilled writer so that the local application to the state will reflect a prosaic style of unparalleled quality. And consider not the reports to the local board to be of lesser importance.
4. Thou shalt provide procedural safeguards for all children and their parents. Likewise, thou shalt not deprive anyone of due process procedures. If thou happen to be an attorney, extra blessings thou may claim, for unless thou art cautious, hearings may consume all of thy time.
5. Thou shalt do thy thing in the least restrictive environment. However, there is no real requirement to drown in the mainstream; avoid the whirlpools of unnecessary segregation.
6. Thou shalt develop uncanny abilities to assess children and determine their problems and their abilities; furthermore, thou shalt determine, without error, the program that is most appropriate to their needs. If thou can use a crystal ball, feel free to do so.
7. Thou shalt be the CA (that's chief advocate) of the IEP. It shall be thy task to convince teachers that the IEP is the hope of the future; but at the same time convince parents that it is only a plan, not a magical solution to their child's problems.
8. Thou shalt not only be an expert in thy field, but shalt also teach

others about it; thou must do this within something called a "comprehensive system of personnel development."

9. Thou shalt cooperate fully with other agencies, including private schools, regional centers, health agencies, and departments of vocational rehabilitation. Whether they see thee as friend or foe, it is thy duty to be pleasant at all times and to avoid due process hearings if possible.

10. Thou shalt work with parents:

Inform them, whether or not they want to hear about it.

Get their permission—do it somehow, even if they won't talk to you.

Tell them how to bring charges against you even though you are doing your best for their child.

Also show them how to appeal, even though they have already lost their case.

And by the way, thou may also work with the other 98 percent of parents who are supportive, cooperative, and helpful.

The special education administrator, though usually expressing a desire to work more with teachers and children, devotes a majority of his/her time to "running the shop." When one is involved with budget preparation and control, ordering supplies, organizing admissions committees, responding to parents, reporting child counts and attendance, attending due process hearings, etc., very little time is left for curriculum development and working with teachers. In larger school systems the special education staff will include other personnel who can fill these roles. There may be some feeling that the tasks listed above are routine or unimportant, but such is not the case. If they are not done, there is no special education program; if they are done poorly, program quality will suffer greatly.

MANAGEMENT AND COORDINATION: THE CENTRAL OFFICE STAFF

The positions included in the central office staff vary greatly, depending on a number of factors such as district size, resources available, and the organizational philosophy of the superintendent and the school board. Small districts have few administrators in the central office, and each person has multiple job assignments. In medium-sized and large districts there are, of course, more staff members, and they tend to function in narrower or more specialized roles.

It is important that each central office administrator be informed about special education and recognize the responsibility that he/she has toward this part of the school program. Obviously, the extent of responsibility varies greatly with different administrative, consultive, or supervisory positions. The director of pupil personnel services has extensive contact with special education, while the consultant for reading programs may have only occasional contact. Table 5–2 gives examples of positions that entail major program responsibilities and those with only occasional program responsibilities.

In addition to those shown in Table 5–2, the special education programs will require services from the directors of elementary and secondary education and from the supervisors of vocational education, attendance and welfare, health services, and bilingual education. There are also some unique program needs that are met by the director of building and maintenance (ramps, bathroom facilities), the director of grounds (special playground equipment), and the director of purchasing (books, instructional equipment, wheelchairs). The expertise required for each of these central office positions does not change significantly when the positions are considered from the special education perspective. What is required is a general knowledge of special pupils' needs and an acceptance that special education programs do not "belong to" the direc-

TABLE 5–2 CENTRAL OFFICE STAFF AND EXAMPLES OF FUNCTIONS
REGARDING SPECIAL EDUCATION

Position	Administrative Functions Regarding Special Education Programs
Director of Pupil Personnel Services	• Establishes procedures for nondiscriminatory testing • Assigns personnel for psychological services • Is responsible for conducting evaluation and placement meetings • Informs parents about assessment procedures; obtaining consent • Provides guidelines for maintaining students' confidential records • Establishes procedures for compliance with the law
Director of Transportation	• Determines bus routes • Develops schedules • Provides special equipment as needed • Projects costs for purposes of budgeting and documents costs for state reimbursement
District Controller	• Provides information about income for special education • Projects all expenditure items • Assists in budget development • Is responsible for budget management and budget control
Supervisor of Reading Programs	• Consults with teachers and principals, as requested, regarding appropriate materials and teaching techniques

tor of special education. Every administrator has some responsibility to the program.

ASSISTANCE FROM SUPPORT STAFF

School programs were first designed to serve only those who were psychologically, behaviorally, and physically compatible with studying and learning academic subjects. In that situation, pupils received most of their instruction and other assistance from the teacher. But as school systems have become more complex, the curricula more varied, and as school programs became mandatory for children with all types of abilities and disabilities, the need for other types of staff members has grown. This need encompasses a range of services that extends from counseling children to reading to the blind. The administration of a school district is continuously pressured to provide more extended services; however, expense of those services is an inhibiting factor. The conflict between the needs of children and the extra costs involved in providing needed services has resulted in a definition of *mandated* services. The federal code, 45 C.F.R. § 121a.13(a) lists thirteen areas of defined related services: (1) audiological services, (2) speech pathology, (3) counseling, (4) medical services, (5) early identification, (6) occupational therapy, (7) parent counseling and training, (8) physical therapy, (9) psychological services, (10) recreation, (11) school health services, (12) social work services, and (13) transportation. These services are mandated if they are necessary for a handicapped child to benefit from special education. This list of services helps one to envision the assistance needed from a support staff and the skills required of staff members.

Depending on the size and resources of the district, one or more of the following may be available to provide supportive/related services to the special education programs:

- School nurse (some districts also have contracted services from an M.D.)
- Speech therapist
- Audiologist (only in large systems; others contract for services)
- School psychologist or counselor
- Occupational or physical therapist (often provided by one of the public health agencies)
- Social worker (this role is often included in the duties of the school nurse)
- Transportation personnel (including bus drivers)
- Braillist, reader for the blind, interpreter for the deaf

As special education has developed, administrators have come to realize the extent and importance of a cadre of people who can provide the various services that supplement and make possible the instructional program.

THE IMPLEMENTERS: PRINCIPALS AND OTHER SITE ADMINISTRATORS

> "Before the handicapped student can receive a more normalized educational program, the administrators of that local school must assume an advocacy role. . . . Administrators must learn that shared responsibility for children, in the final analysis, is related to training and skills of teachers, the attitudinal considerations of educators, and the determination of the most effective, appropriate individually based learning environments for particular children."
>
> (Mann and McClung 1976, pp. 127, 129)

The manner in which the school principal, other school site administrators, and regular classroom teachers relate to handicapped and gifted students has changed dramatically in recent years. This change is due to a philosophical change from a policy of separation to a policy of education in the least restrictive environment. This new viewpoint conceptually places special education personnel within the total system rather than in their own parallel school program. Burrelo and Sage (1979) go one step further and propose a model where special education is a supportive service for all children.

Even though there has been a change in models (emphasizing mainstreaming and deemphasizing rigid categorization), special education administrators and teachers have not "abandoned ship." They still provide special classes, resource rooms, support services, etc. But the mildly handicapped are now at least partially the responsibility of the regular classroom teacher, and local school administrators have direct responsibility for the day-to-day operation of most programs.

Numerous articles, chapters, and books have been written about the school principal's role (Kreps 1972, Heichberger 1975, National Association of Secondary School Principals 1970, Sandin 1974), but very little information can be found in the professional literature concerning the principal's role for special education. This area is wide open for research.

As a means of looking at the principal's role,[1] this author would like to propose six assumptions:

Principals:
1. Perceive the value inherent in special education programs. They provide services that are needed by certain pupils and are beneficial.
2. See special education as helping the regular program, since it relieves the regular classroom teacher of full responsibility for handicapped students.
3. Feel that principals should be in charge of any program placed in their building.
4. Feel somewhat inadequate in their knowledge of handicapping conditions, special curricula, and provisions of the special education laws.
5. Feel overwhelmed with the time commitments required for guidance committees, IEP meetings, notices to parents, annual reviews, record keeping, and reporting.
6. Have a genuine desire to implement and maintain quality special education programs in their building.
7. Must provide leadership to teachers and demonstrate a positive attitude concerning the feasibility and desirability of education in the least restrictive environment.

Keeping in mind the above assumptions, the roles, functions, and tasks that site administrators perform can be placed in the following framework.[2]

Role No. 1: The Principal as the Educational Leader and Program Advocate at the School

   Function 1.1: Create a Climate for Openness, Experimentation, and Change
      • Keep informed about special education programs at other schools and borrow good ideas
      • Encourage new curricular development and ideas
      • Encourage experimentation with new approaches to teaching
      • Assist teachers in implementation

   Function 1.2: Involve Students, Staff, and Community in the Educational Program
      • Encourage participation of teachers in appropriate community affairs
      • Involve teachers and parents in extracurricular activities such as program planning and development

         · Involve staff members and citizens in making
          decisions about the school

Function 1.3:   Plan for Renewal and Improvement of All Aspects of the Program
         · Assist in the development, implementation, and followup of educational goals and objectives
         · Plan and implement changes that are indicated by the various evaluation methods

Function 1.4:   Maintain a Program of Staff Development That Enhances Educational Quality
         · Attend special education meetings for personal growth and in-service education
         · Interview and select new teachers
         · Evaluate the performance of all special education personnel at the site (assisted by the special education administrator, as appropriate)
         · Provide in-service education programs for regular and special education personnel
         · Keep informed about current trends in special education

Function 1.5:   Evaluate School Programs and Initiate Changes That the Evaluation Data Suggests
         · Observe programs and record information; collect data when feasible
         · Utilize evaluative information to support the status quo or to suggest change

Role No. 2:   The Principal as the Organizer and Manager of the School's Special Education Program

Function 2.1:   Implement and Maintain the Instructional Program for Special Education Students
         · Initiate and/or review referrals for special education programs
         · Assist in the assessment process
         · Participate in IEP meetings
         · Participate in the annual review of students
         · Review with teachers special education curriculum requirements
         · Provide a disciplinary system that is supportive of the teachers
         · Facilitate mainstreaming
         · Arrange for instructionally related support services

Function 2.2:   Provide for Effective Utilization of Resources
- Involve teachers in budget planning
- Prepare the school's budget requests
- Monitor expenditures
- Review and approve purchase requests
- Assign regular teachers to assist in placing students in the least restrictive environment

Function 2.3:   Communicate to the Staff and Implement Laws, Policies, and Regulations That Govern the Programs
- Inform staff members about requirements of state and federal laws
- Enforce the provisions of the laws and regulations at the school site
- When appropriate, get involved in suggesting legislation or regulations

Function 2.4:   Establish and Maintain Procedures for Informing Parents, for Involving Them in Decisions Regarding Their Child, and for Assuring Procedural Safeguards and Due Process Procedures
- Prepare and utilize brochures and other materials to keep parents informed about programs
- Involve parents in assessment and educational planning decisions that affect their child, and encourage them to participate in IEP development, review, and modification
- Inform parents of their rights, of procedures to protect their rights, and of due process procedures
- Maintain procedures for obtaining informed parental consent for assessment and program assignment

Role No. 3:   *The Principal as the Organizer and Manager of Supportive Services and Administrative Trivia*

Function 3.1:   Maintain Procedures for Record Keeping, Reporting, and Providing Information
- Fill out special education forms
- Maintain written and verbal communication with central office staff
- Keep individual and program records that are in compliance with laws and regulations

                              • Maintain confidentiality of records as required by law
                              • Complete appropriate reports on time

Function 3.2: Maintain Physical Facilities That Are Appropriate to the Needs of the Program
                              • Identify rooms that allow access to programs
                              • Provide appropriate bathroom facilities for certain handicapping conditions
                              • See that rooms are properly equipped and supplied

No discussion of roles, functions, and tasks at the school site would be complete without recognizing the differences found at the elementary, middle, and secondary levels. A high percentage of elementary schools have only one site administrator—the principal. He/she deals with fewer pupils, but has no one to whom administrative tasks can be delegated. At middle schools and high schools, the administrative staff usually includes assistant principals and deans. Also, some of the organizational and management tasks can be delegated to counselors. But whatever the size of the administrative team at the school site, the principal sets the tone for the special education program. The principal must be an advocate and take the lead in establishing programs and gaining support from teachers and nonhandicapped students. That role cannot be delegated.

SUMMARY

Chapter 5 discusses the roles, functions, and tasks associated with the initiation, maintenance, and improvement of special education programs. A major point of emphasis is the shared responsibility that all persons in leadership positions have for these programs.

The role of the board of education is discussed. The board establishes the philosophy, local policies, and procedures that will govern special education programs in the school district. Several objectives are proposed through which the administrative staff can help board of education members become fully informed about program needs.

The superintendent's leadership and directive roles, as well as those of his/her staff, are discussed, with emphasis placed on planning and organizing programs, working with the board of education, and providing direction for the central office staff and building administrators.

Program leadership and technical expertise and assistance are presented as the responsibility of the administrator of special education programs. Nine distinctive roles (ranging from program advocate to legislative expert) are discussed, and functions within each role are identified. The person in this administrative position usually has both line and staff responsibilities, has the overall major responsibility for ensuring that the district is in compliance with the laws, and must maintain a quality program.

Only a few of the other central office administrative positions are discussed in this chapter, and examples of their functions are provided in Table 5–2. While these functions are often included with the regular duties of these administrators, there are also different or extra responsibilities related to special education programs. The importance of the support services provided by these staff members is emphasized.

A large range of support staff personnel (school nurse, speech therapist, psychologists, counselors) provide services to special education pupils. While these persons are technically classified as "service personnel" rather than administrators, their inclusion in this discussion seems appropriate. They, along with teachers, often implement the items for which administrators have responsibility.

A discussion of the roles, functions, and tasks of the principal and other site administrators comprises this chapter's final section. Greater detail is provided for this administrative position than for other positions. Those who implement programs always play a key role in program success. Responsibilities at the school site have dramatically increased with many new compliance laws and with the emphasis placed on mainstreaming. This writer lists "program advocate and leader" as the number one role of the school principal. Proper fulfillment of this role is crucial to the implementation and maintenance of good special education programs at regular school sites and to the success of handicapped and gifted students in those programs.

NOTES

1. This discussion includes assistant principals and other site administrators to whom the principal can delegate functions and tasks.
2. The roles, functions, and tasks listed represent a modification and combination of items listed by Kreps et al. (1972), Newman (1970), Nevin (1979), Raske (1979), and Rouman (1980).

REFERENCES

American Association of School Administrators. 1971. *Profiles of the administrative team.* Washington, D.C.

Burrello, L. C., and Sage, D. D. 1979. *Leadership and change in special education.* Englewood Cliffs, N.J.: Prentice-Hall, Inc.

Conner, F. E. 1971. Foreword. In *Profiles of the administrative team,* ed. American Association of School Administrators, Washington, D.C.

Heichberger, R. L. 1975. Creating the climate for humanistic change in the elementary school with the principal as change agent. *Education* 96:106–12.

Kreps, D., and the Association of California School Administrators Standing Committee on Secondary Administration. 1972. The role of the on-site school administrator. *ACSA Special Report,* June 5, 1, 8.

Mann, P. H., and McClung, R. M. 1976. Training administrators for shared responsibility roles. In *Shared responsibility for handicapped students: Advocacy and programming,* ed. P. H. Mann, pp. 125–35. Coral Gables, Fla.: University of Miami Training and Technical Assistance Center.

Marro, T. D., and Kohl, J. W. 1972. Normative study of the administrative position in special education. *Exceptional Children,* September, 5–13.

National Association of Secondary School Principals. 1970. *The principalship.* Washington, D.C.

Newman, K. S. 1970. Administrative tasks in special education. *Exceptional Children,* March, 521–24.

Nevin, A. 1979. Special education administration competencies of the general administrator. *Exceptional Children,* February, 45:363–65.

Raske, D. E. 1979. The role of general school administrators responsible for special education programs. *Exceptional Children* 45, 8:645–46.

Rouman, J. 1980. A study of principals' perceptions of their roles between regular and special education in school buildings where learning handicapped children are mainstreamed. Doctoral dissertation, University of Northern Colorado, in process.

Sandin, Adolph A. 1974. Conceptualizing the elementary principal's job. *The Oregon Elementary Principal,* Spring, 13–14.

ADDITIONAL SUGGESTED READINGS

Birch, J. W., and Johnstone, B. K. 1975. *Designing schools and schooling for the handicapped.* Springfield, Ill.: Charles C Thomas, Publisher.

Gearheart, B. R. 1967. *Administration of special education.* Springfield, Ill.: Charles C Thomas, Publisher.

Rasmussen, G. R., et al. 1972. Competence in educational administration. *Thrust for Educational Leadership.* 1,4:23–24.

Relic, P. D., and Griffin, P. J. 1979. Clearing the air on school administrator training. *American Education,* May, 15:6–10.

Reynolds, M. C. 1973. Critical issues in special education leadership. In *Leadership series in education,* vols. 1 and 2, ed. R. A. Johnson et al., pp. 23–33. Minneapolis: University of Minnesota.

Shanks, R. E. 1972. Making the role of the building principal more effective. *Thrust for Educational Leadership* 1980. 1,2:42.

Stile, S. W., and Pettibone, T. J. 1980. Training and certification of administrators of special education. *Exceptional Children* 46, 7:530–33.

Voelker, P. H. 1975. Organization, administration and supervision of special education programs. In *Education of Exceptional Children and Youth,* ed. W. M. Cruickshank and G. O. Johnson, pp. 659–91. Englewood Cliffs, N.J.: Prentice-Hall, Inc.

Wey, H. W. 1966. *Handbook for principals.* New York: Schaum Publishing Co.

Working with Other Agencies and Groups

"It is time for equal opportunity for all handicapped persons in all aspects of . . . society, everyone must assume a role and responsibility in order to ensure these opportunities, present resources— including information—must be used in better ways, and it is only through cooperative efforts that the existing barriers can be 'bridged'."

(Phillips et al. 1977, p. xvii)

INTRODUCTION [1]

The concept that school systems are responsible *only* for instruction in school subjects, once widely accepted, seems now to be totally obsolete. Schools have slowly but surely assumed more and more responsibility for services beyond the three R's, and each year, it seems, new responsibilities are added. While school lunch, counseling, recreation, vision and hearing testing, psychological services, and a whole spectrum of other services were not part of school fifty years ago, they are now fully accepted as proper functions of the schools. Even newer to the schools are many of the related services required for handicapped students. These include early identification (before school age), medical services, occupational therapy, physical therapy, and parental counseling and training. These services must be provided if they are necessary for the child to benefit from special education. Such requirements are very positive in terms of meeting the needs of children, but they necessitate a considerable reorganization of thinking on the part of program administrators.

Obviously, school districts can directly provide many of the services with their own personnel (speech therapists, school nurse), but many of the services must come from other agencies specializing in other education-related programs. School districts sometimes establish formal, working agreements with these agencies, but they also have informal relationships with agencies that provide parents with information, or they may refer parents to agencies for particular services. It is also interesting to observe the two-way street that exists. For example, LEAs frequently provide school programs in the children's ward of a hospital, in rehabilitation centers, and in juvenile correction facilities. These and many other types of facilities are operated by nonschool agencies.

The purpose of this chapter is to enhance the awareness of educational administrators about the services that handicapped pupils and their parents may request and about the resources (both inside and outside of the schools) that are available to help meet these needs.

SERVICES FROM THE NATIONAL LEVEL

On the national level, there are hundreds of public and private agencies that provide a wide variety of services ranging from money for the operation of programs to advocacy and political action. To gain a perspective of these programs, a practicing school administrator might ask two questions: (1) What are these agencies and what services do they provide? (2) Which of these services will assist me and the teachers and pupils for whom I am responsible?

Government Agencies

The Office of Special Education (OSE) (formerly the Bureau of Education for the Handicapped) has, as the name suggests, primary responsibility for many national educational program services. And while a local administrator does not typically deal directly with the office, he/she may benefit from its available services. This agency assists with development and interpretation of the laws (see Chapter 4) and with compliance monitoring. It also distributes federal funds to states and agencies within the states.

Local education agencies may see the major service provided by OSE encompassed by two kinds of grants. Entitlement grants provide a prescribed amount of money that school districts may obtain by meeting certain legal requirements and by submitting an application for funds (often through the state education agency). A limited number of *competitive grants* are then awarded for specific projects deemed most worthy by the OSE. LEA administrators should keep themselves informed about the types of projects being funded so that they can make appropriate decisions about applications for federal funding. Information is available from OSE and is periodically published by the journal *American Education,* but the primary source of information about federal programs, funding sources, and grants is the *Federal Register.*

While OSE is the federal agency with the most direct ties to educational programs for the handicapped and gifted, numerous other federal offices, bureaus, and divisions (The Office of Civil Rights, Bureau of Occupational and Adult Education, National Center on Educational Media for the Handicapped) also provide grants and various types of regulatory or technical assistance.[2]

Nongovernment Agencies

The agencies, foundations, and organizations operating at the national level number in the hundreds. Frequently they are parent organizations for state and local groups of the same name. For example, the Council for Exceptional Children (CEC), an international professional organization with headquarters in Reston, Virginia, is the parent organization for state federations and local chapters throughout the country. The National Association for Retarded Citizens (NARC), basically an organization for parents of the retarded, has its main office in Arlington, Texas, and has state and local chapters located throughout the country.

Each of these agencies has certain objectives and delineated areas of service. CEC and NARC both serve as political advocates for the handicapped, and both organizations publish and disseminate information that is informative and beneficial to educators and parents; but CEC encompasses all handicapped and gifted individuals, while NARC is concerned mostly with individuals who are retarded. Local ARC chapters frequently provide programs that directly serve children, while local CEC chapters do not usually include this type of service.

In order to gain perspective, agencies may be viewed both in terms of types of function and in terms of the clientele they represent. Examples are cited in Tables 6–1 and 6–2. These are only a few of the agencies that could be listed within each category. A more extensive (but still only partial) listing of agencies may be found in other publications. See the references at the end of this chapter.

TABLE 6–1   FUNCTIONS AND AGENCIES PROVIDING SERVICES

Function	Examples of a National Agency Concerned with This Function
Education	National Association of Private Schools for Exceptional Children
Employment	The President's Committee on Employment of the Handicapped
Research	Joseph P. Kennedy Jr. Foundation
Recreation and Leisure Time	National Wheelchair Athletic Association
Health Care	American Health Foundation
Counseling and Guidance	American Rehabilitation Counseling Association
Rehabilitation	Rehabilitation International, U.S.A.
Political Action	Council for Exceptional Children
Parent Advocacy	National Center for Law and the Handicapped

TABLE 6-2 AGENCIES REPRESENTING SPECIFIC AREAS OF EXCEPTIONALITY

Area of Exceptionality	Example of National Agency Concerned with This Population
Mental Retardation	American Association on Mental Deficiency
Epilepsy	Epilepsy Foundation of America
Cerebral Palsy	United Cerebral Palsy Association
Gifted	American Association for Gifted Children
Blind	American Printing House for the Blind
Deaf	National Association of the Deaf

THE STATE EDUCATION AGENCY (SEA)

As defined here, the SEA includes the state board of education, the chief state school officer (superintendent of schools), and the state department of education, whose employees work as the professional staff for the board and the state superintendent. The SEA is charged by the legislature of the state and by many provisions of federal law to carry out educational programs within the state. In most states, the SEA provides few or no direct services to school children (exceptions consist of a few state-operated schools for special purposes). The responsibility for program operation is given to the LEAs, while the SEA facilitates and monitors programs.

As a facilitator, the SEA may assist the state legislature in assessing needs and developing legislation such as school attendance laws and school building codes. The SEA also assists LEAs with such matters as interpretation of the laws, regulations, and guidelines for program operation, consulting services, technical assistance, and training of personnel.

As a monitor, the SEA checks attendance figures, audits fiscal expenditures, conducts program reviews to determine compliance with the laws and regulations, checks for proper credentials, participates in due-process procedures, and responds to reports from parents or other interested individuals with regard to any noncompliance issues.

Occasionally LEA administrators see the SEA as "big brother" or even as "the enemy." This type of relationship, however, is counterproductive, and a cooperative relationship should and usually does exist. Certainly the facilitating functions of the SEA should be very helpful. LEAs can utilize these services in many ways. For example:

- Gaining assistance in curriculum development
- Gaining assistance in personnel in-service education
- Receiving information regarding funding on both state and federal levels
- Receiving information that concerns program development

• Using the agency as an advocate when communicating with the legislature and federal agencies
• Receiving assistance in developing new programs.

It is important for information to flow between the SEA and LEAs. Each SEA has a state director of special education (various titles are used) and a staff of professional people who service special education programs. Local administrators must maintain close communication with state special education staff members. In addition to utilizing the SEA's services, local administrators can give invaluable input about local needs and suggest new legislation or modification of the old. Maintaining this relationship usually becomes one of the functions of the local director of special education.

Even the monitoring function of the SEA can be very helpful to local programs. Most monitoring teams are far more interested in contributing to the upgrading of programs for handicapped children than they are in declaring a district out of compliance. The guidelines that are utilized by the SEA help give a picture of a quality program. They should serve as a model of what a program should be and can sometimes be used by skillful administrators as a lever in getting approval for activities to improve programs.

SUPPORT SERVICES FROM HEALTH-RELATED AGENCIES

Handicapped children are often thought of as sick children. While some of these children do have very fragile conditions or conditions that might be described as a disease, for the most part they are *not sick*. They have a condition that results in a disability or a handicap. This mistaken notion of sickness may cause some problems with health-related services. Many agencies serve normal children who are acutely or chronically ill, but they do not adequately serve the child who is well but has a handicapping condition. The child who has juvenile diabetes or childhood leukemia has a chronic illness that may be totally under control or may be acute. The child who is an amputee or has cerebral palsy may enjoy very good health, but may need other health-related services such as physical therapy or audiological testing.

Fortunately, many public and private agencies do provide appropriate services. Geographic isolation, a sparse population, parents who do not seek out help for their children, and a lack of knowledge about available services are problems that prevent children from receiving necessary attention. While it is difficult to generalize about the availability of services in different geographic areas, certain suggestions seem appropriate:

• School nurses who are oriented to the needs of handicapped children can provide many of the needed services.
• Many LEAs contract with local medical doctors for examinations and consultation.

- Occupational and physical therapy are often provided (sometimes at school sites) by local health agencies.
- College and university clinics often work with school districts to provide therapy, counseling, testing, and treatment.
- Private clinics can be utilized to provide services (school personnel can provide information to parents and the district may pay for the service under certain conditions).

Local health departments frequently have referral systems and publish printed directories that identify service agencies in the area. Making this information available is a service to parents and a necessity if all children are to be properly served. High-quality special education programs invariably work closely with a broad spectrum of health-related agencies.

VOCATIONAL EDUCATION AND REHABILITATION AGENCIES

In discussing agencies that provide vocational education and rehabilitation, it is appropriate to briefly mention the needs of handicapped students as they become adolescents and young adults. They have at least three basic needs: (1) career preparation (a broader term than vocational education); (2) habilitation (a more appropriate term than rehabilitation since most of those discussed here have not yet become successful workers); and (3) employment (including services that help an individual get a job or agencies that provide sheltered employment). Some individuals need only one of these services, while others need all three.

Career Preparation

Career preparation begins in the schools. While a department of vocational education that operates within the same school as a special education program is not an outside agency, the two programs often function independently of each other. Good planning in a school system allows special education students to participate in the vocational training classes the school offers. Students must also have the opportunity to develop job-related knowledge and skills such as work habits, interpersonal relations, vocational mathematics, and career information within the classroom and to accumulate actual job experience. Many agencies can and do assist the school in this endeavor. Career speakers, field trips, job training, and actual employment may be provided by:

- Local businesses (e.g., stores, service stations, restaurants)
- Industrial organizations (e.g., manufacturing plants, distribution centers, construction companies)

- Labor organizations (e.g., building trades unions, teamsters)
- Public organizations (e.g., schools, city government)
- Community service groups (e.g., Lions, Kiwanis, Rotary).

Vocational Rehabilitation Services

Vocational rehabilitation (or habilitation) services and career preparation programs sometimes overlap in function and utilize many of the same resources, but they also offer several distinct services. On the national level are the Office of Human Development Services and the Rehabilitation Services Administration. Each state also has a department of rehabilitation services (various titles are used). Through these government agencies certain services are provided or purchased. Included are:

- Diagnostic services (medical, psychological, vocational assessment)
- Medical restoration (surgery, therapy, prosthetic devices)
- Vocational counseling (assessment of interests, job information)
- Vocational training (academic training, vocational training, on-the-job training)
- Job placement and follow up (making all arrangements for employment and job placement.

For many of the services listed above, the local department of vocational rehabilitation office serves as the facilitator by determining the needs of a client, getting him/her to the agency or individual who can provide the required service, and providing the necessary funds.

School personnel should work closely with rehabilitation agencies in order to be able to refer eligible students who need assistance. Services may begin while the student is still in high school. Eligibility requirements include:

- Presence of a physical or mental disability
- Existence of a substantial employment handicap
- Expectation that rehabilitation services may enable the individual to engage in a gainful occupation.

In addition to government agencies, there are many private agencies involved in providing rehabilitative services. Included are:

- Medical clinics for reconstructive surgery
- Dental clinics for the handicapped
- Public and private services for physical or occupational therapy
- Speech and hearing clinics
- Occupational training centers
- Counseling services.

Employment

The usual concept of employment agencies includes only those public and private agencies that help individuals with job placement or with unemployment compensation. This discussion includes the traditional concept of an employment agency as it relates to handicapped individuals of school age, as well as agencies specifically geared toward employing the handicapped.

Some school personnel may say "Education, not employment, is our business; why should the schools be concerned with employment agencies?" In responding to this type of question, one must indicate that (1) career preparation is an important part of the school program for exceptional students, and (2) traditional employment agencies can contribute to that process. They publish a wealth of information about jobs and job preparation; they have counselors who can be resource people for school programs; and they can help to place students in work-study programs.

For the student who demonstrates less potential for employment, a sheltered workshop may be more appropriate than the previously discussed programs. A sheltered workshop is an employment service created to help handicapped individuals. The workshop's primary function is to train or provide extended employment for handicapped individuals, as opposed to focusing on the production of goods. The workshop does produce goods or services, as does a regular business or industry, but that objective is secondary to its training and employment functions.

School districts frequently establish contracts with sheltered workshops, and students between the ages of sixteen and twenty-one receive part of their instruction and gain applied experience through a workshop.

School and Community Resources in Career Preparation and Vocational Rehabilitation

In a discussion of the available resources that can enhance a special program's quality, there is a tendency to think small instead of considering all of the possibilities. In this field, administrators must not think only of a high school's special education department and a few regular classes in which students can be scheduled. They should consider other resources within the school and the wealth of available community resources. A good summary of these resources was developed by Phelps and Lutz (1977). This information is presented in Figures 6–1 and 6–2.

RECREATION AND LEISURE TIME ACTIVITIES

Schools traditionally include many activities that can be classified as recreation or leisure time activities, such as intra- and interschool athletic programs, pep

FIGURE 6–1 SCHOOL RESOURCES AND THE SPECIAL NEEDS STUDENT

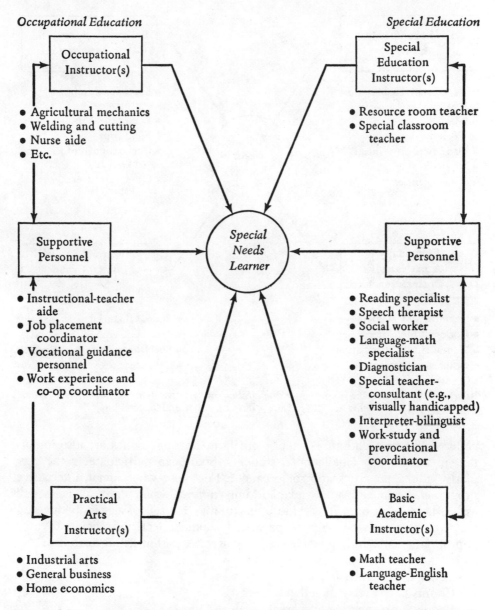

Occupational Education

Special Education

Occupational Instructor(s)
- Agricultural mechanics
- Welding and cutting
- Nurse aide
- Etc.

Special Education Instructor(s)
- Resource room teacher
- Special classroom teacher

Supportive Personnel
- Instructional-teacher aide
- Job placement coordinator
- Vocational guidance personnel
- Work experience and co-op coordinator

Special Needs Learner

Supportive Personnel
- Reading specialist
- Speech therapist
- Social worker
- Language-math specialist
- Diagnostician
- Special teacher-consultant (e.g., visually handicapped)
- Interpreter-bilinguist
- Work-study and prevocational coordinator

Practical Arts Instructor(s)
- Industrial arts
- General business
- Home economics

Basic Academic Instructor(s)
- Math teacher
- Language-English teacher

Reprinted by permission from *Career Exploration and Preparation for the Special Needs Learner,* by L. A. Phelps and R. J. Lutz (Boston: Allyn and Bacon, Inc., 1977).

FIGURE 6–2 COMMUNITY RESOURCES AND THE SPECIAL NEEDS LEARNER

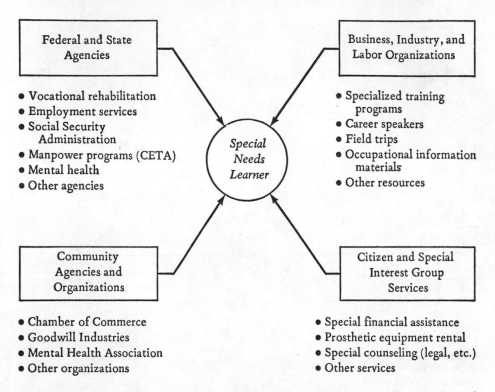

Reprinted by permission from *Career Exploration and Preparation for the Special Needs Learner,* by L. A. Phelps and R. J. Lutz (Boston: Allyn and Bacon, Inc., 1977).

clubs, drill teams, and after-school recreation. These activities are also important in the lives of handicapped students. Some can participate in the regularly offered programs and some cannot. For those who cannot, alternative programs should be made available. Many different community agencies will assist the schools or will provide opportunities for school-age individuals to participate in activities. School personnel should select and cooperate with appropriate community agencies in their area. A partial listing includes:

- Local YMCA and YWCA
- County or city recreation departments
- Recreation committees of parent organizations
- Special services offered by libraries or museums
- Handicapped Artists of America
- Special Olympics, sponsored by the Joseph P. Kennedy, Jr., Foundation
- Boy Scouts, Girl Scouts, Camp Fire Girls, other clubs
- National Wheelchair Athletic Association.

WORKING WITH NONPUBLIC SCHOOLS

Just as children with exceptional needs are enrolled at all levels in the public schools, there are also special students in many nonpublic (both sectarian and nonsectarian) schools. Sometimes they are there incidentally and sometimes by design; some children are placed in nonpublic schools because of parental preference and some because the public school does not provide a needed program.

Students who are in nonpublic schools because of parental preference are still eligible for services provided to handicapped students by the public schools. A student might attend the nonpublic school for most of the day, but come to the public school for speech therapy or physical therapy. The public school program may also take the services to the child, but care must be taken to observe the laws regarding public programs on sectarian school sites.[3]

In instances where the public school program does not meet the needs of an individual child, nonpublic, nonsectarian schools may be used to meet the requirements of a free publicly supported education. The public school system pays the costs of education at the nonpublic school.

Particularly in cases of geographic isolation, low incidence of a particular educational need, or unusual and difficult handicapping conditions, the public school system may turn to the private sector for assistance. Also, parents sometimes challenge the appropriateness of the public school program provided for their child and request placement in a private school program (at public expense). If there is a disagreement between the parent and the school system about which program is appropriate, the matter can be resolved through the due process hearing procedure. If this procedure is utilized, the private school may function as an advocate for the parent and an opponent of the public school system. The potential for adversarial roles between the public and private schools is obvious, but should be avoided whenever possible. A close working relationship should be cultivated. Money is the major contributing factor to potential conflict between private and public schools. Private schools must have funds to operate, and a major source of those funds is the tuition paid by public schools for education of their handicapped students. If the public school is operating a program that is seen as meeting the needs of the child, school personnel may strongly resent the drain on their budget represented by tuition and other costs incurred at nonpublic schools.

It must be remembered that the public school system is still responsible for handicapped students who are placed in nonpublic programs. The public school must ascertain that they are being educated according to an individualized education program (IEP) appropriate to their needs at no cost to the parents.

There are several sources of information about nonpublic schools, including the National Association of Private Schools for Exceptional Children, 7700

Miller Road, Miami, Florida 33155; and various state associations such as the California Association of Private Special Education Schools and state departments of education (consult local sources for mailing addresses).

CHILD AND FAMILY COUNSELING SERVICES

Handicapped children sometimes are a direct cause of emotional stress within the family. The child who has a severe behavioral problem, or one who requires a great deal of care, may make such demands on the parents that serious family problems result. If these problems remain unresolved, there is a strong possibility of rejection of the child, additional learning problems in the school, and perhaps even child abuse. Even though some children have no behavioral problems and do not need extensive care, some parents are so devastated by having a handicapped child that they cannot cope with the situation and thus reject the child. Professional counseling services for the family are then needed to help resolve these problems.

School counselors and school psychologists can frequently handle the counseling needs of the child, but they often do not have the skills or the time to work extensively with families. Until recently, family counseling was not recognized as being a responsibility of the schools. Agencies providing services in this area are National Council of Community Mental Health Centers, 2233 Wisconsin Avenue, N.W., Washington, D.C. 20007; private counseling services for families; and public family counseling services (usually a part of a city or county department of social services or department of health and welfare).

POLITICAL ACTION

The term "political action" usually refers to the exertion of influence to gain one's objectives. Activities ranging from testifying at a local school board meeting to serving as a legislator and voting for a bill can be labeled as political action. Many legislative actions that guarantee full educational rights for handicapped students came about because of the political activities of parent and other political action groups. These groups, on occasion, have even played a major role in electing people to positions on school boards and legislatures.

Steps that might be taken in order to achieve a political goal include:

- identifying specifics of the action that needs to be taken (for example, increase the contribution of state government to programs for the blind);

- assessing the level of support (How many people will help? How much will they help?);
- organizing a group or subgroup that will "carry the ball" for this project;
- finding people in decision-making positions (school board member, legislator) who will support the cause and who will introduce a proposal for consideration by their colleagues;
- helping to write the policy or law needed;
- campaigning for approval—writing letters, sending telegrams, testifying before committees, and demonstrating; and
- showing commitment by having large numbers of supporters make their wishes known.

School administrators are frequently involved in political action activities that will further the interests of their schools. They can also work with other groups in the political process. On occasion, parental and community political action groups are aligned against a position taken by the school system. Special education can be a very emotional issue, and it is not uncommon for political action to be directed against the school administration.

A great deal can be done by alert administrators to avoid any hostile political actions directed against them and the school system. Including parents in all aspects of program planning and utilizing their services in various supportive and advisory roles makes them a part of the team. The schools and the parents can be partners rather than adversaries in political action. The support of political action groups can be very helpful to a school administration, while a hostile group can be very difficult to deal with.

Parental political action groups began with the actions of parents representing children with particular handicaps such as mental retardation and cerebral palsy. In some cases they unintentionally worked against each other. This happened, for example, when they were each lobbying for financial support but competing for the same dollars. The success of the groups increased when they achieved better communication and began to work cooperatively toward common goals. One only needs to look at the volume of legislation affecting special education to recognize that the efforts of political action groups have wrought excellent results.

ADVOCACY GROUPS AND INDIVIDUALS

One frequently hears about "providers of services" and "consumers of services." School districts, departments of rehabilitation, private schools, and clinics are providers of services, while handicapped individuals and their parents are consumers. Of course, consumers often believe that they are not receiving all of the services to which they are entitled by law and by an agency's philosophical or legal obligations. With increasing frequency, consumers are taking action to obtain services that they are not receiving or that they believe to be substandard. This action may be in the form of political activity, due process hearings, or court cases.

As the responsibilities of the providers of services become greater, they may find it difficult to meet these responsibilities. Also, parents are becoming increasingly aware of their rights to services. Thus, a controversial situation arises. Many times the controversy and the solution are very complex, and parents seek assistance in developing their approach to the issue. As a result, a number of agencies and firms that assist or represent parents have arisen. They frequently refer to themselves as "parent/child advocates," and are staffed by lawyers, educators, and psychologists with expertise in the field of education of the handicapped. They have established these private consulting firms to assist parents in due process procedures and other advocacy roles. These sources of assistance are usually well known to local parent groups, and contacts can be made through these groups.

One type of advocacy concerns an individual; a second type of advocacy is a class action representing all individuals in a given class (e.g., all individuals who are mentally retarded); a third type of advocacy is oriented toward changing the system. The complaining party may be a handicapped individual or a parent or guardian. The party brings action on behalf of himself/herself only or on behalf of himself/herself and others. The defendant is usually the agency providing service, although these roles may be reversed in rare instances.

The agencies providing service may be precluded from doing all they would like to do by a lack of funds or other uncontrollable circumstances. In that case, the providers and the consumers will band together in an advocacy role to deal with a third party, such as the state legislature. Also, the providing agency frequently assumes the advocacy role for its clients. More often, however, parents want to obtain greater or different services, and they seek the assistance of individuals or agencies outside of the system.

Since they are independent of the system, a number of public and nonprofit organizations can serve as powerful advocates. They do not provide services; thus, they needn't be concerned about opposing their own organizations. They can help parents understand the issues, seek services, deal with the system, and use the legal process to achieve satisfactory services for handicapped individuals. These agencies include the National Center for Law and the Handicapped, National Association for Retarded Citizens, National Federation of the Blind, and Western Law Center for the Handicapped.

The school administrator should be aware that advocacy groups and individual advocates should perform the following types of activities:

- Advocacy by school personnel for enabling legislation and resources
- Advocacy by school personnel for improvement within the system[4]

• Advocacy by various groups to establish the rights of all handicapped individuals and to establish the procedures and resources whereby these rights can be realized

• Advocacy by individuals or groups representing handicapped individuals or their parents in disputes with the schools or other service-providing agencies.

SUMMARY

Chapter 6 points out the complexity of providing a wide range of mandated services appropriate to the needs of handicapped individuals with many different kinds of educational or education-related problems. Since it is not feasible for schools to provide for all of these needs, other agencies and individuals are needed to complete the spectrum of available services.

The chapter briefly discusses government and nongovernment agencies at the national level, with emphasis given to the Bureau of Education for the Handicapped (a public agency) and to the Council for Exceptional Children (a professional organization). Agency functions are explained in Table 6–1.

The state education agency (SEA) is defined, and its role as a facilitating and monitoring agency is discussed. Since school districts function directly under the SEA, it is important for every school administrator to establish a good working relationship with this agency.

The next section of the chapter discusses health-related services. While most handicapped children would not be classified as sick, many do need therapy, braces, corrective surgery, and other medical care. Ways to meet the health-related needs of the students are proposed.

A high percentage of handicapped individuals can profit from career preparation programs. The school curriculum can be adapted to include this emphasis, but good programs must also utilize many community resources. These resources are discussed as contributors to the overall program of preparation and habilitation for the world of work. The roles of employment agencies and employing organizations are also considered.

A number of community agencies provide special recreational and leisure time activities. Handicapped students have the same needs in this area as do other students, but frequently need modification of facilities and programs. Specific agencies that provide these services are listed.

The next section of Chapter 6 discusses the services provided by private schools and by child and family counseling services. These agencies have a new type of relationship with the school systems as a result of recent legislation. A discussion of political action and advocacy groups is the final portion of the chapter.

A partial list of agencies and organizations that provide services to handicapped individuals, their parents, and school programs is provided in Appendix 3. This list should be used as a reference. School administrators should become familiar with agencies and organizations in their own area.

NOTES

1. Names and mailing address of many agencies that serve the handicapped and gifted are included in Appendix 3.
2. Appendix 3 includes references to many government and private agencies. Detailed information about financial support may be found in the *Guide to OE-Administered Programs for Fiscal Year . . .* , from the Superintendent of Documents, U.S. Government Printing Office, Washington, D.C. 20402; and the *Federal Education Grants Directory*, Capital Publications, Inc., 2430 Pennsylvania Avenue, Washington, D.C. 20037.
3. Individual states have specific statutes that describe the extent to which LEAs may or must provide ancillary services to nonpublic schools.
4. Advocacy by school administrators must be carefully considered from the point of view of loyalty to the organization, job security, etc.

REFERENCES

Federal education grants directory. 1978. Washington, D.C.: Capitol Publications, Inc.

Guide to OE-administered programs for fiscal year . . . . Washington, D.C.: U.S. Government Printing Office (published annually).

Phelps, L. A., and Lutz, R. J .1977. *Career exploration and preparation for the special needs learner.* Boston: Allyn and Bacon, Inc.

Phillips, L., Carmel, L., Renzullo, R., Seymour, L., and Weinheimer, S. R. 1977. *Barriers and bridges.* Sacramento: California Advisory Council on Vocational Education.

ADDITIONAL SUGGESTED READINGS

A guide to organizations, agencies and federal programs for handicapped Americans. 1979. Washington, D.C.: Handicapped American Reports, February. (Note: This guide contains an extensive listing of national agencies and organizations. It also lists the services given by each agency, contacts, and mailing addresses. It can be obtained by writing to Handicapped American Reports, 2626 Pennsylvania Avenue, N.W., Washington, D.C.)

President's Committee on Mental Retardation. 1975. *Mental retardation . . . the known and the unknown.* Washington, D.C.: U.S. Government Printing Office.

Administrative Models
for Special Education
Programs and Services

7

Organizational Structures or Models: An Overview

INTRODUCTION

One who reads professional materials in the field of educational administration would find it very difficult to locate professional textbooks that do not mention administrative structures or models. This is understandable. The utilization of models is a basic tool in discussing the mechanics of providing school programs or the nature of the programs themselves. Utilization of educational models runs the gamut from developing a theoretical, conceptual perspective of a future program to "show and tell" about one that already exists.

The dictionary defines "models" in a variety of ways: a set of plans, a miniature representation of something, an example for imitation, a description or analogy used to help visualize something, or an example or pattern. One can readily see how these definitions apply to educational programs. The understanding, development, and use of educational models can serve these purposes:

- Providing a framework for program planning and operation
- Assisting in promoting communication among administrators, teachers, parents, and students
- Serving as a systems approach to delivery of services

- Helping LEAs comply with laws, regulations, and policies
- Serving as the frame of reference for program evaluation
- Providing the structure for development of verbal or visual pictures of the program
- Serving as the pattern of something that works and that can be replicated
- Providing the necessary structure for obtaining and expending funds
- Providing a means for obtaining some degree of stability for the above functions.

If used appropriately by program administrators, models for special education programs can have a significant and positive effect on school programs. It should also be remembered that models or structures do exist in our programs, either by design or by default. Educators can use them or be used by them.

ALTERNATIVE APPROACHES TO EDUCATIONAL MODELS

As a reader reviews the literature on the development and use of educational models, or as an observer looks at current practices in the schools, it becomes obvious that program models or structures may be discussed from several different perspectives. While the concepts involved in different approaches are often complementary, we frequently fail to integrate views from different models. We might begin by identifying the most common approaches to describing particular models. Included are the following:

- The organizational approach: describes the administrative structure that will provide programs.
- The categorical or noncategorical models approach: outlines the types of programs to be provided to individuals who have been classified according to some category or who are being served cross-categorically.
- The spectrum of services approach: shows, often pictorially, the range of services that are being provided or that will be provided in the future.
- The local school district or building models: defines a plan that applies only to the local district or to one or more school sites in the district.

Remember, these different models are not mutually exclusive. The discussion below looks at each of the major divisions in greater detail.

THE ORGANIZATIONAL APPROACH TO DEVELOPMENT OF MODELS

Federal agencies usually do not prescribe or suggest models for educational programs.[1] Therefore, the basic sources of information about the "what" and "how" of running special education programs are the states' laws and administrative regulations. It is no surprise, then, to find many different organizational models operating in the various states.

The author suggests that administrators who have not previously thought of state laws and regulations as being the basis for a model compare the conditions described below:

- A state that permits or mandates special districts for certain programs, such as special education or vocational education, as opposed to a state that makes no such provisions.
- A state in which county school offices serve as intermediate school districts and often provide direct services to students as opposed to a state that has no such organizational structure.
- A state that organizes special education programs on a categorical basis (EMR, PH, LD, etc.), as opposed to a state that prohibits the use of categories.[2]
- A state where funding patterns encourage LEAs to operate special education programs as opposed to a state where funding patterns place undue burden on the LEAs' general fund.

The reader can readily see how different state philosophies, laws, and regulations affect the development of organizational models. However, by focusing attention on the local level, we can see that the similarities of organizational models are greater than their differences.

Johnson (1967) described six different organizational structures that were available to LEAs. These organizational structures, along with a few added ideas that reflect current trends, are defined in Table 7–1.

Johnson also points out that failure to plan is itself a plan. Although few school officials would admit to having no plans, this situation is sometimes the result of an apathetic attitude toward the needs of special children. Failure to plan can occur when an administrator denies that exceptional individuals exist in a given LEA, fails to identify those students who have special needs, says that it can all be handled without any special services, or procrastinates for a long time. However, the superintendent and school board members who fail to plan can anticipate increasing criticism from parents, lawsuits for noncompliance with the law, due process panels, and possible loss of school operating funds.

Another approach to the organizational model is the administrative flow

TABLE 7–1   EDUCATIONAL MODELS: LEA ORGANIZATIONAL STRUCTURE

Organizational Model	Description	Used by
1. Comprehensive Direct Program Operation	The LEA independently operates special education programs within its own boundaries. It must have a wide variety of facilities, programs, and services to help all handicapped individuals, no matter what their problem is, at all school age levels.	LEAs with a large population base and a philosophy or practical factors favoring independent rather than cooperative action.
2. Limited Direct Program Operation	The LEA, for a variety of reasons, provides programs or services only to selected types of individuals with exceptional needs. It relies upon state schools, privately operated schools, and private clinics to provide services to all other students (as required by federal and state laws). These services are obtained on a contractual basis and many must be paid for by the LEA.	Geographically isolated LEAs may find this model the only feasible way to meet their commitments.
3. Reciprocal Plan	LEAs in close geographic proximity may informally agree to have each one operate a part of the total program and to accept one another's students on a cost-of-operation basis. For example, one LEA might operate the program for the deaf, a second LEA the program for the blind, a third the program for the physically handicapped. Each one would operate its own program for other special needs students with high incidence handicaps. Interdistrict agreements for attendance and cost reimbursement are usually adequate for this type of program. Difficulty may arise (1) when some programs are more expensive than others, (2) when participating districts differ greatly in socioeconomic level or ethnic and racial makeup, or (3) from other unforeseen factors.	Small to medium-sized LEAs where geographic distances are not so great as to prohibit daily transportation of students.
4. Cooperative Plan	This model is more formal than the reciprocal plan. It is based on state laws and/or on formal agreements between LEAs. The cooperative	Small and medium-sized LEAs that are required by law or find it more efficient

TABLE 7-1 *(Cont'd)*

Organizational Model	Description	Used by
	plan operates as a program rather than as a cluster of independent programs. Cooperative plans have a governing board (often representatives of the component LEAs) and their own administrative/support staff and teachers. This model also provides for a budgeting process separated from, but sometimes dependent on, the component LEAs. As described in Chapter 9, cooperative models take different forms in different states, such as the Boards of Cooperative Educational Services in New York, the Collaboratives in Massachusetts, the Special Education Service Areas in Michigan, the special education services of the Offices of the County Superintendents of Schools in California, and the Special School District of St. Louis County, Missouri.	to work together to provide a full spectrum of educational services.
5. Dependent Plan	LEAs are sometimes so small that they feel unable to provide quality programs. They depend on a larger neighbor or on an intermediate district to provide all special education programs and services. While this may be an acceptable position for the very small LEA, it is much less defensible for the larger district that adopts a dependent plan simply because of a "don't want to be involved" philosophy.	Appropriate only for very small LEAs that can receive quality services from a neighboring district or an intermediate district.
6. Combination of Plans	Local considerations frequently indicate that some combination of plans will best meet a district's needs. A particular LEA may find it advantageous to operate its own program for children with learning disabilities, to be involved in a reciprocal plan for students with other types of disabilities, and to utilize the cooperative plan for vocational education and work-study programs for secondary students.	Widely used by LEAs because of its adaptability to local situations.

FIGURE 7-1 SAMPLE ADMINISTRATIVE FLOW CHART FOR SPECIAL EDUCATION SERVICES—LARGE LEA

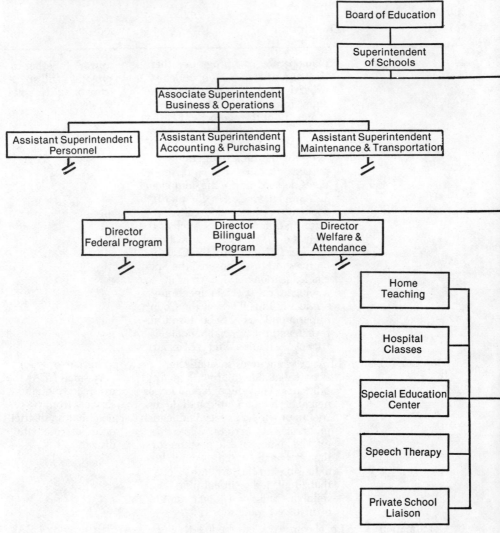

chart. This is a technique used by almost every type of agency to show lines of authority and functions performed (often referred to as line or staff responsibilities). Frequently, the administrative flow chart only shows positions, (e.g. superintendent, director, teachers), but it may also include programs (e.g. EMR, PH, Deaf). It has the advantages of being brief and containing a great deal of information about the position of special education programs relative to other programs in the district. Examples of administrative flow charts for a large and a medium-sized district are presented in Figures 7–1

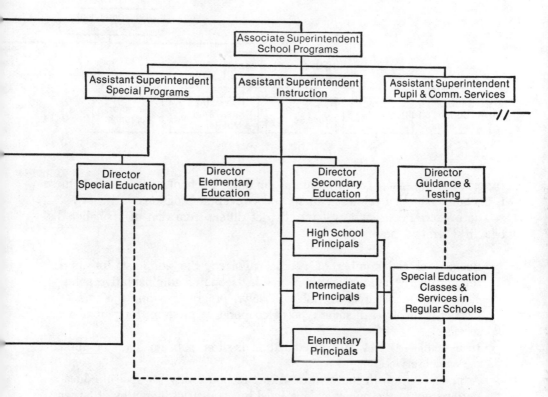

and 7–2. These charts show the lines of responsibility flowing from the board of education to the superintendent to an associate or assistant superintendent; line authority is then dispersed to the director of special education or to school principals. The principal usually has line responsibility for special education programs located in his/her building. The director of special education's staff responsibility toward those programs usually includes curriculum supervision, placement of students, budget development and monitoring, working with parents, in-service staff education, program evaluation, and shared responsibility for teacher evaluation. The director of special education also has line responsibility for several programs and services located at the schools and within the community.

It is important to note that every position listed on a flow chart entails some measure of responsibility for all or part of the students in special education programs. No matter how a position is defined (employing qualified teachers,

FIGURE 7-2   SAMPLE ADMINISTRATIVE FLOW CHART FOR SPECIAL
EDUCATION SERVICES—MEDIUM SIZE LEA

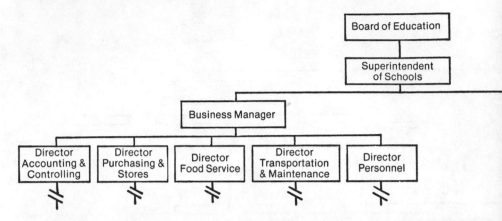

supervising the school lunch program, purchasing school supplies, etc.), there
is a component that relates it to special education programs.

The organization of a very large district differs from that of a smaller district in several ways:

- Because of the number of people involved, the administrator in a
  smaller district usually covers a broader scope of administrative areas.
- The large district operates all of its own programs, while the smaller
  district is involved in some type of cooperative program for part of its
  services.
- In a smaller district, special education is often subsumed under pupil
  personnel services.
- Administrators with the greatest direct responsibility for special education are not at the policy-making level in the district hierarchy of larger
  districts.
- Special education is a hybrid of instructional programs and supportive
  services. It is often difficult to find an effective management system for
  very diverse programs and services, but the problem appears to be more
  manageable in small districts.

Burrello and Sage (1979) suggest that we must study different alternatives
for the future in order to make intelligent decisions about the present organizational structure. For example, if the implementation of education in the
least restrictive environment continues to make handicapped students more
a part of the general education program, building administrators will continue
to be very involved in the administrative process. They will need greater
expertise and a great deal of help from supportive services personnel. Burrello
and Gilliam (1974) propose a model that would establish a dual authority

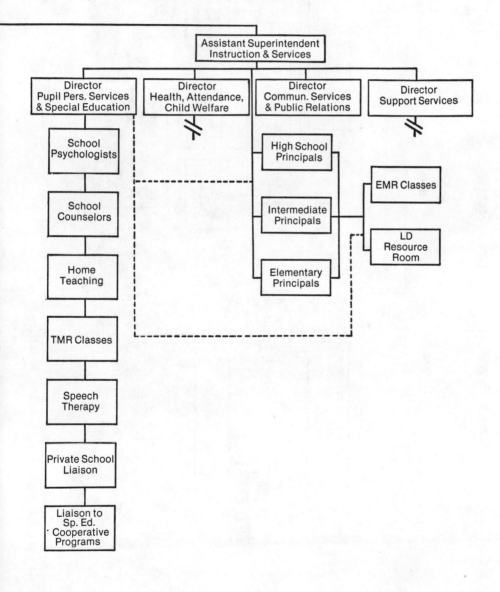

FIGURE 7–3 FORMAL AUTHORITY STRUCTURE OF MATRIX ORGANIZATION

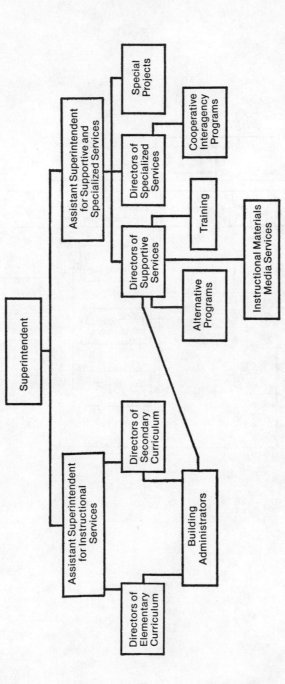

Reprinted from *Leadership and Change in Special Education*, by Leonard C. Burrello and Daniel D. Sage, © 1979, p. 159. Reprinted by permission of Prentice-Hall, Inc., Englewood Cliffs, New Jersey.

relationship, as shown in Figure 7–3. In this model, directors of support services and building administrators share responsibility, rather than one of them having line responsibility and the other one having staff responsibility. As explained in Burrello and Sage (1979, p. 156), the supportive services of this model include (1) consultant teacher services, (2) demonstration resource teacher programs, (3) itinerant services, and (4) training.

CATEGORICAL AND NONCATEGORICAL MODELS

Current educational trends are toward deemphasizing special education categories. At least five major factors have influenced this shift:

- Using categories such as educable retarded, trainable retarded, deaf and hard of hearing, visually handicapped, orthopedically handicapped, and other health impaired to classify students implies that there is a firm boundary between those who are included in a category and those who are not included. This premise simply cannot be supported by the facts.
- The use of categories implies that differences exist between the disabled and the nondisabled and among the different disability groups, when such differences often do not exist.
- Categorical programs have the built-in problem of labeling children. Labels can sometimes produce very negative effects.
- Labeling students for placement in school programs often causes rigidity in assignments and scheduling. Students may experience extreme difficulty getting into regular classes and may find it impossible to attend a class, no matter how appropriate, that is set aside for another category of children.
- In some cases, categorizing, labeling, and tracking students may violate their civil rights. This fact has been supported by numerous court cases.

While the factors discussed above would seem to present a very strong argument against any model based on a categorical system, problems are encountered when a state or LEA attempts to abolish such a model or to substitute a totally noncategorical model. Consider the following:

- When we remove a label that has a negative connotation for some people (e.g., mentally retarded) we usually substitute another label that may seem more positive, such as learning handicapped. However, this label may also become negative over a period of time.
- Without some way to identify a student's problem, we have difficulty deciding which class or group is most appropriate for that student.
- Very few parents or special education professionals want to give up categorical funding. This method of receiving and expending funds is

the greatest single protector of educational programs for the handicapped student.
- The system for reporting information, for obtaining grant funds, and
for requesting special services is geared toward labeling individuals.
This system exists at both federal and state levels and yields to change
slowly and reluctantly.
- Teachers, counselors, social workers, and other professionals are trained
along categorical lines to work with individuals who have very different
needs. It does not seem practical (and may not be possible within reasonable time limits) to train professionals to work across all categories.

Now that we have an overview of factors that argue both for and against
a categorical model, a brief analysis of categorical models can be presented.
This will set the stage for further discussion of movement toward noncategorical structures.

Categorical concepts and models can be applied in a variety of ways. They
can refer to (1) categorical funding, (2) categorical professional training,
(3) categorical programming (with or without the labeling of children), and
(4) categorical identification and assignment of children. Examples of each
of the above may contribute to better understanding.

Categorical funding provides money that is ear-marked for certain purposes.
Examples are funds for adaptive physical education, for vocational education,
for education of the blind, or for vocational rehabilitation of the retarded.
Proponents of special education programs are strong supporters of categorical
funding. For them, it is a matter of survival to have these funds protected
from those who have more votes in the budgeting process. Federal and state
funds presently are entirely or partially allocated on a categorical basis for
special education (and sometimes for categorical disability areas within special
education), but in these days of budget crises categorical funding is under
increasing attack. (See Chapter 15 for a more detailed discussion of funding.)

Several states have experimented with noncategorical professional preparation for a career in special education. It is this writer's opinion that none of
the experiments have been highly successful in preparing a person to teach
across all categories. They usually compromise by (1) training students in
a limited disability area, such as the mildly handicapped or (2) providing a
generic training base for all trainees and specializations from which a person
may choose. The latter type of training is portrayed in Figure 7–4. This second
approach to teacher training would seem to hold the greatest promise and be
the most logical. However, most states still prepare teachers in programs that
are essentially categorical in nature as opposed to programs that are fully
generic or that have a generic base with advanced specializations available.

Categorical programming without categorizing students might be exemplified by an adaptive physical education (APE) program. A student enrolled
in APE should not have to be categorized as physically handicapped, just as

FIGURE 7-4 TEACHER TRAINING MODEL—GENERIC BASE AND
SPECIALIZATION AREAS

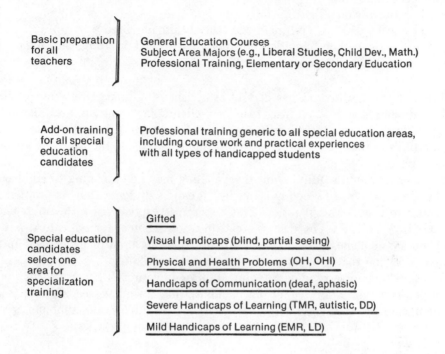

Basic preparation for all teachers

General Education Courses
Subject Area Majors (e.g., Liberal Studies, Child Dev., Math.)
Professional Training, Elementary or Secondary Education

Add-on training for all special education candidates

Professional training generic to all special education areas,
including course work and practical experiences
with all types of handicapped students

Special education candidates select one area for specialization training

Gifted

Visual Handicaps (blind, partial seeing)

Physical and Health Problems (OH, OHI)

Handicaps of Communication (deaf, aphasic)

Severe Handicaps of Learning (TMR, autistic, DD)

Mild Handicaps of Learning (EMR, LD)

a student enrolled in remedial reading does not have to be classified as mentally retarded or learning disabled.

Identification of children and assignment to school programs by category is the heart of the discussion of categorical models. Prior to the 1960s, special education programs were highly categorical in nature. The rigid application of categories has begun to break down because of the research, legislation, and court cases previously cited, but many programs are virtually unchanged. There is always the argument (right or wrong) that we continually group, classify, and label people in all situations—young, old; upper class, lower class; professional, nonprofessional. In school situations we group and label as directed by state laws or a central administration directive—elementary, secondary; first grade, third grade; bilingual, monolingual. We also categorize within each class—group leaders, group members; blue birds, red birds.

The grouping categories that have traditionally been used in special education programs were discussed in Chapters 2 and 3 and are listed below:

1. Educable mentally retarded
2. Trainable mentally retarded
3. Learning disabled or educationally handicapped

4. Hearing impaired
5. Visually handicapped
6. Speech impaired
7. Emotionally disturbed
8. Physically disabled (crippled and other health impaired)
9. Gifted (sometimes included in categorical special programs and sometimes listed under general education).

Each of these categories has had an established funding pattern and established standards as to class size, teacher credentialing program, and methods of providing services. Many states and federal agencies still use the categories as the basis of their laws and regulations, their method of funding LEAs, and their reporting.

Most of us would readily admit that labeling may be damaging to children. Although some type of labeling is needed, it causes students obvious problems. We seek to resolve this paradox. This concern is expressed by Reynolds and Birch (1977, p. 71): "The test of a classification scheme, for educators, is its educational outcome. Does a scheme permit the allocation of each child to a school situation that is most productive for that child?"

It seems that some type of categorization of programs is necessary for purposes of communication, reporting, funding, and assigning teachers. It is a challenge to use a categorical system without negatively affecting children.

Comparison of Plans

NONCATEGORICAL MODELS   Several states have begun to use what they describe as a noncategorical model (critics may say it is only a modified categorical model). One example of this is the program being implemented by the *California Master Plan for Special Education* (California State Board of Education 1974)[3]; a second example comes from Chapter 766 of the Massachusetts Education Code (1972). Many states are moving toward using a noncategorical model. This model usually includes the following concepts:

• A single classification, such as "children with special needs" or "individuals with exceptional needs," is used. The old classifications may be used for data purposes only.
• Classes restricted to one group (e.g., classes for the EMR) are abolished in favor of assignment to classes on the basis of educational need and the ability to change the student's environment.
• The administration is committed to a continuum or cascade of direct programs and supportive services.
• Students are placed in educational settings that range from full-time assignment to special classes (either in regular schools or in more segre-

gated settings) to full-time assignment to a regular class, supplemented with supportive services as needed.
- Appropriate supportive services that will help the student remain in the least restrictive environment are emphasized. Such services include speech therapy, readers for the blind, physical therapy, special transportation, and special equipment.
- Funding is allocated according to the educational service provided, rather than according to a special disability category.

The California Master Plan. The *California Master Plan for Special Education* (California State Board of Education 1974) did not present a pictorial model, but verbally defined eight "program components" through which the schools provide services for all individuals with exceptional needs. Recent legislation has further modified the original Master Plan and authorizes only five program components (SB 1870, 1980).

California Master Plan Program Components

1. *Special Classes and Centers.* Special classes are provided for students with more intensive educational needs. They are designed to enroll pupils for a majority of the school day. Special centers are clusters of special classes. Students are assigned according to educational need rather than according to category.
2. *The Resource Specialist Program.* This component is the key to meeting least restrictive environment provisions for exceptional individuals. It provides instructional planning, special instruction, tutoring assistance, and other services to individuals who spend a majority of their time in the regular class. The service is designed to assist both the student and his/her teacher.
3. *Designated Instruction and Services.* Included in this component are a variety of special services such as:

   Speech/language assessment and remediation
   Audiological services
   Mobility instruction
   Adaptive physical education
   Home or hospital instruction
   Career preparation
   Parent education.
4. *Non–Public School Services.* Non–public school services are made available when these services can more appropriately meet the needs of the individual.
5. *State Schools.* State schools provide diagnostic services and instruction in a residential setting.

Massachusetts Noncategorical Legislation. The approach to noncategorical programming in Massachusetts is explained in excerpts from Chapter 766 of the Massachusetts Education Code (1972).

Section 1, Paragraph 3:

This act is designed to remedy past inadequacies and inequities by defining the needs of children requiring special education in a broad and flexible manner, leaving it to state agencies to provide more detailed definitions which recognize that such children have a variety of characteristics and needs, all of which must be considered if the educational potential of each child is to be realized; by providing the opportunity for a full range of special education programs for children requiring special education; by requiring that a program which holds out the promise of being special actually benefits children assigned thereto; and by replacing the present inadequate and antiequalizing formula for distribution of state aid for special education programs with an equalizing one which encourages cities, towns and regional school districts to develop adequate special education programs within a reasonable period of time.

Section 1, Chapter 71B:

. . . Children receiving or requiring special education shall be entitled to participate in any of the following programs: (1) additional direct and indirect instruction, consultation service, materials, equipment or aid provided children or their regular classroom teachers which directly benefits children requiring special education; (2) supplementary individual or small group instruction or treatment in conjunction with a regular classroom program; (3) integrated programs in which children are assigned to special resource classrooms but attend regular classes to the extent that they are able to function therein; (4) full-time special class teaching or treatment in a public school building; (5) teaching or treatment at home; (6) full-time teaching or treatment in a special day school or other day facility; (7) teaching or treatment at a hospital; (8) teaching or treatment at a short or long-term residential school; (9) occupational and preoccupational training in conjunction with the regular occupational training program in a public school; (10) occupational and preoccupational training in conjunction with full-time special class teaching in a public school building, at home, special day school or other day facility, hospital, or short or long-term residential school; (11) any combination or modification of programs (1) through (10) or other programs, services, treatments or experimental provisions which obtain the prior approval of the department.

It should be readily observable that emphasis is placed on the type of service needed rather than on categories of children.

Vermont's Consulting Teacher Approach. Another approach to a noncategorical model is to adopt a form of mainstreaming, with different variations. In each variation, there is some way of providing service to the regular classroom teacher or to the special student in the regular class. A number of such plans have been described in the literature—Haring (1972); Lilly (1971); Christie, McKenzie, and Burdett (1972); Fox et al. (1974)—under what might generically be called a "consulting teacher" program. Fox et al. (1974, p. 22) describe the implementation of a consulting teacher program in Vermont as follows:

> In this program, consulting teachers assist and train regular-classroom teachers to provide successful learning experiences for children eligible for special educational services.... Regular class placement for all children but the profoundly handicapped is made possible by the inservice training in applied behavior analysis and individualized instruction that provides regular-classroom teachers with the necessary special education skills.

This type of model returns the major responsibility for the child's day-to-day program to the regular classroom teacher. The consulting teacher becomes a trainer of regular teachers in special materials and techniques and a consultant regarding special problems. In some models, the special education person also has a teaching assignment (with the special education children) for a portion of the day. The latter arrangement seems much more acceptable to the regular classroom teacher, who often says, "Don't just tell me how to do it, but show me and help me by sharing the responsibility for the child's instruction."

CATEGORICAL MODELS   In contrast to the above examples, many states have maintained models that are best described as categorical in nature. Even those states that call their programs noncategorical tend to use categorical terms and, by necessity, do some grouping of children in that way.

New York's Categorical Approach. New York is an example of a state that uses a categorical approach. Part 200 of the Regulations of the Commissioner of Education (New York Department of Education 1978) and the New York State Plan (New York Department of Education 1979) identify programs by handicapping condition—educable retarded, trainable retarded, emotionally disturbed, severely speech impaired, deaf, hard of hearing, legally blind, partially sighted, orthopedically physically handicapped, other physically handicapped, specific learning disabled, and other speech impaired.

To serve children in the various categories, several different program alternatives are given: special classes (general), special classes (specific to category), home and hospital instruction. One can see from this listing of programs that integration with the nonhandicapped and mixing of children in the different categories is possible and probably encouraged. It is important to recognize that a categorical model does not require segregation or rigidity of placement, but integration and flexibility are more difficult under this system.

Implementation of mainstreaming for some students and the least restrictive environment for all students is becoming a reality. It is required by law and supported, at least in theory, by educators and by the public. The extent to which children are being served in this way is shown in Figure 7–5.

However, this does not mean that all states and LEAs will adopt a non-

FIGURE 7–5 ENVIRONMENTS IN WHICH HANDICAPPED CHILDREN WERE SERVED, 1976–77

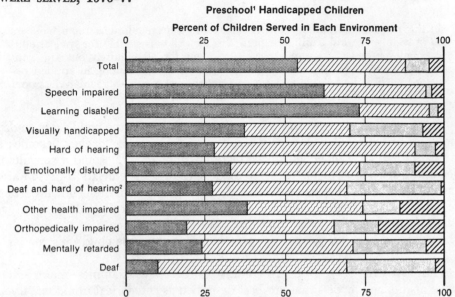

Preschool[1] Handicapped Children

Percent of Children Served in Each Environment

[1]Preschool-aged children are defined here as children ages 3-5.
[2]Those States that combined the deaf and hard of hearing categories are shown here..

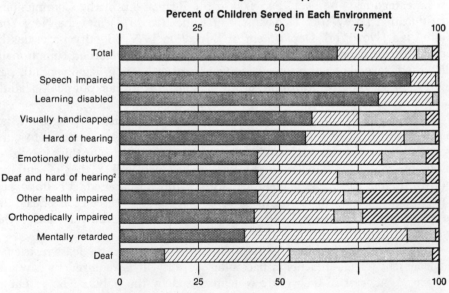

School-Aged[1] Handicapped Children

Percent of Children Served in Each Environment

[1]School-aged children are defined here as children aged 6-17.
[2]Those States that combined the deaf and hard of hearing categories are shown here.

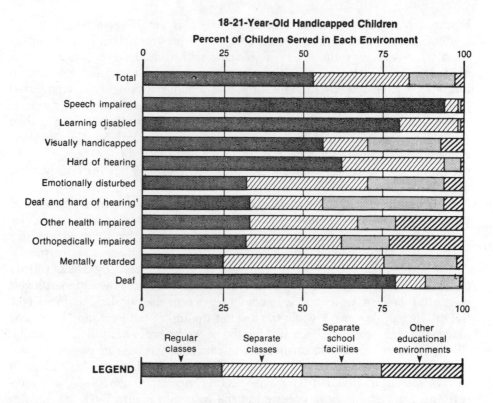

18-21-Year-Old Handicapped Children

Percent of Children Served in Each Environment

'Those States that combined the deaf and hard of hearing categories are shown here.

Reprinted from *Progress Toward a Free Appropriate Public Education. A Report to Congress on the Implementation of Public Law 94–142: The Education for All Handicapped Children Act"* (Washington, D.C.: Department of Health, Education, and Welfare, January 1979), pp. 36, 37, 38.

categorical model. Establishing the least restrictive environment and utilizing noncategorical models are not synonymous. The benefits and problems of both categorical and noncategorical models have been discussed, but some factors for and against should be reemphasized. Labeling of children can be harmful, is really unnecessary, and may be illegal. The use of categories tends to cause rigidity in assigning students to programs. Labels are often misleading. Some form of labeling of programs (not children) may be a necessary part of the communication process. The use of categories has been a definite aid in securing funding for programs. While it may present some problems, developing noncategorical programs for children while continuing to obtain the benefits of categorical funding and data reporting does not seem to be an overwhelming task.

THE SPECTRUM OF SERVICES MODEL

It is not reasonable to suggest that the needs of any diverse population of students can be met by any one type of school program. This fact is emphasized when we study the needs of students with different types and degrees of disabilities. Over the years, the numbers of special education students in the schools have increased significantly, and school personnel have recognized that their needs can only be met by providing a greater range of services. For example, visually handicapped students had been included in public school programs for more than fifty years when programs for the trainable retarded, in significant numbers, were initiated as part of the public school program. The learning problems of these two groups are obviously very different.

As LEAs developed more special programs with an ever increasing range of possibilities, the professional literature began to include numerous articles describing different programs and services. An article by Reynolds (1962) presented a pictorial model as a framework for considering issues in special education. Similar models were presented in greater detail by Deno (1970) and Willenberg (1970). (See Figure 7–6.) These models show different levels of special services. Level one is basically service in the regular classroom (for the mildly handicapped), while the level at the top of the pyramid is full-time placement in a residential school (for the severely/profoundly handicapped). The greatest concentration of special students is at the base of the model and their density gets progressively smaller at the upper levels. Reynolds and Birch (1977) present an updated "Original Special Cascade" (Figure 7–7), and indicate the changes that have occurred in the cascade (Figure 7–8).

These models are basically noncategorical and present a good overview of the different types of administrative arrangements that can be utilized as educational placements for a complete range of student needs. For example, Table 7–2 lists programs that might be appropriate for two different students. The reader can readily see that the different program options presented in Table 7–2 (segregated special class, integrated special class, resource room, itinerant teacher, supportive services) are included in the models shown in Figures 7–5 and 7–7. If additional information were available, one could also relate these options to categorical or noncategorical programs and to organizational models.

THE LOCAL SCHOOL DISTRICT OR BUILDING MODEL

We frequently find that LEAs or individual schools within an LEA utilize the options available through the various laws and regulations in order to develop unique programs to serve their own special education populations. Districts or individual schools are usually responding to philosophical ideas or to their

FIGURE 7-6 LEVELS OF INSTRUCTIONAL INTERVENTION WITHIN
PUBLIC SCHOOL SPECIAL EDUCATION PROGRAMS

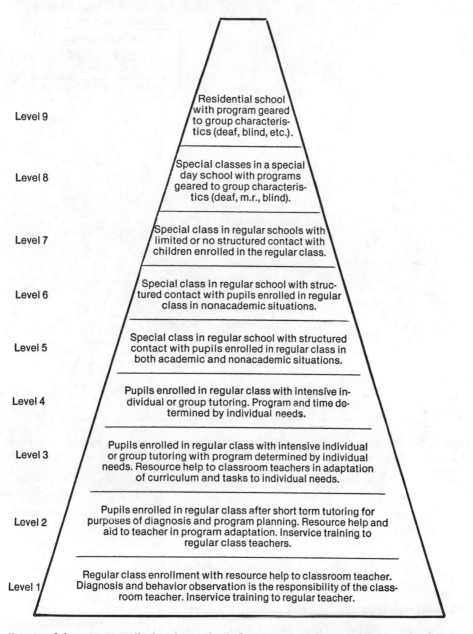

Level 9 — Residential school with program geared to group characteristics (deaf, blind, etc.).

Level 8 — Special classes in a special day school with programs geared to group characteristics (deaf, m.r., blind).

Level 7 — Special class in regular schools with limited or no structured contact with children enrolled in the regular class.

Level 6 — Special class in regular school with structured contact with pupils enrolled in regular class in nonacademic situations.

Level 5 — Special class in regular school with structured contact with pupils enrolled in regular class in both academic and nonacademic situations.

Level 4 — Pupils enrolled in regular class with intensive individual or group tutoring. Program and time determined by individual needs.

Level 3 — Pupils enrolled in regular class with intensive individual or group tutoring with program determined by individual needs. Resource help to classroom teachers in adaptation of curriculum and tasks to individual needs.

Level 2 — Pupils enrolled in regular class after short term tutoring for purposes of diagnosis and program planning. Resource help and aid to teacher in program adaptation. Inservice training to regular class teachers.

Level 1 — Regular class enrollment with resource help to classroom teacher. Diagnosis and behavior observation is the responsibility of the classroom teacher. Inservice training to regular teacher.

Reprinted from E. P. Willenberg's article "Administrative Structures for Special Education. In *The Process of Special Education Administration*, C. H. Meisgeier and J. D. King, eds. (Scranton, Pa.: International Textbook Co., 1970), p. 123. Reprinted by permission of Ernest P. Willenberg.

FIGURE 7-7   THE ORIGINAL SPECIAL EDUCATION CASCADE

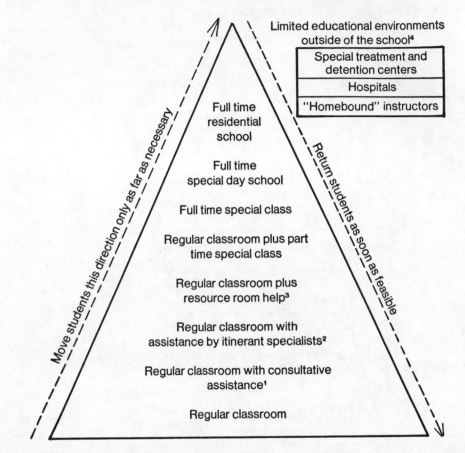

Reprinted from *Teaching Exceptional Children in All America's Schools*, by M. C. Reynolds and J. W. Birch, by permission of the Council for Exceptional Children (Reston, Va: The Council for Exceptional Children, 1977), p. 34.

own specific needs. Innovative programs have frequently been developed in response to:

- Recognition that the old program is not working well;
- Pressure from parents, organizations, the courts, or one's boss;
- A desire to more effectively utilize scarce resources;
- Recognition of the need to eliminate negative labels;
- A desire to introduce greater program flexibility; and
- The need to comply with court directives or legislative mandates regarding such requirements as service in the least restrictive environment.

FIGURE 7–8 CHANGES OCCURRING IN THE CASCADE (FEWER SPECIALIZED PLACES; MORE DIVERSE "REGULAR" PLACES)

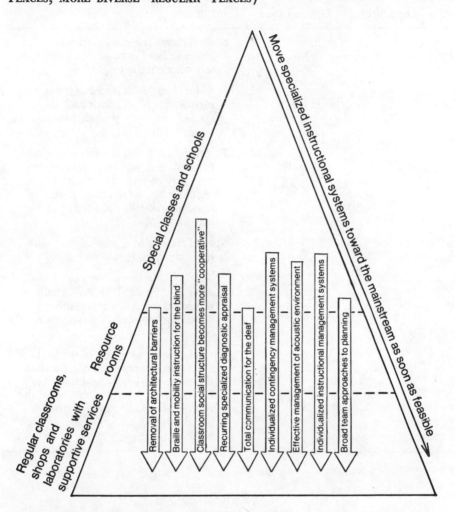

Reprinted from *Teaching Exceptional Children in All America's Schools,* by M. C. Reynolds and J. W. Birch, by permission of the Council for Exceptional Children (Reston, Va: The Council for Exceptional Children, 1977), p. 32.

Descriptions of various districts' special education programs can be found in the professional literature. Only a few will be included in this discussion. They have been selected to provide examples of a range of different programs.

The Houston Plan

One of the most frequently cited programs is the Houston Plan. As described by Meisgeier (1974), the plan was initiated in eighty-five elementary schools to

TABLE 7–2   COMPARISON OF PROGRAMS FOR TWO STUDENTS

Student Disability	Grade Level	Program
Severe Visual Problems	K–3	Special class (with integration) while learning Braille, basic math concepts, school orientation.
	4–8	Regular class (with resource room services for two periods each day) and special assistance provided for regular classroom teacher.
	9–12	Regular class (with the services of an itinerant teacher and a paid reader, who may be another student with a similar schedule of classes), Braille translation service, mobility instruction.
Moderate Mental Retardation	K–3	Special class in a regular school (with limited integration at recess and at lunch time).
	4–8	Special class in regular school (with increased interaction with other students, such as peer tutors from regular classes).
	9–12	Special class on high school campus (all day in grades nine and ten, one-half day in grades eleven and twelve). From ages sixteen to twenty-one, the student should be enrolled in a vocational training center for half of each school day.

help implement a systemwide change in special education programs. It was the Houston Independent School District's response to a self-perceived need and to Texas legislation known as "Plan A." The legislation provided the opportunity to establish new alternatives to meet the needs of exceptional children. The funding model gave impetus to change by providing monies for teachers, supportive personnel, and materials. The funds were based on total student enrollment rather than on the categorization of children.

The Houston Independent School District changed its special education model. Instead of making special education a subsystem of general education, the district formulated an "adaptive" system that responds to the needs of all children. The plan incorporated four major goals (Meisgeier 1974, p. 134):

1. To integrate the special and regular education programs, recognizing that each child is unique in the way he learns and that each child had different educational needs.
2. To make available the technology of a Continuous Progress Learning curriculum to meet the individual needs and differences of the entire educational community through teacher retraining.
3. To provide the regular classroom teacher with additional teacher aides, teacher specialists, and instructional materials.
4. To provide specialists in diagnostic and treatment procedures to support the efforts of the classroom teacher. To individualize the instructional programs and to provide the opportunity for individualized learning.

The Houston Plan attempted to accomplish its goals by utilizing a massive program of in-service education for all teachers, by using a broad range of services in order to integrate students with their nonhandicapped peers, and by establishing at each school a precision learning center that would serve all youngsters according to individual needs.

Burrello and Sage (1979), reporting on the progress made in implementing the Houston Plan, indicate that there is commitment to and implementation of many of the plan's positive aspects at the individual schools, but that the plan has not been fully implemented by the district. This is an interesting development, since more recent requirements might readily be met by the provisions of a plan that predated the law.

The Madison School Plan

In contrast to the Houston Plan, which was developed as a district model that "moves down" and is implemented at the school level, the Madison School Plan (Taylor and Soloway, 1974) was initiated at a local school site in the Santa Monica Unified School District with the intent that it would later become the model for the entire district.

Two major conceptual views were adopted as a means of moving away from a categorical model:

1. All exceptional children are learners, first and foremost. Their handicaps are secondary.
2. Most exceptional children can profit from some experiences in the regular classroom, provided that they are properly scheduled and receive appropriate supportive services.

Thus, children are viewed in terms of their educational abilities and needs rather than in terms of such factors as I.Q., emotional functioning, or motor skills. Each one is seen as a child whose functional ability lies between that of the least efficient learner and that of the most efficient learner and is assessed in terms of readiness for regular class functioning. A child could fall anywhere between the two extremes of the inefficient learner who needs full-time special class placement and the efficient learner who is capable enough to handle full-time regular class placement.

Taylor and Soloway (1974, p. 147) define four levels of competence that reflect readiness for regular-classroom functioning:

1. *Pre-Academic Competence.* This skill relates to the child's ability to function at the *readiness* or *process* level of learning. It includes the abilities of paying attention (A), starting an assignment immediately (S), working continuously without interruption (W), following task directions (F), doing what he is told (D), taking part verbally in discussions (T), and getting along with others (G). Pre-academic skills also relate to adequacy in perceptual-motor functioning and proficiency in language.
2. *Academic Competence.* This level relates to the traditional core subjects that are basic to all school programs: reading, writing, spelling, and arithmetic. The abilities of being right (R) and neat, efficient, and well organized (N) are also included.
3. *Setting Competence.* This level relates to the student's ability to function and profit from instruction in the various settings found in all regular classrooms. Such settings include (a) instruction by the teacher standing in front of the entire classroom (T/LC), (b) the student working independently among the entire classroom (I/LG), (c) the teacher instructing a small group of students (I/SG), (d) the student working independently within the small group (I/SG), (e) the student working alone with the teacher (T/S), or (f) the student working independently with the teacher readily available for assistance (I/S).
4. *Reward Competence.* This level relates to the child's susceptibility to traditional classroom rewards. Does the child work for such incentives as the pure "joy of learning"? to acquire new knowledge and skills? for knowledge of results? or for social praise and recognition? Less traditional types of reinforcement include sensory and activity experience, task completion, social attention, and tangibles.

To bring an appropriate instructional program to the students in the Madison School, two adjacent classrooms were combined by an inner connecting door. This became a learning center with three learning areas: (1) PreAcademic I, (2) PreAcademic II, and (3) Academic I (Academic II is the regular classroom). Such instructional areas allow students to move about according to need and also provide a resource-room facility for regular children in the school. Special education students are not labeled and can receive instruction from teachers trained in special education in the learning center. They can also be integrated into regular classes for one period each day or on a full-time basis.

The Madison School Plan has many advantages from an administrative point of view:

- Most importantly, it gives evidence of working for children.
- It is advantageous to have the option of implementing a particular model at a committed school without requiring the same model at every school in a district.
- Existing facilities (with only minor modifications) meet the needs of the plan.
- This model is probably no more expensive than one that uses categorical special classes.
- Even though regular-class integration is very much a part of the plan, it does not require that regular classroom teachers be overwhelmingly committed to mainstreaming all students; nor does it call for extensive in-service education and retraining of teachers.
- There is a written plan and a defined model.
- The plan encourages flexibility and an unhampered flow of students between special and regular classes.

In 1975, the Santa Monica District became one of the pilot districts to implement the state master plan for special education. This move added new components, such as the resource specialist program, to other parts of the ongoing program. Moving from operating in a single building to a district-wide program retains the model's major benefits at the single building while simultaneously disseminating benefits to others.

DISCUSSION

The models described represent only a few of the many that are mentioned in the professional literature or that may be observed if one takes the time to visit different school programs. They have been arbitrarily classified as (1) organizational models, (2) categorical or noncategorical models, (3) the spectrum of services approach, and (4) local school district or building models, so that the reader might be exposed to a variety of viewpoints.

Models that deliver educational services are important to educational administrators in policy-making roles. They must continually evaluate the success of current programs, new requirements imposed by law, and the needs and abilities of their agency. This should be done at least on an annual basis. As these reviews are conducted and plans for future school years are developed, the following items may serve as a foundation for discussion:

- P.L. 94–142 requires all states to submit a state plan for serving handicapped students. The state plan is the basis for local organizational planning.
- State plans may require that a written plan be developed by LEAs and submitted to the state agency.
- All administrative and teaching personnel must be committed to a model developed for or by an LEA if it is to be successfully implemented. It cannot be imposed on the participants with any prospect of success.
- A model can involve a whole state, a group of LEAs, a single LEA, or one school building.
- Development and dissemination of a written model enhances the communication process because everyone can see "the big picture" and understand the conceptual framework.
- Models should be designed to help people do their jobs more effectively and to promote effective utilization of resources.
- Having a model does not ensure a successful program, but it can provide the foundation for and serve as the system in which successful programs can grow.
- A special education model will probably be more effective if it utilizes the entire system rather than focusing on a small parallel system.
- Models that emphasize integration or mainstreaming must consider the skills, available time, and teaching load of regular classroom teachers as well as their willingness to cooperate. Special education personnel who provide support by doing, rather than telling, will usually succeed.
- Some models are designed solely for the mildly handicapped, while others deal with all disability levels.
- It is highly unlikely that one can develop a particular model that works best in all situations. LEAs must assess their needs and apply the conceptual frameworks, that best meet local needs.

SUMMARY

Chapter 7 discusses organizational structures that help provide educational services to pupils with exceptional needs. These organizational structures are often called models. A description of the models presents a conceptual framework from which to examine various school programs. Alternative approaches to the development of special education models are discussed from four different perspectives. In each of the four approaches (organizational, categorical and noncategorical, spectrum of services, and local district), the model is explained, examples are provided, and pros and cons are presented.

Finally, the chapter presents a discussion of the information provided on special education models and suggests a number of points that may be helpful to administrators when they evaluate and plan programs. One should always remember that "There is no inherent value in any organizational framework. It is nothing more than a vehicle which permits program development. Nonetheless, there must be structure before there can be function." (Isenberg 1966, p. 169)

NOTES

1. Federal agencies provide laws and regulations stating what must be done, check for compliance, and provide funds, but usually leave to the various states the option of developing their own models for how programs are to be organized.
2. For example, New York's special education programs are organized categorically, while Massachusetts' programs are not. California is moving from categorical programs to programs defined by the types of service provided. But until the State Master Plan for Special Education is implemented throughout the entire state, some LEAs will be using one model and other LEAs will use the other.
3. The California Master Plan for Special Education was adopted as a conceptual document by the State Board of Education in 1974 and implemented by the state legislature in AB 4040 (1975), AB 1250 (1977), and SB 1870 (1980).

REFERENCES

Burrello, L. C., and Gilliam, J. 1974. Administering special education programs— an interrelated service model. Unpublished paper.

Burrello, L. C., and Sage, D. D. 1979. *Leadership and change in special education.* Englewood Cliffs, N.J. Prentice-Hall, Inc.

California State Board of Education. 1974. *California master plan for special education.* Sacramento: State Department of Education.

Christie, L. S., McKenzie, H. S., and Burdett, C. S. 1972. The consulting teacher approach to special education: In-service training for regular classroom teachers. *Focus on Exceptional Children,* October, 4,5.

Deno, E. N. 1970. Special education as developmental capital. *Exceptional Children* 37:229–237.

Department of Health, Education, and Welfare. 1979. *Progress toward a free appropriate public education: A report to Congress on the implementation of Public Law 94–142:* The Education for All Handicapped Children Act. Washington, D.C.

Fox, W. L., Egner, A. N., Paolucci, P. E., Perelman, P. F., and McKenzie, H. S. 1974. An introduction to a regular classroom approach to special education. In *Instructional alternatives for exceptional children,* ed. E. N. Deno, pp. 22–46. Reston, Va.: The Council for Exceptional Children.

Haring, N. G. 1972. A strategy for the training of resource teachers for handicapped children. In *Exceptional children in regular classrooms,* eds. M. C. Reynolds and M. D. Davis. Minneapolis: University of Minnesota.

Isenberg, R. M. 1966. Administrative organization. *Sparsely populated areas: Guidelines for research.* Denver: Western Interstate Commission for Higher Education. Reprinted in *The process of special education administration*, eds. C. W. Meisgeier and J. D. King, pp. 169–74. Scranton, Pa.: International Textbook Co., 1970.

Johnson, D. E. 1967. Special education needs met by planning. *California State Federation—Council for Exceptional Children* 16,2:31–33.

Johnson, R. A. 1975. Models for alternative programming: A perspective. In *Alternatives for teaching exceptional children*, eds. E. L. Meyen, G. A. Vergason and R. J. Whelan, pp. 153–72. Denver: Love Publishing Co.

Lilly, M. S. 1971. A training based model for special education. *Exceptional Children* 37:745–49.

Massachusetts Education Code, Chapter 766. 1972.

Meisgeier, C. 1974. The Houston plan: A proactive integrated system plan for education. In *Instructional alternatives for exceptional children*, ed. E. N. Deno. Reston, Va.: The Council for Exceptional Children.

New York Department of Education. 1978. Amendment to the regulations of the Commissioner of Education. Part 200 of the regulations of the Commissioner of Education, Oct. 16. University of the State of New York, The State Department of Education.

New York Department of Education. 1979. *Helping children with handicapping conditions in New York State: The New York State plan submitted under the Education for All Handicapped Children Act* (P.L. 94–142). University of the State of New York, the State Department of Education.

Reynolds, M. C. 1962. A framework for considering some issues in special education. *Exceptional children* 27:367–70.

Reynolds, M. C., and Birch, J. W. 1978. *Teaching exceptional children in all America's schools.* Reston, Va.: The Council for Exceptional Children.

Taylor, F. D., and Soloway, M. M. 1974. The Madison School plan: A functional model for merging the regular and special classrocms. In *Instructional alternatives for exceptional children*, ed. E. N. Deno, pp. 144–55. Reston, Va.: The Council for Exceptional Children.

Willenberg, E. P. 1970. Administrative structures for special education. In *The process of special education administration*, eds. C. W. Meisgeier and J. D. King. Scranton, Pa.: International Textbook Co.

8

Full Program Operation: The Large District

"The bureaucratic organization that is unable to command the support of its clients, the general public and important centers of government power will find survival difficult. Probably no public organization is more dependent on public support than the school system. The system has an almost endless appetite for resources and an almost total accessibility to public scrutiny."

(Bresnick 1974, p. 27)

INTRODUCTION [1]

Major city school systems have become so large and complex that a discussion of special education programs is somewhat difficult. This difficulty is more than a problem of numbers; it also relates to other urban concerns such as decentralization, court-ordered desegregation, socioeconomic differences, geographic distances, and the bureaucracy of most large organizations. Nothing in a large district can be done in isolation. Every decision made and every action taken has a tremendous domino effect. A large district is made up of countless divisions and subdivisions, and each one must plan for itself and with the others. The special education division must help other divisions see their responsibilities to programs for handicapped and gifted children.

Special education is only one of many programs that administrators are responsible for. Thus, administrators tend to resist having new duties laid on their shoulders when they do not get adequate help to do the job. But if administrators are not kept informed about special education, some very volatile situations may arise.

Although large school systems face a number of problems in their special education programs, they also have many advantages when compared to their smaller counterparts. Sheer numbers allow many persons to function in more specialized roles, provide resources for a broader variety of support services, and make it possible to offer programs to children with low incidence handicaps. A discussion of numbers becomes more meaningful when appropriate comparisons are made. A large city school system enrolls more handicapped students than make up the total school population of some other districts. For example, the Los Angeles Unified School District had an unduplicated pupil count of some 45,000 handicapped students served for the 1979 school year.

The material in this chapter focuses on special education in large city school systems. The chapter includes a brief discussion of (1) the power structure and the position of special education within that structure, (2) the issues of centralized versus decentralized special education programs, (3) benefits and problems from a management perspective, and (4) suggested management techniques.

THE POWER STRUCTURE

In most cases, a discussion of a large organization's power structure must be concerned with outside influences as well as the hierarchy existing within the organization itself. If one were discussing a large corporation that manufactures and sells a product, outside influences would include such factors as consumer preference, price and quality of goods from competitors, and a community's tax structure. When the organization being discussed is a large urban school district, outside influences include state and federal laws relating to education, various community groups (such as organizations representing different minority groups), different parent groups (each representing children with a different handicap), and groups representing different geographic areas of the city. Occasionally the different special interest groups unite to champion a certain cause; more often each one is busy with its own interests; and sometimes different special interests are in conflict with one another, as when two groups may be competing for limited funds.

Just as a manufacturing corporation must be influenced by the buyers of its product, a school district must be influenced by its students, by their parents, and by other politically active persons in the community. And while other organizations may operate in relative seclusion, large school districts operate "in a fish bowl." The public is constantly made aware of happenings in the schools by the media.

Recognizing that the fish bowl effect can be an asset rather than a liability, large school systems use this opportunity to help gain the support of individuals and groups who form the outside power structure. Most large districts have a variety of commissions, committees, and volunteer groups that serve in advisory capacities at different levels in the organization. Examples of this type of function are presented in Table 8–1. They are very much a part of the district's power structure.

The administrative structure within a large school system is highly complex, and special education programs compete with all other programs for a favorable position within the system. The administrative flow chart in Figure 8–1

TABLE 8–1   EXAMPLES OF ADVISORY GROUPS

Group	Advises:
Commission on Minority Relations	Board of Education
Committee for Curriculum Adoption	Associate Superintendent, Instruction
Committee for Employment of the Handicapped	Assistant Superintendent, Personnel
Community Advisory Committee for Special Education	Assistant Superintendent, Special Education
School Subcommittee for TMR Program	School Principal

(also see Figures 7–1 and 7–2) is one way of looking at organizational structure. Another approach is to think in terms of levels of administration and the lines for communication and for approval of proposed activities, as presented in Table 8–2.

The reader can trace lines of authority through a flow chart or by considering administrative levels and the various people to whom others report. This presents a picture of how special education is represented in the organization of a given system and how different service needs are channeled through the hierarchy. Lines of authority for special education are shown in Figure 8–2. On the positive side, tracing lines of authority indicates how many different resources can be directed toward the needs of a given student. On the negative side, it illustrates the potential problems of delay in resolving issues and the cumbersome lines of communication weaving throughout the layers of administration.

Individuals who are responsible for the education of handicapped students must know how to utilize the system in order to bring the best possible programs to these students. To do so, they must understand "the pecking order," must establish visibility within the system, and must have influence with top-level administrators. They must find ways to work with separate, sometimes competing, divisions. It is only by understanding the district's power structure and working within it that one can ensure that programs receive the attention they deserve.

CENTRALIZED VERSUS DECENTRALIZED PROGRAMS

A discussion of centralized versus decentralized programs could properly be placed within the preceding section on the power structure, in the chapter on special education models, or as a separate topic. A separate approach is taken

FIGURE 8–1   DADE COUNTY PUBLIC SCHOOLS DISTRICT ORGANIZATIONAL
CHART EXCEPTIONAL STUDENT EDUCATION

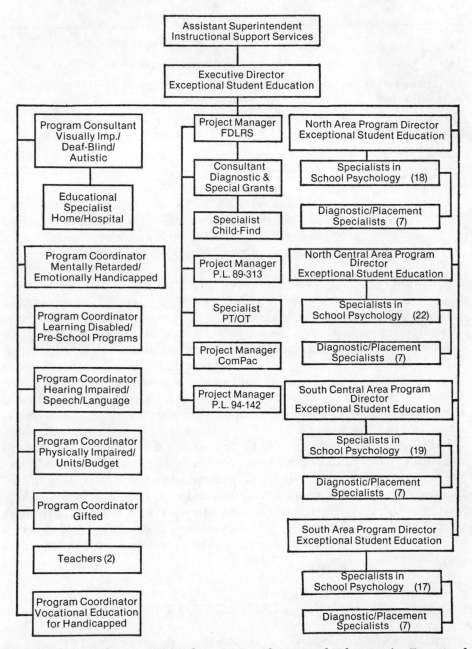

Reprinted from *Dade County Procedures for Providing Special Education for Exceptional
Students, 1976–77,* by permission of the Dade County Superintendent of Schools, Dade
County Public Schools, Miami, Florida. ERIC Document 136 497.

Full Program Operation: The Large District 187

TABLE 8–2 LEVELS OF ADMINISTRATION

	Position	Responsible to:
Level I	Superintendent Deputy Superintendent	Board of Education Superintendent
Level II	Associate Superintendent, Instruction Associate Superintendent, Business Operation Associate Superintendent, Support Services Area Superintendent	Deputy Superintendent
Level III	Assistant Superintendent, Special Education Assistant Superintendent, Personnel Assistant Superintendent, Pupil Personnel Services Assistants to Area Superintendents	Associate Superintendent, Instruction Asssociate Superintendent, Business Associate Superintendent, Support Services Area Superintendent
Level IV	Director, Programs for EMR Director, Certificated Personnel Director, Psychological Services School Principal	Assistant Superintendent, Special Education Assistant Superintendent, Personnel Assistant Superintendent, Pupil Personnel Services Assistant to Area Superintendent

because the issue is primarily related to large city school systems and is of sufficient importance to receive special attention. Bresnick (1974, p. 19) says, "Decentralization and recentralization are continuing phenomena in large bureaucracies, each cyclically emerging to prominence." Special education's position within the cyclical process adds another dimension to questions concerning the benefits of centralized versus decentralized programs.

For the reader who is not familiar with the functions of centralized and decentralized programs, or is not familiar with the way in which special education fits into this issue, two brief definitions are provided.

- A centralized school district has only one board of education, one superintendent, and one administrative structure. All school personnel are directly responsible to this centralized unit. The term "centralized" does *not* refer to moving students to a central location.
- A decentralized school district has divided itself on a geographical basis and has delegated part of its responsibility and part of its authority to each area. Each area has a superintendent, and some systems have area boards of education.

FIGURE 8–2   LINES OF AUTHORITY FOR SPECIAL EDUCATION

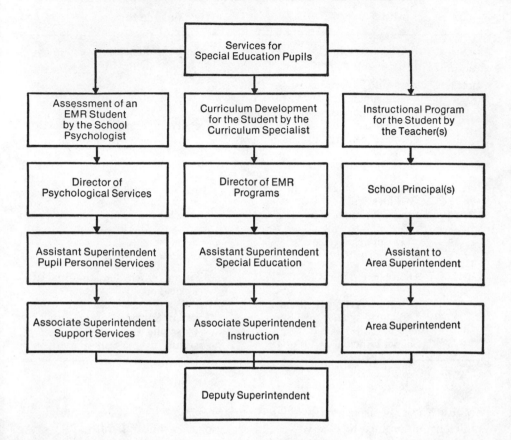

All large decentralized city systems have allowed the central board of education to retain final authority and responsibility. In most instances, functions such as allocation of resources, noneducational support services, and district wide planning are retained at the central level. Most have also maintained special education as a centralized function.

The 1976–77 administrative flow chart for Dade County (Figure 8–3) shows a system that has some decentralized functions administered through area superintendents, and some centralized functions administered through the associate superintendent for instruction. The Los Angeles Unified School District is decentralized into ten administrative areas, but also maintains a centralized special education division. Bresnick (1974) indicates that many special education functions in New York City are centralized for administrative purposes. McKeown (1978) indicates that the Toronto Metropolitan Board serves exceptional children on behalf of the six area boards. A 1973 survey reported by Nash (1975) of twenty of the nation's largest school districts indicated that most decentralized districts had not included special education in the decentralization process. The organization of special education divisions was not significantly changed.

From the above discussion, it may appear that decisions about decentralization of a large school district are not very pertinent to administering special education programs. However, such is not the case, as will subsequently be shown.

Even though the top administrative staff for a special education program may retain a centralized role, its implementers are usually divided between line responsibility to the central administration and responsibility to the different area administrations. Table 8–3 shows how these services may be divided.

Personnel such as speech therapists and school psychologists, while responsible to the central administration, may work within a setting directed by the area administration. Numerous other services such as budget development, transportation, in-service education, and program leadership have usually remained centralized.

Many problems must be resolved in order to decide if a large system should implement a centralized or a decentralized special education program. Problem areas include dual governance, technical expertise versus administrative authority, placement of low incidence programs, maintenance of common standards, and struggles for power.

Obviously, it is difficult to determine whether or not decentralization of a large system produces better results. Perhaps this is the reason for the cyclical phenomena mentioned earlier. There have, however, been some attempts at evaluation. One study reported by Silberman (1977) found that parents feel more favorable toward decentralization than do school personnel. Some of the positive comments by both groups included:

• More local autonomy
• Better access to the administration
• More citizen participation
• More support services.

TABLE 8–3   ADMINISTRATIVE LINES FOR PROGRAM IMPLEMENTERS

Program Implementer	Line Responsibility to:
Teachers of LD, EMR Programs	Area Administration
Principals of LD, EMR Programs	Area Administration
Teacher of Severely Multihandicapped	Central Administration
Principal of Special School	Central Administration
Speech Therapists	Central Administration
School Psychologists	Central Administration

FIGURE 8–3   EXCEPTIONAL CHILD EDUCATION CHART 1976–77, DADE COUNTY
PUBLIC SCHOOLS

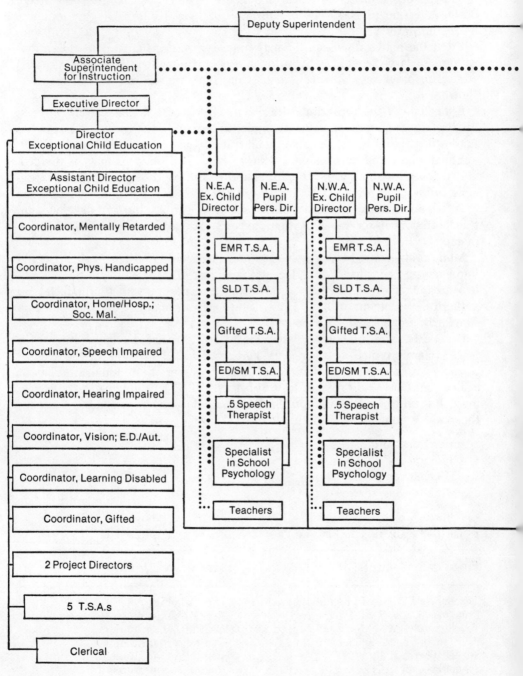

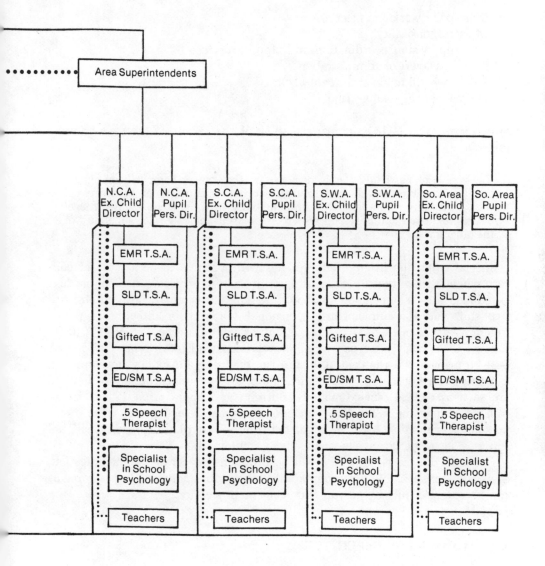

Solid lines connecting boxes indicate direct relationships

•••• Required cooperative relationships

•••••• Staff relationship

Reprinted from *Dade County Procedures for Providing Special Education for Exceptional Students, 1976–77*, by permission of the Dade County Superintendent of Schools, Dade County Public Schools, Miami, Florida. ERIC Document 136 497.

The negative comments included:

- More paperwork and meetings
- More responsibility
- Less supervision, coordination, and support services
- Needless layers of administration
- Decisions still made at the central office
- No real change taking place.

Silberman (1977, p. 16) summarized some of the results of the evaluation as follows:

> The results of our study clearly demonstrate that power has not been significantly re-distributed by decentralization, but that decentralization has increased the equivocality of authority and accountability in the system.... Each level desires increased authority and resources for itself and more accountability of the other levels.

Special education in large city systems will continue to be a topic of concern whenever centralization versus decentralization is discussed. The question is reduced to: "Which functions should be handled by the central administrative staff and the implementing personnel whom they direct, and which functions can more effectively be decentralized?" Burrello and Sage (1979) suggest that program advocacy, public relations, and interagency liaison can best be managed at the central level. Also, planning and policy development, as related to resource allocation, curriculum, and general program evaluation, are seen as central office functions. Burrello and Sage propose that decentralized management functions include personnel selection and placement; personnel evaluation, case management, and pupil placement; instructional supervision; resource management; and parent relations.

However the pie is cut, there will be problems concerning communication, division of responsibility, accountability, and coordination. These problems can be resolved only by careful management procedures.

MANAGEMENT PERSPECTIVES

Benefits of Large Systems

The concept that "bigger is better" can find support in many different special programs. To give a very obvious example, blind or deaf-blind students constitute a very small percentage of the school population. When they are spread throughout the twelve grades of school, the number of these students per grade level becomes extremely small. Large school systems have sufficient numbers of these students to provide programs for them. Their smaller counterparts do not. Likewise, the ability to provide specialized centers and schools requires a large population base. A full range of program alternatives is needed to provide an appropriate educational program for all exceptional children. This is possible within the large system.

In terms of personnel, a school system can benefit from having skilled grant writers, curriculum specialists, assessment specialists, and so on. In large systems, there can be a conscious effort to recruit people with highly specialized skills. They can function in a narrow, specialized assignment and continue to enhance their special skills. In smaller systems, personnel must function in many different roles. Thus, they may not develop the same level of expertise.

While resistance to change in a large system is frequently seen as a problem, it can also be an asset. If a district is committed and has valid priorities, a lack of ability to make rapid changes may serve as a stabilizing factor. Curriculum, budget, facility commitment, capital outlay and many other parts of the program may benefit from this stabilizing influence.

Problems with Large Systems

Large school systems frequently have a unique relationship with policy-making agencies within their state. These systems present an anomaly for legislatures and state boards of education. Laws and regulations that are appropriate for all other school districts within a state may be very inappropriate for a large system. There is a tendency to think, "We must adopt rules that are best for the majority," without realizing that the majority in terms of numbers of school districts may not be the majority in terms of numbers of pupils or school personnel. Four or five large city systems may enroll a majority of the pupils within a given state.

When differences arise over philosophy or compliance issues, there may be a power struggle between the school districts and other agencies. In this case, there is a tendency for the policy-making body to "pick on" the large districts. An agency may believe that "If we can whip Goliath into shape, the rest will follow."

Large districts are plagued by the spotlight effect. Almost anything that happens is subject to extensive coverage from press and broadcast media. Headlines such as "High School Graduate Can't Read" reflect negatively on the district. Any negative reports regarding handicapped students become instant news items because of their emotional appeal.

Because of their sheer numbers of pupils and personnel, many problems are unique to large districts. A presentation by Hannon (1978) helps one to understand size and numbers by utilizing just a few examples. Paraphrasing Hannon's report: Chicago has approximately 130,000 high school students. Fifteen percent are absent each day. At the rate of seven dollars per student per day, that is a loss in state funds of $136,500 per day, or $24,480,000 per year. Substitutes for teachers who are absent, at forty-two dollars each, cost the district $65,000 per day, or $11,700,000 per year.

A second illustration of the tremendous size of large districts comes from the National Institute of Education (1973). Their report indicates that the chancellor of New York City's schools is responsible for the education of more children than are enrolled in thirty-nine of the fifty states. Still another example of sheer numbers may be seen in Table 8–4, which gives some statistics for the Los Angeles Unified School District.

Within the schools enumerated in Table 8–4 are some 45,000 handicapped pupils served in about two dozen different programs. These huge numbers cause difficulty in communicating, planning, maintaining uniform standards, and keeping good human relationships. Sheer numbers in the form of thousands of staff members, hundreds of school sites, and literally *tons* of records may cause an insensitivity to individual needs and to program trouble spots.

Physical distance is another management problem faced by large districts. The tendency to think of a district as a single unit is negated when one may have to drive on an expressway for an hour or more to get from one boundary to the opposite side of the district. Thus, services such as delivery of supplies, transportation, and placement of programs cannot be organized on a district-wide basis. They must be regionalized.

Because a system is large, it is able to develop programs for children with all types of handicaps. This ability to be a full service agency becomes well known and attracts parents whose children have the most severe problems.

TABLE 8–4 STATISTICAL INFORMATION: LOS ANGELES UNIFIED
SCHOOL DISTRICT

Type	Number of Schools
Elementary	429
Junior High	75
Senior High	49
Opportunity	5
Continuation	42
Schools for Handicapped	25
Magnet Schools and Centers	46
Community Adult Schools	27
Regional Occupation Centers	5
Regional Occupation Program Center	1
	704

Note: The school district also operates eighty-nine children's centers, seven skill centers, and two opportunity centers.

Parents frequently move their residence to where they can find appropriate services for their children. This is known as a "magnet effect." The magnet effect may be a positive factor for the district, but it can also have a negative impact since programs for the severely handicapped are the most expensive of all school programs. They also require other resources, such as special transportation, special facilities, and medically related services.

Finally, the problem of finding adequate financial resources plagues a large city school district. Funding methods that work well for an affluent suburb may not work at all for a less affluent urban area. Valdez (1977), discussing urban education problems in Denver, listed numerous difficulties caused by or related to the fiscal status of city school districts. Included were the eroding of the district's financial base, controlled percentage increases, changed methods of financial control, the halting of annexation (which might provide new resources), a high percentage of disadvantaged children, and costly desegregation orders. While these problems are primarily related to general education, special education programs are also greatly affected. Any time a district is having overall financial problems, very costly special education programs will be in trouble.

MANAGEMENT PRACTICES IN LARGE SYSTEMS

Many management techniques are unique (or at least more appropriate) to large systems. For example, a written communication to all principals in a district with four hundred or five hundred principals is quite a different matter from what it is in a small district. Thus, large and small systems require different management styles. Although there are many different management practices, this chapter will provide only three very brief examples of ways in which practices may be different in large systems.

Communication Processes

One of the most perplexing problems facing administrators is how to exchange information about rules, procedures, and program changes. Obviously, communication must be in writing and must utilize a common format. There must be a hierarchy of documents so that everyone can understand the importance of a given piece of paper. For example, communications relating to rules and procedures could be included in any of the following:

- A district's board policies
- A district's administrative regulations
- General bulletins received from top-level administration indicating ongoing policies

- General memoranda sent to all divisions and schools and including general announcements and information
- Reference memoranda containing information that should be retained and limited to a specific audience, and
- Limited memoranda containing information limited to a specific audience and event.

Small districts also follow a process of formal communication, but it is less structured and more information can be informally handled. In addition to means of communication among administrators, there must be an effective means of communicating with teachers and parents. In most cases, these contacts are made by or through school principals so that all parents receive appropriate information from the district office.

Recruitment, Selection, and Training of Staff

As previously stated, large numbers of employees allow for considerable specialization of function. With careful selection a staff can include skilled grant writers, legislative experts, specialists in curriculum development, and skilled in-service leaders, as well as program administrators. Including specialized individuals on a staff enhances the central administration's ability to provide meaningful support service to those at the operational level.

Selecting well-trained teachers is critical to program success. The special education division depends on the proficiency of individuals in the personnel division. The selection process can be enhanced by having people in the personnel division who are knowledgeable about special education programs. Also, working with college and university student teaching programs allows a district to conduct in-depth evaluation before selecting applicants and gives a participating district a recruiting edge.

Large districts have the ability to offer many in-service training programs. Such training, while frequently directed to improving teaching skills, can also be used to inform personnel about district procedures and to solicit communications from the field.

Public Relations

A broad public relations perspective is needed to enhance special education programs. Leadership personnel must maintain good relationships with parents, community leaders, community advisory groups, outside agencies, and policy-making groups. They must also have a good working relationship with other divisions within their school district. Within the system, special education administrators must work with others in many areas. Examples include:

- Planning new programs (several divisions such as budgeting, housing, and instructional services must be involved)
- Assessment (this service may be provided for special education by the pupil personnel services division)
- Locating programs (the divisions of housing and transportation must be involved in decisions regarding program location)
- Assignment of staff (the divisions of instruction, special education, and personnel must work cooperatively in meeting this responsibility).

Outside of the system, public relations work must involve various ethnic population representatives, representatives of different geographic areas, parents of children in different special education groups, and other community groups. Good relationships make possible effective operation and management of the programs. They are more difficult to maintain in a large system, but they can and must be maintained.

SUMMARY

Chapter 8 provides a brief overview of factors that are characteristic of urban education and discusses special education in large city school systems. Since special programs are affected by all other aspects of a large system's unique capabilities and problems, factors that concern the total system form the basis of the chapter. Obviously, one cannot adequately discuss special education without also discussing an agency's power structure, centralization versus decentralization issues, benefits and problems inherent in a large district, and some large system management techniques.

The power structure is discussed in terms of outside influences and in-house organization. The position of special education programs and administrators is presented in narrative discussion and in administrative flow charts. Since the special education administrator is several administrative layers below the top in a large system, special programs depend on general administrators to represent them in the power structure.

Centralized and decentralized programs are discussed. Since most large districts have decentralized some functions, it is important to understand the position of special education in the decentralization process. In most instances, one could say that supportive administrative functions remain centralized while instructional functions are decentralized. This contributes to a balanced organizational structure, as discussed by Featherstone and Hill (1971).

The chapter discusses such benefits of a large system as the ability to serve low incidence groups, the range of specialized support services, personnel's ability to specialize and serve a narrow function, stability, and full program capabilities. It also discusses problems inherent in a large system, such as power struggles with state agencies, the spotlight effect, large numbers of students and of personnel, difficulty of communication, physical distances between one part of a district and another, the attraction of children with the most severe problems, and difficulty obtaining adequate resources.

Finally, Chapter 8 discusses some management techniques that can be helpful to administrators working in large school systems.

NOTES

1. Special appreciation is expressed to Al Casler, Administrative Coordinator, Division of Special Education, Los Angeles Unified School District, for providing materials, ideas, and information used by the author in writing this chapter.

REFERENCES

Bresnick, D. 1974. Cyclical renewal in a large city school district—decentralization and the policy process. *Educational Administration Quarterly* 10,2:19–34.

Burrello, L. C., and Sage, D. D. 1979. *Leadership and change in special education.* Englewood Cliffs, N.J.: Prentice-Hall, Inc.

Dade County Superintendent of Schools. 1974. *Dade county procedures for providing special education for exceptional students.* Miami: Dade County Public Schools. ERIC Document 136 497.

Featherstone, R. L., and Hill, F. W. 1971. Urban school decentralization. In *Urban Education,* ed. R. R. Heidenreich. Arlington: College Readings, Inc.

Hannon, J. P., et al. 1978. Management analysis in the Chicago Public Schools. Paper read at American Educational Research Association Annual Meeting, 27–31 March 1978, at Toronto, Canada. ERIC Document 161 968.

McKeown, E. N. 1978. Planning for the individual needs of exceptional learners in a fast growing metropolitan community. Paper read at First World Congress on Future Special Education, 21 June–1 July 1978, at Stirling, Scotland. ERIC Document 158 508.

Nash, N. 1975. Decentralization and special education in the great city schools: A summary of survey results. In *Special education in school system decentralization,* ed. M. Reynolds. Minneapolis: Leadership Training Institute.

National Institute of Education. 1973. *Building capacity for renewal and reform: An initial report on knowledge production and utilization in education.* Washington, D.C.

Silberman, H. F. 1977. An evaluation of decentralization in a large school district. Paper read at Annual Meeting of the American Education Research Association, 4–8 April 1977, at New York, N.Y. ERIC Document 139 816.

Valdez, B. 1977. Urban education problems: Now and in the future. Paper read at Annual Meeting of the National School Boards Association, 26–28 March 1977, at Houston, Texas. ERIC Document 137 972.

9

Organizing
Cooperative
Programs

"Cooperation is an old and familiar
Yankee characteristic. In earlier
years, it found expression in quilt-
ing bees, corn huskings, and barn
raisings. . . . It is a concept directly
applicable to the need for developing service programs which
school systems individually
cannot provide with efficiency
and economy."

(Isenberg 1964, p. 15)

INTRODUCTION

The term "cooperative program" has no universal meaning in general use by
educators. Instead, the concepts and uses applied to this term range from an
informal agreement between two teachers to legislated cooperative programs
affecting several local school districts. Since administrators frequently deal
with different kinds of cooperative programs, this chapter will discuss: (1)
potential cooperative efforts within a given school or district and (2) mandated and voluntary cooperative programs involving local school districts.

At the local school level, cooperative efforts are directed toward meeting
the needs of individual pupils through sharing pupils' time and applying the
professional expertise of different staff members. A pupil might spend part of
his/her time in a special education class, part in a regular class, and also
receive speech therapy or adaptive physical education. Thus, several staff
members would cooperate to provide an appropriate educational program for
this pupil. Cooperative arrangements can be either informal or formal.

Since special education programs in the schools began, LEAs have found
it difficult to provide programs for very small numbers of children with similar
needs and to efficiently manage available resources. While these problems
have existed in a number of other program areas, special education programs
have presented the most difficult organizational questions. A number of different cooperative models have emerged to resolve these questions.

COOPERATIVE PROGRAMS AT THE SCHOOL SITE

As soon as the one-room schoolhouse was replaced by schools with two or more teachers, informal cooperative agreements began to develop. For example, a teacher might say, "I'll be responsible for teaching gym if you will teach health to all of the kids," or "Send your slow readers to me at ten o'clock and I'll send my advanced readers to work with you." Of course, teachers will continue to make informal arrangements, usually to the benefit of both teachers and pupils.

In terms of organized cooperation, the next step up may be integrating handicapped students into regular classes for a portion of the school day. A secondary school may refer to this as scheduling. Nevertheless, it requires a commitment from the principal and cooperative efforts between teachers.

Many LEAs and several states have broadly implemented a resource teacher plan in order to meet student needs in the least restrictive environment. Under such a plan, a child with learning disabilities may be based in a regular class. The child spends part of the day receiving special instruction in the resource room, or receiving assistance from the resource teacher within the regular classroom. The resource teacher may also aid the regular classroom teacher in identifying specific learning problems and planning remediation techniques.

Resource teachers and resource rooms were successfully used to assist the visually handicapped before they were applied to many other special students. For many years, resource teachers and resource rooms have provided services such as converting printed materials into Braille, offering readers, collecting Braille and large-print materials, and obtaining optical and projection devices. Regular classroom teachers and visually handicapped students use the services of the resource teacher and the facilities of the resource room as they are needed.

INTRA-DISTRICT COOPERATIVE PROGRAMS

While some programs for cooperative action operate only at a given school site, others operate on a districtwide basis. Again, these programs are primarily designed to provide supplementary services.

Speech therapy programs serve the greatest number of children. Speech therapists serve youngsters who have articulation, voice, rhythm (stuttering), and language development problems. Most of these students are in regular classes, but speech therapists also work with students from other special education programs. Teachers and therapists must resolve scheduling conflicts in order for this cooperative effort to work. A child's time must be organized so that time spent outside of class does not cause problems meeting class requirements. For example, what happens if a child is with the speech therapist two mornings each week during the time mathematics is being taught in the classroom?

A different approach is called for when a child has a physical handicap and needs regular physical therapy. Since a physical therapist uses a great deal of equipment, it is not usually feasible to have him/her travel from school to school to serve different children. Instead, all students who need this service usually attend the same school, and the physical therapy facility is located at that school. Thus, a particular school in the district may provide classroom and related services for all physically handicapped children in the district, as illustrated in Figure 9–1. Figure 9–1 shows the number of different services that can be directed toward a child through the cooperative efforts of many

FIGURE 9–1 CLASSROOM AND SUPPORTIVE SERVICES FOR PHYSICALLY HANDICAPPED STUDENTS

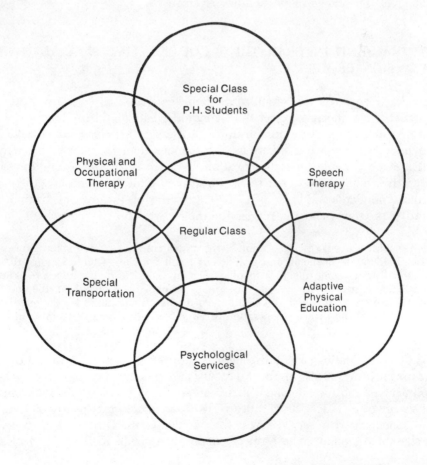

individuals within a system. It also points out the need for good management so that cooperation does not degenerate into competition for a student's time.

Another type of intra-district cooperative effort is a program based on the concept of the helping teacher. This type of program has a number of variations. The Vermont consulting teacher program (Fox et al. 1974), the diagnostic/prescriptive teacher program (Prouty and McGarry 1974), and others are basically designed to provide training and assistance to regular teachers, along with programming for special education students. This program's strengths include mainstreaming children and educating teachers about children's special needs. A possible weakness is that the special education specialist spends less time giving children direct service.

From an administrative point of view, locally designed cooperative efforts have many advantages. They can be worked out to meet local needs, are based on local priorities, can be changed without outside permission, are designed to fully utilize local resources, and usually have greater support at the operational level. The range of possibilities is extensive.

REGIONAL AND INTER-DISTRICT COOPERATIVE SPECIAL EDUCATION PROGRAMS

Educational agencies can organize cooperative action in so many different ways that it is difficult to select those methods that should be described in a book of this nature. Some administrative structures are very formal and defined in legislation, while others are little more than friendly verbal agreements. Some include special education as one aspect of a multipurpose cooperative, while others exist solely for special education purposes.

Lavin and Sanders (1974, p. i) explain some of the reasons behind cooperative programs and the reason for their diversity:

> Faced with a needs-resources crunch, the states consider plans for reorganization. Inadequate financing and insufficient pupil population often require that school districts come together to obtain or to share needed services. At the same time, there is considerable desire to remain autonomous at the local school level. It is precisely this uniqueness mediated with state legislation that has produced the diverse cooperation arrangements that emerge from state to state.

While consolidating school districts has reduced their number in the United States from over 125,000 to about 17,000 (and thereby increased the average enrollment of those remaining), many are still too small to offer a comprehensive program of services. Trudeau (1973) indicated that nearly 60 percent of all school districts served fewer than 1,200 pupils. Obviously, districts of this size must employ some form of cooperative action if they are to offer a range of services for handicapped students. We can identify a number of ways in which districts organize for cooperative action.

Local school organization must conform to state legislative prescriptions or allowances. This leads to a variety of organizational structures. Within these structures, numerous modes for cooperative action are developed. At least three different patterns are found at the state level:

- *Single unit of school governance.* Consists of one statewide unit. For example, in Hawaii all state schools are a part of one district and under the state education agency's direction.
- *Two-level system of school governance.* Consists of the SEA and the LEA. For example, Utah has an SEA and about forty LEAs. The LEA is frequently coterminous with county boundaries, and schools within that county are all part of the same school district. Other examples are in Dade County, Florida, and Montgomery County, Maryland, where the county is the LEA. But whether the districts are county or city schools, there is no intermediate education unit (IEU). Lavin and Sanders (1974) indicated that nineteen states had no legally created IEU.
- *Three-level system of school governance.* Consists of the SEA, the IEU, and the LEA. The IEU may be the county, as in California and Michigan; a board of cooperative educational services, as in Colorado and New York; a supervisory union, as in some New England states; or some form of regional unit.

If a state has only one district, no additional administrative structure is needed in order to initiate cooperative special education programs. If a state has a two-level organizational structure, LEAs may form cooperative groups, but they tend to be directed by the LEAs rather than to function as an IEU. If a state has a three-level organizational structure, the IEU frequently serves as the base for cooperative special education programs, as well as having other supervisory or regulatory functions. A more detailed discussion of the various administrative organizations follows.

The Office of the County Superintendent of Schools

As previously mentioned, the county school office functions as the LEA in some states. In this case, the county board of education and superintendent collect state and federal aid, levy local taxes, and provide all school programs. Special education programs in all towns and cities are operated by the county schools. If needed, inter-district cooperation usually takes the form of contractual services or cooperative programs with a neighboring county school office.

If the county school office is also an IEU, its usual purpose is to assist the

SEA in supervising local programs and/or to help LEAs provide school programs. At first, many of these offices did not directly operate any school programs. They served such functions as supplying fiscal control for the LEAs, serving as instructional media centers, and providing support staff when LEAs could not reasonably have their own specialized staff. However, as vocational education and special education programs developed and individual LEAs did not have adequate numbers or resources to handle them, it became a function of the IEU to operate these programs for LEAs. In essence, the IEU became an LEA for a limited purpose. In many states, county schools have gained recognition for their outstanding special education programs.

Several other factors about the special education programs operated by county schools should be of interest to school administrators:

- Some IEUs have the same type of taxing authority and revenue base as the LEAs. Their broader geographic base is an advantage.
- The IEU frequently serves students from the low incidence groups and the more severely handicapped, while the LEA serves mildly handicapped children.
- The trend is toward establishing larger service areas so that more children can be served more effectively, thus upgrading program quality and efficiency.
- The county district operates successfully as an IEU in both rural and urban areas. For example, according to the most recent unduplicated pupil count, the Los Angeles County Superintendent of Schools Office served some 12,000 children in special education programs, while LEAs within the county served an additional 86,000 special education students.
- County districts usually have an elected or appointed board of education, as opposed to representatives from each component school district.
- Two or more counties may join together as an IEU for special education services.

Although the present trend is toward using more cooperative programs, there appears to be a reaction against having counties serve as the IEU. Presently, movement is toward an area or regional organization that is not limited by county lines.

Other Forms of IEUs

New York and Colorado have IEUs called boards of cooperative educational services (BOCES). According to Lavin and Sanders (1974), the BOCES in New York were initiated in 1948 to meet the needs of rural areas. However, it was soon found that they also meet the needs of metropolitan areas. Currently, New York has some forty-eight BOCES serving more than seven hundred local school districts. Each BOCES has a superintendent who is responsible to a board of education and to the state commissioner of education. The BOCES's governing boards are appointed by component LEA boards. The LEAs frequently appoint one of their own board members.

Observations by this author indicate that BOCES services can be described under two general headings:

- Direct services to students, such as special education and vocational education
- Support services to LEAs, such as consultant services and curriculum development.

BOCES, while technically classified as IEUs, are in most ways subservient to LEAs. Their governing board members are appointed by the LEAs and they have no taxing or regulatory authority over the LEAs. For special education purposes, BOCES are funded by LEAs. Each LEA pays a portion of the administrative costs on a pro-rata basis according to district enrollment and contributes to operating costs according to services utilized. BOCES have legal status throughout the state, and all LEAs are located within a BOCES geographic area. LEAs select the cooperative programs and services in which they wish to participate.

Other forms of intermediate education units are found in other states. In general, their functions are similar to those of the county IEU and the BOCES. Most provide direct services to pupils in limited areas, such as special education, vocational education, and career guidance, and they usually provide other services, such as media centers and curriculum development. Some IEUs have regulatory and supervisory control over LEAs, but many do not. Various states' IEUs are frequently different only in titles. Examples are

- Connecticut: Supervisory Union Districts
- Iowa: Regional Education Service Agencies
- Minnesota: Intermediate School District
- Oregon: Intermediate Education District
- Pennsylvania: Intermediate Unit
- Texas: Regional Education Service Center
- Washington: Intermediate Educational Service Agency
- Wisconsin: Cooperative Educational Services Agency.

The Special School District

One cooperative method of organization available under some state laws is the special school district. Isenberg (1964, p. 17) explained this as follows:

The special school district is an alternative to the voluntary special purpose agency illustrated by the educational cooperative. As an integral part of school government, except for such limitations of function as may be specified in its establishment, it operates in much the same way and with the same powers and responsibilities as any school district. It has distinct boundaries, a board of education, tax-levying authority, and is entitled to direct state financial support as may be provided by the state finance plan.

The most widely known special school district for special education is the St. Louis County, Missouri, district. Its boundaries overlie the total geographic area of the LEAs it serves. While a special district's independence gives it some advantages, these advantages may be overshadowed by the difficulties encountered in placing handicapped children with their nonhandicapped peers. This is certainly not an insurmountable obstacle, but it may be more difficult within this administrative structure than it is in a regular school district.

Formal LEA Cooperatives

School administrators have always recognized that an organizational structure may be appropriate for one kind of service and inappropriate for another. Thus, an elementary school district that has three hundred pupils may be able to do an excellent job with most educational programs, but not be able to adequately provide special education programs. It is often more expedient for a district to join a cooperative organization designed to meet a group's special needs than to consolidate with other LEAs. This type of cooperative action has taken a number of different directions.

As explained in a pamphlet produced by the Bureau of Educational Information Services for the Massachusetts State Board of Education (1977):

> Collaboratives arose to provide local school systems with mechanisms for joint solutions to common problems, the premise being that it is less expensive to perform certain tasks collectively than it is for individual school systems to be involved in separate but parallel efforts. . . .
> The characteristics of collaboratives vary greatly, but basically collaboration involves an agreement, either verbal or written, among two or more school systems to provide educational services or programs. Some agreements maintain the identity of each participating member school system; others provide for the establishment of a host community to act as fiscal agent or provide for the creation of an educational collaborative board. Some agreements seek to solve a single and sometimes isolated problem; others are multi-purpose and multi-service. Some Collaboratives function without any appropriation of monies; others are financed through contributions from participating member school systems and/or government and foundation grants. Some involve only two contiguous towns; others cover a large geographic region.

LEAs officially and usually voluntarily establish a formal cooperative program as an administrative entity. The following characteristics are usually present:

- A governing board (the LEA's superintendents may function in this role)
- An administrative staff
- Funding (received from the state and from component LEAs)
- Employees (may be special program employees or may be the LEA's employees).

The cooperative may provide services for all special students or may only handle low incidence groups, with districts conducting their own programs for the educable mentally retarded and learning disabled. In most cases, cooperatives do not own buildings or major equipment. LEAs furnish facilities through some form of sharing plan or reimbursement schedule.

Because of the voluntary nature of participation in these cooperative programs, LEAs usually are highly supportive. The cooperative exists to meet their needs, they decide the extent of their participation and changes can easily and quickly be made. However, a formal cooperative is stable enough to maintain high standards and good program control. Examples of voluntary (but formal) cooperative programs include:

California: special education service regions (may be one county, multi-county, or multi-district within a county)

Massachusetts: educational collaboratives (about forty-three are currently in operation)

Ohio: councils of independent schools

Tennessee: educational cooperatives.

Informal Agreements and Tuition Contracting

When LEAs elect to use informal agreements rather than organized cooperatives as their mode for providing special education services, the administrative structure (or, more correctly, lack of structure) is quite different. The following items tend to characterize this type of arrangement:

- No centrally employed staff
- An advisory committee instead of a governing board
- Formal fiscal agreements and informal program agreements
- Short-term agreements that are usually annually renewed.

An informal cooperative agreement might involve District A operating a program for deaf and hard-of-hearing children, District B offering a program for visually handicapped students, and District C providing a program for orthopedically handicapped children. Students from all three districts would attend the program that best suited their needs. Since no central administrative staff members are employed, an informal cooperative agreement cuts down expenses.

. Tuition contracting is another form of informal cooperation. In this type of arrangement, one district sends students to another and pays the receiving district for the costs of students' education. In many states, the district of residence collects state revenues for these students and supplements this amount with local funds in order to pay full tuition costs. This type of arrangement is frequently used when one large LEA with considerable program capability is surrounded by smaller, dependent LEAs. The large district agrees to include students from the small districts in its own programs and pro-rate program costs back to the tuition-paying districts.

The implementation of P.L. 94–142 encouraged public schools to tuition contract with nonpublic schools. Sometimes nonpublic schools can provide services that the public schools cannot or choose not to supply. In these cases, the LEA agrees to pay the nonpublic school to provide the required special education programs and services. Some states have specific sections in their educational codes permitting contracting with nonpublic schools; some require contracting under certain circumstances; and others preclude these kinds of contractual arrangements.

Every cooperative program is subject to critical factors that make it work or that contribute to its failure. Some of these factors are unique, but others seem common to the success of all cooperative programs. These include:

- Planning appropriately in order to meet the district's special education needs.
- Giving one administrator authority to identify space and location for the programs.
- Defining the administrative structure for the cooperative programs (if several districts are involved, superintendents must be accessible to the special education administration).
- Identifying a person who is responsible for staff supervision and evaluation.
- Assigning responsibility for budget preparation and management of fiscal resources to the program administrator.
- Establishing methods that assure cooperation with the general education program's philosophy and compliance with laws, rules, and regulations.

SUMMARY

Chapter 9 explains many different administrative cooperative arrangements that provide special education programs. This information is intended to help administrators look at their own areas of responsibility and ask, "How can we improve special education programs by cooperative action?" The models discussed may suggest some answers to that question.

Various reasons for using a cooperative model are discussed. They include the unique problems of some children, high costs, the low incidence of children with certain needs, requirements for program leadership, and cost effectiveness.

Cooperative programs really begin at a school site when two or more professionals serve the same student. Even departmentalization may be considered a form of cooperative action, but usually the format is different. Certainly, programs that serve handicapped students in the least restrictive environment require a great deal of cooperation between teachers.

Intra-district cooperative programs involve two or more schools within a district. Personnel serve in more than one school or serve children from more than one school. Depending on one's definition of cooperative programming, the services that might be included under this heading are speech therapy, physical therapy, itinerant teachers, resource rooms, and adaptive physical education.

To most school administrators, a cooperative program means cooperation in administrative arrangements. It also means that two or more school districts join together for some specific purpose. Regional or inter-district programs are discussed in terms of the intermediate education unit (IEU), which includes county school offices, boards of cooperative educational services, intermediate school districts, and so on. Cooperative programs also include the special school district, formal cooperatives, informal agreements, and tuition contracting with other public schools or with nonpublic schools.

Probably no other instructional program is more dependent on cooperative action than the special education program. Cooperation with other persons and other school districts is the key to success for many special education programs.

REFERENCES

Bureau of Educational Information Services. 1977. *Policy on educational collaboratives.* Boston: Massachusetts State Board of Education.

Fox, W. L. et al. 1974. An introduction to a regular classroom approach to special education. In *Instructional alternatives for exceptional children,* ed. E. N. Deno, pp. 22–46. Reston, Va.: The Council for Exceptional Children.

Isenberg, R. M. 1964. Various approaches to developing area programs. In *Cooperative programs in special education,* eds. F. E. Lord and R. M. Isenberg, pp. 9–21. Reston, Va.: The Council for Exceptional Children.

Lavin, R. J., and Sanders, J. E. 1974. A review of educational cooperatives and their various forms. *Organizing for improving delivery of educational services in Massachusetts,* vol. 2. Boston: Governor's Commission on School District Organization and Collaboration, and the Massachusetts Advisory Council on Education.

Prouty, R. W., and McGarry, F. M. 1974. The diagnostic/prescriptive teacher. In

Instructional alternatives for exceptional children, ed. E. N. Deno, pp. 47–57. Reston, Va.: The Council for Exceptional Children.

Trudeau, E. 1973. *Legal provisions for delivery of educational services on a cooperative basis to handicapped children.* Arlington, Va.: State-Federal Clearinghouse for Exceptional Children. ERIC Document 081 126.

10

Unique Capabilities/Problems: Rural Areas, Low Incidence Programs, Special Education in the Secondary Schools

"Country schools are the rural version of city ghetto schools with one difference: Not much of an attempt is being made to improve the country schools."

(Sasser 1975, p. 35)

"The new belief that 'small' can also mean 'quality' is spawning new efforts and new programs."

(Alexander 1978, p. 111)

INTRODUCTION

Special education programs in any type of school setting present many problems that challenge the system, but these programs also help the schools to resolve problems by meeting the needs of many pupils who do not fit easily into the system. These capabilities and problems are different in different situations. They are related to such factors as numbers of children to be served, numbers of children with similar needs, and types of programs that can function successfully in a given school.

Special education programs in rural areas[1] are faced with the problem of very small numbers; low incidence programs, such as programs for deaf-blind students, face similar problems whether located in rural or urban areas. The unique ways in which LEAs meet the needs of special education pupils in rural areas and the low incidence programs are discussed in the first two sections of the chapter.

The third section of the chapter discusses secondary school programs. While this topic deals with different types of problems and capabilities, it seems appropriate for inclusion in a chapter that emphasizes the unique factors found in school systems. Secondary school administrators are very aware of the fact that special education programs in secondary schools face a set of circumstances different from that found in the elementary schools. These different circumstances are discussed, and suggestions for the operation of effective programs are made.

EDUCATIONAL PROGRAMS IN RURAL AREAS

State departments of education, intermediate education units, and local education agencies throughout this country are faced with the problem of how to best meet the needs of children living in rural areas and attending rural schools. This statement in no way implies that rural schools are inferior to urban schools. It does indicate that circumstances are different in rural areas, and that these differences require a unique educational approach.

Over the past five decades, there has been a trend toward consolidating and reducing the number of local school districts throughout the country. The number has decreased from more than 125,000 districts to less than 17,000. This decrease reflects an attempt to ensure sufficient numbers of students, trained personnel, and adequate resources to operate effectively. However, a report from the National Institute of Education (1973) indicated that 41 percent of the school districts still had fewer than three hundred pupils each. If one spreads this population over the twelve or thirteen years of school, it becomes obvious that the number of pupils per grade level is often very small. Also, when a district covers a large geographic area, the children in a given age group may live miles apart. Consolidation in this type of area is probably not practical. Even in areas where geography is favorable, the trend toward consolidation of districts has slowed to a near stop. This situation may be influenced by indications of a migration back to the rural areas. If this movement is real, the country school may again start to grow.

Special education is an additional variable to consider when looking at rural programs. Children with all types of handicaps at all grade levels make up approximately 10 percent of the rural school population. These children may live in an area that covers several hundred square miles, a situation that makes it difficult to establish appropriate programs in a centralized location.

The problems faced by rural educators have long been recognized. Nearly forty years ago at a White House conference a Charter of Education for Rural Children was developed (National Education Association of the United States 1944, pp. 14–15). The rights that were proposed seem as appropriate today as they were at that time. Briefly, they are as follows:

1. Every rural child has the right to a satisfactory, modern elementary education.
2. Every rural child has the right to a satisfactory, modern secondary education.
3. Every rural child has the right to an educational program that bridges the gap between home and school, and between school and adult life.
4. Every rural child has the right through his school to health services, educational and vocational guidance, library facilities, recreational

activities, and, where needed, school lunches and pupil transportation facilities at public expense.

5. Every rural child has the right to teachers, supervisors, and administrators who know rural life and who are educated to deal effectively with the problems peculiar to rural schools.

6. Every rural child has the right to educational services and guidance during the entire year and full-time attendance in a school that is open for not less than nine months in each year for at least twelve years.

7. Every rural child has the right to attend school in a satisfactory, modern building.

8. Every rural child has the right through the school to participate in community life and culture.

9. Every rural child has the right to a local school system sufficiently strong to provide all the services required for a modern education.

10. Every rural child has the right to have the tax resources of his community, state, and nation used to guarantee him an American standard of educational opportunity.

Since numbers of children, distances, available resources, community attitudes, qualifications of teachers, and a number of other factors have an effect on all programs, we must first be concerned with rural education in general. Special education programs share all of the concerns of regular educational programs and have some that are uniquely their own. These concerns are discussed on the subsequent pages.

General Capabilities/Problems of Rural Education

Sher (1978) indicates that more than fifteen million children are enrolled in nonmetropolitan schools. This is approximately one-third of all students in U.S. public schools. Similarly, more than 11,000 school districts (two-thirds of the U.S. total) are located in nonmetropolitan areas.[2] Every state has many rural school districts, some of which are within fifty to one hundred miles of the major population centers. California, New York, Illinois, Texas, and other states that have very large school enrollments are dotted with geographically isolated areas that have very small school populations. Obviously, states with small populations such as Alaska, Wyoming, and Nevada, are predominantly rural in nature.

To gain perspective, the reader should consider specific examples:

• Johnson County School District, Wyoming, measures about seventy-five miles by seventy-five miles, covering an area of 4,175 square miles. It serves a total of 1,435 students in kindergarten through twelfth grade in six elementary schools, two middle schools, and two high schools. Most of the schools are considerable distances apart. Served in these geographically distant schools are a total of 121 handicapped children three to twenty-one years old. Most handicapping conditions are represented.

- Peshkin (1978) describes Mansfield School District (a pseudonym for an unidentified community in Illinois), which has 500 students in kindergarten through twelfth grade. The village, covering only four or five square miles, has one elementary school and one high school. It is entirely different from the large geographic area described above, but still is very much a rural setting.
- Alexander (1978) gives examples of several rural school districts. For example, the North Haven, Maine, school, located on an island off the coast of Rockland, has only about eighty pupils in kindergarten through twelfth grade.
- Students in the Gunnison–Watershed School District in Colorado may ride the bus for as long as two hours to reach their small school.

Whether one talks about Barrow (Alaska), or upstate New York, western Kansas, or northern California, many rural education problems are similar. Administrators must deal with:

- Providing programs for small numbers of children;
- Locating school sites and services in appropriate geographic areas;
- Arranging transportation;
- Hiring teachers who can cover several grade levels or subjects;
- Hiring staff members who can serve in a variety of capacities;
- Qualifying for state and federal funds;
- Obtaining an income that will adequately finance school programs; and
- Obtaining such resources as books, equipment, and supplies.

It would be inappropriate to discuss problems without also discussing benefits and successful practices. Some personal and professional success stories are reflected in the professional literature. A few promising titles include: "The Lingering Lure of the Little Red School House," "Is the Country School the Newest thing in Education?" "A Lot We Can Learn from Those Not-So-Second-Rate Rural Schools," and "Growing Up American."

Alexander (1978) lists a number of advantages of rural schools. Included are

- Students, parents, teachers, and the community are a closely knit group;
- School board members take a personal interest in the school;
- Children have a feeling of belonging;
- Small groups are easier to manage;

• There is greater student participation in school activities;
• Schools are the center of community activities; and
• Smallness allows flexibility.

The effective rural area administrator will emphasize advantages and utilize procedures that enhance them. A number of techniques have proven effective in rural schools. Some are new ideas and some are old; many work equally well in urban schools. For example, individualized instruction may be a new idea to some teachers, but it has always been used by teachers in the one-room schoolhouse. The same could be said for cross-age teaching, peer tutoring, and use of parent volunteers.

Rural schools are also using other available resources. These include community resources people (to teach vocational skills or provide work experience), technological resources (television, radio, telephone programs), traveling teachers, traveling support personnel, cooperative programs with other districts, and programs with local colleges or universities. Special education is very much a part of the total picture of rural school systems. Actions that improve the quality of general programs generally contribute positively to special education programs.

Capabilities/Problems Specific to Rural Special Education

From the examples of different rural districts previously described, one can see the need for different kinds of approaches to providing special education programs. While one district covers hundreds of square miles, another is located in a rural village of five square miles that is within commuting distance of other districts, and a third is isolated on an island, each district's approach to a similar problem will be different. Number of students needing service is another critical factor. Alaska, for example, serves 10,242 handicapped students at all grade levels; Wyoming serves 9,873. Of these, only about 50 in each state are visually handicapped and about 200 are hearing handicapped (Bureau of Education for the Handicapped 1980). These students are spread throughout the states and their ages range from five to eighteen. Under such circumstances, the problems of providing for small numbers become obvious. Table 10–1 gives a complete listing of enrollment by category and by state.

To develop a concept of other challenges and possible solutions, one should consider the following:

• Total number of students needing special services;
• Breakdown of students by type of need and by age level;
• Geographical location of each student and each school program;
• Transportation (time, resources, distance, weather);

TABLE 10-1 NUMBER OF HANDICAPPED CHILDREN REPORTED SERVED UNDER
P.L. 94-142 AND P.L. 89-313 FOR SCHOOL YEAR 1979-80

STATE	SPEECH IMPAIRED	LEARNING DISABLED	MENTALLY RETARDED	EMOTIONALLY DISTURBED
ALABAMA	14,106	15,670	35,127	3,503
ALASKA	2,739	5,716	906	333
ARIZONA	11,275	22,372	6,879	4,359
ARKANSAS	11,475	13,250	17,433	475
CALIFORNIA -	108,284	117,974	39,810	28,525
COLORADO	10,478	20,501	6,808	6,405
CONNECTICUT	14,342	25,019	8,212	11,585
DELAWARE	1,898	6,528	2,629	2,726
DISTRICT OF COLUMBIA	1,602	1,128	1,309	450
FLORIDA	41,072	47,829	29,973	10,931
GEORGIA	23,729	27,098	30,274	13,960
HAWAII	1,202	6,938	2,120	371
IDAHO	4,176	7,891	3,021	538
ILLINOIS	78,684	72,697	50,770	31,540
INDIANA	47,783	17,373	27,165	2,053
IOWA	16,044	23,961	12,955	3,243
KANSAS	12,886	12,528	7,780	2,590
KENTUCKY	22,958	14,205	23,321	2,623
LOUISIANA	24,640	29,416	20,713	5,201
MAINE	5,575	7,640	5,293	3,681
MARYLAND	24,488	46,118	11,870	3,616
MASSACHUSETTS	40,908	35,246	26,822	24,787
MICHIGAN	54,127	43,472	31,188	18,063
MINNESOTA	23,248	35,201	14,894	3,945
MISSISSIPPI	14,064	8,136	18,720	255
MISSOURI	33,337	30,592	23,192	6,000
MONTANA	3,879	5,266	1,780	459
NEBRASKA	10,548	9,952	7,015	1,386
NEVADA	3,086	5,380	1,365	320
NEW HAMPSHIRE	1,626	6,320	2,453	1,058
NEW JERSEY	60,544	45,335	18,849	13,493
NEW MEXICO	4,103	9,956	3,439	1,623
NEW YORK	43,751	30,975	47,960	45,692
NORTH CAROLINA	26,946	34,017	43,507	3,692
NORTH DAKOTA	3,258	3,474	2,083	291
OHIO	65,439	58,214	64,422	4,277
OKLAHOMA	19,109	25,035	13,781	558
OREGON	11,819	19,801	5,991	2,265
PENNSYLVANIA	72,127	46,307	49,276	12,494
PUERTO RICO	989	2,670	10,539	1,459
RHODE ISLAND	3,437	8,728	1,989	1,092
SOUTH CAROLINA	21,021	16,240	26,090	4,882
SOUTH DAKOTA	4,847	2,437	1,245	309
TENNESSEE	31,824	27,221	23,302	3,084
TEXAS	70,555	123,751	31,033	11,084
UTAH	7,834	12,760	3,327	9,650
VERMONT	3,168	4,481	3,363	328
VIRGINIA	32,101	27,842	18,950	5,025
WASHINGTON	11,495	20,782	11,063	5,466
WEST VIRGINIA	10,089	9,174	11,552	828
WISCONSIN	15,780	23,283	15,004	7,475
WYOMING	2,697	4,689	1,044	630
AMERICAN SAMOA	0	49	65	0
GUAM	382	200	921	27
NORTHERN MARIANAS	0	22	9	0
TRUST TERRITORIES	225	92	19	33
VIRGIN ISLANDS	285	146	732	43
BUR. OF INDIAN AFFAIRS	883	2,281	821	286
U.S. AND TERRITORIES	1,188,967	1,281,379	882,173	331,067

OTHER HEALTH IMPAIRED	ORTHO-PEDICALLY IMPAIRED	DEAF AND HARD OF HEARING	VISUALLY HANDI-CAPPED	MULTI-HANDI-CAPPED	DEAF AND BLIND	TOTAL
516	408	1,157	521	1,307	63	72,378
59	156	205	48	68	12	10,242
609	856	898	331	708	16	48,303
450	442	718	317	438	29	45,027
35,453	15,194	7,172	2,854	0	267	355,533
0	702	913	285	1,103	33	47,228
944	537	1,233	642	36	1	62,551
16	252	182	124	48	31	14,434
180	234	50	55	168	41	5,217
0	2,735	2,060	853	1,492	18	136,963
1,483	560	2,092	804	1,809	38	101,847
4	165	322	52	184	24	11,382
575	483	483	250	629	20	18,066
2,408	4,402	5,177	2,147	2,450	188	250,463
400	863	1,429	601	1,123	28	98,818
3	673	1,063	321	667	39	58,969
703	339	765	251	852	39	38,733
1,013	629	1,059	447	649	183	67,087
1,483	734	1,681	551	1,183	38	85,640
310	346	459	135	860	8	24,307
1,838	1,102	1,868	673	2,152	38	93,763
5,640	285	6,487	1,128	283	283	141,869
0	4,128	3,205	1,149	53	0	155,385
1,661	1,246	1,615	474	42	20	82,346
18	322	543	228	130	14	42,430
1,056	717	1,195	430	1,564	51	98,134
111	129	290	190	660	17	12,781
0	461	511	187	326	0	30,386
194	266	194	74	319	9	11,207
198	206	293	257	213	3	12,627
2,177	1,882	2,259	1,428	3,551	60	149,578
17	182	470	156	487	46	20,479
35,407	6,920	5,208	2,081	542	51	218,587
900	1,146	2,246	845	1,542	53	114,894
60	104	206	87	198	15	9,776
0	3,543	2,676	1,023	1,662	96	201,352
352	365	796	323	643	35	60,997
639	1,243	1,688	599	85	15	44,145
289	2,096	4,804	2,318	525	8	190,244
663	662	1,372	1,217	1,377	87	21,035
187	184	258	61	115	20	16,071
72	847	1,098	576	622	18	71,466
19	163	445	55	327	3	9,850
1,534	1,170	2,358	796	1,706	9	93,004
3,102	2,736	4,578	1,465	19,067	241	267,612
108	211	680	303	1,231	23	36,127
185	264	293	85	241	16	12,424
530	513	1,495	1,642	2,908	45	91,051
1,199	1,018	1,302	418	1,265	41	54,049
767	321	410	256	545	22	33,964
572	915	1,264	414	855	49	65,611
100	109	203	46	334	21	9,873
1	3	22	5	18	4	167
0	1	97	27	127	8	1,790
0	0	15	2	9	1	58
57	26	1,140	18	109	23	1,742
0	13	57	12	15	15	1,318
30	39	114	42	343	0	4,839
106,292	66,248	82,873	32,679	61,965	2,576	4,036,219

Reprinted from figures released by the Bureau of Education for the Handicapped (BEH), U.S. Office of Education, on May 14, 1980.

· Possibilities for cooperative action with other districts;
· Administrative and community support;
· Resources available (money, facilities, equipment); and
· Personnel (numbers, skills, location).

Consideration of the above items should help an administrator to formulate a special education plan. Under the law, LEAs no longer have the option of deciding whether or not they will provide needed services. The question is "How will we do it?" To give examples of a needs assessment and considerations in planning, we will consider a mythical district, District A.

District A's boundaries are identical to the village boundaries. The village is a small farming community about fifty miles away from a large industrial city. There are no other school districts with which District A can develop cooperative plans. The district has a four-year high school, a middle school for grades six, seven, and eight, and two elementary schools. The total school population is approximately 1,000 students. Table 10–2 shows the distribution of handicapped and gifted students according to the most recent unduplicated pupil count.

For many years, District A has had a very active special education parent group. Even prior to P.L. 94–142, the district was providing services to most students with special needs. Both the board and the administration are com-

TABLE 10–2   REPORT OF UNDUPLICATED PUPIL COUNT FOR DISTRICT A

Special Education Area	Count	Grade Levels
Pregnant Minors	2	10, 11
Drug Dependent	1	11
Language and Speech Disordered	18	K–6
Physically and Health Impaired	22	All
Blind	1	12
Partially Seeing	3	2, 5, 11
Deaf	2	K, 9
Severely Hard of Hearing	9	2, 4, 5, 8, 9
Learning Disabled	15	All
Severely Language Disordered/Aphasic	1	2
Educable Mentally Retarded (EMR)	15	All
Moderately/Severely Mentally Retarded	5	1, 2, 4, 9, 10
Severely Behavior Disordered	2	6, 9
Multi-Handicapped	1	12
Autistic	0	—
Gifted	20	All
TOTAL	117	All

mitted to providing a full range of services. This is also a matter of community pride. Following are descriptions of the district's programs:

- *Pregnant Minors* attend regular classes until their physician indicates that they should not do so. They receive special health instruction from the school nurse and a home teacher prior to and following delivery.
- *Drug Dependent* students are provided with educational services by contractual arrangement. The only student currently receiving this service is in a residential treatment center in the city. The district is paying for this student's educational program.
- *Language and Speech Disordered* students are provided a program only in the elementary schools. Students receive speech therapy two times a week from a full-time speech therapist. This person has taken extra professional training at the district's expense so she can also serve as the resource teacher for the hearing impaired.
- *Physically and Health Impaired* students receive service as needed from the following sources: one full-time teacher operates a resource room at one elementary school four mornings each week, and is also an itinerant specialist for the middle school and the high school; home and hospital teaching is provided by regular teachers on a "moonlighting" basis; services are provided by the school nurse; and physical therapy is available from the visiting clinic team, which comes twice each month and whose therapists teach parents how to assist their children with the appropriate exercises.
- *Blind and Partially Seeing* students receive a variety of services, depending on need. The partially seeing are all print readers. Thus, the district resource teacher works with state consultants to obtain large-print books, projectors, and optical devices as needed. The blind student attended the state residential school for four years and then returned home. He now attends regular classes. The district employs a senior high school student as his reader and a woman from the community as a Braillist. Each employee is available for a maximum of two hours each day.
- *Deaf and Severely Hard of Hearing* students have audiological testing and receive their hearing aids at a clinic in the city. Parents and district personnel work together to make these arrangements. The speech/language specialist is also the resource teacher for the hearing impaired. Two students attend the state residential school.
- *Learning Disabled* students are served by a special day class teacher or through small-group instruction by the transition teacher. Youngsters who need a special class are in the noncategorical special class at one of the elementary schools, the middle school, or the high school. There is

one special class at each level. Students are integrated into regular classes as appropriate.

• *Severely Language Disordered/Aphasic* students do not yet have a program at the local level. The one student identified as aphasic is currently attending a residential school.

• *Educable Mentally Retarded* students are served in the noncategorical program that serves learning disabled students.

• *Trainable Mentally Retarded, Severely Behavior Disordered, and Multi-Handicapped* students are served by a teacher and an aide, whose students range from six to seventeen years of age.

• *Gifted* students have no special program, as such. But several teachers have taken special training in this area and are in contact with the state consultant. They attempt to provide enrichment experiences for their gifted students.

It can be seen from the above example that mythical District A is able to provide a program for its special education students. Obviously, there are some problem areas, but it is a workable situation. However, it would be much less workable if the district were half that size, or if it were spread over four hundred square miles, or if no services were available from the city.

Glenn and Summers (1973) believe that many of the problems of special education in rural areas are induced by rigid categorical grouping. They recognize the possible benefits to be derived from categorization in terms of funding and public support, but feel that many problems are side effects of our categorizing methods. Instead of traditional categorical groups, Glenn and Summers (1973) propose grouping *only* on the basis of common learning characteristics. Appropriate flexibility allows group membership to change as children move from one subject area to another or from one program to another.

One has only to visit some rural special education programs to know that rural schools can and do provide quality programs. Likewise, one can also see programs of questionable quality. To offer good programs is a responsibility of the administration of the rural LEAs. Administrators must seek out the methods that will work in their particular situation, considering every viable possibility. Possibilities previously mentioned include, but are not limited to:

• Cooperative programs with other districts
• Tuition contracting
• Traveling/itinerant teachers or specialists
• Telecommunication programs
• Teacher consultation
• Resource rooms
• Noncategorical special classes
• Community resources for part-time employment
• Community volunteers
• Residential schools.

The number of special education pupils being served and the district's financial status will usually determine the organizational structure for management and support services. While large systems can divide administrative functions among many individuals, small rural districts must combine many functions into one position. One individual may only be responsible for a small number of students but will probably have very broad leadership assignments, such as responsibility for all special education programs, psychological services, counseling services, and other support functions. As such, he/she must be a specialist in curriculum development, teaching techniques, grant application writing, evaluation and reporting, and so on. Being a successful rural administrator requires a broad range of knowledge and a high level of skills. As in all other settings, a committed and supportive superintendent and appropriately active site principals are necessary for the operation of quality programs.

EDUCATIONAL PROGRAMS SERVING LOW INCIDENCE POPULATIONS

The problems of providing appropriate programs for students with unique conditions and needs are frequently related to the small number of students who share the same disability. If a district has only one or two students with a given handicap, such as deafness, it is difficult to obtain the resources needed to provide for the needs of the student(s). In rural settings, this dilemma is caused by a small general population. However, children with low incidence handicaps may also be difficult to serve in urban settings because there may not be enough children with a particular handicap to justify the development and maintenance of a special program.

Perhaps the best known low incidence handicap is being both deaf and blind. While most Americans are familiar with the Helen Keller story, few have given much thought to public school educational programs for the deaf-blind student.

In 1963–67, the nation had a rubella epidemic. More than 4,000 women who contracted the disease during their first trimester of pregnancy gave birth to deaf-blind children. Dantona (1974) indicates that between 1969 and 1974 the Regional Center for Deaf-Blind Children had located 4,414 children who

... have auditory and visual handicaps, the combination of which causes such severe communication and other developmental and educational problems that they cannot properly be accommodated in special education programs solely for the hearing handicapped child or for the visually handicapped child.

Currently, the total number of deaf-blind children ranges from a low of 1 child in Colorado to a high of 285 in Massachusetts. And while this group has the lowest incidence in the school population, other groups are also small in number. Beginning with the smallest group, the deaf-blind children, and moving up to the biggest group, the low incidence handicaps include: deaf-blind, drug dependent (recognized by some states as a physical handicap), blind, autistic, partially seeing, deaf, severely hard of hearing, seriously emotionally disturbed, aphasic, and orthopedically handicapped. Of some fifty-one million school-aged children in the United States, .0086 percent are deaf-blind and .08 percent are visually handicapped. Table 10–1 shows the number of special education children served in each state.

Low incidence handicapping conditions usually severely interfere with the educational process. To meet the needs of students with these conditions, highly skilled teachers are required. Specialized support services, specialized equipment, and specialized materials are also needed. Program administrators face many challenges in finding ways to meet these needs. Even in urban areas, the sparse population of children with similar needs in the low incidence groups can tax the ingenuity of administrators seeking effective models for delivery of services.

SECONDARY SCHOOL SPECIAL EDUCATION PROGRAMS

The advantages or problems inherent in rural programs and low incidence populations are present in secondary programs as well as at the elementary level. Many are even more pronounced at the secondary level. But secondary schools also have advantages and problems that elementary schools do not have. This discussion is aimed at the secondary school's unique situation.

Special education had its roots in the elementary schools, and for many years functioned mostly at that level. Many secondary schools felt that their role was to offer academic preparation for academically oriented students. Since handicapped students did not go on to college, high school was not an appropriate step for them to take. Elementary schools provided the basic educational program, and handicapped pupils terminated their schooling before they reached the secondary level.

Although few secondary educators today would publicly express a philosophy such as the one described above, some peoples' attitudes have not significantly changed. Many schools are primarily geared to college preparation.

Certain factors contribute to the success or failure of special education programs. Secondary schools have several unique characteristics, some which contribute to good special education programs and some which make it difficult to implement and maintain good programs. To list a few:

• Middle schools and high schools are usually much larger than elementary schools, and the administrative structures are different.

- Most secondary schools are departmentalized. Teachers work with large numbers of pupils and are usually not as well acquainted with them.
- Secondary school teachers tend to be more oriented toward subject matter than toward pupils. The relationship between a teacher and an adolescent student is different from that between a teacher and a six-year-old student.
- As students get older, there is a greater discrepancy between the "average" student and the handicapped learner in terms of achievement.
- Secondary schools have certain proficiency and graduation requirements. These factors are not a concern at the elementary level.
- Various secondary school programs diverge more than elementary school programs.
- Special education models were basically designed for the elementary schools, with the assumption that they would also be appropriate for the secondary schools. Some are, but others are not.

Less than a decade ago, Metz (1973) reported that only 20 percent of the students receiving special education services were in secondary programs, although 40 percent of the total student population attended secondary school. Thus, recent requirements stipulating that all handicapped pupils (up to age twenty-one) be served have stimulated the secondary programs' rapid growth. This rate of growth has caused a shortage of trained special education teachers. One solution has been to recruit special education teachers with an elementary school background. While this practice has some advantages, it can also cause many problems if a teacher cannot adapt to the needs of older students and to the orientation of a secondary school.

One of the most difficult problems secondary schools face as they expand to accommodate all types of handicapped students is scheduling these students into secondary coursework. Scheduling involves much more than simply signing up students for five or six periods of courses. It involves mainstreaming, determining course equivalency for graduation purposes (when courses are in a special class and at a lower level of difficulty), establishing differential proficiency standards for handicapped students who have academic problems, and developing special courses that meet the needs of these students.

The social adjustment of students who may be less mature than regular students has also been a problem. Special education students who have been in a very sheltered environment in the elementary schools may have difficulty handling the transition to a more independent setting.

In this writer's opinion, the area of greatest concern is the development of appropriate curricular experiences for secondary students in special education programs. A curriculum based solely on extending the elementary program (even though students may be functioning at an elementary academic level) is totally inappropriate. In this area, some secondary schools have made little progress, while others have developed high-quality programs that meet the needs of secondary age students. (See Chapter 14 for additional discussion of curriculum items.) This may be the greatest challenge that secondary school administrators face when they design special education programs.

This discussion of problem areas is not intended to imply that secondary schools cannot or do not offer high quality special education programs. It does imply that many needs are different at this level and that educational approaches should also be different. Many secondary schools have recognized these differences and are providing appropriate programs. The following suggestions are based on observation of successful programs:

- Special education teachers in secondary programs should have secondary school training and orientation.
- In-service education for regular teachers, counselors, and administrators is a *must*.
- Regular teachers must cooperate with special teachers in order for a good special education program to exist. The principal can facilitate this cooperation.
- A secondary school curriculum that meets the needs of handicapped students is usually not just an extension of the elementary school curriculum or a watered-down secondary school curriculum.
- Provisions must be made for the student who is not academically able. This student must learn to apply his/her limited academic skills to daily life situations.
- The practice of having teachers and students spend "five periods in class" may need to be modified.
- Administrative models that meet the needs of the secondary school should be developed and implemented.

SUMMARY

Chapter 10 considers the unique problems and advantages that rural areas have in connection with providing educational programs in general and, more specifically, with providing a full range of special educational programs. It also discusses low incidence handicapping conditions and the special needs of secondary school programs.

The chapter discusses the prior practice of consolidating districts and the apparent current trend toward "moving back to the country." Statistics are provided on the percentage of rural districts and rural school district enrollment. A summary of the "Charter of Education for Rural Children" is included.

Different types of rural settings are discussed. The fact that every state has some rural areas is stressed. A partial listing of items that rural administrators must deal with is provided, as is a partial listing of the advantages of rural schools.

Special education in rural areas constitutes a "small within small" situation in terms of the number of students. A list of items that must receive administrative consideration is presented. A mythical school district is described to illustrate how many and what sorts of handicaps might be expected and to suggest the breadth of programs that a small district might provide. Options for administrative models are suggested.

The chapter's next section discusses low incidence handicaps. Even in urban areas, numbers are small. Statistics on the incidence of deaf-blind students in different states are given, and other low incidence populations are identified.

The last section of Chapter 10 covers the unique problems/abilities of secondary schools in the area of special education. The philosophies and models inherited from earlier time periods may be appropriate for elementary programs, but secondary programs call for new approaches. Factors that are unique to secondary schools are discussed, and suggestions are made for further development of secondary programs. Finally, administrators are presented with the challenge of utilizing innovative procedures and models to develop appropriate special education programs. Table 10-1 supplies detailed statistics on the number of different types of handicapped individuals served in different states.

NOTES

1. Appreciation is expressed to Dr. Marilyn R. White, Coordinator of Special Services, Johnson County, Wyoming Public Schools, for information and suggestions that were helpful to the author in writing the portion of this chapter that discusses programs in rural areas.
2. Information is based on U.S. Census reports.

REFERENCES

Alexander, R. 1978. Is the country school the newest thing in education? *Instructor,* October, 88:106–11.

Bureau of Education for the Handicapped. 1980. Washington, D.C.: U.S. Office of Education 1980. (Figures released on May 14, 1980) *Number of Handicapped Children Reported Served Under P.L. 94–142 and P.L. 89–313 for School Year 1979–80).*

Dantona, R. 1974. Demographic data and status of service for deaf-blind children in the United States. Paper read at Conference on the Future of Deaf-Blind Children, John Tracy Clinic.

Department of Health, Education and Welfare. 1979. *Progress toward a free appropriate public education: A report to Congress on the implementation of Public Law 94–142: The Education for All Handicapped Children Act.* Washington, D.C.

Elam, S. M. 1978. The lingering lure of the little red school house. *Phi Delta Kappan,* December, 60:265.

Glenn, G. L., and Summers, W. C. 1973. Problems of rural special education—unique or induced? *Thrust for Educational Leadership* 2,6:17–19.

Metz, A. S. 1973. *Number of pupils with handicaps in local public schools.* Bureau of Education for the Handicapped report no. DHEW-OE-73-11107. Washington, D.C.: U.S. Government Printing Office.

National Education Association. 1944. *The White House Conference on Rural Education.* Washington, D.C.

National Institute of Education. 1973. *Building capacity for renewal and reform: An initial report on knowledge, production, and utilization in education.* Washington, D.C.

Peshkin, A. 1978. *Growing up American.* Chicago: The University of Chicago Press.

Sasser, C. W. 1975. What's wrong with rural schools? Everything, says this ex-teacher. *The American School Board Journal,* January, 35–36.

Sher, J. P. 1978. A proposal to end federal neglect of rural schools. *Phi Delta Kappan,* December, 60:280–82.

Thompson, M. 1978. A lot we can learn from those not-so-second-rate rural schools. *The American School Board Journal,* June, 165:36–38.

ADDITIONAL SUGGESTED READINGS

Cordell, D. 1978. The disabled child in rural areas. *The Exceptional Parent,* February, 8:D21–24.

Cosby, A. G., et al. 1978. Education and work in rural America. Paper read at the Annual Meeting of the American Educational Research Association, March, Toronto, Canada. ERIC Document 158 898.

Lowell, E. L., and Rouin, C. C., eds. 1977. *State of the art: Perspective on serving deaf-blind children.* Sacramento: California State Department of Education.

Sanche, B., et al. 1976. Implementing the SEECC model of special education in rural Saskatchewan. Paper read at the National Congress of the Council for Exceptional Children, 2 October 1976, at Saskatoon, Saskatchewan, Canada. ERIC Document 158 900.

Tawney, J. W., et al. Using telecommunications technology to instruct rural severely handicapped children. *Exceptional Children* 46,2:118–25.

*Organizing
for
Action*

11

Screening, Assessing, and Placing Students

"The hope is that by identifying specific developmental deficits in children at as young an age as possible, one can design appropriate programs to prevent the deficits from accumulating and/or to reduce the children's vulnerability to learning and behavior disorders."

(Ullman and Kausch 1979, p. 8)

INTRODUCTION

Screening, assessing characteristics, and placing individuals in some group or classification is not a new process, nor is it peculiar to educational programs for individuals with exceptional needs. This process is frequently used by businesses, industry, the military, and other organizations.

For example, in a time of war the nation may require all males within a certain age bracket to register for the draft and to have a physical examination. By so doing, the selective service agency screens the general population and identifies individuals who are (1) male, (2) ages eighteen to twenty-six, (3) physically fit for military service. Next, the selective service may administer a series of aptitude and skill tests to determine an individual's characteristics and abilities. This is followed by induction and assignment to a unit that can effectively utilize the individual's skills. Business and industry frequently screen potential employees by listing job requirements (e.g., applicants must type fifty words per minute). Thus, all nontypists are screened out. A test is given to all applicants to assess typing ability, and qualified individuals are placed in positions that will use their skills.

Schools are very much involved in screening, assessing, and placing potential employees in jobs or students in educational programs. School administrators are very familiar with some aspects of the process, such as group testing and assigning students to teachers; but they are not always familiar with the detailed process required for placing students in special education programs. Also, administrators tend to think of screening, assessing, and placing students as nonadministrative functions that should be handled by the school psychologist and other pupil personnel services staff. Although these persons are mainly responsible for the services being discussed, administrators (especially school principals) should play a major role in defining and implementing special education services.

Instead of stressing knowledge about tests and their administration, this chapter emphasizes the process through which assessment, identification, and placement of students are accomplished. The former type of knowledge is the "territory" of the pupil services person. The process is discussed by Wallace and Larsen (1978) in terms of (1) screening or "finding" youngsters who have possible handicapping conditions, (2) administering specific tests to identify, verify, and diagnose abilities and disabilities, and (3) conducting thorough case studies. While this model is appropriate for other professionals, administrators usually need a slightly different approach. Administrators' concerns may be more effectively addressed by considering the following: (1) establishing a process for screening and referral, (2) assessing student capabilities and needs, and (3) establishing procedures for program placement and student movement. These three topics define the content of this chapter.

ESTABLISHING A PROCESS FOR SCREENING AND REFERRAL

Screening handicapped individuals has taken on new meaning in recent years, since federal and state laws now require an active *seeking out* of individuals who must have special education services in order to realize the equal educational opportunities that are their legal right. It is no longer permissible to provide these services only on parental demand. The law clearly requires schools to conduct a search for those children who need services. This requirement is first applied to those who are not currently being served by the schools (unserved), and second to those who are not receiving all the services they need (inappropriately served). The unserved are not in school (usually because of age), and the inappropriately served are usually found in regular classes that do not fulfill their needs for different or supplementary services. Since the passive approach to identification is not sufficient, states and LEAs must adopt policies and procedures that will help them locate, identify, and evaluate children who may need special education and related services (U.S.C. 1412 (12)(C) and 1414 (a)(1)(A); 45 C.F.R. § 121a.128 and 121a.220).

Locating the Unserved

Locating unserved handicapped children is discussed in the literature under a number of different headings. These include "child find," "search," and "early identification."[1] Over the past several decades, the need to locate unserved children has been shown through hard data. These data indicated that large numbers of handicapped children were not participating in any educational program. A more subtle indication of the need to locate unserved children is the fact that some schools do not identify handicapped students in order to avoid serving them.

Legal provisions mandating efforts to locate handicapped children seem to have been developed on the basis of three factors: (1) court actions regarding equal protection under the law; (2) increasing pressures to establish corrective laws; and (3) professional theories or evidence indicating that early identification may result in more effective remedial action. This latter belief is expressed in the following statements:

> The roots of the delivery of special education services are founded in the early detection of any form of handicapping condition, rapid remedial assistance in learning, and return to or placement in the least restrictive educational environment. [Magliocca et al. 1977, p. 414]
> Early identification refers to the practice of screening infants and preschool children in an attempt to predict those likely to experience school problems. . . . Interest in the practice rests on the assumption that predicted school problems may be reduced via early treatment. [Mercer et al. 1979, p. 52]

The processes by which the unserved are located may be thought of as a form of screening. The total population is known, but a method of identifying handicapped individuals within the total population is needed. The identification process involves federal, state, and local educational agencies. The screening procedure's ultimate goal is to acquaint the local education agency with every unserved handicapped individual in its area so that the agency can plan and provide appropriate services. This procedure may include a number of activities:

- *An ongoing media campaign.* This usually consists of radio and television announcements, local newspaper notices, and posters strategically placed so that they will be seen by parents of young children.
- *Cooperative efforts with hospitals, clinics, and agencies that provide social services.* Cooperation increases schools' awareness of preschool-age children who have observable handicaps or who are believed to have handicaps.
- *Written notices to parents.* Written notices inform parents that all handicapped children have a right to an education and explain available services. (See Appendix 4 for sample material.)
- *Other procedures.* Depending on local situations, a number of other individuals and groups may help locate unserved handicapped individuals. Law enforcement agencies, lawyers, the courts, and government agencies are in contact with families who have handicapped members. Also, "preschool kindergarten roundups" are an ideal time for locating and identifying these children.

Identifying the Inadequately Served

When children are already in school, the screening process may be approached in many different ways (e.g., kindergarten observation, review of group test scores, parent requests, teacher referrals). Some LEAs have well-planned kindergarten screening programs that note children's developmental levels. This is usually done by observing motor skills, perceptual skills, self-help abilities, speech and language usage, quantitative thinking, reading readiness, and personal or social skills. Students found to be significantly below the expected developmental level for children of that age are thought of as academically "at risk." In such a case, the teacher would attempt to provide extra help for remedial purposes and would investigate the possibility that the problem might really be one of delayed maturation. (If a child is significantly ahead of the class, the challenge is to provide suitable enrichment experiences.)

If problems persist through three-fourths of the kindergarten year, the teacher requests assistance from the school psychologist. The psychologist visits the classroom to get acquainted with the children and to observe particular children in the classroom setting. If necessary, formal testing can be initiated.

Figure 11–1 suggests a form that teachers can use to record observations. An organized observational approach helps alert teachers to the needs of advanced students who require extra challenges and to the needs of special students who require extra help. Observation provides general guidelines for identifying areas that may require further assessment.

Children who have no observable physical problems and whose handicaps are related to learning or behavioral disabilities are frequently not identified until the primary grades. Problems may be recognized through a teacher's observations or through district group testing results. In the latter process, the district may adopt a practice that makes any student who scores below a certain level a candidate for further observation or testing. Since many states and LEAs have a regular group testing schedule (e.g., in first, third, and sixth grades), it is relatively easy to identify students who have academic problems and refer them for additional assessment. Teacher observation and group testing scores provide both an informal and a formal procedure for identifying children who need extra challenges or extra help. Children who are singled out may or may not need special education programs. That can only be determined by a more extensive assessment process.

Procedures may vary from one LEA to another, but one approach that seems to work well emphasizes solving problems in the regular classroom and conducting formal assessment procedures only if regular classroom intervention is not successful. Figure 11–2 outlines the steps involved in this type of procedure. Step one of the identification and referral process is recognition of a problem. While the explanation indicates that teachers bear most of the responsibility of this stage, the process should be as broadly based as possible.

FIGURE 11-1   KINDERGARTEN OBSERVATION RECORDING FORM

Student's Name	Gross Motor Skills		Fine Motor Skills		Visual Perceptual Skills		Self-Help Abilities		Speech and Lang. Dev.		Quantitative Thinking		Reading Readiness		Personal-Social Skills	
	9th wk	27th wk	9th wk	27th wk	9th wk	27th wk	9th wk	27th wk	9th wk	27th wk	9th wk	27th wk	9th wk	27th wk	9th wk	27th wk
1.																
2.																
3.																
4.																
5.																
6.																
7.																
etc.																

Directions: This form is to be used only to assist the teacher in recording his/her observations. It should be used only after the teacher has become well acquainted with the children.

1. List all students' names alphabetically.
2. Identify the four students who seem to have the most advanced gross motor skills and mark the column with a " + ."
3. Identify the four students who seem to have the greatest problems with gross motor skills and mark the column with a "—."
4. Repeat #'s 2 and 3 for fine motor skills, visual perceptual skills, etc.
5. About ¾ of the way through the school year repeat the same observations.

The information obtained by using an organized approach to observation may help identify students who should be referred for additional assessment.

FIGURE 11-2 STEPS IN THE IDENTIFICATION AND REFERRAL PROCESS

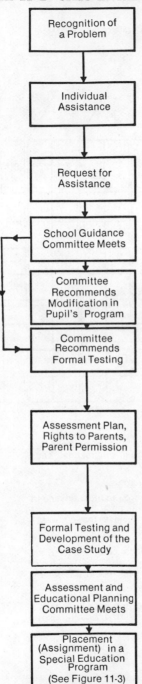

Recognition of a Problem

The teacher identifies the child as having a problem which manifests itself in some type of school-related difficulty, or group testing indicates a problem, or a parent indicates a problem.

Individual Assistance

The teacher devises a plan for working with the pupil to help overcome the problem. The teacher may request help from the principal or other school support staff. Parents are made aware of the problem through a teacher/parent conference and are asked to assist in resolving the problem.

Request for Assistance

The teacher prepares a summary of his/her observations and attempts to ameliorate the pupil's problems. This is given to the School Guidance Committee along with a request for assistance.

School Guidance Committee Meets

The School Guidance Committee meets to review material from the teacher and any other pertinent information—e.g., records from previous teachers.

Committee Recommends Modification in Pupil's Program

The Committee makes suggestions to the teacher, principal or support staff regarding program changes which may be helpful or recommends formal testing for possible special education placement.

Committee Recommends Formal Testing

The Committee recommends formal testing and initiates the referral process.

Assessment Plan, Rights to Parents, Parent Permission

Under the direction of the local administrator, an assessment plan is developed and presented for parental approval. The program options are also explained. Written consent from the parent is a requisite for proceeding with the formal assessment. The notice to parents must explain all of the procedural safeguards, describe the action which is proposed (or refused), describe the proposed assessment procedure, include any other information which is relevant. The notice must be in the native language of the parent — if feasible.

Formal Testing and Development of the Case Study

Testing as indicated by the child's individual problem is conducted (e.g., speech/language, achievement, intelligence), and all relevant information is collected.

Assessment and Educational Planning Committee Meets

The Committee—(administrator, teacher, parent, child (if appropriate), plus others as appropriate—meets to discuss the assessment information, develop an IEP (see Chapter 14), and recommend a special program, if needed.

Placement (Assignment) in a Special Education Program (See Figure 11-3)

The Administrator arranges the program assignments and notifies appropriate school personnel (e.g., the receiving principal, transportation).

Figure 11-2 "borrows" ideas from several school districts' materials. Montebello Unified School District's "Referral and Placement Procedures" were particularly helpful.

If a problem is noted by a parent, a school nurse, a playground supervisor, or even the affected child, it should be brought to the teacher's attention. The reader should note that the first five steps shown in Figure 11–2 are screening and remedial activities; the remaining steps relate to formal testing, identification, and placement.

Administrators must assume a major role in the screening process. If procedures are not carefully planned and implemented, some children will not get into school and others will continue to be inappropriately served. Generally speaking, the special education administrator should establish identification procedures for out-of-school children; the pupil personnel services administrator should establish teacher observation and group testing procedures for children in school; and the building site administrator should help to implement all of these procedures. *It must be clearly understood that screening and identification procedures do not certify that a pupil needs or is eligible for special education services.* That determination is made through a more formal assessment of a pupil's abilities. The screening process may be thought of as a "red flag mechanism" that does not affect most students in the general population. A good screening process might "flag" 15 percent to 20 percent of the total school population. Further assessment may identify less than half of these individuals as needing special education services. Establishing a general screening procedure is the first step toward developing more specific identification activities.

ASSESSING STUDENT CAPABILITIES AND NEEDS

There are many reasons for educational assessment. The most obvious rationale is improving children's instructional programs. Assessment assists teachers in (1) grouping, (2) selecting instructional materials, and (3) measuring progress. Assessment may also be a formal identification process that helps school personnel recognize individuals who need special education services. As such, it is the next step in the placement program. Wallace and Larsen (1978, p. 5) say:

> ... children with specific learning problems are administered various educational assessment techniques for two major purposes: (1) to identify and sometimes label for administrative purposes those children experiencing learning problems who will probably require special educational help; and (2) to gather additional information that might be helpful in establishing instructional objectives and remedial strategies for those children identified as handicapped learners.

A variety of abilities and disabilities may be considered in the assessment process, including intelligence, academic achievement, sensory deficits (e.g., hearing and vision problems), speech and language difficulties, physical abili-

TABLE 11-1   AREAS OF ASSESSMENT

Area of Assessment	Conducted By
Health	School Nurse, Physician
Vision	Ophthalmologist, Optometrist
Hearing	Otologist, Audiologist
Speech and Language	Speech Therapist
Social and Emotional Status	School Psychologist, Nurse
General Intelligence	School Psychologist
Academic Performance	School Psychologist, Teacher
Motor Abilities	Physician, Nurse, Adaptive P.E. Teacher

Note: Teachers and parents are prime sources of information about functional levels in any of the above assessment areas.

ties, and behavioral characteristics. Note that this partial listing is similar to, but not identical to, the list in Table 11-1. This is because the functions of various members of the professional team differ. For example, a teacher may assess visual perceptual skills, but does not test visual acuity. A teacher may also identify delayed speech patterns or articulation problems, but a speech pathologist conducts formal tests and diagnoses specific problems. Thus, assessment done for placement purposes is directed to individual needs, involves the professional skills of different team members, and uses many criteria to determine placement. Since there are more than a dozen major functional areas that can be assessed and literally hundreds of different assessment instruments that can be used, it is difficult to develop efficient and inexpensive procedures.

Developing a Practical Approach

Common sense tells us that we needn't assess a child's every characteristic. For example, if no speech or language problems are apparent, the speech pathologist and clinical audiologist probably need not be members of the assessment team. A child's parents and teacher know him/her best and will probably supply most of the preliminary information about a problem. An administrator can play a key role by ensuring that this information is properly used in the assessment process.

If the regular classroom teacher (acting independently or with the assistance of other school personnel) is not able to meet a student's needs, more extensive assessment may be indicated. Table 11-1 suggests disability areas that might be assessed and the school personnel most likely to conduct the assessment.

The site administrator should organize school resources in a way that assures that assessment will be conducted in the appropriate areas. He/she must work with other professional staff members to see that testing, materials, and procedures:

- are conducted *only* when the parent has given informed consent;
- are selected and administered so as not to be racially or culturally discriminatory;
- are provided in the child's primary language or mode of communication;
- are validated for the purposes for which they are used;
- are administered by trained personnel in conformance with test instructions;
- are designed to assess specific areas of educational need instead of providing a single score such as an intelligence quotient;
- are administered so that test scores reflect factors that the test purports to measure rather than reflecting a physical deficiency, such as a sensory loss or a speech impairment, that inhibits maximum performance;
- are designed so that no single procedure is used as the sole determiner of an appropriate educational program;
- are organized so that evaluation is made by a multidisciplinary team that includes a teacher or specialist in the area of suspected disability; and
- are geared toward assessing all areas of a child's suspected disability.[2]

The safeguards written into laws and regulations regarding assessment reflect the concern that many educators and parents have about the assessment process. Deno (1971, p. 4) asks a very pertinent question: "How many ways must a child or an educational problem be characterized before educators can achieve the most effective educational decisions?" One must also inquire about the effect that a particular assessment procedure will have on a child, the resources it will require, and how much time (both professional and student) it will take. These questions are relevant to the decision-making process.

Assessment for Instructional Purposes

As suggested by Wallace and Larsen (1978), information gathered during the evaluation process should help teachers understand a child's specific difficulties and should suggest instructional strategies and materials. Teachers should have access to assessment information collected for identification and placement purposes. Appropriate personnel (e.g., physicians, speech therapists, psychologists) should help teachers interpret assessment information and use it to plan IEPs. After IEPs have been developed, teachers assume the major responsibility for ongoing functional assessment. This type of assessment helps to establish each child's instructional level. Teachers always should be aware of each child's functional level in every subject area being taught. Without this knowledge, instruction cannot be specifically geared to the learner's needs.

If one accepts the premise that good teaching requires a continuous process of assessment and reassessment and that the site administrator is responsible for the quality of teaching at his/her school, it follows that assessment must be one of the site administrator's major concerns. As indicated by Wallace and Larsen (1978, p. 9), "Teachers are quite capable of using both formal and informal assessment procedures." Special education teachers should be trained to observe and functionally assess children. They can help to provide in-service education for other teachers who need to develop these skills.

ESTABLISHING PROCEDURES FOR PROGRAM PLACEMENT AND STUDENT MOVEMENT

Picture a child taking a bus, arriving at a local school, and not knowing where his/her classroom is. The principal is notified, finds out the name of the child's previous school, and makes a telephone call. The principal is informed that this child has been assigned to a special class and was told to take the school bus to his/her new school. While this may seem absurd, such a situation is not uncommon. The above example shows how *not* to arrange a pupil's placement or transfer.

In response to the emphasis placed on guaranteeing pupil and parental rights, most LEAs have developed well-defined and well-organized assignment procedures. Thus, the type of situation described above would not usually happen. The following people should be involved in the assessment process:

- The parents
- The principal of the child's school of residence
- The child's teacher
- A special education teacher or specialist
- The school psychologist
- Others as needed (e.g., audiologists, speech pathologists).

If the receiving principal and teacher are included in the above list, assessment and placement are transformed from two distinct activities into one continuous process.

In past years, the assessment process looked like this:

Assessment $\longrightarrow$ Categorization of the child (e.g., EMR, OH) $\longrightarrow$ Placement on the basis of category.

More recent trends de-emphasize the use of categories and concentrate on placing a child on the basis of educational need. Thus, the assessment process currently looks like this:

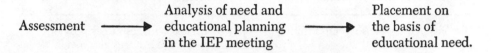

Assessment   ⟶   Analysis of need and educational planning in the IEP meeting   ⟶   Placement on the basis of educational need.

Although the special education administrator has usually been responsible for managing the placement procedure, he/she has also had to work closely with other personnel. Principals and teachers from both schools involved in a student's transfer must participate in educational planning and the final placement decision. Parents also have a legal right to participate in the decision-making process. Even if they choose not to participate, placement may not be made without parents' permission.[3]

Assuming that a full spectrum of programs is available, pupils should be placed in the least restrictive environment that best meets their needs.[4] Examples of placement in the least restrictive environment are provided in Table 11–2.

Models and examples of appropriate placements may sometimes be limiting and inaccurate. However, the listings in Table 11–2 are neither all-inclusive nor limiting. The severely handicapped, for example, may be appropriately served in a regular school rather than in a special school. Administrators should keep open minds about program location and use separate facilities only when necessary. Administrators are responsible for complying with requirements stating that a pupil's progress be annually reviewed and that a pupil's abilities and his/her placement be completely reevaluated every three years.

In past years, the administrative procedures used to determine a pupil's appropriate placement and needed services, actual placement in a given instructional program, and follow up of that placement were often not properly organized. Children were improperly placed and "forgotten," or left, in that improper placement. Recent changes in federal laws and regulations have more carefully defined procedural safeguards, and parents who have become more sophisticated and knowledgeable about their children's rights demand that greater attention be paid to appropriate placement procedures. Figure 11–3 explains steps that must be included in the process of assigning students to special education programs and services.

Screening, testing, identifying and placing students require extensive communication with parents. Communication *should* include informal activities such as telephone calls and personal discussions, but formal written communication is a *must*. Formal communication is required by law and is one of the topics included in most compliance reviews. Written communication must be

TABLE 11–2 PROGRAM PLACEMENTS FOR DIFFERENT INDIVIDUALS

Type and Extent of Handicap	Examples of Alternative Placements/Services
Mild Physical or Sensory Disabilities	Regular class with resources provided as needed (e.g., hearing aid, special transportation, adaptive P.E., low vision aids); itinerant teacher
Mild Learning Disabilities (EMR, LD)	Regular class with resource room, learning disability group, tutoring; or special class with partial integration in regular classes
Mild Emotional/Behavioral Disabilities	Regular class with resource room, time-out facilities, counseling
Mild Speech and Language Disabilities	Regular class with speech therapy
Moderate Physical or Sensory Disabilities	Regular class with resource room, physical and occupational therapy (PT, OT); facilities without architectural barriers; speech therapy; itinerant teacher
Moderate Learning Handicaps	Special class with or without integration in regular classes; integration for non-academic activities; work-study or workshop training; tutoring
Moderate Emotional/Behavioral Disabilities	Special class with or without integration in regular classes; counseling; non–public school placement; tutoring; use of behavior modification techniques; work-study or workshop training
Moderate Speech and Language Disabilities	Regular class with intensive speech and language therapy/instruction; special class for language development with regular class integration; work-study or workshop training
Severe Physical or Sensory Disabilities	Special class in regular school; special class in special school; residential school (probably in an orthopedic hospital or school for the deaf or blind); PT and OT; speech therapy; interpreter, reader service; home instruction
Severe/Profound Learning Disabilities	Special class in special school; development center; sheltered work training center; nonpublic school; residential center
Severe Emotional/Behavioral Disabilities	Special class in special school; nonpublic school; counseling/therapy; sheltered work training center; residential treatment clinic or hospital; home instruction

TABLE 11-2 (*Cont'd*)

Type and Extent of Handicap	Examples of Alternative Placements/Services
Severe Speech and Language Disabilities	Special class in regular school; intensive speech/language therapy and instruction; work-study or workshop training

Note: The above listing of possible program placements and services is only a partial listing. All related services needed to assure an appropriate educational opportunity must be made available for each pupil.

readable, concise, and informative. It must also meet the provisions of the codes. Appendix 4 provides samples of form letters that may be used to communicate with parents.

SUMMARY

Chapter 11 discusses material concerning screening, assessing, and placing pupils with special education needs.

The screening, assessing, and placing process is compared to similar activities in business, industry, and the military. Even just in education, these activities are not unique to special education; they are used throughout the local education agency. However, special education activities are extensive and many have stringent legal requirements.

The need to establish a screening and referral process is discussed, and suggestions on locating unserved children are given. Methods of identifying inadequately served children (those needing special education programs) are also discussed. These methods include an organized approach to kindergarten observation, along with utilization of group test results and teacher observation in the other grades. Figure 11-2 summarizes steps in the identification and referral process. A list of the areas of assessment is provided in the chapter's text. A practical approach to assessing, identifying, and referring pupils for special education programs is then given, and the need to assess for instructional purposes is explained.

Procedures for assigning students to special programs are derived from a combination of legal requirements and practical needs of the children and the schools. A changing trend (from assessment–categorization–placement on the basis of category, to assessment–analysis of educational need–placement for appropriate educational service) is explored and linked to the necessity of having a full spectrum of services available. Table 11-2 gives examples of

FIGURE 11–3   THE PROCESS OF SPECIAL EDUCATION PLACEMENT

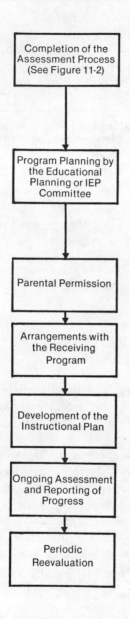

Completion of the Assessment Process (See Figure 11-2)

The preassessment process emphasizes efforts to remediate or ameliorate problems in the regular classroom, if feasible. If not, an assessment plan is developed. Informed parental consent is a prerequisite for formal testing. There must be a full and individual evaluation of the child's educational needs.

Program Planning by the Educational Planning or IEP Committee

The Committee (see Chapter 14 for membership) plans a program according to educational need and makes a determination as to which programs/services best meet that need. The following conditions must be met: the assessment information must come from a variety of sources; the information must be documented; the placement decision must be made by persons who are knowledgeable about the child, the evaluation data, and the placement options; the placement must be in conformity with least restrictive rules; the IEP must be developed and approved.

Parental Permission

Parental permission must be obtained prior to formal testing and whenever the LEA proposes (or refuses) to initiate or change the identification, evaluation, or educational placement of the child.

Arrangements with the Receiving Program

The Administrator of Special Education communicates with the receiving site administrator and teacher regarding student transfer procedures. All information relevant to the instructional program is provided.

Development of the Instructional Plan

The teacher reviews the IEP and develops the daily plans for implementation of the defined goals and objectives.

Ongoing Assessment and Reporting of Progress

The teacher and site administrator assume responsibility for ongoing assessment as needed for effective instruction and for the purpose of reporting on progress toward the objectives defined in the IEP.

Periodic Reevaluation

Every child must be reevaluated at least every 3 years, or more frequently if needed.

alternative placements for individuals with different types and degrees of disability. Requirements for making this continuum of placement possibilities available to all students involve all school administrators.

Finally, Chapter 11 provides a graphic explanation of the steps that must be followed in special education placement (Figure 11–3). These steps can help administrators meet both practical and legal special education placement requirements.

NOTES

1. The terms used imply that this practice relates only to preschool-age children. While that group constitutes a large percentage of the unserved population, older children and youth are also included.
2. These assessment procedures may be found in 45 C.F.R. § 121a.530–532.
3. If parents refuse to participate in the placement process or to give permission for placement, the LEA has the option of redress through a due process hearing.
4. The concept of establishing the least restrictive environment has been extensively discussed in previous chapters. Some educators are embracing another concept, called "normalization," which suggests that all students, if possible, should move toward a "normal" educational program. This author believes that the former concept is more productive. Although it is realistic to talk about creating the least restrictive environment for even the most severely handicapped, it may not be practical to try to "normalize" these students.

REFERENCES

45 C.F.R. § 121a.128, 121a.133, 12a.220, 500–505, 530–534.

Deno, E. 1971. Some reflections on the use and interpretation of tests for teachers. *Focus on Exceptional Children* 2,8:1–11.

Education for All Handicapped Children Act, P.L. 94–142, § 612(5)(e).

Magliocca, L. A., et al. 1977. Early identification of handicapped children through a frequency sampling technique. *Exceptional Children*, April, 43:414–20.

Mercer, C. D., Algozzine, B., and Trifiletti, J. J. 1979. Early identification: Issues and considerations. *Exceptional Children*, September, 46:52–54.

Ullman, D. G., and Kausch, D. F. 1979. Early identification of developmental strengths and weaknesses in preschool children. *Exceptional Children*, September, 46:8–13.

Wallace, G., and Larsen, S. C. 1978. *Educational assessment of learning problems: testing for teaching*. Boston: Allyn and Bacon, Inc.

ADDITIONAL SUGGESTED READINGS

Gearheart, B. R., and Wright, W. S. 1979. *Organization and administration of educational programs for exceptional children*, 2nd ed. Springfield, Ill.: Charles C Thomas, Publisher.

How to find the children in your schools who most need special education. 1976. *The American School Board Journal*, November, 163:44–45.

Keogh, B. K., and Becker, L. D. 1973. Early detection of learning problems: Questions, cautions, and guidelines. *Exceptional Children*, September, 5–11.

Mauser, A. J. 1977. *Assessing the learning disabled: Selected instruments*, 2nd ed. San Rafael, Ca.: Academic Therapy Publications. (Note: This publication describes more than three hundred assessment tools which may be applicable to evaluating individuals with learning disabilities. It is an excellent source of information about testing instruments that can be used for different types of tests, ranging from intelligence tests to vocational tests.)

Salvia, J., and Ysseldyke, J. E. 1978. *Assessment in special and remedial education*. Boston: Houghton Mifflin Company.

12

Working with Parents and Community Groups

"Each minute of the day, a young couple in a maternity ward, in a hospital clinic or in a physician's office, somewhere in the world is confronted with the news that their child has a handicap. They must absorb, assimilate, recognize, and accept the fact that perhaps their child will never walk as other children do, talk as others do, see or hear as others do, or grow as others do.... Some parents feel personally responsible for the child's defect. Others are relieved in the knowledge that an accident over which they could not possibly have control is the responsible agent. Some accept their problem, some will learn to accept it, and some will never accept it."

(Barsh 1968, pp. 8–9)

INTRODUCTION

If one accepts the saying that "everyone has a boss," school personnel should probably define "the boss" as the parents of the children whom they serve. Perhaps a better way to define the relationship between school personnel and parents is to call it a partnership formed for the purpose of educating children. If this partnership is to work, it must be a cooperative effort. It cannot survive if parents must fight to have their children included in school programs or are continuously made to feel guilty about their children's school problems.

If one were to analyze the types of situations in which parent-school relationships are most easily developed, it would probably be shown that teachers and administrators work best with parents whose youngsters are gifted or above-average achievers and with those whose children present no behavior problems. But if a child presents severe behavior or learning problems, communication with parents is of a different nature and feelings tend to be less cordial. This can cause unnecessary problems for all concerned—the child, the parent, the teacher, and the school administrator. A report by the Carnegie

Council on Children (Gliedman and Roth, 1980) says that schools still ride roughshod over the rights of parents, even with the protection of P.L. 94–142, and expect parents to agree with the "experts" on what is best for their child. Parents often feel that the school administrator is more concerned about the school he/she represents and about teachers' attitudes and acceptance than about the needs of the child who has problems and who causes problems for the school.

Although the negative relationships discussed above are found at some schools, observation at many other school sites indicates that conditions can be quite the opposite. Parents of handicapped students are frequently the most active and avid supporters of school programs. The school-parent partnership can be a positive working relationship. Chapter 12 is directed toward helping administrators establish such a partnership with parents at their schools. School administrators should focus their efforts on the following seven areas: (1) developing an understanding of parents' feelings, needs, and hopes for their children, (2) establishing parent education programs, (3) involving parents in the school, (4) ensuring due process rights and parental rights and responsibilities, (5) working with parent organizations, (6) initiating parental advisory committees, (7) handling parental advocacy and political action.

UNDERSTANDING PARENTS

Parents learn that they have a handicapped child in a variety of ways and at different stages of their child's development. If a child has Down's Syndrome or a congenital amputation, parents may know very soon after birth; if a child is deaf or has cerebral palsy, parents' suspicions may be confirmed when the child is a few months old; if a child is seriously hyperactive, it may be recognized that he/she is more than just an unhappy baby sometime around his/her first birthday; if a child is mildly to moderately learning disabled, the kindergarten teacher may give the first clue and confirmation may come in the primary grades. Whenever and from whatever source parents learn that their child is handicapped, it is a very traumatic experience. Some parents are totally devastated; some cope immediately; some eventually learn to handle the problem.

A parent's first reaction is frequently: "Why me? Why am I being punished?" They may feel angry, full of self-pity, or guilty. They may blame themselves or others and feel very hostile. Behmer (1976) explains that grieving for the perfect child one has lost is a genuine part of parents' feelings. In most cases, these feelings are gradually replaced by acceptance of what has happened and a strong desire to do whatever is necessary to eliminate or ameliorate the disability.

Parents must also confront the difference between eliminating and ameliorating the disability. Many parents hope that problems will go away with time and maturity, or that a "cure" can be prescribed if only the right physician can be located. This is a realistic goal for some children, but for others it is obviously unrealistic. Parents must determine if there is (1) a potential problem that may be prevented, (2) a disability that can be overcome or eliminated, or (3) a disability that may be permanent in nature, but that can be ameliorated through appropriate action. In any case, *no* child's problem should be seen as being beyond help. Most handicapped children can learn, can make progress toward achieving independence, and can profit from school programs. School personnel must convey a positive, constructive attitude to parents. A positive attitude produces the effect described by Mayer (1979, p. vii):

> The educators and parents of the handicapped in these schools do not ask such questions as "Should we provide school programs?" or "Can these children be educated?" These questions have long since been answered in the affirmative for them. Instead they ask, "What are the most effective strategies for teaching these students?" and "What content and which materials should teachers and parents use?"

Parents seem to be sending a message to school administrators. They are saying:

1. Know about my child. If you don't already know, please learn. You can't function as an educational leader by saying, "I don't know very much about these children."
2. Don't blame me any more than you blame other parents for the problems of their children. I'm doing the best I can, and I hope you will too.
3. Let's work together. Let me know what the school is doing and I will try to help. Conversely, I'll let you know about our goals. Perhaps you can help with those.
4. I know about the new laws which guarantee me and my child certain rights. I hope you are doing everything possible to implement and maintain services that are in compliance with those laws.
5. If you need political support with the superintendent, the school board, the legislature, or anyone else, our parent organization will help to represent the cause of handicapped individuals.
6. Remember that all parents have problems. We are experiencing all of those situations plus problems that are unique to being parents of a handicapped child. We don't want sympathy, but your understanding of our problems would be appreciated.

Parents of handicapped pupils are individuals, and their personal, social, and emotional traits will vary as much as traits of other pupils' parents vary. Different parental characteristics to keep in mind include age, economic status, emotional maturity, social status, level of education, and intellectual ability.

Some parents are unable to cope with problems; some are apathetic; but most do cope with the problem and most do care. Some have developed an impressive store of knowledge about medical, legal and educational issues related to handicapping conditions. Trying to work successfully with different types of parents is an exciting challenge.

Since the site administrator is the individual who most often works with parents, it is particularly important for him/her to develop special education knowledge and skills. Site administrators should have a good working knowledge of handicapping conditions and realize that these conditions may require different educational programs. They should recognize the feelings that parents have for their children so they can work effectively with individual parents and parent groups. They should also know which educational programs are appropriate for children with special needs. Fulfilling these realistic requirements is the key to developing a good parent-school relationship. Site administrators needn't devote unrealistic amounts of time to acquiring this essential knowledge; they can easily make it part of their professional training.

One very sensitive situation involves placing students in private schools or returning students from private schools to public school programs. When public schools are unable to provide an appropriate school program for any particular student, they sometimes contract with private schools to offer the needed program.

Parents are sometimes dissatisfied with public school programs and are "turned off" by the treatment they receive from public school personnel. They may request or demand that their child be given the opportunity to attend a private school at public expense. Resolving this type of issue, whether through informal parental counseling or through a due process hearing, requires great skill and understanding on the part of school personnel.

Placements in private school programs are frequently made on a temporary basis. If the district implements new programs or if a child's situation changes, the school district brings the child back to its own programs. The parents of such a student may have become accustomed to the protective, supportive environment provided by the private school. They will be reluctant to return to the public school scene, which they view with hostility and suspicion. It is to be hoped that public school personnel will be sensitive to parents' needs and will treat them with courtesy and respect. Unfortunately, this has not always been the case. Public school staff members may learn a lesson from observing the way that private school personnel work with parents.

PARENT EDUCATION PROGRAMS

Parent education programs may be approached in a number of different ways. The most effective approach is probably one that says, "Let's get together and discuss a particular group's common concerns. From these discussions, we may develop ideas that will help parents, the group, and the school."

The most common approach to parental education is to establish a local parent group. A group might be composed of parents whose children attend the same school, or parents whose children have similar problems but attend different schools. Parent education programs should be run by parents. Parents identify their needs, arrange for speakers, encourage other parents to participate in the group's program, and assume general educational responsibility. School administrators play a supportive role, and school personnel help by providing facilities and other needed resources. They can also explain school programs.

As indicated by Prescott and Hulnick (1979, p. 263): "Parenting a handicapped child often presents situations and problems for which few parents have been trained or prepared to deal effectively." Thus, parent meetings can be directed toward helping parents cope with these new challenges. Just as parents of nonhandicapped children have changing needs as their children go through different developmental stages, parents of exceptional children have different concerns about their children at different times in their lives.

Relevant topics for parent education meetings might include the following items:

- Aids for New Parents
- Accepting Your New Child and Yourself
- Where to Get Medical, Social, and Educational Services
- Management Techniques for Parents of Disabled Children
- Respite Care for Children; Rest and Relaxation for Parents
- Finding and Training Babysitters
- Parent-Child and Sibling Relationships—What About the Nonhandicapped Children in the Family?
- What Can We Expect from the Schools?
- Parent-School Partnerships—Understanding Each Other
- The Individualized Education Program: A Positive Approach to Planning
- Career Preparation Programs in the Schools
- Sex Education Programs for Special Education Pupils
- How Much Independence Can We Expect?
- Programs for the Adult Handicapped
- What Happens When I Am Gone?

The reader should note that the topics progress from the interests of parents of a young child to those of a young adult. Again, let me stress that even though parents themselves should and will take an active part in planning and organizing parent education programs, school administrators can and should be very actively involved in the process. An enlightened and cooperative parent group is a key factor in achieving a successful school program.

INVOLVING PARENTS IN THE SCHOOLS

In a report to the Ford Foundation, Hobbs et al. (1979, p. 43) point out that although some educators are reluctant to involve parents, more parental involvement in a school's educational programs will reap benefits for the school:

> It may be a bit like rediscovering the wheel, but special educators have rediscovered parents. The inclusion of parents in planning and carrying out programs helps children learn. . . . Programs work less well when parents are excluded, yet that is the normal pattern of operation in most schools.
>
> There are a thousand familiar reasons given why parents should not be involved in the formal teaching of their own children. Parents of the most difficult children, the most deprived, are said not to care. Parents are said to be too close to their children to teach them. Parents are assumed not to know enough of the techniques needed to help their children read or add or subtract. Parents are often perceived as unreliable. In some schools, the only contact between parents and teachers is at the mutually dreaded "parent-teacher conference." Such schools regard parents as a nuisance and have as little to do with them as possible. But many special educators (and regular educators as well) are discovering that there is probably no source of assistance to schools so promising, so high in potential, as the utilization of parents in regular school programs.

Even if an administrator chose to do so (and it would be a serious error), there is no legitimate way to avoid involving parents in the schools. Under existing laws, parents must be involved in assessing and planning their child's educational program. Of course, there are many other ways in which parents may be involved in school programs. Some of these methods (e.g., serving on advisory committees and becoming politically involved) are described in this chapter. Parents may also be involved at their child's local school.

Some schools benefit greatly from time donated by volunteer teacher-aides. An organized volunteer program allows a teacher to effectively plan his/her use of volunteers. In this way, the pupil-teacher ratio is significantly reduced and pupils can receive more individualized instruction. There is some controversy over the advisability of having a parent volunteer work in his/her own child's class, but this can be resolved by developing a policy that suits local preference. Also, parents frequently assist when "extra hands" are needed. Classroom parties, field trips, playground monitoring, and similar activities require more adult supervision than is usually available.

Some schools utilize another approach. They adopt senior citizens as foster grandparents. These people often find working with handicapped children very rewarding. They can help meet the school's need for assistance; their involvement helps to create a good school-community relationship; and they form a base for community support. Also, since senior citizens frequently employ other people to do general housekeeping, heavy cleaning, and yardwork, they can help employ students in a work-study program that stresses these vocational skills.

One way to ensure the success of mainstreaming special education pupils may be to "mainstream" their parents. Parents of handicapped pupils should be encouraged to participate in both general and special education school activities. Parents who accept one another encourage children to accept one another.

If there are so many benefits to be derived from involving parents in the schools, one might ask why it is not done more extensively. Of course, part of the answer is found in the reluctance of both parents and school personnel. Feldman, Byalick, and Rosedale (1975, p. 551) have explained some parents' feelings:

> Parents have learned that a minimum of contact with their children's school is best. Being called to school often results in having to deal with the school's contention that their child is not coping adequately, either academically or behaviorally. Parents are then left with the burden of trying to resolve these difficulties and are generally as perplexed about what to do as is the school.

School personnel frequently try to avoid seeing parents at the school. They prefer that parents only occasionally visit the school. When parents visit the classroom frequently, teachers may feel that they are spying (which is possible) rather than showing their genuine interest (which is more often the case). This concern may be eliminated by adjusting the focus of parental involvement. Observers tend to be critics; helpers tend to be supporters.

To assist the reader in his/her thinking about parental involvement in the schools, a few specific suggestions are listed below:

- Give parents of special education students the opportunity to supply or to withhold permission for their child's testing and placement (as required by law). Do this in a positive manner; emphasize benefits. Use clear language in written and verbal communication.
- Give parents an opportunity to participate in developing the IEP. Accept them as partners and encourage their planning suggestions. Avoid treating parents like novices whose arms must be twisted until they accept the professionals' plan.
- Let parents know that you do not blame them for their child's learning and behavioral problems. It is the child's problem, and the parent and the school personnel should work together to solve it.
- Encourage parents to volunteer to help with school activities. School personnel can decide the nature and extent of the help they would like to have.

• Emphasize that the parent-school relationship is a partnership. Parents and school personnel should have complementary goals.

DUE PROCESS AND PARENTAL RIGHTS AND RESPONSIBILITIES

School personnel have always recognized that parents have certain responsibilities to their children and to the schools that their children attend. Most school personnel have also recognized that parents and children have certain rights. However, these rights have been mainly determined by the school, and parents have had no voice in the matter.

Parent/student rights have frequently been withheld or unevenly administered. For example, compulsory attendance laws have essentially stated that all children of certain ages must attend school and that local school districts must make schooling available for them. But when it came to considering handicapped children, these laws were frequently ignored. Opportunities were not provided, so compulsory attendance was not enforced.

As has been shown in previous chapters, codes have been revised and expanded in order to give greater protection to parent/pupil rights. Also, specific due process procedures exist to guarantee these rights and allow parents to appeal if they feel that schools are not following the codes' provisions.

P.L. 94–142 and P.L. 93–112, their accompanying federal regulations, and a number of state codes currently protect parents' and pupils' civil rights. These rights can be described under five general headings, each with several sub-topics:

1. *General Parental Rights*
   All parents and children are guaranteed the rights to:
   • Attend school, as prescribed by laws of the various states.
   • Have a child's records kept private and confidential (in accordance with the Family, Educational Rights and Privacy Act of 1974), and have complete access to records.
   • Have equal educational opportunities, as provided by federal, state, and local codes and policies.
2. *Specific Special Education Rights*
   Special education parents and children are guaranteed the rights to:
   • Receive a free and appropriate public education.
   • Have access to a range of different programs—depending on a child's current need.
   • Be placed in the least restrictive environment and be educated with nonhandicapped peers if appropriate.
   • Examine and obtain copies of a child's educational records before attending meetings that concern a child's program.

- Have all procedural safeguards and appeal rights fully explained.
- Be represented by a surrogate parent if a parent or guardian is unknown or not available.
3. *Pupil Assessment Rights*
   Parents are guaranteed the rights to:
   - Initiate a request that their child be assessed.
   - Give or withhold informed consent to assess.
   - Have an assessment proceeding that is designed to be free of racial or cultural discrimination.
   - Obtain an "outside" assessment. (If the LEA's assessment is inadequate, the LEA must pay for outside testing.)
   - Obtain a description of procedures and tests to be used in the assessment.
   - Be fully informed of assessment results.
4. *Educational Planning and Implementation Rights*
   Parents and children are guaranteed the rights to:
   - Be notified in advance in writing and in a parent's primary language, of any meeting to discuss placing a child in a special education program or modifying his/her program.
   - Participate in the development of the individualized education program (IEP).
   - Have the IEP meeting within a prescribed time limit.
   - Have the meeting conducted in or translated into a parent's primary language.
   - Have the IEP reviewed annually (or more frequently, if needed or requested).
   - Appeal any committee decision.
5. *Disagreement and Appeals Rights*
   Parents are guaranteed the rights to:
   - Request an impartial due process hearing.
   - Be informed of free or low-cost legal services.
   - Be accompanied and advised by counsel.
   - Present evidence and witnesses and cross-examine LEA witnesses.
   - Appeal decisions to the state education agency or to civil courts.

School administrators must recognize the new-found realization by parents that they have rights as well as responsibilities. If schools aggressively develop procedures to provide these rights, instead of reluctantly providing rights, parents and school personnel will work together as child advocates. If schools take a negative approach, they will invite an adversary relationship. This may result in numerous complaints, due process hearings, and political activities that are counterproductive to a school program's operation. Administrative time is far more productively spent when it is directed toward achieving a quality program rather than toward avoiding responsibilities.

WORKING WITH PARENT ORGANIZATIONS

Wirtz (1977, pp. 65–66) says, "The best salesmen a good program has are satisfied parents and, of course, satisfied children." Satisfied parents have even more impact if they form an organized group that speaks out in favor of a school's programs. This is one of the reasons why many administrators work closely with parent organizations and help parents organize new groups.

Local groups support parents by providing counseling services, sponsoring parental education programs, locating resources, handling day-to-day problems, and planning for the future. Group members can also serve as spokespeople for special education programs at a given school or for children who have similar problems (e.g., parents of the deaf). More often, organizations function along categorical lines.

Although most parent organizations were initiated for the purposes listed above, many have evolved into advocacy groups for individuals with the handicap possessed by their children. For example, parental members of the Association for Retarded Children assumed a major advocacy role when they fought for legislation that would mandate school programs for their children. These groups organized at the local, state, and national levels. At first, parent groups provided school programs themselves while concurrently working to get legislatures and school districts to accept educational programs as their legitimate responsibility. Much of the credit for progress made should be given to parent organizations.

Most parent groups really want to work cooperatively and closely with school administrators, and the converse is also true. Difficulties are frequently related to the question "How much can be done, and when can it be done?" Parent groups are usually pushing for more programs and services and for more rapid implementation. Parents may feel that administrators are not doing as much as could be expected. A wise administrator tries to dispel this perception by working with parents in a common cause rather than working as adversaries.

PARENT ADVISORY COMMITTEES

School districts sometimes use advisory committees to involve parents and other citizens in the decision-making process. Some committees serve an entire district, while others only serve a local school. Involving parents in special education programs is both desirable and required by federal regulations. Title 45 of the Code of Federal Regulations (Sections 121a.120, 121a.147 and 121a.650, *et seq.*) explain the requirements for giving public notice of meetings and for establishing participation by parents and other persons on state ad-

visory committees. Many states also have their own requirements in this area.
A local education agency's application for P.L. 93–142 funds also requires
parental involvement (45 C.F.R. § 121a.226) at the local level:

> Each application must include procedures to insure that, in meeting the goal
> under Section 121a.222, the local education agency makes provision for par-
> ticipation of and consultation with parents or guardians of handicapped
> children.

As one form of technical assistance to LEAs, the California State Department of Education arranged for a parent member of a successful local advisory
committee to visit other LEAs that were developing advisory committees for
special education programs. The report that resulted from those visits (Yusim,
1979) is a major source of information for the suggestions made below. Since
school administrators are very involved in forming and working with these
committees, a few guidelines may be helpful:

- Committees should have a balanced membership that represents different geographic areas, different special education programs, and different
  types of expertise.
- Members should be people who are committed to attending meetings,
  representing their constituency, and taking an active role in committee
  work.
- Parents of the mildly handicapped have the largest group of children
  needing service, but are frequently underrepresented on the committee;
  this should be avoided.
- Committees will be more effective if professional personnel from the
  schools and other agencies are members—even if they are nonvoting,
  ex officio members.
- School personnel and experienced committee members should plan and
  conduct training sessions for new members.
- School administrators have a definite role to play within a committee.
  They should disseminate information, make suggestions, provide technical assistance, and facilitate communication with the LEA's policy
  makers. They should not dominate committee discussions.
- Committees must remain visible and must communicate with their con-
  stituencies, with the public, and with the right people in the school
  organization.
- Committees must have a "mission." If members can see themselves in
  challenging roles, they will be active participants. Bylaws can define
  each committee's "mission."
- Committee chairpersons assisted by school personnel, should produce
  well-planned agendas.

PARENTAL ADVOCACY AND POLITICAL ACTION

Advocacy is defined and explained by Davis (1980, p. 8) as:

> A program in which agencies or individuals, serving mostly as volunteers, act on behalf of the interests of others; e.g., child advocates. Generally the major goal of an advocacy program is to ensure that the rights of a particular individual or group are protected. As a result of federal and state legislation and litigation in recent years, advocacy programs for the handicapped are developing at a rapid rate. Advocates for the handicapped frequently function in such areas as school placement, housing discrimination, vocational placement, and barrier-free access to public buildings.

Most people in leadership positions tend to feel positive about advocacy and political action—as long as it is directed toward someone else. However, if an individual is made the target of advocacy and political action, he/she may feel very threatened. The opposition is saying, "You are not doing everything that can and should be done to resolve this important issue. That is why public opinion and pressure are being directed toward you."

Of course, parents have a natural desire to be advocates for their own children. Most parents want the "best" they can get. Frequently, they feel that handicapped children do not get the best from the schools. Parents feel that many educators work with handicapped children only because it is a part of their job and that these persons are not really helping their children obtain quality services. Altman (1980, p. 3) says, "It is our individual and collective responsibility to aggressively demand sensitivity of ourselves and others ... think about and evaluate the situations and opportunities wherein *your* advocacy can have an impact or make a difference."

The following examples will more fully explain the different advocacy roles pursued by parents.[1]

EXAMPLE ONE

Child A's case study is brought to the evaluation and placement committee in order for the committee to develop an IEP. There is some debate about whether placement in an EMR program or a TMR program would be more appropriate. Since the former program has no vacancy, the committee votes for placement in the TMR class. The parents disagree and request a due process hearing. At the hearing, the parents are represented by the president of the local Association for Retarded Children. He/she serves as an advocate for Child A's rights to an appropriate education.

EXAMPLE TWO

Physically handicapped children in District B are routinely bussed to District C for their school program. This causes many pupils to spend two hours each day on the bus. Some parents feel that this situation is unjustified and unnecessary. Joining together, these parents petition the board of education to place mildly handicapped children in regular classes and to have a resource room teacher available. These parents function as advocates by gathering information that shows the feasibility of their plan, by developing support at the local school, by running a public relations campaign, and by putting group pressure on school board members at meetings.

EXAMPLE THREE

The local high school program for mildly handicapped students has developed a good career preparation program for its students, but is being stymied by lack of cooperation from community employers. These potential employers are not offering off-campus training opportunities. Parents solicit the assistance of a labor leader and three of the community's business leaders. Together, they form a committee that will work with employers to resolve this problem. They are serving as program advocates in an attempt to encourage community support.

In the examples given above, one can see different situations that may be either easy or difficult for a school administrator to confront. In the third example, joining the advocacy group does not constitute a conflict of interest. It has, in all likelihood, been encouraged by school personnel. Conversely, in example number one, the administrator may turn out to be the "defendant." The budget makes no provisions for another EMR class and a teacher is not available, so the administrator is in the position of opposing the parents' desires.

Thus, depending on the situation, administrators may find themselves in one of several positions regarding parental requests or demands. They say, "Come and see our school programs. We are abiding by the law, and—even more—we are providing quality programs for your children. Let's work together to improve them." Or they may have to say, "You are correct. We need to take some corrective action, and will do so as soon as possible." Finally, they might say, "We disagree with your contention, and think we are meeting your child's needs." Sometimes, school personnel can join forces with parents who are filling an advocacy role; sometimes they are the "target" of advocacy action. Obviously, it is most desirable to operate good programs and to be allied with parents.

Political Action

Although it is sometimes difficult to differentiate between advocacy and political action, one might arbitrarily define a political action as one directed toward those who hold political offices (e.g., board members, legislators) and one that is initiated by a class or group of people rather than an individual.

Parents of the handicapped have been very active and very successful in many types of political activities. They have been vigorous campaigners for political candidates who favor programs for the handicapped and have been instrumental in obtaining political support for many of the proposed laws under which we now function.

School administrators also become involved in political activities when a school's interests are at stake. Since both groups are interested in providing better education for children, they are natural political allies. This alliance should be cultivated, not only for its political benefits, but because it will improve parent-school relationships.

Political action conducted by school personnel sometimes is ineffective because elected officials and the public see it as self-serving. While this might also be said of political action by parent groups, parents frequently have greater impact than school personnel or professional organizations. As indicated by Buffer (1980, p. 113):

> Certainly, highly motivated and articulate volunteers who realize, from personal experience, that special education needs require legislative and public support are in a good position to lobby for such support.

Political action by parents and parent groups has affected the legislative actions of law-making and policy-making groups at all levels of government. It has also affected many of the court decisions cited in this text. Parental political action groups have been successful in bringing about current school programs. Administrators should recognize the potential of these groups to provide assistance in obtaining favorable laws, regulations, and policies.

SUMMARY

Chapter 12 is designed to help school administrators understand the parents of handicapped children and ways in which school personnel and parents can work together more effectively. Parents' needs and the feelings they have for their children are discussed. An important part of this discussion is the concept of amelioration versus elimination of the child's disability. A message from parents to school administrators is presented.

Since few parents have received specialized training in how to cope with a handicapped child, most are not well prepared for this task. This chapter provides suggestions for parent education programs. It also makes a strong argument in favor of increasing parental involvement in the schools. Parent volunteers can greatly enhance school programs if they are given the opportunity.

The requirements of recent state and federal laws place new emphasis on parental rights and responsibilities and on due process procedures. These are discussed under the general headings (1) general parental rights; (2) specific special education rights; (3) assessment rights; (4) educational planning and implementation rights; and (5) disagreement and appeals rights.

Next, working with parent organizations and parent advisory groups is discussed. The point is made that having the support of parents is essential to program success. Parents possess tremendous energy and knowledge that can be utilized to help develop quality programs. Organizing and running advisory committees is looked at, and some general guidelines are given.

The final section of the chapter discusses parental advocacy and political action. Different examples are provided to show that although administrators and parents frequently join forces as advocates, school personnel may also be the target of parental advocacy activities. Various types of parental political action are examined as many school programs for handicapped students find their "roots" in parents' political activities.

NOTES

1. Parent advocacy for the handicapped may usually be classified in three different ways: (1) individual advocacy, which assures that all rights guaranteed to a given class of people are also guaranteed to individuals within that class; (2) class advocacy, which assures that all members of a given class of people receive the same privileges as the rest of society; and (3) systems advocacy, which works within or outside of a system in order to initiate positive changes with regard to a given set of criteria.

REFERENCES

Altman, R. 1980. President's message: Special education and advocacy for the handicapped. *Education and Training of the Mentally Retarded* 15,1:3.

Barsh, R. H. 1968. *The parent of the handicapped child: The study of child rearing practices.* Springfield, Ill.: Charles C Thomas, Publisher.

Behmer, M. R. 1976. Coping with our children's disabilities: Some basic principles. *The Exceptional Parent* 6,2:35–38.

Buffer, L. C. 1980. Recruit retired adults as volunteers in special education. *Teaching Exceptional Children* 12,3:113–15.

45 C.F.R. § 121a.120, 121a.147, 121a.226, 121a.650 *et seq.*

Davis, W. E. 1980. *Educator's resource guide to special education.* Boston: Allyn and Bacon, Inc.

Feldman, M. A., Byalick, R., and Rosedale, M. P. 1975. Parents and professionals: A partnership in special education. *Exceptional Children* 41,8:551–54.

Gliedman, J., and Roth, W. 1980. *The unexpected minority: Handicapped children in America.* A report from the Carnegie Council on Children. New York: Harcourt Brace Jovanovich, Inc.

Hobbs, N., et al. 1979. *Exceptional teaching for exceptional learning.* A report to the Ford Foundation. New York: Ford Foundation.

Mayer, C. L. 1979. Foreword. In *Parent partnership training program: A comprehensive skills program for the handicapped,* by M. H. Moore, p. vii. New York: Walker Educational Book Corporation.

Prescott, M. R., and Hulnick, H. R. 1979. Counseling parents of handicapped children. *The Personnel and Guidance Journal* 58,4:263–66.

Wirtz, M. A. 1977. *An administrator's handbook of special education: A guide to better education for the handicapped.* Springfield, Ill.: Charles C Thomas, Publisher.

Yusim, C. 1979. A report on Master Plan for Special Education Community Advisory Committees. A report to the California State Department of Education. August 28.

ADDITIONAL SUGGESTED READINGS

California State Department of Education. 1978. *Parents can be partners* (pamplet). Sacramento.

Gorham, K. A. 1975. A lost generation of parents. *Exceptional Children* 41,8: 521–25.

Kelly, C., Mullins, P., Caliendo, G., and Sweet, N. 1976. Parent-professional communication: Practical communication. *The Exceptional Parent* 82:F15–18.

Kerr, D. A. 1978. Too special can be too much. *The Exceptional Parent* 8,2:F3–4.

Klein, S. D., and Schleifer, M. J. 1976. Parents and educators—bases of effective relationships. *The Exceptional Parent* 6,4:10.

LaVor, M. L., ed. 1976. Understanding the political process. In *Public policy and the education of exceptional children,* ed. F. J. Weintraub et al., pp. 259–330. Reston, Va.: The Council for Exceptional Children.

Lichter, P. 1976. Communicating with parents: It begins with listening. *Teaching Exceptional Children* 8,2:67–71.

Losen, S. M., and Diament, B. 1978. *Parent conferences in the schools: Procedures for developing an effective relationship.* Boston: Allyn and Bacon, Inc.

McLaughlin, J. A., and London, S. B. 1979. Surrogate parenting: The extent to which state education agencies have begun to comply. *Exceptional Children* 43,3:211–16.

Santa Monica Unified School District. No date. *Handbook for parents* (pamphlet). Santa Monica, Ca.

Schleifer, M. J. 1971. Let us all stop blaming the parents. *The Exceptional Parent* 1,2:3–5.

FILMS

Stanfield Film Associates. 1980. *Parenting the Child Who Is Handicapped.* Santa Monica, Ca. A series of three 16mm films:
What Was I Supposed to Do?
A Matter of Expectations
Early Intervention

13

Working with Teachers and Instructional Support Personnel

"The school building principal, by virtue of his leadership role, must be considered a key person in instituting this change [mainstreaming]. If the principal is supportive of the integration of the handicapped child, then as educational leader, he can insure the success of an integrative program. On the other hand, if the principal is nonsupportive, the chances of developing an integrative program are diminished correspondingly."

(Payne and Murray
1974, p. 123)

INTRODUCTION

As special education programs in the schools have grown in number and have increased in complexity, the personnel needs of the schools have also grown and become more complex. Programs have changed from a simple organizational mode, consisting mostly of a few special classes, to a highly sophisticated mode that includes special classes, a host of other instructional models, and many related educational services. The new programs require trained special education teachers and regular classroom teachers who can work effectively with these students. They also require the services of other professionals such as school psychologists, counselors, speech therapists, school nurses, physical and occupational therapists, audiologists, work-study counselors, social workers, orientation and mobility specialists, and transportation coordinators.

The addition of more personnel and new personnel functions increases administrative responsibilities. Special education people must be selected, employed, assigned to specific functions in particular locations, supervised, evaluated, and provided with in-service training. Administrative roles have obviously changed: e.g., the director of personnel must screen, select, and employ people who have non-teaching training and skills; the principal must supervise regular classroom teachers during the mainstreaming process; the director of special education must organize and supervise individuals who provide a broad variety of instructionally related services. The purpose of this chapter is to help administrators more clearly understand the roles that they fulfill when they work with other school personnel who are involved in the education of special education pupils.

THE NEED FOR DIFFERENT PROFESSIONAL SKILLS

As discussed in other chapters, the needs of handicapped children and the requirements of the law dictate that school districts provide a range of different programs and services. These programs and services require that school personnel have certain professional skills. Some of these skills have always been required of school personnel, but others are new.

In the past, regular classroom teachers had the option of *not* dealing with handicapped pupils—they could refer them to the special education program. However, requirements for education in the least restrictive environment place many regular classroom teachers in the position of working with special education pupils for at least part of the school day.

The requirement that each special education pupil have an IEP has also created a need for new professional skills. Although developing an IEP may not appear to be a significant problem, teachers, psychologists, nurses, administrators, and others have had to develop different skills in order to handle this new task.

Special education teachers who formerly taught a self-contained special class may now be working as resource teachers and assisting regular classroom teachers with their handicapped, mainstreamed pupils. A bus driver who brings nonambulatory children to school may need some important new skills. A school nurse who serves as a member of an IEP committee is using his/her skills in a different way. And so it goes; different models for school programs, additional services that help a child benefit from special education, and new program mandates all contribute to the need for diverse professional skills. School administrators must find the right people, supervise their work, provide them with in-service education, and evaluate their performance. It is an important challenge.

RECRUITING TRAINED, QUALIFIED PERSONNEL

Traditionally, teacher recruitment has consisted of a personnel director interviewing candidates at local universities or advertising available positions and waiting for applicants to come to the personnel office. But in special education, recruitment has frequently followed a different pattern.

Public school special education programs predated college and university teacher preparation programs. Thus school districts selected teachers from within their own ranks, asked them to take whatever training was available in their geographic area, and then placed them in special education programs.

In many cases, this procedure worked reasonably well because administrators selected their best teachers to initiate new programs.

In 1958, Congress passed P.L. 85–926. This law provided funds for student fellowships and for program development at the universities. Subsequent laws and amendments still fund this program, and it has become one of the major forces behind the development of professional preparation programs. Even though training programs have expanded rapidly and hundreds of colleges and universities now train special education personnel, there continues to be a shortage of fully trained people. Thus, recruiting qualified personnel has been an ongoing problem.

Paradoxically, the number of special education teachers needed has increased at a time when the number of regular teachers needed has decreased. There are fewer regular classroom teachers in many school districts because of the declining birth rate and the overall decline in school population. At the same time, there are more special education teachers because of laws mandating that school services be provided for all handicapped children and because of the growing number of children served through special education programs.

Many school administrators feel that there is an obvious solution to these two problems. Regular classroom teachers who are losing their jobs due to declining enrollment can be placed in special education programs, where there is a personnel shortage. However, when one drafts people from within the system, deciding what procedures to follow and determining who will change jobs can be difficult. Some teachers enjoy working with handicapped students, but others feel very negative about it. Also, teaching in special education programs usually requires special credentials and additional training. Some teachers are willing to "retread," but others are not. Administrators must determine their priorities and decide where the best teachers should be assigned. Administrators' attitudes have ranged from "Let's put our best teachers with the children who have the greatest problems" to "Let's put those who can't teach with those who can't learn." Obviously, the latter attitude spells disaster for special education programs. Placing teachers in special education programs just to solve a personnel problem can never be justified.

One can take several positive approaches to recruiting qualified special education personnel. Some of these approaches are short-term efforts that provide immediate results, while others are long-term activities that will bear fruit in the future. Specific suggestions for recruitment activities might be grouped under two headings: (1) working with colleges and universities and (2) recruiting within the system.

Working with Colleges and Universities

Special education and personnel services administrators should identify nearby and distant college and university training programs that are recognized as producing quality graduates. Most colleges and universities have placement offices that will help LEAs find interested applicants. The district can post its listing of job opportunities and can arrange interview schedules.[1] The placement office will provide references, evaluations, and other pertinent data that will assist the LEA in its selection process.

Another way to work with colleges and universities is to provide students with opportunities to gain practical experience. Activities might include observation, early experiences with pupils, student teaching, clinical assignments (for testing, therapy, etc.), and graduate field placement. Student trainees learn about the school district, and the district's administrators are able to observe their work. In many districts, the earliest employment offers go to student teachers who have shown that they have the greatest potential for becoming successful teachers. Close relationships between LEAs and training institutions are usually advantageous to both parties.[2]

Recruiting within the System

School district employees frequently look for job opportunities available within the system. They may want to find a position that is more in keeping with personal goals, pays more money, has greater prestige, or appears to be more enjoyable. For example, a teacher aide may take university courses that lead to teaching credentials while continuing to work as an aide. Also, some regular classroom teachers find that they enjoy working with special education pupils and take the additional training required for certification.

The most important factor involved in recruiting within the system is planning in advance. Given adequate time and encouragement, classroom aides and regular classroom teachers can obtain needed training and certification and can become fully qualified special education teachers (assuming, of course, that a university training program is available).[3] If a district uses an internal recruitment system but does not allow adequate time for additional professional training, the result may be very unsatisfactory. If teachers are assigned to special education when they do not want this type of assignment, this too can be disastrous for the pupils with whom they work.

Many of the principles applied to recruiting and selecting teachers may also be applied to recruiting other personnel. LEAs must employ school psychologists, speech therapists, work-study coordinators, resource teachers, and other special education personnel. Teachers who find these positions desirable might be trained to fill them.

Administrators sometimes do not give recruitment efforts the high priority they deserve. This is a serious error and may result in a less capable staff. The greatest factor in program success is a capable, enthusiastic staff. An administrator's success or failure is partly based on his/her staff's competence. An administrator who pays attention to the selection process will solve many problems and prevent countless others.

WORKING WITH REGULAR CLASSROOM TEACHERS

Recent legislation mandating service in the least restrictive environment (main-streaming) accelerated an existing trend. This practice has been accepted by some teachers, questioned by others, and vigorously opposed by still others.[4] Feelings of concern or opposition are exemplified by quotations from the literature:

> The classroom teacher must assume responsibility for all of the children in the class, regardless of the range of capabilities. . . . There is a process of passing the child along—waiting for a psychological test, an opening in a special class, or for June to come and social promotion to another teacher. Educators must come to grips with the problems of these children and stop looking for easy outs, dumping grounds. [Edmonds 1976, p. 425]

> If human attitudes toward the retarded have at all improved, feelings of resentment and rejection toward the handicapped are still embedded deep down in most of our minds, yet knowing that such feelings are not acceptable to society any longer, we try to suppress and hide them. [Wong and Perkins 1978, p. 9]

Since administrators (particularly principals) must deal with their teachers' perceptions and attitudes, they should try to understand them and to gain teachers' acceptance of special children. If teachers do not accept these children, problems will result. Vallveturri (1969, p. 404) explained the problem:

> The integration of special children into regular classes may also be destructive if they are returned to teachers whose attitudes toward deviance are debilitating. One wonders what effect the nonperforming, nonproducing, special child has on the teacher's self image. . . . Ideally, before placing a special child into any class, the attitudes and values of the teacher should be carefully and precisely delineated.

The Annual Report of the National Advisory Committee of the Handicapped (1976, p. 4) also discusses the importance of teachers' attitudes:

> The crucial central issue goes far beyond optimum pedagogical practices, or research or funding, or the mechanics of moving youngsters into different settings. The overriding issue in this and all other provisions affecting the handicapped is the matter of attitudes.

The range of feelings that regular teachers express may be further explained by three brief examples.

EXAMPLE ONE

Teacher A was approached by the resource room teacher for physically handicapped students regarding Teacher A's willingness to have a pupil who was confined to a wheelchair placed in his regular classroom. They talked about the pupil's school abilities, the child's need for certain support services which would be provided in the resource room, and the ways in which the other pupils might react. Teacher A indicated a willingness to accept the pupil and expressed a desire to work closely with the resource teacher in order to provide the best possible program.

EXAMPLE TWO

Teacher B was a kindergarten teacher assigned by the principal to include a totally blind pupil in her class. The teacher expressed concern over this assignment, since she knew nothing about educating blind pupils. Support services were not explained. Teacher B felt very threatened by this assignment.

EXAMPLE THREE

Teacher C, a junior high school teacher, was informed that each regular classroom teacher was responsible for mainstreaming one or more learning disabled pupils. Since Teacher C was academically oriented and concerned about the class's overall academic progress, he resisted this change. This resistance turned to anger when Teacher C walked by the LD teacher's room and saw the teacher working with only eight pupils.

These examples show some possible reactions of teachers to working with special education pupils—acceptance, fear, and rejection. In all probability, the child in the first example will succeed while the other two children will have a difficult time.

In a study designed to measure the attitudes of regular classroom teachers, Stephens and Braun (1980) received responses from 795 teachers. Of these teachers, 481 (61 percent) indicated that they were willing to integrate handicapped pupils into their classes. The other 314 (39 percent) said that they would be unwilling to do so. Primary and middle grade teachers were more willing to integrate than were seventh and eighth grade teachers. High school teachers were not included in the study, but experience indicates that these teachers are less likely to accept handicapped students. This information emphasizes the fact that administrators must carefully select teachers who will work with mainstreamed pupils. It may also indicate a need to institute an in-service training program for large numbers of regular classroom teachers.[5]

The school principal and the special education administrator can influence regular classroom teachers' attitudes toward special education pupils. The principal must set the tone for teachers' acceptance of and cooperation with these students; the special education administrator must provide appropriate support services. Given the proper circumstances, many regular teachers will support the special education program and accept special education students. Actions that may contribute to success include the following:

- The school principal must show that he/she has a positive attitude toward handicapped students.
- The principal must lead the way when it comes to designing the school's plan for serving special education students.
- The school's philosophy should be that all students belong in the regular classroom, unless they cannot be properly served in that environment.
- The special education administrator must implement a plan that ensures regular classroom teachers a prompt supply of needed support services.
- Regular classroom teachers must be involved in any decisions made about placing special education pupils.
- Regular classroom teachers must have the opportunity to obtain information about handicapped pupils. In-service education programs should be made available through the resources and cooperative efforts of the principal and the special education administrator.
- The special education administrator must provide guidelines and procedures that will enhance the entire mainstreaming process.

If special education services are properly planned and provided, regular classroom teachers can have a positive experience with special pupils. Handicapped children can reinforce teachers as much as other pupils do. They can be loving and affectionate toward the teacher; they can appreciate the teacher's efforts; they can make progress in academic areas, and their social skills can improve. Problems that may crop up are unacceptable behavior (on the part of a few) and slower-than-expected academic progress on the part of others. If regular classroom teachers receive proper training and support to help them cope with these problems, and if mainstreamed pupils and regular classroom teachers are carefully selected, there is every reason to expect program success.

The premise that special education training will make regular classroom teachers more willing to accept special students was supported by Stephens and Braun's study (1980). This study found that acceptance was related to: (1) coursework taken in special education; (2) confidence in one's abilities to work with these pupils; (3) the belief that handicapped children can become useful members of society; and (4) the belief that public schools should educate exceptional children. The study also indicated that willingness to integrate special education students increased with the number of professional special education courses taken. These findings support the need to require special education training for all teachers.

Where general educators are required to take special education coursework, the requirements are part of the state's credential laws and regulations. Smith and Schindler (1980) indicate that twenty-five states and the District of Columbia have no such requirement and no immediate plans to include special education training in regular certification programs. The other twenty-five states have a coursework requirement and/or a competency requirement, or they contemplate having such a requirement in the near future. In many cases, the requirement is for a single course, usually entitled "Education and Psychology of Exceptional Children." This type of course usually provides information about the characteristics of exceptional individuals and an overview of educational programs. It is helpful, but should be supplemented by training that stresses the techniques used to teach pupils with special problems.

Both empirical and research evidence indicates that regular classroom teachers can and will work effectively with children who have special needs. Their attitudes, their willingness to be involved, and the amount of effort they expend are related to other factors such as: (1) the principal's attitude toward handicapped individuals; (2) the school's philosophy; (3) exposure to special education through pre-service or in-service training; (4) the care with which they were selected and placed; and (5) availability of support services.

WORKING WITH SPECIAL EDUCATION TEACHERS

Even when special education programs are located at a school site, they may essentially constitute a separate entity. This separation is occasionally an administrative problem (e.g., the special program is operated by an intermediate district in rented space), but more often it is caused by artificial barriers. These barriers must be removed if segregation problems are to be resolved.

True integration of special education programs first requires integrating special education teachers. They must accept and be accepted by the school's other staff members. They must be included in the school's activities and in general staff responsibilities. They must report to the building principal the same way a regular classroom teacher does. The special education administrator should provide support, but should not be seen as the special education teacher's "real" principal.

Special education teachers who work at regular school sites typically take regular turns lining up children who ride the bus, supervising children in the schoolyard, serving as faculty advisors to student activities, and working on faculty committees. If they are not involved in these activities, other teachers interpret it as favoritism or self-imposed isolation. A person who is seen by his/her colleagues as receiving special treatment and having fewer responsibilities is seldom really accepted as a "regular" member of the faculty. This can have a detrimental effect on a special education teacher's pupils, since regular teachers may extend their feelings about a particular teacher to his/her students. Most special education teachers have learned a great deal about working with pupils who have behavioral problems. They also utilize materials and techniques designed for youngsters with learning problems. These special teachers can help other teachers who are experiencing problems in these areas.

Many teachers have been involved in special education programs for long periods of time. Because these teachers have spent extended periods of time with pupils who exhibit serious learning or behavioral problems, some of them feel "burned out." If left unresolved, this situation can cause teachers to leave the field or to do a less-than-adequate teaching job. Sometimes a brief change —teaching a regular class during summer session or as a part of one's teaching assignment—can help. Sometimes a teacher needs some sort of psychological support, such as positive recognition; other times a teacher really needs to be reassigned to another position. Administrators would do well to be attentive to signs of burnout in teachers and to suggest remedial procedures.[6]

There continues to be a serious shortage of trained special education teachers. Based on program growth and a normal 6 percent attrition rate for teachers, it is projected that for several years the need for new teachers in this field will range from 65,000 to 85,000 teachers per year. (Department of Health, Education and Welfare 1979, p. 56.) Despite intensive efforts to increase the number of people trained by colleges and universities, supply has fallen far short of demand. This will continue to be a problem in the foreseeable future.

WORKING WITH RELATED SERVICE PERSONNEL

Recent laws dictate that schools provide a variety of related services that help handicapped students to benefit from the educational program. These requirements are based on the premise that certain factors interfere with the educational process. For example, a pupil cannot benefit from school if he/she cannot get there. Thus, special transportation is necessary for someone in a wheelchair. Similarly, a person with deficient hearing may not be doing well in school, but this problem may be ameliorated if an audiologist's services and a hearing aid are made available.

This discussion will not attempt to make a clear distinction between an instructional service and a related service. These functions are closely connected and frequently overlap. For example, a speech therapist may be working on developing language concepts and correcting articulation problems. Certainly no one would want to debate whether these are instructional functions or related functions. The therapist is providing a service the child needs. The numbers of available and needed school staff members, other than special education teachers, are shown in Figure 13-1. Although the needs for 1982 and subsequent years may differ slightly, the information provided demonstrates the relative numbers of people in different positions and highlights the needs versus availability problem. The following discussion will include some, but not all, of the positions listed.

FIGURE 13–1 SCHOOL STAFF OTHER THAN SPECIAL EDUCATION
TEACHERS AVAILABLE AND NEEDED

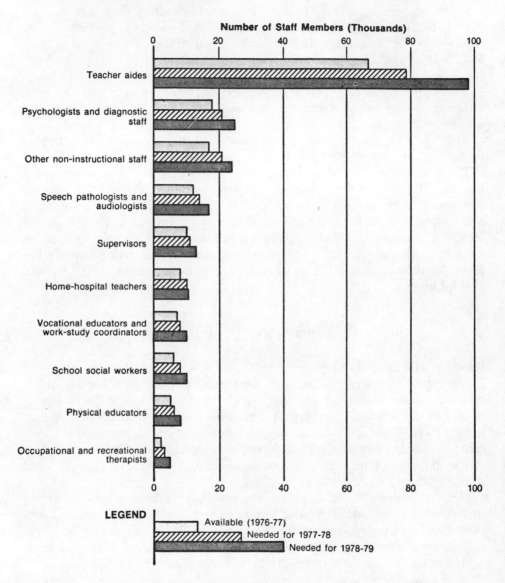

Reproduced from Department of Health, Education and Welfare, *Progress Toward a Free
Appropriate Public Education: A Report to Congress on the Implementation of Public Law
94–142: The Education for All Handicapped Children Act* (Washington, D.C., 1979), p. 57.

Teacher Aides

Any special education teacher will attest to the importance of having good teacher aides. Aides have become a necessary part of a special education program. Teacher aides (many districts use the title assistant teacher) have made it possible to establish realistic pupil-adult ratios without unrealistic expenses.

Some states have established pre-service training requirements for special education aides, and some have initiated good in-service education programs. Some aides are working toward a teaching credential and are almost as well prepared as the teacher. Unfortunately, most teachers and administrators have not been trained to work with teacher aides. Too often, teachers and pupils do not fully benefit from the availability of this "extra teacher." The aide can help with day-to-day routine tasks, but should also instruct pupils (under the teacher's direction). The school principal, assisted by the special education administrator, can be instrumental in training aides to function as assistant teachers and in training teachers to properly utilize the aides' services.

Speech/Language Specialists

Speech/language disorders occur more often than any other disability. Information on the distribution of children served by handicapping condition shows that more than 30 percent of all special education pupils are listed as speech impaired (Department of Health, Education and Welfare 1979, p. 10). From these figures, one might conclude that speech therapists constitute the largest professional group involved in special education. This, however, would be incorrect. Speech/language specialists frequently have a very large case load (ranging from very few children to as many as ninety) and are not as numerous in the school system as teachers of the high incidence handicapped groups.

Speech/language specialists play several different roles in the schools; thus, they have different professional relationships with individuals in different administrative positions. If a specialist functions as an itinerant speech therapist and serves youngsters who have mild speech problems (usually articulation difficulties), he/she may serve two or more schools. In this case, a special education administrator would have general supervisory responsibility. A school principal would only have supervisory responsibility if the specialist worked at his/her building.

To more fully understand the administrator's working relationship with speech/language specialists, it is necessary to be acquainted with the different services provided:

- *Itinerant speech therapist:* works with pupils enrolled full-time in regular classes who need speech correction, but who do not require other special education services.

• *Speech therapist (or language development specialist):* works with special education pupils who also need other special education services (e.g., pupils in programs for the hard of hearing or for the cerebral palsied).
• *Special class teacher:* works with pupils who have severe language disorders, such as aphasia.

Administrators should work with the speech/language specialist to establish schedules for testing and for providing children with direct service. Time should also be planned to let teachers and parents know how they can assist. One of this program's most challenging administrative problems is scheduling these special services. Classroom teachers must be involved in the scheduling process, so that children will leave their classrooms for speech therapy at the time that will be least harmul to their educational progress in other areas. Since administrators have a broader understanding of a child's total program, they can help specialists establish their own time priorities and properly schedule a pupil's time.

School Psychologists

School psychologists are usually responsible to a pupil personnel services administrator. Depending on the LEA's size, this administrator may also supervise special education programs. Whatever the arrangement may be, the psychologist often works at one or more school sites. If this is the case, he/she is obligated to work as a member of each school's special education team.

The school psychologist's role has changed significantly in the past decade. Many psychologists have exchanged their test-giving roles for the roles of diagnostician and prescriber of educational programs. School psychologists also spend a considerable amount of time working with parents during the assessment and educational planning process. Teachers and site administrators feel that school psychologists meet pupils' needs much more effectively in their new expanded roles.

A school psychologist must fulfill a broad range of functions in order to meet the needs of children, their parents, teachers, and program administrators. These functions include:

• Consulting with regular classroom teachers about the learning and behavioral problems of children in their classes
• Observing children and recommending approaches to remediation
• Informally and formally assessing pupils who are referred through the school principal
• Gathering information and preparing case studies
• Presenting case studies at educational placement and/or IEP meetings
• Helping to plan educational strategies

- Conferring with parents
- Participating in the reevaluation process.

A school psychologist provides supportive services. He/she is a specialist in assessment and learning and behavioral problems. Supportive services are essential to a properly functioning special education team. Administrative responsibilities related to working with school psychologists include planning for and budgeting supportive services; assigning a psychologist to each school for an adequate amount of time; handling any scheduling difficulties; and setting up operational procedures.

Physical and Occupational Therapists

Because of the population served and the facilities and equipment needed, physical therapists and occupational therapists are not always housed on a regular school campus. They may be housed at a special school or at a nearby separate facility.

These therapists serve physically handicapped children and multihandicapped children who have one or more problems of a physical nature. In their work, these professionals attempt to help an individual restore some functional use to disabled parts of the body. They utilize exercises, braces, splints, and a variety of orthotic devices to help an individual more effectively use weak muscles, stiff joints, and defective bone structures.

Physical and occupational therapists may be employed by a school district or by another agency and assigned to the schools by some type of inter-agency agreement. In either case, the school administrator must bring these professionals and the pupils who need their services together. The schools may also have to provide space and equipment. Since physical therapists work to develop the large muscles and gross motor skills, they particularly need large rooms and a great deal of equipment.

The School Nurse

The school nurse is a very important member of the special education team. In order to properly plan an instructional program for a child, one must have a thorough knowledge of that child's overall health status. A nurse can interpret medical information supplied by doctors and school health records and can explain the educational implications of a child's problems. The importance of the role of the school nurse is evident when we recognize that acute health problems may alter a child's ability to participate in certain school activities, may require a shorter school day, or may even prevent any attendance at school for extended time periods. A nurse may also serve as a liaison between the home and school by advising parents of their child's needs.

Educators often have the mistaken perception that all handicapped children are sick. While acute illness may be a problem for some special education children, most of them are not ill. The school nurse helps educational personnel deal with a child's medical problems and reduce their impact on a child's educational program. For example, the school nurse might serve as a member of the IEP team, gathering and presenting all medically relevant information.

The Orientation and Mobility Specialist

One daily living skill that is essential to achieving independence is the ability to move about in one's environment. To do this effectively, an individual must be able to relate himself/herself to a location (orientation) and to move from place to place (mobility). The orientation and mobility specialist teaches these skills and does much more besides. Handicapped individuals must be able to learn through exploration and to utilize intact sensory modalities.

In past years, the orientation and mobility specialist served only visually handicapped pupils. School personnel now realize that other handicapped pupils may also need specialized training in this area; thus, the service has expanded to include other individuals. For example, a moderately retarded young adult may have good work-related skills and would be considered employable except for the fact that he/she cannot travel alone. The orientation and mobility specialist can provide this type of training.

Since orientation and mobility specialists serve a very low incidence population, they are usually employed by large LEAs or shared by several districts. Schools sometimes contract with other agencies for these specialists' services.

Other Support Personnel

Space does not permit a separate discussion of each professional discipline that provides supportive services for the education of special needs pupils. However, school administrators must become familiar with these services in order to effectively operate programs and serve children.[7]

Sometimes, total program success depends on resolving one problem. This point can be emphasized by illustrating three pupils' problems.

EXAMPLE ONE

Pupil A attends the local high school for only three hours each day, even though she is an excellent student. Pupil A's day is limited because of a transportation problem for wheelchair students. A transportation specialist may be able to resolve this problem so that Pupil A can attend school for the same amount of time that the other students do.

EXAMPLE TWO

Pupil B has a severe hearing loss and is assigned to a special class for the deaf. He has been placed in integrated programs without success. A rehabilitative school audiologist may be able to help this pupil obtain a more effective hearing aid and better utilize his residual hearing ability. This could enhance Pupil B's ability to function with nonhandicapped people.

EXAMPLE THREE

Pupil C has a serious learning disability. Even though she is in the eleventh grade, Pupil C has only a fourth grade reading and mathematics ability. Recognizing this as a functional level for many everyday needs, the special education teacher recommended involvement in a work-study program. The work-study coordinator can provide job placement and training opportunities. The coordinator can also help the teacher plan lessons that will focus on the development of practical, job-related skills.

The brief examples given above are only samples of the ways in which other professional support personnel can contribute to the educational program of pupils with special needs. In some school districts, services are available for the asking; in others, the potential is waiting to be developed. In either case, school administrators should seek out services that will contribute to a pupil's educational success.

PROVIDING IN-SERVICE EDUCATION

Most people would agree that periodically updating their professional knowledge and skills is a good idea. This can be done in many different ways.

A common method of in-service education utilized by school personnel is completing additional university coursework. Classes may be taken in the evening, on weekends, or during the summer. Courses may be located on a university campus or may be "taken to the field" through extension divisions. Salary schedules that base an individual's pay partially on the number of university units completed encourage this type of in-service education.

In-service education programs are also provided by local school districts, intermediate districts, state education agencies, and nonpublic agencies. These agencies are being encouraged to provide in-service education programs with monies available from federally funded grants. Each state education agency must include a comprehensive plan for personnel development in its annual program plan for P.L. 94–142 funding. Thus, the SEA must commit part of the funds it receives to providing additional training for people who serve handicapped students. In turn, SEAs require local school districts to include the ways in which they will provide in-service education in their annual plan. This requirement involves providing training opportunities for administrators, parents, support personnel, and teachers.

The need for in-service education is intensified when a school program undergoes a significant change. Since special education programs have changed significantly in recent years, training needs are evident in certain areas. These areas include:

- Characteristics and needs of handicapped pupils
- Due process and procedural safeguards
- Identification and assessment procedures
- Continuity of alternative programs (including mainstreaming)
- IEP development and implementation
- Program evaluation.

Administrators have a responsibility not only to provide in-service educational opportunities for others, but to participate in these programs themselves. A well-informed professional staff is essential to program success.

SUMMARY

Chapter 13 discusses methods that will improve an administrator's interpersonal skills and help him/her with teachers and instructional support personnel. As educational programs become more complex and the numbers and types of professional personnel increase, an administrator's ability to work effectively with many people becomes increasingly important.

The range of programs required by law dictates the need for staff members with a great variety of professional skills. This chapter outlines these skills and suggests ways to recruit qualified staff members. Recruiting methods include working with colleges and universities and drawing on personnel already working within the system. The problem of "drafting" unqualified and unwilling regular classroom teachers is also discussed.

Regular classroom teachers have many fears about working with handicapped pupils. Chapter discussion helps the administrator understand these teachers' feelings and offers ways of dealing with these feelings. Administrators must also work with special education teachers to help them feel that they are a part of the total system. Suggestions for supervising and improving the work of these teachers are included.

Related service professionals include speech and language specialists, teacher aides, school psychologists, physical and occupational therapists, school nurses, orientation and mobility specialists, and many others. These people provide additional specialized services that help a handicapped individual profit from his/her educational program. Services offered by these professionals are discussed from an administrative perspective.

Finally, Chapter 13 discusses in-service education programs. Educators' needs to update their skills are emphasized, and different approaches to providing in-service education are presented.

NOTES

1. Interviewing candidates for special education positions is a very important part of the employment process. No matter what position is to be filled (e.g., teacher, speech pathologist, or school psychologist), the interviewing team should include a school principal and a special education specialist (e.g., a special education director or a special education teacher). Interview questions should be carefully developed to help the committee learn as much as possible about a candidate's expertise and job-related skills. Sample questions are included in Appendix 5. Some LEAs have taken an even more organized approach to the interviewing process. They use a standardized, structured interviewing format.

2. Although establishing a cooperative relationship between LEAs and colleges/universities makes sense, some teachers' unions have sometimes restricted the use of student teachers or forbidden teachers to accept student teachers in their classrooms. The rationale behind this restriction has been that while large numbers of trained persons remained unemployed, the use of student teachers would only help to create a greater surplus.

3. LEAs sometimes arrange for university training courses to be offered within the district. Teachers may be encouraged to participate in these courses if costs are paid by personnel development funds provided through P.L. 94–142.

4. Teacher organizations have sometimes militantly opposed mainstreaming and tried to give regular classroom teachers veto power over placing special education pupils in their classes.

5. The way to assure an in-service education program's success is to have participants identify their training needs and help plan their in-service education activities.

6. Teachers who work with the severely disabled (e.g., autistic children, the severely behaviorally disordered, and severely multi-handicapped pupils) may need occasional reassignment to a different program. Others who teach an extended school year (e.g., 220–230 days) may function more effectively on a nontraditional schedule. The Plymouth-Canton Community School District in Michigan has reported significant success in utilizing a 45–15 schedule with both general and special education programs. Many LEAs are experimenting with similar arrangements.

7. Parents and school districts strongly disagree about the extent of educational services required by law and about which specialists LEAs must provide. Some parents request such services as chiropractic treatment, vision therapy, psychotherapy, family counseling, and tongue-thrust therapy. Because of a lack of funds, LEAs are resisting these requests. They feel that some of these services are not essential to a student's ability to profit from an educational program and that these requests open a Pandora's box of parental demands that cannot be met.

REFERENCES

Department of Health, Education and Welfare. 1979. *Progress toward a free appropriate public education: A report to Congress on the implementation of Public Law 94–142: The Education for All Handicapped Children Act.* Washington, D.C.

Edmonds, M. 1976. Accountability for all children in the regular class. *Language Arts*, April, 53:425.

National Advisory Committee on the Handicapped. 1978. Education of the handicapped today. *Readings in psychology of exceptional children*, 1st ed. Special education series. Gilford, Conn.: Special Learning Corporation, pp. 2–4.

Payne, R., and Murray, C. 1974. Principals' attitudes toward integration of the handicapped. *Exceptional Children*, October, 41:123–24.

Public Law 85–926 (An act to encourage expansion of the training of leadership personnel in education of the mentally retarded through grants to institutions of higher education and state education agencies). 1958.

Smith, J., and Schindler, W. J. 1980. Certification requirements of general educators concerning exceptional pupils. *Exceptional Children* 46,5:394–96.

Stephens, T., and Braun, B. 1980. Measures of regular classroom teachers' attitudes toward handicapped children. *Exceptional Children* 46,4:292–94.

Vallveturri, P. 1969. Integration vs. segregation: A useless dialectic. *The Journal of Special Education*, Winter, 3:406.

Wong, M., and Perkins, S. A. 1978. Attitudes toward the mentally retarded: A review of the selected literature. Paper read at the First World Congress on Special Education, Stirling, Scotland. ERIC Document 158 486, p. 9.

14

The Special Education Curriculum

"The individualized education program requirement . . . does not promote a type of curriculum or dictate methodology. It does not require that children be individually taught, nor does it necessarily embrace behaviorism. It is a management tool designed to assure that, when a child requires special education, the special education designed for that child is appropriate to his or her special learning needs, and that the special education designed is actually delivered and monitored."

(Torres 1977, p. 1)

INTRODUCTION

The principles and procedures used to develop, implement, and monitor the special education curriculum do not significantly differ from those used in the regular curriculum. Procedural similarities should help general administrators, since they are already able to easily handle their curricular responsibilities. Because of their training and experience, administrators feel well prepared to cope with this part of their leadership role. However, some aspects of the special education curriculum are unique, and a general administrator may not be familiar with them. Thus, he/she may need assistance from a special education expert. Assistance should be available from special education directors, disability specialists, teachers, and outside consultants. A general administrator has a legitimate right to expect specialists' help.

What do curriculum development, implementation, and modeling mean? To some, the term "curriculum" means everything that happens in a school; to others, it refers to the courses taught; to still others, it encompasses a school's philosophy, course content, learners, and teaching techniques. This chapter will focus on course content, but will explain how other factors are related to content. One factor that affects a curriculum's content is a special education student's abilities or disabilities. A second influencing factor is a special education student's environment. Another factor that should be taken into consideration is special techniques that may enable special needs pupils to learn the content that is presented.

One curriculum item is now (by law) common to all special education programs throughout the nation. This common element is the individualized education program. The requirements, format, content, benefits, and problems of the IEP will be discussed. Its effect on children, teachers, other school personnel, and parents will also be considered.

IS IT DIFFERENT? HOW?

Curricular content that is appropriate for handicapped students is usually also appropriate for nonhandicapped students. The reverse may or may not be true. Sometimes a regular student's curriculum is also appropriate for a handicapped student, but not always. The emphasis that is usually placed on the three R's provides an exaggerated example. Although reading, writing, and arithmetic are very important to regular students and to most special education students, the development of these skills may be less important (or of no importance) to the very severely retarded. Their primary area of curricular concentration may be developing *self-help skills*.

The following situation provides another example of curricular content being influenced by handicapping conditions.

EXAMPLE

Jill was an average student in a third grade class until she contracted rheumatic fever. She was absent from school for three weeks and was too ill to have a home teacher. During the fourth week of her illness, Jill's doctor indicated that she would need six months to recuperate, but could have a home teacher and spend a maximum of one hour each day on schoolwork. Obviously, physical education will have to be removed from her curriculum; health, social studies, penmanship, and science also will probably be deleted. Her total curricular experience may now be composed of reading and arithmetic.

There are many other reasons for varying curricular content:

- Some children are not ready for certain types of curricular content at the usual age (e.g., educable mentally retarded children may not be ready to read until nine years of age or later).
- Some disabilities prevent or make difficult participation in certain learning experiences (e.g., oil painting for the blind student, tumbling for the paraplegic).
- Time is a factor; some pupils spend less time in school.
- Different levels of ability may limit or encourage participation in certain school subjects.

- Need should influence a curricular choice (e.g., a twelfth grade student who has a serious reading disability needs a vocational training class more than a literature class).
- Deaf children will not develop reading, writing, or spelling skills until they have developed adequate language concepts.

Some characteristics of a regular curriculum may make it inappropriate for some special education students. For example, a particular LEA may have very extensive academic curricular requirements. Although completing these requirements may help many students who plan to go to college, a college-preparatory curriculum is obviously inappropriate for some learning disabled students. Also, it is well known that textbooks greatly influence curricular content. If a special education student reads significantly below his/her grade level, it will be very difficult for that student to compete with his/her peers.

How does the special education curriculum differ from the regular curriculum? It is not different for some students; its content differs for others; and its instructional techniques are different for still others. For example:

- A paraplegic student who has no associated learning handicaps may need slightly different school facilities, but the curricular content and teaching techniques can be the same as those applied to his/her non-handicapped peers.
- A secondary school blind student may require special learning materials and different teaching techniques, but curricular content can be virtually unchanged.
- A mentally retarded student will probably have great difficulty with a curriculum's academic areas, but can apply his/her knowledge to on-the-job training. Thus, the curricular content is modified.

WHERE IS THE EMPHASIS?

The most extensive efforts to develop materials, guides, frameworks, and learning packages have probably been directed toward the mildly retarded student. Some of the best known curriculum development work has been conducted by Goldstein (1976).[1] His Social Learning Curriculum is based on research showing that these students need to develop competence in practical social skills. His curriculum materials are divided into sixteen phases, beginning with the self and expanding to include a broader environment as students mature. The phase titles given below indicate the areas that Goldstein emphasizes:

Phase 1. Perceiving Individuality
Phase 2. Recognizing the Environment

Phase 3.   Recognizing Independence
Phase 4.   Recognizing the Body
Phase 5.   Recognizing and Reacting to Emotions
Phase 6.   Recognizing What the Senses Do
Phase 7.   Communicating with Others
Phase 8.   Getting Along with Others
Phase 9.   Identifying Helpers
Phase 10.   Maintaining Body Function
Phase 11.   Identifying Family and Home
Phase 12.   Recognizing Basic Physical Needs
Phase 13.   Recognizing Personal Needs
Phase 14.   Acting on Independence
Phase 15.   Maintaining Self and Environment
Phase 16.   Communicating Effectively.

Shryock and Hanson (1974, pp. 54–60) list ten major headings for curriculum goals. They suggest orienting goals toward skills and application instead of general knowledge. The ten goals areas are listed below:

· Skills related to personal and social growth
· Skills related to maintaining health
· Skills related to communicating ideas
· Skills related to money
· Skills related to working with measurements
· Skills related to getting along in an expanding community
· Skills related to coping with the physical environment
· Skills related to maintaining a home
· Skills related to using leisure time
· Skills related to career development.

Since these goal areas do not mention reading or arithmetic, one might ask if the basics have not been omitted from the curriculum. In reality, the basic skills have become a means rather than an end and are considered to be fundamental tools needed to achieve each goal.

For some students, emphasis may be placed on techniques rather than on content. This is exemplified by the case of a blind, academically talented student. This student's academic curriculum will be identical to a nonhandicapped student's curriculum, but the blind student must also learn Braille, acquire orientation and mobility skills, and master notetaking and typing. These special techniques will allow the blind student to pursue a regular curriculum.

For students with hearing impairments, emphasis is placed on developing language concepts and understandable speech patterns. These students would study such special techniques as speechreading, oral speech development, and manual or total communication skills.

Textbook Emphasis

It is almost impossible to overstate the influence that textbooks have on a general education curriculum. Some educators might even say that textbooks *are* the curriculum. But that statement would not necessarily be true for some exceptional individuals. Since these students frequently read below their grade level, they are unable to use the text prescribed for their age group. They may have to use different materials and frequently use no text.

Some educators have maintained that regular textbooks are appropriate for exceptional students and that teachers can adapt material by "watering down" or "slowing down" the curriculum. "Watering down" means to simplify or cover less of the content; "slowing down" means to begin instruction at a later age or to extend the amount of time spent on any given material. This general approach assumes that (1) all topics in the regular curriculum are relevant and essential to the special student and (2) all material in the regular curriculum can be learned by the special education student, if he/she is given enough time. Obviously, both assumptions are incorrect.

A further problem encountered with the watered down curriculum is that it sometimes sacrifices depth of study in important areas in the interest of covering a total curriculum. The slowed down curriculum tends to be inadequate because some learning handicapped students may only reach fifth or sixth grade level content. That would hardly prepare them for adult living.

This does not imply that the use of textbooks is inappropriate or that simplifying content or slowing down the coverage of content is always inappropriate. These procedures all have legitimate uses, but they should not form the foundation for a special education curriculum.

Emphasis on Individualization of Content and Instructional Techniques

Reading about special education curricula or observing teaching and learning techniques inevitably leads one to recognize the importance of individualization. If individualizing is important for general education students (and it is), it is even more crucial for disabled or gifted students. Special students are just as diverse as general education students. One can no more say that all deaf children are alike than that all children are alike.

Individualizing instruction is primarily a teacher's responsibility. However, it can only be fully successful if administrators provide needed resources and help to establish a supportive environment. A special education teacher can benefit from the help of a teacher's aide and the use of multi-level texts and special equipment. The opportunity to be included in regular classes and to participate in vocational training programs will also aid students.

Individualizing instruction involves several types of activities:

- Assessing functional abilities
- Specifying general strengths and problem areas
- Determining a curriculum's goals
- Establishing instructional objectives
- Analyzing learning tasks
- Implementing appropriate teaching techniques and learning activities.

Table 14–1 shows how one might carry out the first three steps listed above with three different sixteen-year-old students. It illustrates the need for individual consideration of curricular needs. The latter three topics will be discussed later in this chapter.

Emphasis on Independent Living Skills and Career Preparation

One of the most important outcomes of a successful school program for handicapped students is to have students develop skills that will enable them to be independent and to contribute to society.[2] Society expects this, and it is an attainable goal (within reasonable limits) for all but the profoundly handicapped. A moderately to severely handicapped individual can learn adequate personal hygiene habits, food preparation skills, home cleaning and maintenance skills, and good social habits. Thus, he/she can become independent within a somewhat sheltered environment. To meet this expectation, an educational leader will have to monitor carefully a student's special curriculum to assure inclusion of goals, objectives, materials, and activities designed to teach independent living skills.

Career preparation may well be the most neglected aspect of an exceptional individual's curriculum. Educators "talk a good show" but seldom produce learning experiences. Mayer (1976) reported that observations of secondary programs often showed that a career preparation program existed on paper, but not in practice. Career preparation is frequently ignored, despite the encouragement of federal agencies and appropriations for vocational education, despite laws in many states mandating that career preparation be included in the curriculum, and despite the fact that most educators support, in theory, the need for career preparation. Perhaps the greatest irony of all is to identify students as learning handicapped when it comes to academic subjects and then to continue to emphasize academic skills year after year instead of emphasizing living skills. A student who might be able to succeed in a variety of vocational situations thus may never be allowed to develop job-related skills.

Why do educators so often fail to prepare students for the world of work? A few observations may be enlightening:

- Special education teachers seldom have vocational training in or experiences with the entry level jobs that are appropriate for a teenaged, handicapped student.
- Vocational education teachers often know very little about handicapping conditions and exclude or limit their experiences with these students.
- Work experience teachers and counselors have very large caseloads and not enough work situations. They select the best workers, not those who have problems. Handicapped students are thus frequently excluded.
- Principals want their students and teachers to be on campus, but job training sites are usually off campus.

Fortunately, many LEAs have resolved their curricular problems and do offer good career preparation programs. While space will not allow a detailed discussion, we can briefly show how a school program can focus on career preparation programs and independent living skills. Figure 14–1 shows how curriculum emphasis is changing at elementary, intermediate, junior high, and high schools. Figure 14–2 suggests course content. These suggestions are aimed at students who are learning handicapped in academic areas. A student who is taking college preparatory courses may have quite a different curriculum.

Task Analysis

As previously stated, one distinction that can be made between special education curricula and general education curricula is that different teaching techniques are used. Exceptional individuals have learning problems. Educational experiences are provided and materials are presented, but the student often does not learn. There are several explanations for this failure to learn, including difficulty identifying what is to be learned and demonstrating that material has been learned, not being ready to learn, and trying to digest too much material at one time. One way to resolve these problems is to use a technique called "task analysis."

Mayer (1978, p. 2) describes task analysis as:

- a technique which is often used by successful teachers to bring objectivity and specificity to the teaching/learning process. It is an attempt to look at all of the details of that process so that *learning* does occur. The learning of any given skill or concept involves a sequential series of many small steps. If any of these steps is *short circuited* or missed the desired result may not come about, and a student fails to become a

TABLE 14-1   CURRICULAR EMPHASIS FOR DIFFERENT INDIVIDUALS

Individual's Ability/Disability	Specific Strengths or Problems	Possible Curricular Emphasis
1. A sixteen-year-old student with a general learning disability (mild to moderate mental retardation). No other observable disabilities.	Student is socially adept, has good physical appearance and stamina, good oral language development, and fair peer and adult relationships. Reading ability measured at fourth grade level, math ability at sixth grade level.	• Functional use of basic academic skills in home, school, community, and work environments. • Social skills and habits, interpersonal relationships. • Personal hygiene and health habits. • Skills of independent living, e.g., cooking, caring for clothing, budgeting, consumer buying. • Work information and exploration. • Skills related to getting and holding a job. • General work attitudes, habits, and skills.
2. A sixteen-year-old blind student. No other observable disabilities.	Student has some social adjustment problems. Relates well with adults, but has problems with peer relationships. Scores well above average on academic aptitude tests (adapted for the blind), has good Braille and typing skills, but is very "dependent" in travel abilities. Is immature in physical development.	• College preparatory courses. • Adaptive P.E.—body building. • Mobility training. • Social skills and interpersonal relationships. • Independent living skills—cooking, personal budgeting, clothing selection and care. • Work information—selecting a career.
3. A sixteen-year-old student with moderate to severe behavioral disorders. Average academic aptitude (I.Q. score of 104), but below average achievement (reading, 4.3 grade level; math, 5.1). No other observable disabilities.	A handsome youngster with good physical development, good motor coordination, good athletic skills. Attention problems—does not attend to learning tasks for sustained periods of time. Aggressive, acting-out behavior. Poor relationships with adults and rejected by most peers.	• Behavior management program to develop attention span and commitment to task completion. • Structured program to develop basic skills. • Self-analysis and analysis of peer relationships. • Controlling one's own actions. • Work information and exploration. • Working with peers, superiors. • Getting and holding a job. • General work attitudes, habits, and skills.

FIGURE 14-1 CURRICULUM EMPHASIS

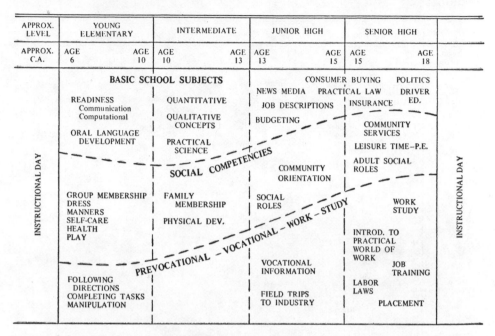

Reprinted from *Work-Study Handbook for Educable Mentally Retarded Minors Enrolled in High School Programs in California Public Schools*, prepared by L. Wayne Campbell, Medford Todd, and Everett V. O'Rourke (Sacramento: California State Department of Education, 1971), p. 24.

learner. Thus, the teacher has not taught. Analysis of the learning task may reveal to the teacher the problem area when learning difficulty occurs.

• a process or a way of thinking as well as an instructional technique. When utilized by a skillful teacher it can become an approach to evaluation of learning problems, a way of planning, a method of programming, and an aid in remediation.

• a teaching/learning procedure which logically follows the writing of behavioral or performance objectives. The objective tells "what" is to be learned. Task analysis tells the sequential learning steps involved in developing the skill to perform a particular objective.

• an essential skill for the development of *individual education programs* and the implementation of prescriptive teaching techniques.

Mayer (1978) lists six steps that are involved in doing a formal task analysis.[3] Of course, in an actual teaching situation, a teacher would not analyze each task for each student (time prohibits this), but would apply the appro-

FIGURE 14-2 GENERAL SUGGESTED CURRICULUM EMPHASIS IN SECONDARY SCHOOLS

Approximate level	JUNIOR HIGH SCHOOL			SENIOR HIGH SCHOOL			
Year of school	7	8	9	10	11	12	
Basic skills	*Basic mathematics	*General mathematics (application)	*Functional mathematics (vocational, homemaking)	*Health and safety Practical science	*Consumer education	Applied mathematics *Adult roles	
	*Basic reading skills	*Reading laboratory		*Practical mathematics (application)			
	*Basic communication		*Functional communication	(Reading will be incorporated into communications sequence.)			
		*Communication skills					
				*Mass media communication	*Communications laboratory	*Communications laboratory	
	*Science	*Community studies	*Cultural and social patterns	*Driver education mobility series	American studies		INSTRUCTIONAL DAY
	*Personal development				P.E. Recreation	P.E. Recreation	
Social competencies and leisure-time activities				Fine arts Recreation P.E.			
			Fine arts Recreation P.E.				
		Fine arts Recreation P.E.					
	Fine arts Recreation P.E.						
				*Vocational exploration	*Vocational guidance	*Vocational laboratory	
			*Vocational orientation	*Work-study, on-campus/on-site	Work-study, on-campus/on-site; *on-campus/off-site	Work-study, on-campus on-site; on-campus/ off-site	
Vocational work-study	*Consumer and homemaking education Vocational arts	*Vocational arts Consumer and homemaking education	Work-study, on-campus/ on-site	Homemaking Industrial arts	Work-study, off-campus	*Work-study, off-campus	

*Recommended emphasis.

Reprinted from *Work-Study Handbook for Educable Mentally Retarded Minors Enrolled in High School Programs in California Public Schools,* prepared by L. Wayne Campbell, Medford Todd, and Everett V. O'Rourke (Sacramento: California State Department of Education, 1971), p. 26.

priate techniques. The steps involved in task analysis are listed below. An example follows each step.

1. Define the task to be learned (say specifically what the learner is to do).

    Given a *telephone trainer,* the student will demonstrate the use of the telephone to call the local fire department and report a fire.

2. State the expected learner outcomes.

   Immediate: The learner can correctly report a fire.

   Long Range: The learner will develop skills in the use of the telephone which may be used in many life situations.

3. List the prerequisite skills (if the learner can not demonstrate the prerequisite abilities or skills, the task is inappropriate).

   The learner must
   - recognize the printed numerals 0 through 9
   - have adequate finger dexterity and strength to operate the telephone dial
   - remember a sequence of 7 numbers, or be able to read the number, and dial it
   - have oral language which is easily understood.

4. Analyze the task for its sequential learning steps (the steps should be listed in sequence. Many tasks cannot be mastered if steps are omitted).

   Using a *telephone trainer* the learner:
   1. picks up the telephone receiver
   2. waits for the dial tone
   3. dials the correct number
   4. waits for an answer by the person receiving the call
   5. properly identifies self by name
   6. states that he/she wishes to report a fire
   7. gives the correct address
   8. responds to questions which are asked
   9. hangs up the receiver of the telephone.

5. Outline the teaching procedures.

   Teaching should be specific to each step in the task rather than to the whole task, and should be designed for a specific student (learner). Examples of teaching procedures include:
   - demonstration by the teacher
   - guiding or cuing each motor and verbal response
   - using manipulative materials
   - reinforcing each step when successfully completed.

6. State the rationale.

   The teacher should be able to answer two questions:
   1. Why should this task be included in the curriculum of this student at this time?
   2. Are the teaching methods and materials which are most appropriate for this student being used?

The preceding discussion presents an overview of the different types of emphasis that may be found in special education programs. As with other children, goals may be different for different individuals. Also, techniques may have to be altered for blind, deaf, retarded, or learning handicapped individuals. Curriculum emphasis must be individualized according to need. This point is expressed by Olivero (1973, p. 4):

> I believe we should not be promoting the concept of individualization—if we mean everyone gets the same thing—even though we take considerable pains to let children move at their own pace. I would argue that not all the children need the same thing, especially if they all must travel the same path to the enlightened terminal objectives. No matter what we do with the pace of learning (which incidentally, is a commendable improvement over the lock-step approach that typified our traditional schools), if we teach the same thing to all children we are likely to miss quite a few by not matching their needs with what we can offer.

THE INDIVIDUALIZED EDUCATION PROGRAM (IEP)

One of the most significant occurrences in the recent history of education for the handicapped (in terms of curriculum development and implementation) has been the introduction of the formal requirement that an IEP be provided for every handicapped student. Public Law 94–142 (discussed in Chapter 4) stipulates that there must be an individualized education program for every student covered under this law. The statutory requirement for IEPs and regulatory procedures included in Title 45 of the Code of Federal Regulations have far-reaching implications for administrators (e.g., parental involvement, organization of IEP meetings, procedural safeguards, time limitations on actions taken, and appeals) and for teachers (e.g., writing objectives, counseling parents, accounting for student progress).

Appendix 6 presents excerpts of laws and regulations related to the IEP. It should help educational leaders focus attention on the provisions most important to them. State education agencies require local administrators to show that they:

- Have an operational IEP for every handicapped student
- Are fully informed (and have informed appropriate staff members) about definition, content, and procedures
- Conduct IEP planning and review meetings according to specified procedures
- Ensure parents the opportunity to participate
- Maintain responsibility for the IEPs of students placed in private schools
- Know what they themselves are accountable for and what agencies, teachers, and others are accountable for.

In their educational codes and regulations, many states have also provided details about developing and using IEPs. Administrators should carefully review mandates regarding the proper development and use of IEPs. Table 14–2 provides a format for conducting a self-analysis of how well one is complying with IEP mandates.

The IEP requirement has been met with great interest and great concern by administrators, teachers, and parents. Discussions with many teachers and administrators have uncovered the following positive remarks about the IEP:

- It extends full rights to the handicapped.
- It helps in planning and organizing instruction.
- It helps establish curricular emphasis through specific goals and objectives.
- It helps teachers keep the instructional program on target.
- It provides a more efficient way of planning daily lessons.
- It provides a better approach to documenting student progress.
- It provides an accountability structure.
- It identifies who is responsible for what—including personnel other than teachers.
- It provides a way for teachers and parents to share information about a child; helps the communication process.
- It assures parents that teachers and other school personnel have their child's best interests at heart.

However, professionals also expressed concerns about the IEP:

- It is extremely time consuming (the number one concern of teachers).
- It often causes a duplication of efforts. Teachers still need daily lesson plans and still have to record progress in grade books.
- The goals developed by the IEP committee may be inappropriate (in the teacher's opinion).
- Short-term objectives must be continually revised.
- Secondary teachers are overwhelmed by the large numbers of IEPs they must handle.
- It requires accountability on the part of the teacher, but not on the part of the parent.
- The IEP meeting intimidates parents.
- It does not provide assessment that is related to a child's day-to-day instruction.
- There is no evidence that the process makes a difference in a child's progress.

TABLE 14–2   SELF-CHECK LIST FOR IEP COMPLIANCE

Area/Task/Concern	Statutory/Regulatory Provisions	We Are OK	We Need to Improve
IEP Requirements	• Every enrolled special education student at the beginning of each school year must have an IEP. • Transfer special education students must have an IEP. • Special education students in private schools must have an IEP. • An IEP must be implemented without undue delay. • An IEP must be reviewed and revised at least annually.		
Definition	IEPs must: • Be written statements • Be developed by a committee • Contain certain required content.		
Committee	The IEP committee must include: • An LEA representative qualified to provide or supervise the student's program (usually an administrator) • The teacher • The parent or guardian • The child (when appropriate) • Others as needed.		
Content	The IEP must include: • A statement of present levels of school performance • A statement of annual goals • Statements of short-term instructional objectives • A statement of the specific educational services to be provided • An explanation of the extent to which the student will participate in regular program • A projected date for initiation and duration of services • Objective criteria and evaluation procedures • A schedule (at least annually) for determining success.		
Meeting Requirements	The LEA is responsible for: • Conducting a meeting to develop an IEP for each handicapped student • Meeting to review (at least annually) the IEP of each student		

TABLE 14-2 (*Cont'd*)

Area/Task/Concern	Statutory/Regulatory Provisions	We Are OK	We Need to Improve
	• Including the following participants: (1) a representative of the LEA (other than the teacher) who is qualified to provide or supervise special education programs, (2) the child's teacher, (3) one or both of the parents, (4) the child, if appropriate, (5) others as needed, and (6) for first-time consideration of a child, a member of the evaluation team.		
Parent Participation	The LEA must: • Give parents "timely" notification of the meeting • Schedule the meeting at a mutually agreed upon time and place • Develop a notice to parents that indicates purpose, time, location and who will attend • Involve parents by telephone if they cannot attend • Keep records of correspondence and contacts with parents • Provide an interpreter, if needed • Provide a copy of the IEP for the parent.		
Private School Placements	For children placed in private schools, the LEA must: • Develop an IEP prior to referral • Ensure that a private school representative attends an IEP meeting • Revise and review the IEP as needed • Ensure parent participation as described above.		
Accountability	• The agency is accountable for providing special education and related services. • The agency, teachers, and other persons involved are *not* held accountable for a child's failure to meet the projected growth which is indicated by the goals and objectives.		

* Refers only to federal laws and regulations. Some states have added provisions.

The IEP requirements are still too new to have significant support from research studies. However, we do have teachers' perceptions. Administrators should use teachers' positive feelings to improve compliance and (we hope) program quality. Teachers' concerns should also receive an educational leader's attention. Many of these concerns can be alleviated. Duplication of efforts, use of time, and excessive concerns about accountability may be reduced by good management techniques and by providing teachers with support services. The IEP process holds great promise and should be given every chance to succeed. A better curriculum for special students will be the result of administrative efforts.

As long as statutory and regulatory requirements are met, the actual format used to write IEPs is usually a matter of local choice. Table 14–3 presents a sample IEP format. It is in the context of this type of format that the curriculum for each handicapped student must be developed. Figure 14–3 presents a graphic picture of the IEP process.

PRESCHOOL THROUGH POST-SECONDARY PROGRAMS

It is not the objective of this chapter to outline a complete curriculum for a very diverse population of students. This chapter's aim is to create a general awareness of those programs that can contribute to curricular planning and decision making.

Educational planners must become familiar with the scope of special programs if they are to be effective managers. Federal law, as of September 1, 1980, required that educational programs be available for special education students between the ages of three and twenty-one, unless this requirement would conflict with state laws designed for the three-to-five-year and eighteen-to-twenty-one-year age groups (P.L. 94–142, Section 612(2)(B)).

For several years, many states have been providing preschool education for children who can be significantly assisted by an early education program. For example, children with hearing, speech, visual, and physical problems need early education programs to help them develop skills that will enable them to learn school subjects. Thus, preschool programs are expanding.

Very few educators would suggest that general education students have acquired all of the formal school training they will need at age eighteen. They can usually profit from additional education at colleges, universities, technical schools, and trade schools. Handicapped students also need continuing education. Some can profit from colleges and universities, some from technical and trade schools, some should continue in a high school program, and some should be trained in a sheltered workshop. Public school officials have a responsibility to see that educational opportunities are available until a student becomes twenty-one years old.

FIGURE 14-3 THE IEP PROCESS

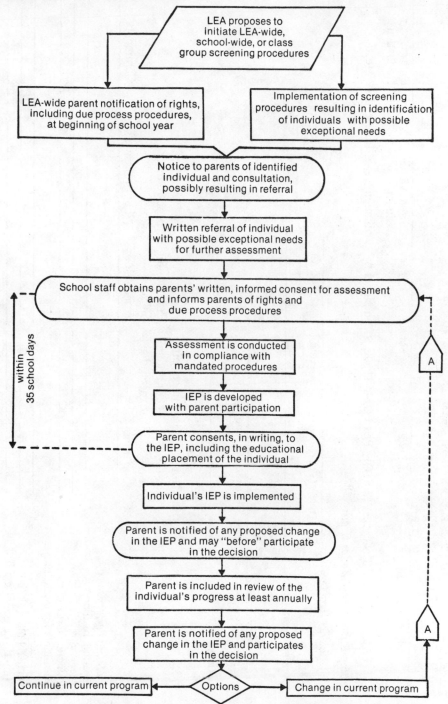

From *The Individualized Education Program: A Developmental Process.* Sacramento: California State Department of Education, Office of Special Education, 1977.

TABLE 14-3 INDIVIDUALIZED EDUCATION PROGRAM (SAMPLE FORMAT)

Student's Name	Birth Date	School	Current Grade Assignment	Date of Evaluation

PART I. CURRENT LEVELS OF PERFORMANCE (Completed by Evaluation Team Prior to IEP Meeting)

Testing Instruments/Modes Used:

Intelligence Tests _____ name(s) _____ V score _____ P score _____

Achievement Tests _____ name(s) _____ score(s) _____

Teacher Evaluation _____ teacher(s) name(s) _____

Other _____

	Not assessed or not applicable	Functioning at or above expected level	Functioning below expectations	Actual functioning level (if appropriate)	Comments
Academic Performance					
reading readiness					
general reading skills					
functional use of reading					
readiness for quantitative concepts					
general math skills					
functional use of math skills					
mechanics of writing					

penmanship
spelling skills
functional writing skills

Speech/Language Development
use of oral language
speech clarity
nonverbal communication

Social Areas
self-concept
relations with peers and adults
social customs and expectations

Physical or Psychomotor Skills
perception skills
gross motor skills
fine motor skills
physical activities

Self-Help Skills
personal care, health and safety
mobility and transportation
home and family living
community living skills
leisure time

Prevocational/Vocational Skills
career awareness
work attitudes and habits
employment seeking skills
interpersonal relationships—
on the job
specific job skills

297

PART II. RECOMMENDED SERVICES, INITIATION DATES, AND ANTICIPATED DURATION

1. Program Assignment:

After consideration of all relevant information the evaluation team recommends assignment to the _____ program. Suggested date _____ (date). This assignment will be reviewed by _____ so that continuation or program change can be made.

2. Least Restrictive Environment and Educational Service

Check as appropriate	Percent of the day	Date to be initiated	Anticipated duration
(a) ___ regular class	_____	_____	_____
___ special class	_____	_____	_____
___ resource room	_____	_____	_____

Check as appropriate		Date to be initiated	Anticipated duration
(b) ___ remedial speech		_____	_____
___ special transportation		_____	_____
___ adaptive P.E.		_____	_____
___ student counseling		_____	_____
___ school-related parent counseling		_____	_____
___ vocational education		_____	_____
___ work experience		_____	_____
___ auditory evaluation/training		_____	_____
___ habilitative services		_____	_____
___ physical and/or occupational therapy		_____	_____
___ special diagnostic evaluation		_____	_____
___ special health services		_____	_____

Comments and/or Explanations:

_____

PART III. GOALS, OBJECTIVES, EVALUATION MONITORING

Goals and Objective Areas (circle appropriate number and letter)
Code: B = Begin, D = Develop, I = Improve, M = Master, U = Use

			Evaluation Monitoring
Goals for Reading			
___ 1. reading readiness skills	___ 2. general reading skills	___ 3. functional use of reading skills	
a. personal readiness	a. vocabulary development	a. study skills	
b. tactile readiness	b. phonetic analysis	b. reading for information	
c. auditory readiness	c. structural word analysis	c. reading for pleasure	
d. visual readiness	d. comprehension	d. reading skills for daily living	
e. letters of the alphabet	e. silent and oral reading	e. reading skills for vocational situations	

Short-term Instructional Objectives (one or more for each goal)

established _____
revised _____
achieved _____
evaluated by _____ *dates*
(person responsible)

Short-term Instructional Objectives (one or more for each goal)

established _____
revised _____
achieved _____
evaluated by _____ *dates*
(person responsible)

299

PART IV. IEP COMMITTEE REMARKS, ACTIONS, SIGNATURE

Initial Planning Meeting   *Periodic (at least annual) Review*

Comments/Suggestions by the Committee: Comments/Suggestions by the Committee:

I have had the opportunity to participate in the development of this IEP.   I have reviewed the progress made by the student and have had an opportunity to participate in revisions to the IEP.

	Agree with committee recommendations	Disagree with recommendations**		Agree with committee recommendations	Disagree with recommendations**
signature of parent*	_____	_____	signature of parent*	_____	_____
the pupil—if appropriate	_____	_____	the pupil—if appropriate	_____	_____
administrator	_____	_____	administrator	_____	_____
teacher of the student	_____	_____	teacher of the student	_____	_____
other (specify)	_____	_____	other (specify)	_____	_____
other (specify)	_____	_____	other (specify)	_____	_____

Note: The IEP is a plan for delivery of educational services. It is not a contract that guarantees the accomplishment of the proposed goals and objectives. (45 C.F.R. § 121a.349).

* If the parent could not be present, a copy of the IEP will be mailed by the administrator.

** Appeal procedures are outlined in the regulations, if dissenters wish to appeal a decision.

SUMMARY

Chapter 14 introduces the special education curriculum and compares it to the more familiar general education curriculum. "Curriculum" is defined in terms of content, but it also involves abilities and disabilities, environmental factors, and special techniques.

The ways in which a special education curriculum is different, the reasons it is different, and curricular emphasis are discussed. Aspects of curricular emphasis presented include social needs, functional application, textbook influence, individualization, the need to develop independent living skills, career preparation, and special techniques (e.g., task analysis).

The individualized education program (IEP) is currently the most significant factor involved in special education curriculum development. This chapter presents relevant excerpts from P.L. 94–142 and Title 45 of the Code of Federal Regulations and suggests a format a district might use to evaluate its compliance with the law.

The author's observations of teachers' and administrators' perceptions of the IEP process are presented, and a sample format for developing the IEP is included.

Finally, the chapter contains a brief discussion of the need to develop a curriculum for exceptional individuals in preschool through postsecondary programs.

NOTES

1. Dr. Herbert Goldstein, a special education professor at New York University, has directed the development of the Social Learning Curriculum. The materials are published by Charles E. Merrill Publishing Company.
2. In our complex society, few people are totally independent. We are dependent on the farmer, on our auto mechanic, on our dentist. Thus, independence takes on a somewhat altered meaning. We depend on others and they depend on us, up to a point. Within this context, independence is a realistic goal for the handicapped.
3. Reprinted by permission of the author.

REFERENCES

California State Department of Education. 1977. *The individualized education program: A developmental process.* Sacramento: Office of Special Education.
Campbell, L. W., Todd, M., and O'Rourke, E. V. 1971. *Work-study handbook for educable mentally retarded minors in high school programs in California public schools.* Sacramento: California State Department of Education.
45 C.F.R. § 121a.340 to 121a.349.
Education for All Handicapped Children Act, P.L. 94–142; Section 612(2)(B).

Goldstein, H. 1976. *The social learning curriculum.* Columbus, Ohio: Charles E. Merrill Publishing Company.

Mayer, C. L. 1976. A study of high school career development programs for handicapped students. Unpublished consultant report to the California State Department of Education.

Mayer, C. L. 1978. Task analysis for teaching and learning. 1552 Trumbower Ave., Monterey Park, Cal. 91754.

Olivero, J. L. 1973. What's wrong with individualizing instruction—educators? *Thrust for Educational Leadership* 2,5:4–6.

Shyrock, C., and Hanson, F. M. 1974. *Programs for the educable mentally retarded in California public schools.* Sacramento: California State Department of Education.

Torres, S. 1977. *A primer on individualized education programs for handicapped children.* Reston, Va.: The Council for Exceptional Children.

15

Budgets, Facilities, Equipment, and Supplies

"The direction and magnitude of special education are determined and controlled by the level of funding provided, the distribution of monies to various programs based on specific formulas, and the conditions and qualifications attached to the funding."

(Bernstein et al. 1976b, p. ix)

INTRODUCTION

The old saying "Money and things do not guarantee a quality program" is true. However, it is also true that trying to operate a program without these resources is difficult, if not impossible. Very early in their careers, school administrators learn that someone must be responsible for (1) knowing the sources of funding and the means by which funding may be obtained, (2) utilizing appropriate funding formulas to project income, (3) preparing, controlling, and monitoring the budget, (4) matching available facilities to student needs, and (5) equipping and supplying the program.

This chapter presents background information on how special education programs are financed and some suggestions about the practical aspects of budget development, budget control, housing the programs, and providing the necessary equipment and supplies.

FUNDING SOURCES

Funds for the operation of school programs come from the three main levels of government: federal, state, and local. Contributions from federal sources are considerably smaller, less reliable, and more controversial than those from the other two sources. A brief overview of historical information helps one understand the reasons for this.

Schools, as they first developed in this country, were very much a local phenomenon. They were funded and controlled first by families and later by community government. Still later, as state government grew, education became the state's responsibility. Most state constitutions declared that education was one of state government's major responsibilities. Even so, states delegated most of their policy-making and funding responsibility to the local government. With few exceptions, actual school operation is still a local responsibility. Citizens have jealousy protected their schools from encroaching federal control and many have seen federal funding and federal control as nearly inseparable. Citizens today still want to maintain local control, but are willing to give up some autonomy because they find it difficult or impossible to finance their schools without federal funds. Thus, it is only in recent years that federal sources of money have become significant in the funding of school programs.

Basically, federal funds that help support special education programs may be described in two ways:

1. *Entitlement funds* are available to LEAs on the basis of formulas that usually take into account the number of students enrolled in a particular program. For example, an LEA may claim a given number of dollars each year for each student placed in a special education program. This is authorized by P.L. 94–142. The LEA must meet certain criteria, but when these are met the LEA is entitled to receive funds. They are channeled through the state education agency to the local education agency.
2. *Competitive funds* are available through application for grants. The applicant competes with other LEAs for the available funds. Grants are awarded to provide a stimulus for development of programs that have been assigned a high priority by the granting agency. Obviously, funds are limited and there is a great deal of competition for the available dollars.

Probably the best and most accessible source of information about federal funds is the "Guide to Office of Education Programs" published annually in *American Education*. Table 15–1 reproduces a section of the 1980 "Guide" on education for the handicapped. It describes fourteen different funding options that provide over $1,049,000,000 in funds each year.

Although the federal appropriation for education of the handicapped exceeds one billion dollars annually, many local school boards and administrators feel that the federal government is rather unreliable. Frequently, money received from a competitive grant covers only a one- to three-year period. The LEA may be left with a highly successful program that can no longer be funded. Entitlement funds tend to be more permanent, but they seldom reach the payment level anticipated in enabling legislation. When Congress passes a bill that requires special funding, a dollar amount is authorized for implementation. Each year, Congress then appropriates money for the given purpose. The problem is that the appropriation is usually considerably less than the authorization. For example, P.L. 94–142 authorizes federal funding to cover 40 percent of the excess cost of special education programs based on the national average per pupil expenditure. However, the current policy is to appropriate money to cover only about 12 percent of these costs. For the 1981–82 school year, this comes to about $239 per pupil—less than expected, but still a significant contribution to a local administrator's budget.

State funds contribute part of the money needed to run educational programs in every state. Gearheart and Wright (1979, p. 170) discuss patterns of state and local funding:

> ... traditionally the Midwest has tended to rely more on local support of public education, depending heavily on local property tax.... In contrast, the mid-southern and the southeastern states have historically tended to lean toward state support with limited responsibility for fiscal support of the schools at the local level.

In most cases, money for school programs comes from a state's general fund and is, constitutionally or by practice, a high priority item.

Lately, more special education funds have come from state sources and less have come from local sources. The argument in favor of this system is that LEAs do not all have equal resources; thus, "poor" LEAs are unable to provide mandated programs. Some local officials suggest that responsibility for special education funding should rest entirely with the state. Bernstein, Hartman, and Marshall (1976) discuss three items that may justify greater state (or federal) funding:

1. The parents of severely handicapped children have selectively migrated to certain areas where services are available. Thus, some districts have higher costs than others.
2. Some LEAs tend to ignore the needs of children who have more severe problems because providing programs for these children is too costly.
3. Wealth is unevenly distributed among various LEAs or states. Thus, providing special education programs is a greater burden for poorer districts or states.

In most states part of the cost of education comes from the local tax dollar. A tax on real property provides most local money. Historically, this practice seemed to be well accepted by the public. But in the 1960s, many people began to feel that property taxes were excessive or even oppressive. School fund tax proposals were regularly defeated in local elections. Public resistance and dissatisfaction were strongly expressed when an overwhelming majority of California residents voted for Proposition 13 (the Jarvis Amendment) in 1978. Thus, by the initiative process, California's constitution was amended to limit the local tax on real property. It appears that some state governments have no choice but to increase their share of the cost of education.

Figure 15–1 presents a general funding picture. Obviously, the different funding approaches of fifty states cannot be shown in one figure, but a gen-

TABLE 15-1 FEDERAL FUNDS FOR EDUCATION OF THE HANDICAPPED

PROGRAM	AUTHORIZING LEGISLATION	WHO MAY APPLY	APPLICATIONS OR INFORMATION
70. **Captioned Films for the Deaf** (13.446). Free loan program of captioned films for the deaf.	Education of the Handicapped Act, Part F	Schools and programs for the deaf, groups of deaf persons	Bureau of Education for the Handicapped, Division of Media Services 472-1165 472-1256 TTY
71. **Centers and Services for Deaf-Blind Children** (13.445). To provide specialized intensive educational and therapeutic services to deaf-blind children and their families through state and regional centers.	Education of the Handicapped Act, Part C, Sec. 622	Public and private nonprofit organizations (Requests for proposals appear in the *Commerce Business Daily.*)	Bureau of Education for the Handicapped, Division of Assistance to States 472-4825
72. **Early Education for Handicapped Children** (13.444). To aid public and private nonprofit agencies in demonstrating model programs for handicapped children from birth through age 8. Closing dates: 1) Demonstration (13.444A): October 18, 1979; 2) Outreach (13.444B)—Projects formerly funded under 13.444A or JDRP-Approved—February 29, 1980; 3) State Implementation Grants (13.444C)—State agencies only—April 2, 1980	Education of the Handicapped Act, Part C, Sec. 623	State and local education agencies, public and private nonprofit organizations	Bureau of Education for the Handicapped, Division of Innovation and Development 245-9722
73. **Handicapped Regional Resource Centers** (13.450). To establish regional resource centers to advise and offer technical services, primarily to state departments of education, for improving education of handicapped children.	Education of the Handicapped Act, Part C, Sec. 621	State and local education agencies, postsecondary schools (Requests for proposals appear in the *Commerce Business Daily.*)	Bureau of Education for the Handicapped, Division of Media Services 472-1366
74. **Information and Recruitment** (13.452). To disseminate information, to provide referral services for parents of handicapped children, to recruit educational personnel into hard-to-staff areas.	Education of the Handicapped Act, Part D, Sec. 633	Public and private nonprofit organizations	Bureau of Education for the Handicapped, Rm. 2403, JFK Federal Bldg., Boston, MA 02203 (617) 223-7227
75. **Media Services and Captioned Film Program—Centers** (13.446). To establish and operate centers for materials for the handicapped, through contracts.	Education of the Handicapped Act, Part F	Requests for proposals appear in the *Commerce Business Daily*	Bureau of Education for the Handicapped, Division of Media Services 472-1165 472-1256 TTY
76. **Media Services and Captioned Film Program—Film** (13.446). To advance the handicapped through media and technology.	Education of the Handicapped Act, Part F	State and local education agencies, public and private nonprofit organizations	Bureau of Education for the Handicapped, Division of Media Services 472-1165 472-1256 TTY

PROGRAM	AUTHORIZING LEGISLATION	WHO MAY APPLY	APPLICATIONS OR INFORMATION
77. **Media Services and Captioned Film Loan Program—Research** (13.446). To provide contracts and grants for media research, development, training and services for the handicapped. Closing date: Feb. 18, 1980	Education of the Handicapped Act, Part F	Requests for proposals appear in the *Commerce Business Daily;* grant announcements appear in the *Federal Register*	Bureau of Education for the Handicapped, Division of Media Services 472-1165 472-1256 TTY
78. **Model Programs for Severely Handicapped and Deaf-blind Children and Youth** (13.568). To award contracts to build innovative educational models or service-delivery components onto ongoing educational services.	Education of the Handicapped Act, Part C, Sec. 624	State and local education agencies, public and private non-profit organizations (Requests for proposals appear in the *Commerce Business Daily.*)	Bureau of Education for the Handicapped, Special Needs Section 472-2535
79. **Personnel Training for the Education of the Handicapped** (13.451). To prepare and inform educators and other personnel who work with handicapped children, through preservice and inservice training. Closing date: Oct. 15, 1979	Education of the Handicapped Act, Part D	State and local education agencies, postsecondary schools, public and private nonprofit organizations (Individuals must apply to participating organizations.)	Bureau of Education for the Handicapped, Division of Personnel Preparation 245-9886
80. **Preschool Incentive Grants—State Grant Program** (13.499-B). To provide an incentive to states to serve and further develop services for handicapped children ages 3 through 5.	Education of the Handicapped Act, Part B, Sec. 619	State education agencies in states which provided programs for handicapped children ages 3 through 5 in previous years and organizations (Individuals and organizations must apply through state agencies.)	For state agencies: Bureau of Education for the Handicapped, Division of Assistance to States 245-9815
81. **Regional Education Programs for the Handicapped** (13.560). To develop or modify specially designed programs for deaf or other handicapped postsecondary students.	Education of the Handicapped Act, as amended, Part C, Sec. 625	Postsecondary schools and public and private nonprofit organizations (Requests for proposals appear in the *Commerce Business Daily.*)	Bureau of Education for the Handicapped, Division of Innovation and Development 245-9722
82. **State Aid Programs for the Handicapped—State Grant Program** (13.449). To assist in initiation, expansion, and improvement of programs and projects for the handicapped at preschool, elementary, and secondary levels.	Education of the Handicapped Act, as amended, part B	State education agencies	Bureau of Education for the Handicapped, Division of Assistance to States 472-2263
83. **State-Supported School Programs for the Handicapped—State Grant Program** (13.427). To strengthen programs for children in state-operated and state-supported schools.	Elementary and Secondary Education Act, Title I, Sec. 121	State education agencies	Bureau of Education for the Handicapped, Division of Assistance to States 472-2263

eralization may be helpful to the reader. On a nationwide basis, state funds account for about 55 percent of an operating LEA's income.[1] These funds frequently include (1) an appropriation made for all pupils (including an equalization factor for low-wealth districts) and (2) extra categorical funding designated for special education pupils.

Local real property taxes contribute about 31 percent of special education programs' income. There may also be an allowable special tax for special education programs, but most funds come from the general property tax. They are not "earmarked" funds, so the amount of funding that goes to special programs is determined by the local board of education.

Federal funds currently provide from 12 percent to 14 percent of the special

FIGURE 15-1   FUNDS FOR SPECIAL EDUCATION PROGRAMS

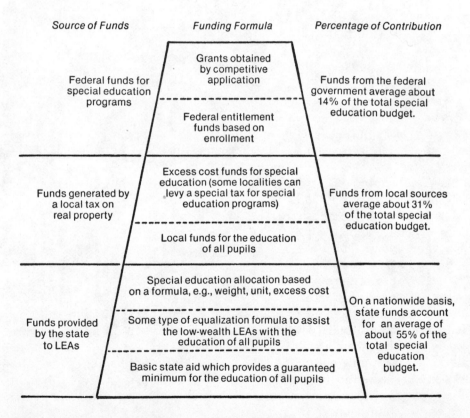

Information regarding percentage of contributions is from the U.S. Department of Health, Education and Welfare, *Progress toward a Free Appropriate Public Education: A Report to Congress on the Implementation of Public Law 94–142: The Education for All Handicapped Children Act* (Washington, D.C., 1979), p. 113.

education budget. Most of this money comes from entitlement funds, but some LEAs also obtain funding from competitive grants.

The above information illustrates that the sources and amounts of funding for education programs in general and for special education programs in particular are somewhat uncertain from year to year. The programs are mandated; the funds to operate the programs are not. Programs are dependent upon support from the public and upon the activities of legislative and executive officials. An administrator must thoroughly understand funding sources, formulas used to distribute funds, and ways of obtaining funds for his/her LEA. This information is of crucial importance to successful program operation.

FINANCING SPECIAL EDUCATION PROGRAMS: FUNDING FORMULAS AND PROCEDURES

Because funding procedures vary from state to state, it is difficult to come up with a broadly applicable description. However, certain characteristics of funding can be described. First, the formula used to fund general education programs usually serves as the base for funding special education programs. Second, funds required for special education programs are usually calculated by some type of "add-on formula." Third, the amount of funding needed is directly related to how severely handicapped pupils are. Fourth, funds that exceed the costs for regular education programs are categorical in nature and are appropriated for special education programs. They must be used *only* for that purpose.

Bernstein et al. (1976a) studied methods used by the various states and LEAs to finance special education services under a grant from the Bureau of Education for the Handicapped. This study added information to those previously conducted by Weintraub et al. (1971) and Thomas (1973). All of these studies have shown that methods of funding in the different states may be categorized by types of expense and by the different formulas they adopt. The three types of expenses that special education programs are subject to follow: (1) extra costs incurred in employing professional personnel needed to operate special programs; (2) costs that are related to pupils with different kinds of handicaps; and (3) costs incurred by a given program component. Strictly speaking, these are three different ways of looking at the same costs, rather than three different types of costs. However, the different formulas developed from these funding concepts may encourage or discourage LEAs from following a particular course of action. For example, providing transportation may be encouraged under program component funding, since the LEA may have received state money that it is only allowed to use to supply transportation. On the other hand, an LEA that receives a given amount of money for each blind or deaf pupil it serves may be discouraged from providing transportation, since this is very expensive and will not increase the amount of state funds the LEA receives.

In contrast to the above example, an excess cost formula (reimbursement related to the number of pupils served) might encourage an LEA to initiate and operate special programs, whereas a percentage formula (program component reimbursement) may discourage an LEA from this type of action. Under the first formula, all excess costs may be reimbursed; the second formula covers only a percentage of the costs.

School administrators, of course, must work with their states' funding formulas. However, if a formula does not serve the best interests of the local district and its pupils, it is certainly an appropriate topic for political action. Action can be taken through professional organizations and through parent groups. Legislators must know the effects that their funding formulas have on local programs.

As can be seen from the above discussion, state reimbursement to LEAs is based on one of three concepts. Each concept is further defined by two or three different types of funding formulas. These include the following formulas:

- Unit funding
- Personnel funding
- Weight funding
- Excess cost funding
- Straight sum funding
- Percentage funding
- Service component funding.

The relationship of the above formulas to the funding concepts previously described is shown in Table 15–2. The method of calculating reimbursement for each formula is also explained in the table.

As was shown in Chapter 5, different individuals in the administrative structure have different roles and functions. Many administrators need only have an awareness level of knowledge with the financial details involved in running special education programs. For example, a site administrator will probably not deal extensively with finances. Conversely, special education administrators and business managers must be intimately acquainted with funding procedures. If they don't know the formulas and use them to good advantage, the district may lose out on large sums of available monies.

Projecting each program's income is an integral part of the budget planning process. This will be described in the next section of this chapter. Income projection utilizes several types of information, including estimates of enrollment and average daily attendance (ADA), state and local basic allowances for all pupils, state formulas for receiving special education funds, federal entitlements and grants, special apportionments for extra services such as transportation, and tuition income from other districts. Although a form used to project income would be different in each state and in each program, an example of such a form may be helpful. Table 15–3 shows how such a form can be developed; it can be modified to meet individual needs.

Most LEAs are currently experiencing financial difficulties. Thus, most school administrators are facing issues such as utilizing resources more economically, coping with an unequal tax base, providing equal funding for all, and defining the connection between available resources and program quality. Inflation, eroding tax bases in the cities, declining enrollments, rising levels of teacher absenteeism, increasing personnel salaries and benefits, and skyrocketing transportation and insurance costs contribute to financial worries. These problems are generic to financing general school programs. They are also specifically related to funding special education programs, since the cost per student is much greater in special programs.

The concept that pupils who live in low wealth districts may be deprived of equal educational opportunities has been the basis for court cases such as *Rodriquez v. San Antonio Independent School District* and *Serrano v. Priest.* The legislature has also made many attempts to remedy this situation. While some progress has been made, most states are still seeking the means to more evenly distribute available funds among different LEAs. Only the state of Hawaii is excluded from these problems, since it only has one school district and one tax base.

Although most people agree that resources for pupils in different districts should be somewhat equal, few people feel that the resources for each pupil within a district should be equal. Burrello and Sage (1979, p. 246) refer to this as "the concept of inequity of need." They indicate that "... the only way to treat children equally is to disperse funds unequally to meet children's unequal needs." For example, the educational costs of educating a nonhandicapped child are much less than those of educating a deaf-blind child. The needs and the costs are highly disparate.

To make sure that LEAs would not use the inequitable costs concept as a way of avoiding their responsibilities to handicapped children, state legislatures have designated certain funds for special education programs. Frequently referred to as "categorical" or "ear-marked" funds, they have been awarded to districts according to the complex formulas described in Table 15–2. Some school administrators feel that this is unnecessary and propose that all federal and state funds be sent to local districts as general funds, with no strings attached. Decisions on how to disperse the funds would be made at the local level. Many special educators and parents feel that this would be disastrous and that more expensive programs would lose out to low-cost programs that serve more students. Thus, securing sufficient income, developing acceptable funding formulas, deciding on categorical or noncategorical funding, and relating costs to specific accomplishments remain unresolved issues. However, this lack of resolution does not absolve general administrators, special educa-

TABLE 15–2   CONCEPTS AND FORMULAS FOR DISBURSEMENT OF STATE FUNDS FOR SPECIAL EDUCATION

Concept on Which Reimbursement Is Based	Type of Formula	Method of Calculating Reimbursement
1.0 Reimbursement Related to Costs of Professional Personnel	1.1 Unit funding formula	The LEA receives a given sum of money for each designated unit; e.g., classroom, or special service unit, transportation unit.
	1.2 Personnel funding formula	The LEA receives a specified sum of money for each professional person who is covered in the formula; e.g., teacher, school psychologist, classroom aide. The amount varies by personnel classification.
2.0 Reimbursement Related to Pupils	2.1 Weight funding formula	Different categories of children are assigned a "weight" based on historical information comparing their educational costs to those incurred educating the nonhandicapped; e.g., if EMR programs cost twice as much per pupil, these students receive a weight of two. The state reimburses on the basis of two times the reimbursement amount for regular students. The weighting factor might be three for TMRs, four for deaf-blind students, etc.
	2.2 Excess cost formula	The LEA computes excess costs (the cost of educating the handicapped minus the cost of educating regular students) and is fully or partially reimbursed at a certain rate per child (e.g., $504/EMR student; $841/deaf student).
	2.3 Straight sum formula	A given sum is designated in advance (on the basis of category or type of service), and the LEA receives that amount for each pupil served, regardless of the amount of excess cost.

TABLE 15-2 (*Cont'd*)

Concept on Which Reimbursement Is Based	Type of Formula	Method of Calculating Reimbursement
3.0 Reimbursement Related to Program Component	3.1 Percentage formula	The LEA computes the total cost of all special program components and is reimbursed by the state for a specified percentage.
	3.2 Differentiated formula according to service provided	Different services (e.g., special class, transportation, resource room, instructional support, management, assessment) are each funded at a specified rate. Categorical classification of children is not a factor in the formula.

tion administrators, and school business managers from trying to find funding that encourages the development of good special education programs. Since funding formulas are constantly in flux, one must make a continuing effort to keep informed.

PREPARING, CONTROLLING, AND MONITORING THE BUDGET

Planning and Preparation

The California School Accounting Manual (State Department of Education 1976, p. xiii) defines a budget as follows:

> The budget is a proposed plan of expenditures, taking into account the necessary legal requirements. The annual financial and budget reports are fiscal documents exhibiting actual income.

Planning and preparing the budget requires a coordinated effort on the part of many individuals in the school system. Many people in different positions have information that is vital for the preparation of a workable budget. Also, employee relations are enhanced when everyone concerned has an opportunity to contribute their ideas. Examples of necessary information and the persons who might supply that information are listed below:

- Additional personnel—principals
- Instructional materials and equipment—teachers
- Space, facilities improvement—director of housing
- Projected personnel costs—director of personnel services

TABLE 15–3   SPECIAL EDUCATION REVENUE ESTIMATE

---

1. Program identification————————————————————.
2. Estimated enrollment————————————. Estimated ADA——————.
3. Number of classes to be operated————————————————.
4. Program level (elementary or secondary)——————————.

Computation of Basic Revenue

5. Basic state revenue per pupil $————————————————.
6. Basic local revenue per pupil $————————————————.
7. Total basic revenue (ADA × the sum of state and local
   revenue) $————————————————.

Revenue from State Special Education Formula

8. Number of units of reimbursement (ADA ÷ the minimum
   class size)————————————.
9. Unit reimbursement according to formula——————————.
10. Projected special education revenue (number of units × the unit
    reimbursement) $————————————————.
11. Special allowance for transportation $————————————.
12. Total revenue from state special education funds (item 10
    plus item 11)—————————————.

Revenue from Federal Sources

13. Entitlement funds (ADA × the per pupil allowance)——————.
14. Competitive grant funds $——————————————.
15. Total revenue from federal sources (the sum of items 13
    and 14) $————————————————.

Revenue from Tuition Charges to Other Local Districts

16. Number of out-of-district students served———————————.
17. Costs per pupil in excess of federal and state
    reimbursement $——————————————.
18. Total revenue from tuition charges to other districts
    (item 16 × item 17) $————————————————.

Total Program Income* (the sum of items 7, 12, 15, 18) $——————.

---

* Since funding formulas for different categorical programs vary, a revenue projection sheet is needed for each program.

- Projected enrollments—director of pupil personnel services
- Transportation costs—director of transportation
- Projected management costs—director of special education
- Current year's expenditures—district controller
- Projected income—business manager.

The most common approach to budget planning is the historical approach. In this method next year's budget is planned on the basis of this year's budget. It has a number of advantages (e.g., most of the different accounts needed have already been identified and current personnel and supply costs are known). Once an inflation factor has been added, the figures may be appropriate for next year's budget. Also, knowing current expenditures helps control future expectations. Table 15–4 shows a planning sheet that might be used in the historical approach to budget planning.

When planning the budget for special education programs, several factors should be considered.[2]

- A budget should consider pupils' needs first.
- Special education programs are mandatory. They must be available, just as first grades are available to qualified pupils.
- The average per pupil expenditure for educating handicapped children in 1980 was about $3,636.
- It costs about twice as much to educate the handicapped as it does to educate the nonhandicapped.[3]
- Employee fringe benefits may be 30 percent of salaries, or more.
- It costs twice as much to educate handicapped children outside of a school district as it does to educate them within the district.
- Residential placements cost about four times as much as local day programs.
- Any new programs will have extra start-up costs.
- Transportation costs are increasing rapidly.
- Programs or classes that have a low average daily attendance (ADA) may be very costly (e.g., a program might be staffed for ninety pupils but have only sixty). This would create a surplus of materials and waste manpower.
- Personnel costs are the least flexible part of the budget. They may require 80 to 85 percent of the budget.
- All expenditures authorized in the budget must be related to identifiable income.

The budget development process requires great effort over an extended period of time. The budget frequently goes through three or four major revisions before the official budget is recommended by the superintendent and adopted by the local board of education. The process usually involves the following sequence of events:

1. Preparation of budget planning sheets. These sheets list the current year's figures, account numbers, budget item explanations, and other pertinent data. The LEA's budget director provides blank columns for proposed budget amounts.
2. Input from teachers, principals, parents, and others regarding program needs (information is collated by the special education di-

TABLE 15–4 BUDGET PLANNING SHEET FOR SPECIAL EDUCATION PROGRAMS

Account Number	Budget Item	Current Year Actual Expenditures	Longevity Increases	Salary Increase	Additional Personnel	Proposed Budget (1+2+3+4)
	Certified Personnel Salaries					
____	Special classroom teachers	____	____	____	____	____
____	Resource room teachers	____	____	____	____	____
____	Speech therapists	____	____	____	____	____
____	Home teachers	____	____	____	____	____
____	Adaptive P.E. teachers	____	____	____	____	____
____	School psychologists	____	____	____	____	____
____	Administrators	____	____	____	____	____
____	Other certificated personnel	____	____	____	____	____
	Noncertificated Personnel Salaries					
____	Instructional aides	____	____	____	____	____
____	Clerical workers	____	____	____	____	____
____	Transportation personnel	____	____	____	____	____
____	Other (percentage of maintenance food service staff—based on special education enrollment)	____	____	____	____	____

Account Number	Budget Item	Current Year	Increased Costs	Additional Personnel	Proposed Budget
	Employee Benefits				
____	State retirement fund	____	____	____	____
____	OASDI	____	____	____	____
____	Health insurance benefits	____	____	____	____
____	Other benefits	____	____	____	____

Account Number	Budget Item	Current Year Actual Expenditures	Projected Increases in Costs	Additional Needs	Proposed Budget
	Books, Supplies, and Equipment Replacement				
	Textbooks	____	____	____	____
	Other books	____	____	____	____
	Instructional materials	____	____	____	____
	Instructional supplies	____	____	____	____
	Other supplies	____	____	____	____
	Replacement of equipment	____	____	____	____
	Contracted Services				
	Non-public school services	____	____	____	____
	Medical assessment services	____	____	____	____
	In-service education consultants	____	____	____	____
	Program development consultants	____	____	____	____
	Classroom rents	____	____	____	____
	Other Expenses				
	Conference travel	____	____	____	____
	Equipment purchases	____	____	____	____
	Improvement of sites	____	____	____	____

rector). Early input from the board of education regarding program priorities is of crucial importance.
3. Identification of all priorities and proposed program changes (e.g., new classes, increased services) for the budget period (coordinated by the special education director).
4. Projection of personnel costs, including longevity step increases, increases for additional professional training, negotiated salary increases, and new-personnel costs (supplied by the personnel director).
5. Projection of income from all sources for special education programs (by the special education director and budget director).
6. Inclusion of the special education portion of the budget in the overall budget and preparation of a working draft for consideration by the superintendent's cabinet (by the budget director).
7. Revision of the working draft and preparation of a tentative budget to be presented to the board of education for their suggestions (under the superintendent's direction).
8. Preparation of the proposed budget document (by the budget director).
9. Publication and opportunity for public comment (under direction of the board of education).
10. Revision and recommendation by the superintendent and adoption by the board of education.

Consultation is very important. Lobsenz (1977) indicates the importance of the school board's early involvement, and Dersh (1976) says to citizens, "The school budget is your business." Lobsenz (1977) suggests that school boards begin the budgeting process by stating their goals and priorities and by setting a dollar limit that directs the development of the proposed budget. Those goals and priorities must include provisions for appropriate special education programs and services, as directed by law. A school board would never debate whether or not they should operate a first grade class; they should be as committed to special education programs.

Controlling and Monitoring the Budget

Once the budget is developed so that programs can be identified (with mandates and priorities met) and so that income and proposed expenditures are in balance, the document can be adopted by the local board of education. In some states and local areas it must also be approved by another agency, such as a city council or county board of supervisors. Administrative responsibilities then shift from utilizing the budget as a means of program planning toward utilizing it as a tool that guides the distribution of resources and spending.

Controlling and monitoring expenditures is usually done at two different levels and from two different perspectives. A business services administrator is responsible for the fiscal aspects of the budget. The special education administrator is responsible for the programs provided for in the budget. He/she analyzes current spending trends and gathers information for future budget planning.

Obviously, many expenditures are fixed. Items such as personnel salaries, fringe benefits, and utilities can be accurately projected. The funds are encumbered and expenditure becomes an accounting function. Other items, such as supplies, equipment, and contracted services, are much more flexible, and the program administrator must plan and approve any expenditures. The data processing systems now used by most local districts make it possible to be well informed and current on budgetary status. In spite of this capability, LEAs are frequently in trouble because of deficit spending. This may be partly due to improper budgeting, but more often it is due to inadequate monitoring and control. Polinsky (1977) studied the budgeting process of Boston and other large city schools and reported many problems with planning and controlling expenditures; thus, these LEAs had large cost overruns. Prohibition of deficit spending, as contained in some states' codes, precludes cost overruns in other LEAs. The special education program budget should be carefully monitored so that it does not cause overall district financial difficulties.

Planning the budget can be vital to the development and operation of special education programs. Program administrators should devote a great deal of time to this task. Also, decisions about what to buy should be given adequate attention. But monitoring the cash flow, preparing fiscal reports, and accounting are the business administrator's responsibilities. It is not a good use of time to duplicate functions, although it is to be hoped that the business administrator and the special education administrator will both develop a working knowledge of program and fiscal matters.

MATCHING FACILITIES AND STUDENT NEEDS

When considering program resources, one tends to think only of money and the budget. Of course, this is a very narrow view of the total resources needed for a program. Other, physical resources also play an important role. School facilities may be a minor consideration or may be so important that they determine whether or not an individual can attend school.

A common misconception is to think of facility needs in terms of a given category of pupils (e.g., all EMR students need one type of facility, and all OH students need another type). This sort of matching is inappropriate. Planning should be based on the needs of individual pupils and the needs of the instructional program.

If school districts were suddenly given enough money to build brand new school buildings, they could be planned without steps, with wide doors, appropriate bathroom facilities, enough storage space, and all the other features that would accommodate special pupils. Unfortunately, many new buildings are being built without considering these students' needs. And school buildings that have already been built will be used for many years. Thus, school planners must deal with modifying buildings, placing programs in appropriate spaces, and properly designing new facilities whenever the opportunity arises.

Whether a district is building new facilities, modifying old ones, or planning so as to effectively use space without paying for major modifications, certain factors must be considered. Boles (1965) identified five planning considerations that are as appropriate for the 1980s as they were when written. These are planning for (1) function, (2) future use, (3) health, safety, and comfort, (4) beauty, and (5) economy. Birth and Johnstone (1975) have devoted a large portion of their book, *Designing Schools and Schooling for the Handicapped,* to providing detailed suggestions on building adequate facilities for pupils with special needs. Wirtz (1977) also provided a comprehensive discussion of these pupils' facilities needs.

A few general statements may be made about the needs of all special education pupils:

· Facilities that allow program access must be provided.
· Facilities must make mainstreaming possible whenever it is appropriate.
· The safety and comfort of the pupils must be assured.
· The needs of the instructional program must be met.

Since there are so many different student needs, it is appropriate for administrators to develop some type of checklist so they can give detailed consideration to matching facilities and students' needs. A format is suggested in Table 15–5. The use of a checklist helps identify problems and contributes to action-oriented planning.

Special education programs are sometimes discussed in relation to their degree of inclusion or separation from the regular classroom:

· Residential school—a totally separate facility with live-in quarters
· Special school—a separate facility for day classes
· Special wing in a regular school—a cluster of special classes physically grouped together
· Special classroom in a regular school—a regular classroom (may have been modified) located anywhere in the school building.

All of the above facilities have appropriate uses. However, administrators should not allow facilities to dictate program content. Students should not be placed in an inappropriate educational program just because a certain building is not being used.

Pupils who have severe problems and who cannot be taken care of at home

TABLE 15-5 MATCHING FACILITIES TO STUDENT NEEDS

Item	Do Pupils Need This?	O.K.	Provisions by the District	
			Needs Improvement	Needed, But Not Provided
1. Program is accessible through use of ramps and elevators.				
2. Program location enhances opportunities for mainstreaming.				
3. Bathroom facilities are appropriate (e.g., wide doors and stalls, wall bars, low sinks).				
4. Safety hazards have been removed.				
5. Emergency evacuation procedures are operational and known to staff and pupils.				
6. Furniture is appropriate to pupils' ages.				
7. Furniture is available according to need (e.g., standing tables, lap boards, adjustable tables).				
8. Parking space for wheelchairs is available.				
9. Floor surfaces are not slippery or dangerous.				
10. Adequate space is provided for storage of special materials/equipment.				
11. Class size has been considered, and appropriate space is provided for each pupil.				
12. Vocational education training facilities are provided.				
13. Loading docks, ramps, and hallways are protected from the weather.				
14. Acoustic characteristics are appropriate.				
15. A "quiet place" for time-out or individual study is available.				
16. A protected outside play area is available.				
17. The cafeteria, library, and auditorium are easily accessible.				
18. Special lighting provisions have been made.				

Note: Other items may be added to reflect the needs of the local school district.

are usually placed in residential schools. A youngster may need physical care or psychiatric care that parents are unable to provide. It is always hoped that residential school placement will be temporary and that another type of facility will be more appropriate later on.

Special schools have usually been built to provide facilities that are not found on a regular campus. Where occupational or physical therapy treatment centers, therapy pools, special vocational training facilities, and special recreation facilities are needed, they can be provided in one school building. They can not be provided economically in every school building throughout a district. The problem with this type of arrangement is that it has contributed to segregation of the handicapped. However, this problem can be overcome by building the special school adjacent to a regular school or by having regular students attend the special school.

A special wing in a regular school has several advantages if it is used properly. It should be used not to promote a greater-than-necessary separation of students, but to encourage grouping of children with similar needs for common use of facilities. This setting realizes many of the special school's advantages without incurring its inherent disadvantages.

A special classroom in a regular school may have to be physically adapted to meet a variety of needs. For pupils with learning disabilities, few (if any) physical changes are needed. Conversely, a hearing impaired pupil may need an environment with special acoustical qualities, or a teacher who serves blind students may need additional storage space for instructional materials and equipment. Again, care should be exercised in selecting the location of special classrooms. Placing these programs in the basement or in the "outer forty" may negate all other efforts being made to educate special children with their nonhandicapped peers, as is required by law.

There is a lesson to be learned from the historical perspective. Special education programs frequently had their beginnings in buildings that other programs found undesirable. Basement classrooms, abandoned schools, church classrooms, and converted storage rooms were the norm rather than the exception. Architectural barriers, lack of transportation, and inadequate bathroom facilities made it difficult or impossible for many special students to attend school. These "facilities" were eventually replaced by separate special facilities. Although this approach often provided facilities of high-quality, it also caused a great deal of unnecessary segregation from nonhandicapped peers. It is hoped that educators have learned from these experiences and that programs will benefit from more enlightened planning in the future. Administrators, teachers, parents, school board members, and architects should all work together to plan facilities that will meet students' needs. Too often, planning has been limited to asking "Where do we have some empty space?"

Birch and Johnstone (1975, p. 9) outlined three main themes in their book. LEAs might want to adopt these themes as their goals:

1. Common architectural barriers to total building use can be eliminated.
2. Subtle space adjustments can be arranged to produce significant positive impacts on quality of teaching and learning.
3. School building design should maximize the opportunity for handicapped children to stay in the mainstream of education.

EQUIPPING AND SUPPLYING PROGRAMS

School administrators are familiar with the task of selecting and purchasing equipment for school programs. Each school district has contacts with manufacturers and distributors of different types of routinely purchased equipment. Supplies range from an inexpensive classroom desk to a very expensive school bus. Just as there are many competing companies that produce and sell equipment for regular programs, there are numerous companies that produce and sell equipment for special programs.

Certain kinds of special equipment are essential to some children's instructional programs, whereas other pupils need little or no special equipment. Administrators must carefully plan to meet individual program needs. A few examples will suffice for this discussion.

Pupils with physical disabilities may need such equipment as buses with lifts, spaces for wheelchairs or gurneys, adjustable tables and desks, standing boards, modified typewriters, book holders, page turners, lap boards, physical therapy equipment, regular and battery-operated wheelchairs, and padded chairs. These are only a few of the items that may be needed. Pupils with visual problems may need Braille writers, cassette recorders, projection equipment, special television screens, magnifying devices, machines to duplicate Braille materials, and long canes. Pupils with hearing problems may need special amplification equipment or instructional equipment that emphasizes visual learning.

Special education administrators and special education teachers should be the local experts on the equipment needed and where it can be obtained. They should serve as consultants to the district's purchasing officer, director of transportation, or whoever is directly responsible for purchasing equipment.

Program materials and supplies can be divided into three categories: (1) instructional materials; (2) supplies that are a part of the instructional program (e.g., writing paper); and (3) supplies that support instruction (e.g., cleaning supplies and facial tissue). Just as different pupils need different types of equipment, they also need different instructional materials. A physically disabled child who needs special facilities and equipment may be able to utilize the same instructional materials as the regular class. On the other hand, a pupil who has no special facilities or equipment needs may not be able to use regular instructional materials because they are too complex.

A few years ago, very few commercial publishers were producing instructional materials aimed at pupils with serious learning problems. That situation no longer exists. Hundreds of commercial companies now produce special materials. Teachers and curriculum people have an extensive amount of material to choose from.

For the person unfamiliar with available materials, the author makes three suggestions:

1. Teachers can supply a great deal of information about instructional materials. Recent graduates of training programs often have the most up-to-date information.
2. Administrators can be placed on a publishing company's mailing list. Many companies furnish catalogs of materials and instructional equipment.
3. Publishers, distributors, and supply houses often display materials at meetings of professional organizations (e.g., The Council for Exceptional Children, The American Council on Learning Disabilities).

SUMMARY

Chapter 15 discusses some of the resources required to operate special education programs. The chapter focuses on (1) identifying the sources of funding for special education; (2) applying the funding formulas and projecting income from local, state, and federal funds; (3) planning, preparing, controlling, and monitoring the budget; (4) developing the school's facilities to meet each student's needs; and (5) equipping and supplying special education programs.

The three main levels of government (federal, state, and local) provide school programs with funds. The types and amounts of funding provided by each level of government are discussed and then are shown graphically in Figure 15–1. Federal funds come in the form of entitlement grants and competitive grants. Table 15–1 lists the types of grants available and agencies from which grant information can be obtained.

The different states all provide money for special education programs. State funds are based on formulas that pay part of the educational costs for all pupils and then pay an additional amount to help alleviate the higher costs of educating handicapped students. Several different types of state formulas are utilized; they are summarized in Table 15–2. Additional state funds provided to help educate the handicapped are usually categorical funds. This means that they are designated for special education programs and may not be used for any other purpose. Designating funds for a particular segment of the school population is a continuing topic of controversy. Some people feel that this is absolutely essential in order to maintain special education programs;

others feel that state money should be deposited in the LEA's general fund and spending decisions should be made there. These funds are frequently referred to as "state excess cost monies."

Local funds come primarily from a tax on real property within the local education agency's boundaries. For the most part, these funds are not categorical in nature; the local board of education decides how to apportion them. In some instances, a special tax on local property provides additional funds for particular school programs.

Planning and preparing the special education budget is discussed. The author suggests what information is needed to prepare the budget and lists some of the school personnel who should be involved in providing that information. A few "factors to remember" are listed, and a sequence of budget events is suggested. Table 15–4 is a budget planning sheet that follows the historical approach to budget planning.

Proper budget controlling and monitoring procedures are strongly emphasized. Special education is one of the LEA's most expensive programs. As such, its budget is scrutinized and sometimes attacked by personnel in other school programs that are competing for funds. When cost overruns and poor management create problems with the local agency's budget, the commitment to the special education program of the board of education and top-level administrators is often weakened. Good management procedures can prevent this from happening.

Chapter 15 also discusses other resources needed by special education programs. Providing proper facilities is essential. Facilities are discussed in terms of students' needs, not in categorical terms. Program accessibility and the ways in which facilities may dictate the forms that programs take are considered. The type of facility chosen and its location strongly influence whether or not a child will be educated in the least restrictive environment. Table 15–5 provides a checklist for matching school facilities with students' needs.

The final section of the chapter deals with equipping and supplying special education programs. General equipment and supply needs are discussed, and a limited number of specific examples are provided. Suggestions are given on obtaining more detailed information about commercially available equipment, instructional materials, and supplies.

NOTES

1. In the past, agencies other than education agencies (e.g., departments of mental hygiene) have been responsible for the educational programs of some groups of handicapped individuals. Since the implementation of P.L. 94–142, this responsibility has often been transferred to state and local education agencies. Unfortunately, state funding has not always followed the transfer of programs to the new agency. This places an additional strain on the availability of state funds.
2. While many budget factors can be accurately predicted, there are also other

factors that cannot always be controlled (e.g., energy costs, contract settlements, tax revenues).
3. Costs cited are findings and estimates from a survey by the National School Board Association reported in *Report on Education Research* (June 27, 1979).

REFERENCES

Bernstein, C. D., Hartman, W. T., and Marshall, R. S. 1976a. Major policy issues in financing special education. *Journal of Education Finance* 1,3:299–317.

Bernstein, C. D., Kirst, M. W., Hartman, W. T., and Marshall, R. S. 1976b. *Financing educational services for the handicapped.* Reston, Va.: The Council for Exceptional Children.

Birch, J. W., and Johnstone, B. K. 1975. *Designing schools and schooling for the handicapped.* Springfield, Ill.: Charles C Thomas, Publisher.

Boles, H. W. 1965. *Step by step to better school facilities.* New York: Holt, Rinehart & Winston.

Burello, L. C., and Sage, D. D. 1979. *Leadership and change in special education.* Englewood Cliffs, N.J.: Prentice-Hall, Inc.

California State Department of Education. 1976. *California school accounting manual.* Sacramento: Bureau of Publications, State Department of Education.

Dersh, R. E. 1976. *The school budget is your business: A handbook for citizens.* Reading, Pa.: Public School Budget Study Project, December. ERIC Document 146 677.

Gearheart, B. R., and Wright, W. S. 1979. *Organization and administration of educational programs for exceptional children,* 2nd ed. Springfield, Ill.: Charles C Thomas, Publisher.

Lobsenz, H. M. 1977. The right and the wrong way to cut a school budget. *The American School Board Journal,* September, 164:27–78.

Polinsky, M. 1977. An examination of the Boston School System's budgetary process. Boston: Boston University Department of Political Science, December. ERIC Document 165 227.

Smith, G. D., and Wexler, H. 1979. 1980 guide to Office of Education programs. *American Education* 15,9:17–29.

Thomas, M. A. 1973. Finance: Without which there is no special education. *Exceptional Children* 39:475–80.

Weintraub, F. J., Abeson, A. R., and Braddock, D. L. 1971. *State law and education of handicapped children: Issues and recommendations.* Arlington, Va.: The Council for Exceptional Children.

Wirtz, M. A. 1977. *An administrator's handbook of special education: A guide to better education for the handicapped.* Springfield, Ill.: Charles C Thomas, Publisher.

COURT CASES

Rodriquez v. San Antonio Independent School District, 337 F. Supp. 1280 (W.D. Tex. 1971).

Serrano v. Priest, 483 P.2d 1241, 1244 (Cal. 1971).

ADDITIONAL SUGGESTED READINGS

Cronin, J. M. 1976. The federal takeover: Should the junior partner run the firm? *Phi Delta Kappan* 57:499.

Marinelli, J. J. 1976. Financing the education of exceptional children. In *Public policy and the education of exceptional children*, ed. F. J. Weintraub et al., pp. 151–94. Reston, Va.: The Council for Exceptional Children.

Sage, D. D., and Riley, D. 1975. *The bounty hunters*. Syracuse, N.Y.: Human Policy Press.

Walters, D. L. 1975. Accounting and financial planning—top priorities for school business administrators. Paper read at the Annual Meeting of the Association of School Business Officials, 1–5 Oct. 1978, Washington, D.C. ERIC Document 163 604.

16

Evaluating the Program

> "Keeping track of how the program looks in actual practice is one of the program evaluator's major responsibilities. You cannot evaluate something without describing what that something is."
>
> (Morris and Fitz-Gibbon 1978, p. 7)

INTRODUCTION

School district program evaluation is carried out for a number of different purposes and by a variety of methods. The content of educational evaluation is also different—what one person describes as program evaluation, another identifies as program description, and someone else calls record keeping. Because of this diversity, Chapter 16 will broadly define program evaluation and include program description, record keeping, and other data gathering as different types of program evaluation. Thus, gathering data in order to determine a program's quality is only one of the many purposes of evaluation.

Program evaluation has existed almost as long as the programs themselves. Popham (1975, p. 2) says:

> Through the centuries teachers and others involved in education have also done their share of evaluating. Teachers have evaluated students, their own instructional efforts, textbooks, and the size of their paychecks. Educational writers have also lauded evaluation, in the more limited sense of having teachers evaluate their instructional efforts. . . . All in all, evaluation has been seen as a worthwhile effort.

Bonnet (1977, p. 2) provides a justification for utilizing a broad definition:

> . . . Another reason for using a broad definition of evaluation is that data alone which are only descriptive often serve as crucial components of evaluation systems and lead to evaluative conclusions when interpreted in conjunction with other components of the system.

One must accept the fact that it is not possible, or even desirable, to evaluate every aspect of every program each year. However, instead of leaving evaluative efforts to chance, an LEA should follow a plan that identifies its need for information and determines in which areas information will be obtained. Some data gathering is absolutely necessary each year (e.g., a summary of expenditures of funds, the attendance and excused absences of pupils), while other information can be collected less frequently (e.g., success of pupils in mainstreamed programs). A broadly defined district plan for program evaluation will help administrators to identify what information they need, the procedures they must follow to obtain that information, and how the information will be used.

The above statements indicate that an LEA's evaluative design must address the "what? how? why?" questions for each topic being studied. Obviously, it would be a waste of time to collect information that can never be used because no one knows why data were gathered. On the other hand, an educational agency frequently finds that needed information has not been collected. Retrieving data on a post-hoc basis can be difficult, if not impossible.

WHAT DO WE NEED TO KNOW?

The top priority for gathering of information is usually assigned to the descriptive and numerical data needed for the day-to-day operation of the system. (This information is usually not qualitative in nature.)

One type of information that contributes to a special education program's effective day-to-day operation may be described simply as program information. Although the special education administrator may know this descriptive information by heart, it must be kept up to date and be available, in written form, for use by anyone in the system. Program information should include at least the following items:

• A list of programs offered
• Program locations
• Personnel who have program responsibility
• Pupil data
• A list of pupils organized by program.

Tables 16–1 and 16–2 show formats that can be utilized to collect and update program information for daily use and future reference. Table 16–1 tells the reader which programs are offered, where they are located, the age range of pupils served in each class, the administrator in charge of each program, and the classroom teachers involved. It also provides quantitative data about maximum allowable enrollment, the current number of students enrolled in each class, and number and location of vacancies. Obviously, this type of information is crucial to the daily operation of programs.

Table 16–2 does not provide a wide scope of information, but locates each pupil who is currently enrolled and may be very useful in planning next year's classes. It also provides a record of evaluation and annual assessment dates and thus serves as a reminder of future deadlines. This is descriptive data/

record keeping which assists administrators in the day-to-day operation of the programs.

The second type of data essential to the daily operation of programs concerns fiscal information and budget control. Program managers must deal with the following formula:

Number of Dollars Budgeted → Amount Encumbered
and Spent → Balance Remaining.

Generally, an LEA's budget control will be kept track of through a data processing system and regular printouts will be available. No matter what system is used, administrators must have information on the current status of their programs' funds (see Chapter 15 for additional information).

The third important area of data collection involves maintaining a "child count" to meet federal requirements and keeping records on average daily attendance (ADA) to ensure that students comply with state compulsory attendance laws. Also, ADA is usually the basis for receiving state funds. State education agencies usually delineate a format for keeping these records and for reporting to different agencies.

The fourth area of importance is program reporting. This activity can provide updates about ongoing programs or it can measure the extent to which new programs are being implemented. It may also be directed toward qualitative evaluation and reporting.

Informing policy makers and funding groups about a program's status is a major program reporting goal. Top-level administration and members of local boards of education want and need to know "how it goes" with the programs they authorize and fund. They will utilize this information when they decide whether or not to support the programs in the future. The publication *Progress toward a Free Appropriate Public Education: A Report to Congress on the Implementation of Public Law 94–142: The Education for All Handicapped Children Act* (Department of Health, Education and Welfare, 1979, p. vii) provides a good example of data gathering to measure program implementation. The table of contents indicates the types of data gathered for this report:

- Are the intended beneficiaries being served?
- In what settings are beneficiaries being served?
- What services are being provided?
- What administrative mechanisms are in place?
- What are the consequences of implementing the act?
- To what extent is the intent of the act being met?

Each question listed above is related to the implementation process. The only qualitative question asked concerns the consequences of passing the act.

Framing similar questions at the local level would help administrators design

TABLE 16–1 PROGRAM SUMMARY FORM

Program Identification	Location	Age Range	Enrollment Data		Administrator	Teacher	Program Vacancy
			Maximum Number	Current Number			
Learning Disabilities Special Day Class	Jefferson School	6–9	10	10	Mr. Anders	Ms. Guiterra	no
	Maze School	9–11	10	9	Ms. Gell	Ms. Belanka	yes 1
	Thomas School	12–14	12	11	Ms. Aka	Ms. Wong	yes 1
	Bell High School	14–18	12	12	Mr. Rios	Mr. Kiterha	no
Total LD/SDC Four classes			44	42			2
TMR	Jefferson School (1)	3–7	12	10	Mr. Anders	Ms. Johns	yes 2
	(2)	8–13	12	9		Ms. Zackey	yes 3
	Special Education Center (1)	14–18	12	10	Ms. Catona	Mr. Krup	yes 2
	(2)	18–22	12	11		Mr. Zello	yes 1
Total TMR Four classes			48	40			8

TABLE 16-2 PROGRAM AND PUPIL INFORMATION

Program Information: _____ (Program) _____ (School) _____ (Principal) _____ (Teacher)

Pupil's Name	Birthdate	Parent or Guardian	Home Address	Telephone Number	Date Entered Sp. Ed.	Date of Annual Review*	Date of Assessment or Reassessment*	Date of Initial IEP

* Each pupil's IEP must be reviewed at least annually, and there must be a reassessment at least every three years.

333

the types of data they want to gather. For example, an administrator might ask if all of the handicapped and gifted pupils in his/her district were being served.

The fifth type of information needed concerns program improvement. Program improvement objectives may focus on improving the implementation process, or on improving a program's outcome, or on both. A program's implementation process and its final product must be compared with those of other programs, if one is to obtain meaningful information on which program's procedures are better. An example showing both process and product evaluation is described below:

EXAMPLE

A special education administrator expressed concern about the process used to develop IEPs and their lack of quality. The committee was taking too long to develop IEPs, and the objectives they were developing did not have measurable outcomes. It was suggested that a new IEP form be developed and that a resource handbook of goals and objectives be used with the IEP.

To evaluate the results of implementing this suggestion, half of the schools in the district stayed with the old program and the other half used the new program. Both groups were randomly selected; neither group was informed that data were being collected. The special education administrator maintained a time log for IEP development and had two outside consultants review an equal number of IEPs from both groups and rate the objectives for their measurable outcomes.

The results indicated that IEPs developed the new way were completed about twenty minutes faster. Ninety percent of the newly developed IEPs had objectives with measurable outcomes, while only 60 percent of the IEPs developed the old way had objectives with measurable outcomes.

While this was not a sophisticated study, it did provide some objective data on which to base a program improvement decision.

The sixth type of information needed in order to properly administer programs relates to compliance with the laws. Preparing for compliance reviews (which districts now undergo at least once every three years) is very important. Inadequate preparation may result in a judgment of noncompliance, which can cause an LEA serious problems. When LEAs are out of compliance (and many are on minor issues), they are given required corrective actions (RCAs). LEAs that fail to respond to these RCAs can lose their funding and can also be subject to legal action.

A program evaluation conducted in order to prepare for compliance reviews should gather data on at least the following topics:

- Verification of LEA child find activities (federal law requires LEAs to seek out and serve all handicapped children).
- Documentation that appropriate assessment procedures have been followed (e.g., records of notices to parents, proper recording of testing data).
- Information regarding IEPs (e.g., verification of parental notice and opportunity to participate, verification of participation by all required team members, dates services were initiated).
- Verification that a free appropriate public education is being provided to each eligible handicapped pupil. (This includes a description of the continuum of educational programs available to the pupil and documentation that all eligible pupils are being served.)
- Documentation that all procedural safeguards are followed for pupils and their parents. (This includes notices to parents regarding assessment and placement, obtaining informed consent prior to taking any actions, and informing parents of their rights concerning due process procedures.)
- Evidence of a plan for personnel development and documentation that the plan is operational. (This requires a written plan for in-service education and records of activities and participants.)
- Records of cooperation with nonpublic schools. (This includes placement of pupils, contacts with parents, and participation in IEP development.)

When each of the areas described in this section has been carefully reviewed, the program administrator has a picture of what he/she needs to know and a basic idea of what should be included in the evaluation design.

GETTING THE DATA

The method by which information is obtained depends on what is to be collected and the purpose for which it is to be used. Sometimes it is collected by the person responsible for the program, but that may introduce bias into the collection process. Sometimes it is collected by an external evaluator; this process is less apt to introduce bias. Again, the nature of information collected and the way it is to be used will determine who should be the evaluator. It is important to remember that data collected by someone close to the program are less believable than similar data collected by a third party evaluator.

Wall (1974) indicates that one component of the evaluation procedure is "the object to be evaluated." This may be a total special education program, a curriculum, a process, or a given child. Obviously, a precise definition of what is to be evaluated is necessary in order to determine how the descriptive data are to be obtained.

One problem that is continuously encountered in program evaluation is finding the time to collect necessary information. Administrators frequently say, "I am so busy running the program that I don't have time to evaluate it too." While this statement contains some truth, it may be the same as saying, "I am so busy doing my job that I don't have time to find out if my methods are effective or if my product has value." Having a workable evaluation design may actually prove to be a time saver.

A responsible administrator need not think that he/she must personally collect all of the information or data for the evaluative process. Others who may assist in the process are outside evaluators, school principals, teachers, pupils, paraprofessionals and secretaries. The evaluator must identify the questions to be answered, the process to be employed to obtain data, the instruments to be used, and the amount of time to be spent on data collection. Other people can then engage in the actual process.

The two examples below will illustrate the point that different people can effectively collect descriptive and evaluative data:

EXAMPLE ONE

The special education administrator knows that she must provide an unduplicated pupil count each year in order to meet the requirements of P.L. 94–142. She is aware that the superintendent frequently calls (on short notice) to obtain information about certain programs, the ratio of enrollment to maximum class limits, and how much time psychologists need to conduct tests. The administrator also knows that accurate assessment records must be kept and that pupils must be reviewed annually in order to fulfill code requirements and to be prepared for compliance reviews.

All of the above information has been included in the special education evaluation design, and forms have been developed for recording the information (see Tables 16–1 and 16–2). A secretary must keep this information up to date on a weekly basis. Although the administrator supervises the secretary's work, it takes her a minimal amount of time to keep this descriptive data current.

EXAMPLE TWO

The local district has provided vocational training for its handicapped pupils for several years. Now, it has an opportunity to participate in a regional occupational training program. The district decides to participate on a pilot basis and to compare the effectiveness of the two programs. The programs will be compared on the basis of achieved student skills; costs will also be analyzed and other possible benefits compared.

The local school board plans to employ a third party evaluator who will design the study and collect the data. In this way, the board will be assured an unbiased evaluation. The special education and vocational education administrators will serve as advisors, but will have no direct control over the evaluation process.

Principals, teachers, and even parents may collect data. The main point is that many people can and will assist in the collection process. But the data, the method, and the study's purpose must all be included in the evaluation design, and administrators (a school principal, a special education administrator, or a person in charge of an LEA's evaluation efforts) are responsible for the evaluation design.

Although this discussion shows that collecting data is not usually an overwhelming task and that different people can help collect data, the author does not wish to minimize the importance of this part of the evaluation process. It is the key to meaningful findings and accurate conclusions. No type of evaluation, regardless of how simple or complex, can be effective if the data collection process is not appropriate.

USING THE INFORMATION

Many professional evaluators discuss the evaluation process in terms of performing *formative* evaluations or *summative* evaluations. Morris and Fitz-Gibbon (1978, p. 11) say:

> The job of program evaluator takes on one of two characters, and at times both, depending upon the tasks that have been assigned:
> 1. You may have the responsibility for producing a summary statement about the effectiveness of the program. In this case, you probably will report to a funding agency, governmental office, or some other representative of the program's constituency. You may be expected to describe the program, to produce a statement concerning the program's achievement of announced goals, to note any unanticipated outcomes, and possibly to make comparisons with alternative programs. If these are the features of your job, you are a *summative evaluator*.
> 2. Your evaluation task may characterize you as a helper and advisor to the program planners and developers or even as a planner yourself. You may then be called on to look out for potential problems, identify areas where the program needs improvement, describe and monitor program activities, and periodically test for progress in achievement or attitude change. In this situation you are a *jack of all trades*, a person whose overall task is not well defined. You may or may not be required to produce a report at the end of your activities. If this more loosely defined job role seems closer to yours, then you are a *formative evaluator*.

While the above material was written to describe the possible roles of a program evaluator, the reader is required to make only minor interpretations to see how it describes the ways in which summative or formative data are used by educational programs. The data may be used to enhance daily program operation, to assist in making decisions about the program or any part of it, to provide information and verification for the reports that must be prepared, to prepare for compliance reviews or other audits by outside agencies, and for a variety of other purposes. These ways of using data are discussed below in greater detail.

Using the Information to Enhance Daily Program Operation

An administrator might take a look at the programs for which he/she is responsible by asking two general questions: What are we doing? How are we doing it? To answer these questions, he/she may have to describe the programs and the procedures followed in their operation. This formative information does not address goals or quality of programs, but the information obtained is essential to administrators. A formative evaluation examines a program's process and helps program managers do their jobs more effectively.

Using Information to Assist in Program Improvement

There are at least two major ways in which programs may be improved: (1) program operation may become more efficient, and (2) program output may be quantitatively or qualitatively increased. In order to achieve either goal, the existing program must be compared to the planned program, or two or more different existing programs may be compared in terms of process or output.

Such comparisons are often carried out in the business world. This can be demonstrated by discussing the automobile manufacturing industry. A car manufacturer may be satisfied with a product's quality, but he/she may still need to reduce costs by using more efficient production methods. In this case, the evaluative process will compare different production techniques in order to find the technique that is least expensive and still allows the manufacturer to maintain the product's quality. If the manufacturer's goal is to improve quality in order to please the consumer, the evaluation may study consumer preference without altering the manufacturing process. However, it is more likely that the evaluation will examine both the manufacturing process and the finished product.

To educators, program improvement usually means such things as increased academic skills, improved behavior, greater vocational skills, and increased parent participation. The number of pupils receiving high school diplomas and improved attendance may be seen as qualitative program measures, but that is debatable. Measuring qualitative improvements in a school program is a much more abstract process than measuring qualitative improvements in an automobile. However, in both cases goals can be established, attained, and measured with some degree of accuracy.

An evaluative design that will be used to improve a program must be carefully planned to (1) identify outcomes that, if achieved, would justify using a different approach from the one being followed, and (2) use ways to obtain data that policy makers will find meaningful and believable. LEAs should also be committed to using the evaluation's results to change programs or to justify existing programs. Without a commitment, it may not be worthwhile to conduct the evaluation.

Of course, some major stumbling blocks are encountered when one evaluates a program in order to improve it. The most difficult problem may be to specify what is meant by a "better" program. If "better" means improved academic learning, almost everyone may be in agreement; but proving that one method enables students to learn better than another method may be difficult. If "better" is defined as promoting greater interaction among students, people may disagree about whether or not this is really a program improvement. It is easier to obtain data showing that teachers, parents, or pupils like a program better than it is to document better academic progress. It is a "softer" type of data, but decision makers may accept it.

Using the Information for Accountability and Compliance Reviews

In the past decade, accountability has become a very popular term in the vocabulary of educators. However, lest they think they invented the term, let us read what Plutarch wrote over two thousand years ago (Ulich 1948, p. 6):

> Fathers, themselves, ought every few days to test their children, and not rest their hopes on the disposition of a hired teacher; for even those persons will devote more attention to the children if they know they must from time to time render an account.

Parents have begun to follow Plutarch's advice and demand that the schools account for their children's educational progress. There are also many laws that require teachers or entire systems to account for their actions.

When people or systems are required to answer as to their accountability, at least two different approaches to evaluation are commonly used: (1) a discrepancy model and (2) an *ex post facto* design. A discrepancy model evaluates a person or an agency by measuring how well that person or agency achieves stated objectives. Obviously, exceeding objectives (a positive discrepancy) is good; failing to achieve objectives (a negative discrepancy) is bad.

A discrepancy evaluation's major flaw is that it must assume that predetermined goals are appropriate. The people being evaluated may tend to set up easily reached objectives in order to assure themselves a positive evaluation.

Another way to evaluate accountability is to compare current data to data previously collected in the same program or to data collected from a normative sample. Tuckman (1979) describes this as *ex post facto* evaluation. The advantage of this method is that the new program (experimental group) is aware in advance of the old program's (normative group) accomplishments and can establish its goals and objectives accordingly.

Educators are constantly required to demonstrate program success because of parental and legislative vigilance. Special education compliance reviews are one form of accountability requirement. P.L. 94–142 requires state education agencies (SEAs) to show that their state is in compliance with the law. In order to carry out this mandate, SEAs must evaluate local education agencies. This is usually done every three years. The previous section, listed five general areas of information needed to prepare for a compliance review. Knowing this well in advance, the administrator can design a process for collecting the data on a continuous basis. Table 16–3 gives a few examples of how information can be used to demonstrate legal compliance. The determination of what data to collect is based on prior identification of the compliance items.

Preparing for special education compliance reviews can be very time consuming, and no one should suggest that it can be done easily. However, an evaluative plan that complements good management procedures can help an LEA simultaneously improve programs, comply with the codes, and document compliance.

TABLE 16–3   USING DATA TO DOCUMENT COMPLIANCE WITH THE CODES

Examples of Compliance Items*	Documentation of LEA Compliance
1. The LEA must have a method for finding all unserved handicapped children (Sec. 121a.220).	1. The LEA has implemented a plan that includes newspaper, radio, and television spots; brochures; posters; in-service education for teachers; letters to parents; and letters to medical organizations. Documentation is on file in the special education office.
2. An IEP must be developed for each handicapped individual in the school system (Sec. 121a.341).	2. A form entitled "Program and Pupil Information" lists the date when the initial IEP was developed and the date of the most recent annual review. IEPs are on file at each school site.
3. An IEP must be in effect before special education and related services are provided (Sec. 121a.342(b)(1)).	3. Services are not initiated until the IEP is in effect. Documentation is included on the "Program and Pupil Information" form and on each pupil's IEP.
4. Written notice must be given to parents prior to any change in a child's educational program (Sec. 121a.504(a)(1)).	4. A copy of letters sent to parents, a log of notices sent, and parental responses provide the information. Documentation is on file in the special education office.

* Examples refer to compliance items in Title 45, Code of Federal Regulations.

Using the Information to Make Decisions

Administrators must make decisions about the daily operation of programs, program improvement, and accountability and compliance. If more decisions are based on good evaluative information, programs will function more effectively and achieve better results.

Popham (1975, pp. 33–42) discusses "decision-facilitation models" of evaluation. In his discussion, Popham quotes other authors' definitions of the evaluation process. These definitions emphasize the process's decision-making role. They should help the reader to relate his/her decision-making process to the evaluation process:

> Evaluation is the process of delineating, obtaining, and providing useful information for judging decision alternatives. [Stufflebeam et al. 1971]

> Evaluation is the process of determining the kinds of decisions that have to be made; selecting, collecting, and analyzing the information needed in making these decisions; and reporting this information to appropriate decision-makers. [Alkin 1974]

The determining factor in making an evaluative design should be the decision maker's need for information. Administrators do not have the time or the resources to collect information that is not directly related to their systems' operation or their pupils' programs. Tuckman (1979, p. 145) believes that a district's best source of comparison is itself and suggests that decisions should be based on questions such as, "Does it move up? Does it improve? Do more students demonstrate mastery of more objectives?" Other questions that decision makers must ask include: Does it take more time or require more resources? Do our people have the skills to implement it? Does it comply with the codes? Will it have the support of teachers and parents? Do we have the necessary funding now and will we have it in the future? Should it be a pilot program at first?

All administrators, regardless of their position in the hierarchy, must make some decisions about special education programs. They can only make the best possible decision if they have appropriate information, and the only way to obtain this information is to implement an evaluation plan. Evaluation is not a luxury; it is a necessity.

REPORTING

Special education is a relatively young field. As such, it is deeply affected by information that shows either good or bad program results. Consider the possible effects of two mythical newspaper headlines highlighting different evaluative findings:

- Study of Special Education Classes Reveals Poor Academic Progress
- Handicapped Seniors Have Better Employment Records Than Other Kids.

Obviously, reporting of evaluation results (whether or not it is accurate) can profoundly affect programs and decisions made about those programs. The evaluator's mission is to accurately report information that facilitates the decision-making process and to provide other information, as previously described. The evaluator's report must meet the needs of the person(s) for whom it is designed.

Special education evaluation can be a small-scale informal process that relates only to a given class or school; it can also be a very complex process that compares different delivery systems within a state. Thus, the reporting process will be different for different evaluations. Some reports are informal, verbal, and directed toward a small audience; others are more in-depth, full of data, and directed toward a wider audience. Some reporting hints include:

- Identify the audience and report accordingly; only give them as much information as they want and need.
- Get input from those who were involved in the evaluation and let them preview the report and suggest changes.
- Be brief and to the point; report only pertinent information.
- Organize the report well so that it is easy to listen to or read.
- Provide a good abstract or summary for the person who will not read the entire report.
- Give your conclusions and recommendations, if it is appropriate to do so.

Administrators who are directly responsible for special education programs sometimes receive evaluation reports concerning their programs. More frequently, however, administrators must prepare reports for other decision makers. This is a tremendously important assignment, and it should be done correctly. Morris and Fitz-Gibbon (1978) and Popham (1975) provide very practical suggestions and outlines for preparing evaluation reports. Their suggestions are mandatory reading for administrators who prepare evaluation reports.

SUMMARY

Chapter 16 discusses program evaluation from the practical viewpoint of one who must manage and make decisions about programs. Evaluation is broadly defined in order to encourage readers to include in their thinking the concept that for different types of evaluations it may be appropriate to collect data that describe a program's process or output, document activities, or compare quality.

This chapter emphasizes the importance of advance planning when a local education agency is conducting an evaluation. This will ensure that data are collected systematically and are targeted to programs where the efforts will produce the desired information. The what, how, and why questions should guide administrators as they develop their evaluative designs.

In responding to the question "What do we need to know?" the author suggests that six types of data be collected: (1) the system's day-to-day operation, (2) fiscal status and budget control, (3) an unduplicated count of pupils and average daily attendance, (4) program reports, (5) program quality, and (6) legal compliance.

The data-collecting process is a major concern of the evaluation design. The chapter presents information about who should collect the data, the amount of time that should be allocated to collecting data, and the ways in which data are collected. Administrators frequently avoid designing evaluations by saying that they don't have time to do it. The author contends that program managers and decision makers must have the information that comes from the evaluation process and that time must be allocated for this purpose. The fact that collecting data is not always as complex and time consuming as one may think is also discussed. Teachers, parents, and secretaries can collect data; data do not always have to be gathered by a professional evaluator.

The purpose of evaluation is to obtain information that serves a specific need. Chapter 16 discusses using evaluative information for five purposes: (1) to enhance daily program operations; (2) to assist in program improvement; (3) to prepare for compliance reviews and enhance accountability; (4) to serve as the basis for decision making; and (5) to provide information needed to report to one's superiors.

NOTE

1. Additional information and sample compliance review questions can be found in Chapter 4 and in Appendix 1.

REFERENCES

Alkin, M. C. 1974. *Evaluation theory development: An introduction to the Center.* Los Angeles: Center for the Study of Evaluation, University of California.

Bonnet, D. G. 1977. *Evaluating design and reporting in career education.* Washington, D.C.: Office of Career Education, Department of Health, Education and Welfare. ERIC Document 171 903.

Morris, L. L., and Fitz-Gibbon, C. T. 1978. *How to measure program implementa-
tion.* Beverly Hills, Ca.: Sage Publications, Inc.
Popham, W. J. 1975. *Educational evaluation.* Englewood Cliffs, N.J.: Prentice-Hall,
Inc.
Stufflebeam, D. L., et al. 1971. *Educational evaluation and decision making.* Itasca,
Ill.: F. E. Peacock.
Tuckman, B. W. 1979. *Evaluating instructional programs.* Boston: Allyn and Bacon,
Inc.
Ulich, R. 1948. *Three thousand years of educational wisdom.* Cambridge, Mass.:
Harvard University Press.
Wall, H. V. 1974. Evaluation of programs for the trainable mentally retarded. In
*Adaptive education and program components for the trainable mentally retarded
in California public schools,* ed. J. C. Edwards and V. Templeton, pp. 59–66.
Sacramento: Office of State Printing.

ADDITIONAL SUGGESTED READINGS

Alvir, H. P. 1979. *Program evaluation by objectives (you're held accountable only
for what you claim your objectives are).* Technical document. Albany, N.Y., April.
ERIC Document 175 223.
Armstrong, M. L. 1978. Developing and monitoring individual education plans for
handicapped children. Doctoral study, Nova University, Fort Lauderdale, Fla.,
September. ERIC Document 176 453.
Dunst, C. J. 1979. Program evaluation and the Education for All Handicapped Chil-
dren Act. *Exceptional Children,* September, 46:24–31.
Holland, R. P. 1980. An analysis of the decision making process in special education.
Exceptional Children, April, 46:551–53.

Examples of Questions from Checklists Utilized by Compliance Review Teams

Sample Questions	Yes	No	Partial Compliance

Public Awareness and Child Search

1. Is there evidence of appropriate effort to inform the public of programs for handicapped children?
2. Is there a process in the LEA for receiving and acting upon referrals from outside agencies/individuals?

Identification and Assessment

3. Does the LEA have a defined process for identification and assessment?
4. Is an assessment of needs conducted prior to placement in a special program?
5. Is written consent of the parent or guardian obtained prior to assessment?

Free Appropriate Public Education

6. Are all identified handicapped children being served?
7. Has an IEP been developed and implemented for each child?
8. Is the instructional program directed toward accomplishment of the IEP?
9. Are the required related services being provided?

Development and Implementation of IEPs

10. Does each IEP include a statement of the child's present levels of educational performance?
11. Does each IEP include a statement of annual goals?
12. Does each IEP include short-term instructional objectives?

Sample Questions	Yes	No	Partial Compli- ance

13. Does each IEP include a statement of special education and related services to be provided?
14. Does each IEP include the degree to which the child will be able to participate in regular education programs?
15. Does each IEP include projected dates for initiation of services?
16. Does each IEP include the expected duration of services?

Local Plan and Application

17. Does the LEA have a written plan, policies, and guidelines for its special education programs?
18. Does the plan meet the compliance regulations of the law?

Procedural Safeguards and Due Process

19. Are parents informed of their rights?
20. Are notices to parents in their primary language?
21. Do parents have access to all records relevant to their child?

Least Restrictive Environment

22. Are all handicapped children placed in the least restrictive environment?
23. Does the LEA make available a full range of programs and services?

Personnel Development

24. Does the LEA have a plan for personnel development?
25. Is the plan based on a needs assessment?
26. Are both general and special educators receiving in-service training regarding education of exceptional individuals?

Local Board Policies
and
Administrative Regulations

A SUGGESTED OUTLINE FOR DEVELOPMENT OF BOARD POLICIES (BP) AND ADMINISTRATIVE REGULATIONS (AR)

BP 1.0   *General Statement of Philosophy and Board Policy*

AR 1.1   Definition of Individuals to Be Served
1.2   Child Identification
1.3   Ages Served
1.4   Eligibility Criteria
1.5   Placement Procedures

BP 2.0   *Comprehensive Planning*

AR 2.1   Annual Plan
2.2   Local Application for Federal Funding Allocations
2.3   Policies, Regulations, and Procedures
2.4   Budgeting
2.5   Program Evaluation and Review

BP 3.0   *Personnel Preparation*

AR 3.1   Selection and Assignment of Personnel
3.2   In-service Education for Special Education Personnel
3.3   In-service Education for Regular Education Personnel

BP 4.0   *Procedural Safeguards, Due Process Procedures, Fair Hearings*

AR 4.1   Notification of Rights
4.2   Informed Consent
4.3   Right of Appeal
4.4   Due Process Hearing Procedures

BP 5.0   *Referral, Assessment, Assignment to Programs or Services*

AR 5.1   Referral Procedures
5.2   Assessment Procedures
5.3   Assignment of Pupils

BP 6.0   *Most Appropriate Placement (Mainstreaming, Least Restrictive Environment): Defining the Range of Alternative Programs or Services*

AR 6.1 Special Classes
    6.2 Hospital School
    6.3 Learning Disability Groups
    6.4 Speech
    6.5 Transportation
    6.6 Health Services
    6.7 Nonpublic Schools

BP 7.0 *Individualized Education Programs (IEPs) and Curriculum Development*

AR 7.1 Parental Involvement
    7.2 Content of IEP
    7.3 Process of IEP Development
    7.4 Accountability
    7.5 Review
    7.6 Career Preparation, Driver Training, Adapted Physical Education
    7.7 Graduation Requirements (Units, Proficiency)

BP 8.0 *Working with Parents*

AR 8.1 Parent Advisory Groups
    8.2 Involvement in School Programs

BP 9.0 *Cooperation with Other Agencies*

AR 9.1 Cooperative Planning
    9.2 Contracting
    9.3 Supplementary/Complementary Services

BP 10.0 *Record Keeping, Evaluation, and Confidentiality of Information*

AR 10.1 Student Records
    10.2 Access Procedures
    10.3 Program Review
    10.4 Compliance

BP 11.0 *Standards for Exceptional Pupil Behavior and Disciplinary Guidelines*

AR 11.1 Procedures for Behavior Management
    11.2 Suspension, Expulsion, Exclusion
    11.3 Exemption
    11.4 Disciplinary Guidelines

For each board policy and administrative regulation, the local education agency develops written statements that are designed to help the program operate effectively at the local level. Space limitations do not allow the presentation of examples for each BP and AR listed, but examples from numbers 1.0 and 4.0 are provided.

EXAMPLES OF LOCAL BOARD POLICIES AND ADMINISTRATIVE REGULATIONS

General Statement of Philosophy and Board Policy (BP 1.0)

The board of education believes in the value of special education programs and services for children who have need for these programs and services, and is committed to the concept of helping all children to develop to their ultimate potential.

It shall be the policy of the board of education to provide appropriate, publicly supported educational programs and related services for *all* individuals with exceptional needs within the legally defined eligibility criteria and age requirements. It shall also be the policy of the board of education to seek out these individuals and to assure appropriate rights and safeguards for pupils and their parents. The superintendent shall identify and direct the regulations and procedures necessary to implement this policy.

References:

45 C.F.R. § 884.4.

45 C.F.R. § 121a.128(a), and 121a.220.

Education for all Handicapped Children Act of 1975, P.L. 94–142, Sec. 601(c).

Vocational Rehabilitation Act of 1973, P.L. 93–112, Sec. 504.

DEFINITIONS OF INDIVIDUALS TO BE SERVED (AR 1.1) The commitment to serve *all* individuals with exceptional needs refers to the definitions for handicapped children used in C.F.R. 121a.5, and to Education Code Section 56000. The following handicapped conditions are included: deaf and hard of hearing, orthopedic and other health impaired, blind and partially seeing, severe language disorders (aphasic), other physically handicapped, mentally retarded, educationally handicapped (including the autistic), and the multihandicapped.

CHILD IDENTIFICATION (AR 1.2) It shall be the responsibility of the superintendent to maintain procedures that ensure that all individuals with exceptional needs who reside in the district are located and evaluated to determine their educational needs. The process of identifying these individuals shall include district activities designed to inform parents as well as participation in public awareness activities that are conducted for larger geographical areas. In general, this means an active program to "seek out" and serve the children in this population.

References:

45 C.F.R. § 121a.220.

Procedural Safeguards, Due Process Procedures, Fair Hearings (BP 4.0)

It is the intent of the board of education to comply with the provisions of P.L. 94–142, P.L. 93–112, and the state regulations regarding parent and pupil rights, procedural safeguards, and due process procedures. Whenever there is a disagreement with parents regarding compliance, the parent or the district may request that informal negotiation or a due process hearing be initiated.

References:

Education for all Handicapped Children Act of 1975, P.L. 94–142.
Vocational Rehabilitation Act of 1973, P.L. 93–112, Sec. 504.

NOTIFICATION OF RIGHTS (AR 4.1)   Parents of individuals with exceptional needs shall be fully informed (in their native language, if feasible) of their rights regarding education of their children. This information shall explain:

1. The right to a free appropriate public education;
2. The right to give informed consent regarding assessment and placement;
3. The right to an independent educational evaluation if the district's evaluation is inadequate;
4. The necessity for written prior notice to parents whenever the district proposes or refuses to initiate change in the identification, evaluation, or placement of the child;
5. The right of a parent to examine all relevant records;
6. The right to confidentiality of personal information;
7. The right to present complaints regarding assessment or placement of the pupil;
8. The opportunity for a due process hearing if differences cannot be resolved informally;
9. The opportunity for parents (and pupils, when appropriate) to participate in development of the IEP and in the periodic review;
10. The right to a timely response by the district to parental request;
11. The right of a child to remain in school during any proceeding, except as described in state code provisions; and
12. The right to a full explanation of all procedural safeguards available to parents.

References:

Education for all Handicapped Children Act of 1975, P.L. 94–142, Sec. 615.

45 C.F.R. § 121a.237, 121a.500–514.

INFORMED CONSENT (AR 4.2)   Parents are guaranteed the right to give "informed consent" regarding assessment and placement. Informed consent means that:

1. The parent has been fully informed of all information relevant to the activity for which consent is sought in his/her primary language or other mode of communication;
2. The parent understands and agrees in writing to the activity for which consent is sought;
3. The parent understands what records will be kept and to whom they will be available; and
4. The parent knows that granting of consent is voluntary and may be revoked at any time.

References:

45 C.F.R. § 121a.500.
E.C. Sec. 56021.

RIGHT OF APPEAL (AR 4.3)   The district will identify, upon request, the procedures whereby a parent may present complaints regarding identification, evaluation, or educational placement. The parent may also appeal a decision by the district and request an informal review or a formal due process hearing.

PROCEDURES FOR DUE PROCESS HEARINGS (AR 4.4)   The hearing process is defined in terms of five different levels:

1. Preventing disagreements with parents by providing quality programs, complying with all statutory and regulatory provisions, and keeping parents fully informed and involved as participating members of the educational effort;
2. Utilizing the "informal review" to resolve issues whenever possible;
3. Establishing a hearing panel when the informal review fails to resolve the issue;
4. Appealing decisions at the local level to the state superintendent of public instruction; and
5. Bringing a civil action in court.

When a disagreement is unresolved, a parent or the district may request that a due process hearing be conducted P.L. 94–142, Sec. 615(b)(2). The matters for hearing are described in 45 C.F.R. § 121a.504.

If the district receives a written request from a parent for a hearing panel, the superintendent or designee shall within ten school days meet with the parent for an informal review to attempt to resolve the issue. If this fails, the superintendent shall implement formal hearing procedures.

The hearing before the panel shall be held within thirty-five days following the receipt, in writing, of a request for hearing before a hearing panel. The hearing shall be conducted according to procedures described in the state code.

If either party disagrees with the decision of the hearing panel, they may file, within twenty days, a written petition for review before the state superintendent of public instruction. Civil action in court is the final step for unresolved issues.

References:

Education for all Handicapped Children Act of 1975, P.L. 94–142, Sec. 615(b)(2).
45 C.F.R. § 504(a)(1,2).
45 C.F.R. § 506–514.
45 C.F.R. § 580–583.

Organizations and Agencies Providing Information and Services for Handicapped Individuals

Alexander Graham Bell Association
for the Deaf
3417 Volta Place, N.W.
Washington, D.C. 20007

American Academy for Cerebral
Palsy
1255 New Hampshire Avenue, N.W.
Washington, D.C. 20036

American Association for Rehabili-
tation Therapy
P.O. Box 93
North Little Rock, Ark. 72116

American Association for the Educa-
tion of the Severely/Profoundly
Handicapped
P.O.Box 15287
Seattle, Wa. 98115

American Association of Mental
Deficiency
5201 Connecticut Avenue, N.W.
Washington, D.C. 20015

American Association of Workers
for the Blind
1511 K Street, N.W.
Washington, D.C. 20005

American Civil Liberties Union
85 5th Avenue
New York, N.Y. 10017

American Corrective Therapy
Association
6622 Spring Hollow
San Antonio, Tex. 78249

American Diabetes Association
1 West 48th Street
New York, N.Y. 10020

American Epilepsy Society
Division of Neurosurgery
University of Texas Medical Branch
Galveston, Tex. 77550

American Foundation for the Blind
15 West 16th Street
New York, N.Y. 10011

American Health Foundation
1370 Avenue of the Americas
New York, N.Y. 10019

American Printing House for
the Blind
1839 Frankfort Avenue
Louisville, Ky. 40206

American Psychological Association
1200 17th Street, N.W.
Washington, D.C. 20036

American School Health Association
Kent, Ohio 44240

American Speech and Hearing
Association
9030 Old Georgetown Road
Washington, D.C. 20014

Architectural Barriers Committee
National Association of the
Physically Handicapped
6473 Grandville Avenue
Detroit, Mi. 48228

Association for Children with
Learning Disabilities
5225 Grace Street
Pittsburgh, Pa. 15236

Boy Scouts of America, Scouting for
the Handicapped Division
North Brunswick, N.J. 08902

Braille Institute of America
741 North Vermont Avenue
Los Angeles, Ca. 90029

California Advisory Council on
Vocational Education
708 10th Street
Sacramento, Ca. 95814

Center for Independent Living
2539 Telegraph Avenue
Berkeley, Ca. 94704

Center for Law and Social Policy
1751 N Street, N.W.
Washington, D.C. 20009

Closer Look: National Information
Center for the Handicapped
Box 1492
Washington, D.C. 20013

Committee for the Handicapped,
People to People Program
1028 Connecticut Avenue
Washington, D.C. 20036

Council for Exceptional Children
1920 Association Drive
Reston, Va. 22091

Disabled American Veterans
3725 Alexandria Pike
Cold Spring, Ky. 41076

Down's Syndrome Congress
1709 Frederick Street
Cumberland, Md. 21502

Epilepsy Foundation of America
1828 L Street, N.W., Suite 406
Washington, D.C. 20036

Girl Scouts of the U.S.A., Scouting
for Handicapped Girls Program
830 3rd Avenue
New York, N.Y. 10022

Goodwill Industries of America
9200 Wisconsin Avenue
Washington, D.C. 20014

Handicapped Artists of America
8 Sandy Lane
Salisbury, Ma. 01950

Joseph P. Kennedy, Jr. Foundation
1701 K Street, N.W., Suite 205
Washington, D.C. 20006

Kiwanis International
101 East Erie Street
Chicago, Ill. 60611

Lions International
New York Road and Cermak Road
Oak Brook, Ill. 60521

Muscular Dystrophy Associations
of America
810 7th Avenue
New York, N.Y. 10019

National Association for Retarded
Citizens
2709 Avenue E East
Arlington, Tex. 76011

National Association for Visually
Handicapped
3201 Balboa Street
San Francisco, Ca. 94121

National Association of Hearing and
Speech Agencies
814 Thayer Avenue
Silver Springs, Md. 20910

National Association of Private
Schools for Exceptional Children
7700 Miller Road
Miami, Fla. 33155

National Association of State
Directors of Special Education
1510 H Street, N.W.
Washington, D.C. 20005

National Association of the Deaf
814 Thayer Avenue
Silver Springs, Md. 20910

National Association of the
Physically Handicapped
6473 Grandville Avenue
Detroit, Mi. 48228

National Association of Vocational
Education Special Needs
Personnel
54 Langer Circle
West St. Paul, Mn. 55118

National Center for a Barrier-Free
Environment
8401 Connecticut Avenue, Suite 402
Washington, D.C. 20015

National Center for Child Advocacy
U.S. Department of Health, Education and Welfare, Office of Child
Development
P.O. Box 1182
Washington, D.C. 20013

National Center for Law and the
Handicapped
1236 North Eddy Street
South Bend, Ind. 46617

National Center on Educational
Media and Materials for the
Handicapped
The Ohio State University
220 West 12th Avenue
Columbus, Oh. 43210

National Council of Community
Mental Health Centers
2233 Wisconsin Avenue, N.W.
Washington, D.C. 20007

National Easter Seal Society for
Crippled Children and Adults
2023 West Ogden Avenue
Chicago, Ill. 60612

National Education Association
1201 16th Street, N.W.
Washington, D.C. 20036

National Federation of the Blind
218 Randolph Hotel Building
Des Moines, Ia. 50309

National Rehabilitation Association
1522 K Street, N.W.
Washington, D.C. 20005

National Wheelchair Athletic
Association
40–24 62nd Street
Woodside, N.Y. 11377

Physical Education and Recreation
for the Handicapped
Information and Research
Utilization Center
1201 16th Street, N.W.
Washington, D.C. 20036

President's Committee on
Employment of the Handicapped
1111 20th Street, N.W.
Washington, D.C. 20210

President's Committee on Mental
Retardation
7th and D Streets, S.W.
Washington, D.C. 20201

United Cerebral Palsy Association
66 East 34th Street
New York, N.Y. 10016

Volunteers of America
340 West 85th Street
New York, N.Y. 10024

Formal communication with parents must cover certain information specified in federal laws and regulations. Included are the following:

- Notification of the right to a free appropriate public education
- Notification of all due process rights
- Notification of intent to conduct an assessment and an opportunity for the parent to approve or disapprove the assessment plan or to have an independent assessment
- Notification of the meeting to develop an IEP and the opportunity to participate in the development process
- Notification of placement decisions and the opportunity to dissent and challenge these decisions
- Information regarding all records concerning the child
- Information regarding the procedure for due process hearings or other legal actions.

Several of the above items can be covered in a single letter, but the same information is not always appropriate. Thus, more than one letter or form is needed. Different school districts use different approaches, but the materials are basically similar. Different state laws account for the inclusion of additional information. Sample letters follow.

SAMPLE LETTER 1: XYZ SCHOOL DISTRICT

Dear Parents or Guardians:

As parents [or guardians] of a student who is enrolled in one of the school district's special education programs [or who is being considered for one of these programs], you have certain rights that are guaranteed by law. We want to advise you of those rights and to provide information that will help us to work as partners in our attempt to provide the best school programs for your child.

We encourage you to read this information carefully. If you have any questions, please call Mr. _____. So we may know that you have received this information, please sign and return the enclosed duplicate copy of this letter.

You and your child have the right to:

1. Have an assessment determine the nature of your child's school problems.
   (a) Receive advance notice of the assessment proceeding and a copy of the assessment plan.
   (b) Have an assessment conducted only if you give written permission.
   (c) Choose to have an independent assessment provided by other professionals, but this is done at parental expense unless the District's assessment is shown to be inappropriate.
2. Examine all school records that concern your child. You may have copies of any records if you pay the cost of reproduction. If any records are inaccurate, you may request that they be amended. When records are no longer needed, you may request that they be destroyed.
3. Have a free appropriate education for your child. This education will be provided by the District whenever possible. For certain special program needs the District may seek the assistance of other school districts or agencies.
4. Have your child's special education program defined by an *individualized education program* (IEP). You are encouraged to participate as a member of the IEP committee to develop the plan. You have the right to:
   (a) Give information in person, in writing, or through a representative.
   (b) Participate in the development of the IEP.
   (c) Be informed in writing of the IEP committee's recommendations.
   (d) Have a copy of the written IEP.
   (e) Give written consent for the special education placement.
5. Have your child spend as much time as possible with students who are not handicapped. Students are only placed in separate classes or in special services when regular classes do not appropriately serve their needs.
6. Have information translated into your native language to enable you to understand your rights and your child's program.
7. Appeal any District decision that involves identification or special education placement.
8. File a written complaint regarding any matter which, if true, would show that the District is not in compliance with federal or state laws and regulations.

I have received and read a copy of this notice of parent/student rights and protections. I know that I may request explanation of any of the items, and I acknowledge that I fully understand this information.

_____   _____
Signature of Parent/Guardian   Date

_____
Name of Child

SAMPLE LETTER 2: XYZ SCHOOL DISTRICT

Dear Parent or Guardian:

The District Admissions and Educational Planning Committee will meet in order to develop a written individualized education program (IEP) for your child. The IEP will set your child's annual instructional goals and objectives. Several developmental areas will be considered: academic ability, overall behavior pattern, social development, prevocational and vocational skills, motor skills, and self-help skills. If your child qualifies for special education programs, a decision will also be made about his/her most appropriate educational placement.

MEETING INFORMATION

DATE_____

TIME_____

PLACE_____

The following committee members will attend:

_____School Administrator   _____Nurse

_____Special Education Teacher   _____OTHER_____

_____School Psychologist   _____OTHER_____

Parents/guardians are encouraged to attend the meeting or to have a representative present, although this is not required. Pupils

are_____
are not_____

invited to attend.

To help us plan this meeting, please complete the form below and return it to this office. Feel free to call the office at (telephone number) if you have any questions about this meeting.

Sincerely,

_____

MARSHA SALLE, Director
Special Education Programs
Enclosure

Please return to the Special Education Office in the enclosed envelope.

_____ I plan to attend the meeting as scheduled, but please proceed without me if I am not there.

_____ I will not be able to attend the meeting. I understand that if I am not present, I will be contacted to sign the individualized education program (IEP) form, since a parent's/guardian's signature is required in order for a pupil to continue in the approved special education program.

_____   _____   _____
Parent's Signature   Date   Pupil's Name

SAMPLE LETTER 3: XYZ SCHOOL DISTRICT

Dear Parent or Guardian:

At an Educational Planning Meeting held on_____(date)_____, to which you were invited, a written individualized education program (IEP) was prepared for_____(child's name)_____. A copy of this form is enclosed for your records. The Planning Committee feels that the most appropriate program for _____(child's name)_____ at this time is_____. This is subject to your approval. If you approve, please sign and return the enclosed consent form.

The classroom teacher will plan and prepare specific activities to help your child accomplish the IEP's instructional goals. You are encouraged to assist in any way you can. We are always more successful when parents and teachers work together to accomplish the same goals.

If you have any questions or would like to discuss the goals, please contact your child's teacher.

Sincerely,

_____

MARSHA SALLE, Director
Special Education Programs
Enclosure

SAMPLE FORM: XYZ SCHOOL DISTRICT

CONSENT FOR EDUCATIONAL SERVICE
IN SPECIAL EDUCATION PROGRAMS

I have talked with school personnel and have been advised of the recommended program and special education placement. I understand that this placement is subject to continued review and that an annual formal review of the placement's appropriateness is made. Continuous assessment by staff members may be appropriate during my child's participation and enrollment in the special education program.

Statement of Rights Regarding Educational Planning/Special Education Placement

1. Assignment to a special education class or a special service is based upon committee recommendation and parental consent. Parental consent may be revoked at any time, or parents may challenge their child's placement through a due process hearing.
2. Placement in a special class or program is determined by the nature and severity of a child's disability.
3. Individuals with exceptional needs will be educated with pupils who are not disabled as long as neither handicapped nor nonhandicapped students are adversely affected.
4. A child's progress and the appropriateness of his/her placement are continually reviewed and an annual review is held. Parents are advised of and involved with the results of the annual review.
5. The committee will review any additional information supplied that may influence a child's placement or the district's educational plan for that child.
6. Parents are invited to participate in the educational planning process and to help their children meet instructional goals.
7. All progress reports are available to parents.

I have been advised of my rights concerning this program recommendation. I agree to assist the school so that it will be possible for my child to receive the program's maximum benefits.

_____ Permission is granted for placement in the_____

_____special education program.

_____ Permission is not granted for placement.

_____ _____   _____
Signature of Parent/Guardian   Pupil's Name   Date

Sample Questions for Interviewing Candidates for Special Education Positions

Special Classroom Teachers

1. Some teachers say that special education teachers get all of the most difficult students in the schools. Why do you want to teach in a special education class?
2. Tell me about your professional training program. I am particularly interested in your field experiences with different types of handicapped children.
3. Have you had experience developing and using IEPs? If so, tell me how you feel about the IEP process.
4. Who should assess children in special classes so that their week-to-week instructional program can be planned? How should the assessment be done?
5. How do you "pull together" and use assessment information, IEPs, and daily lesson plans?
6. Briefly describe the components of (1) a good work-study program and (2) a good preparation for daily living program.

Resource Room Teachers

1. If your school principal put you in charge of planning the in-service training program for regular classroom teachers for the coming year, how would you do it? What special education training would you include?
2. As a resource teacher, you will be required to provide consultative services for regular classroom teachers who have special education students in their classes. How would you go about providing these services?
3. Suppose your principal tells you that the school's relationships with parents have been "shakey," and he/she gives you the task of helping him/her improve these relationships. What course(s) of action might you suggest?
4. If you were told to organize and conduct the annual reviews of the students' IEPs, would you feel comfortable with that assignment? Why or why not?
5. Being a resource teacher means teaching students, working with other teachers, and sometimes serving as a quasi-administrator. It demands highly developed skills and takes a great deal of time. So why do you want this job?

The Individualized Education Program

Following are excerpts from P.L. 94–142 (Sections 602–614) and from Sections 121a.340 to 121a.349 of the Code of Federal Regulations.

IEP REQUIRED FOR EVERY HANDICAPPED STUDENT

Sec. 612. In order to qualify for assistance under this part in any fiscal year, a State shall demonstrate to the Commissioner that the following conditions are met:

(4) Each local educational agency in the State will maintain records of the individualized education program for each handicapped child, and such program shall be established, reviewed, and revised as provided in section 614(a)(5). (see below)

Sec. 614. (a) A local educational agency or an intermediate educational unit which desires to receive payments under section 611(d) for any fiscal year shall submit an application to the appropriate State educational agency. Such application shall ...

(5) provide assurances that the local educational agency or intermediate educational unit will establish, or revise, whichever is appropriate, an individualized education program for each handicapped child at the beginning of each school year and will then review and, if appropriate, revise its provisions periodically, but not less than annually ...

Sec. 121a.341 State educational agency responsibility.

(a) *Public agencies.* The State educational agency shall insure that each public agency develops and implements an individualized education program for each of its handicapped children.

(b) *Private schools and facilities.* The State educational agency shall insure that an individualized education program is developed and implemented for each handicapped child who:

(1) Is placed in or referred to a private school or facility by a public agency; or

(2) Is enrolled in a parochial or other private school and receives special education or related services from a public agency.

(20 U.S.C. 1412(4),(6); 1413(a)(4))

Comment. This section applies to all public agencies, including other State agencies (e.g., departments of mental health and welfare), which provide special education to a handicapped child either directly, by contract or through other arrangements. Thus, if a State welfare agency contracts with a private school or facility to provide special education to a handicapped child, that agency would be responsible for insuring that an individualized education program is developed for the child.

Sec. 121a.342 When individualized education programs must be in effect.
  (a) On October 1, 1977, and at the beginning of each school year thereafter, each public agency shall have in effect an individualized education program for every handicapped child who is receiving special education from that agency.
  (b) An individualized education program must:
    (1) Be in effect before special education and related services are provided to a child; and
    (2) Be implemented as soon as possible following the meetings under Sec. 121a.343.
(20 U.S.C. 1412(2)(B),(4),(6); 1414(a)(5); Pub. L. 94–142, Sec. *(c) (1975).)
Comment. Under paragraph (b)(2), it is expected that a handicapped child's individualized education program (IEP) will be implemented immediately following the meetings under Sec. 121a.343. An exception to this would be (1) when the meetings occur during the summer or a vacation period, or (2) where there are circumstances which require a short delay (e.g., working out transportation arrangements). However, there can be no undue delay in providing special education and related services to the child.

DEFINITION, CONTENT AND PROCEDURES FOR DEVELOPING IEPs

Section 4.(a) Section 602 of the Act (20 U.S.C. 1402) is amended...
  (19) The term "individualized education program" means a written statement for each handicapped child developed in any meeting by a representative of the local educational agency or an intermediate educational unit who shall be qualified to provide, or supervise the provision of, specially designed instruction to meet the unique needs of handicapped children, the teacher, the parents or guardian of such child, and, whenever appropriate, such child, which statement shall include (A) a statement of the present levels of educational performance of such child, (B) a statement of annual goals, including short-term instructional objectives, (C) a statement of the specific educational services to be provided to such child, and the extent to which such child will be able to participate in regular educational programs, (D)

the projected date for initiation and anticipated duration of such services, and (E) appropriate objective criteria and evaluation procedures and schedules for determining, on at least an annual basis, whether instructional objectives are being achieved.

Sec. 614(a)(5) The State has established (A) procedural safeguards as required by section 615, (B) procedures to assure that, to the maximum extent appropriate, handicapped children, including children in public or private institutions or other care facilities, are educated with children who are not handicapped, and that special classes, separate schooling, or other removal of handicapped children from the regular educational environment occurs only when the nature or severity of the handicap is such that education in regular classes with the use of supplementary aids and services cannot be achieved satisfactorily, and (C) procedures to assure that testing and evaluation materials and procedures utilized for the purposes of evaluation and placement of handicapped children will be selected and administered so as not to be racially or culturally discriminatory. Such materials or procedures shall be provided and administered in the child's native language or mode of communication, unless it clearly is not feasible to do so, and no single procedure shall be the sole criterion for determining an appropriate educational program for a child.

Sec. 121a.340 Definition.
As used in this part, the term "individualized education program" means a written statement for a handicapped child that is developed and implemented in accordance with Sections 121a.341–121a.349.
(20 U.S.C. 1401 (19).)

Sec. 121a.346 Content of individualized education program. The individualized education program for each child must include:
   (a) A statement of the child's present levels of educational performance;
   (b) A statement of annual goals, including short term instructional objectives;
   (c) A statement of the specific special education and related services to be provided to the child, and the extent to which the child will be able to participate in regular educational programs;
   (d) The projected dates for initiation of services and the anticipated duration of the services; and
   (e) Appropriate objective criteria and evaluation procedures and schedules for determining, on at least an annual basis, whether the short term instructional objectives are being achieved.
(20 U.S.C. 1401(19); 1412(2)(B),(4),(6), 1414(a)(5); Senate Report No. 94–168, p. 11 (1975).)

REQUIREMENTS FOR MEETINGS

Sec. 121a.343 Meetings.

(a) *General.* Each public agency is responsible for initiating and conducting meetings for the purpose of developing, reviewing, and revising a handicapped child's individualized education program.

(b) *Handicapped children currently served.* If the public agency has determined that a handicapped child will receive special education during school year 1977–1978, a meeting must be held early enough to insure that an individualized education program is developed by October 1, 1977.

(c) *Other handicapped children.* For a handicapped child who is not included under paragraph (b) of this action, a meeting must be held within thirty calendar days of a determination that the child needs special education and related services.

(d) *Review.* Each public agency shall initiate and conduct meetings to periodically review each child's individualized education program and if appropriate revise its provisions. A meeting must be held for this purpose at least once a year.

(20 U.S.C. 1412(2)(B),(4),(6); 1414(a)(5).)

Comment. The dates on which agencies must have individualized education programs (IEPs) in effect are specified in Sec. 121a.342 (October 1, 1977, and the beginning of each school year thereafter). However, except for new handicapped children (i.e., those evaluated and determined to need special education after October 1, 1977), the timing of meetings to develop, review, and revise IEPs is left to the discretion of each agency.

In order to have IEPs in effect by the dates in Sec. 121a.342, agencies could hold meetings at the end of the school year or during the summer preceding those dates. In meeting the October 1, 1977 timeline, meetings could be conducted up through the October 1 date. Thereafter, meetings may be held any time throughout the year, as long as IEPs are in effect at the beginning of each school year.

The statute requires agencies to hold a meeting at least once each year in order to review, and if appropriate revise, each child's IEP. The timing of those meetings could be on the anniversary date of the last IEP meeting on the child, but this is left to the discretion of the agency.

Sec. 121a.344 Participants in meetings.

(a) *General.* The public agency shall insure that each meeting includes the following participants:

(1) A representative of the public agency, other than the child's teacher, who is qualified to provide, or supervise the provision of, special education.

(2) The child's teacher.

(3) One or both of the child's parents, subject to Sec. 121a.345.

(4) The child, where appropriate.

(5) Other individuals at the discretion of the parent or agency.

(b) *Evaluation personnel.* For a handicapped child who has been evaluated for the first time, the public agency shall insure:

(1) That a member of the evaluation team participates in the meeting; or

(2) That the representative of the public agency, the child's teacher, or some other person is present at the meeting, who is knowledgeable about the evaluation procedures used with the child and is familiar with the results of the evaluation.

(20 U.S.C. 1401(19); 1412(2)(B),(4),(6); 1414(a)(5).)

Comment.

1. In deciding which teacher will participate in meetings on a child's individualized education program, the agency may wish to consider the following possibilities:

(a) For a handicapped child who is receiving special education, the "teacher" could be the child's special education teacher. If the child's handicap is a speech impairment, the "teacher" could be the speech-language pathologist.

(b) For a handicapped child who is being considered for placement in special education, the "teacher" could be the child's regular teacher, or a teacher qualified to provide education in the type of program in which the child may be placed, or both.

(c) If the child is not in school or has more than one teacher, the agency may designate which teacher will partipate in the meeting.

2. Either the teacher or the agency representative should be qualified in the area of the child's suspected disability.

3. For a child whose primary handicap is a speech impairment, the evaluation personnel participating under paragraph (b)(1) of this section would normally be the speech-language pathologist.

PARTICIPATION BY PARENTS

Sec. 121a.345 Parent participation.

(a) Each public agency shall take steps to insure that one or both of the parents of the handicapped child are present at each meeting or are afforded the opportunity to participate, including:

(1) Notifying parents of the meeting early enough to insure that they will have an opportunity to attend; and

(2) Scheduling the meeting at a mutually agreed on time and place.

(b) The notice under paragraph (a)(1) of this section must indicate the

purpose, time, and location of the meeting, and who will be in attendance.
(c) If neither parent can attend, the public agency shall use other methods to insure parent participation, including individual or conference telephone calls.

(d) A meeting may be conducted without a parent in attendance if the public agency is unable to convince the parents that they should attend. In this case the public agency must have a record of its attempts to arrange a mutually agreed on time and place such as:

(1) Detailed records of telephone calls made or attempted and the results of those calls.

(2) Copies of correspondence sent to the parents and any responses received, and

(3) Detailed records of visits made to the parent's home or place of employment and the results of those visits.

(e) The public agency shall take whatever action is necessary to insure that the parent understands the proceedings at a meeting, including arranging for an interpreter for parents who are deaf or whose native language is other than English.

(f) The public agency shall give the parent, on request, a copy of the individualized education program.

(20 U.S.C. 1401(19); 1412(2)(B),(4),(6); 1414(a)(5).)

Comment. The notice in paragraph (a) could also inform parents that they may bring other people to the meeting. As indicated in paragraph (c), the procedure used to notify parents (whether oral or written or both) is left to the discretion of the agency, but the agency must keep a record of its efforts to contact parents.

IEPs FOR STUDENTS IN PRIVATE SCHOOLS

Sec. 121a.347 Private school placements.

(a) *Developing individualized education programs.*

(1) Before a public agency places a handicapped child in, or refers a child to, a private school or facility, the agency shall initiate and conduct a meeting to develop an individualized education program for the child in accordance with Sec. 121a.343.

(2) The agency shall insure that a representative of the private school facility attends the meeting. If the representative cannot attend, the agency shall use other methods to insure participation by the private school or facility, including individual or conference telephone calls.

(3) The public agency shall also develop an individualized educational program for each handicapped child who was placed in a private school or facility by the agency before the effective date of these regulations.

(b) *Reviewing and revising individualized education programs.*
(1) After a handicapped child enters a private school or facility, any meetings to review and revise the child's individualized education program may be initiated and conducted by the private school or facility at the discretion of the public agency.
(2) If the private school or facility initiates and conducts these meetings, the public agency shall insure that the parents and an agency representative:
(i) Are involved in any decision about the child's individualized education program, and
(ii) Agree to any proposed changes in the program before those changes are implemented.
(c) *Responsibility.* Even if a private school or facility implements a child's individualized education program, responsibility for compliance with this part remains with the public agency and the State educational agency.
(20 U.S.C. 1413(a)(4)(B).)

Sec. 121a.348 Handicapped children in parochial or other private schools.
If a handicapped child is enrolled in a parochial or other private school and receives special education or related services from a public agency, the public agency shall:
(a) Initiate and conduct meetings to develop, review, and revise an individualized education program for the child, in accordance with Sec. 121a.343; and
(b) Insure that a representative of the parochial or other private school attends each meeting. If the representative cannot attend, the agency shall use other methods to insure participation by the private school, including individual or conference telephone calls.
(20 U.S.C. 1413(a)(4)(A).)

ACCOUNTABILITY OF AGENCIES, TEACHERS, OTHER PERSONS

Sec. 121a.349 Individualized education program—accountability.
Each public agency must provide special education and related services to a handicapped child in accordance with an individualized education program. However, Part B of the Act does not require that any agency, teacher, or other person be held accountable if a child does not achieve the growth projected in the annual goals and objectives.
(20 U.S.C. 1412(2)(B); 1414(a)(5),(6); Cong. Rec. at H 7152 (daily ed., July 21, 1975).)
Comment. This section is intended to relieve concerns that the individualized education program constitutes a guarantee by the public agency and the

teacher that a child will progress at a specified rate. However, this section does not relieve agencies and teachers from making good faith efforts to assist the child in achieving the objectives and goals listed in the individualized education program. Further, the section does not limit a parent's right to complain and ask for revisions of the child's program, or to invoke due process procedures, if the parent feels that these efforts are not being made.

Glossary

The reader who wishes to have an extensive listing and definition of terms, an explanation of acronyms and abbreviations, a description of assessment instruments, a list of related legislation, and a reference guide to organizations concerned with exceptional individuals is referred to the *Educator's Resource Guide to Special Education: Terms–Laws–Tests–Organizations,* by W. E. Davis, Boston: Allyn and Bacon, Inc., 1980.

Advocacy: Actions taken by individuals or agencies on behalf of others. Advocacy for handicapped individuals usually involves attempts to secure for them equal educational, housing, or vocational opportunities.

Behavioral Disorders: Chronic, excessive, and deviant behavior which violates cultural norms and social expectations for an individual of a particular age. Abnormal behavior may range from total withdrawal to overt aggression.

Board Policy: An official statement adopted by a local school district's board of education that defines the procedures under which a district's schools will operate. A board policy must conform to federal and state statutory and regulatory codes.

Budget Monitoring: Controlling the expenditure of funds and/or keeping oneself and others in a system informed about the current status of various budget accounts.

Career Preparation: Programs that provide educational and vocational skill development, job experience, activities to develop good work attitude and ethical growth or habilitation and are directed toward helping an individual become a productive and successful worker. Career preparation is a broad term and is inclusive of such terms as vocational education and work experience.

Categorical Funding: Funding that is designated for a particular purpose and limited to that specific purpose (e.g., special education or bilingual education funds). Within special education, funds designated for MR or LD programs, as opposed to special education programs in general, would be described as categorical funds.

Categorical Program: An educational program organized, funded, and provided for handicapped individuals with a specific type of disability (e.g., a program for the mentally retarded or the visually handicapped).

Code: A statutory code is a set of rules enacted by a legislative body. A regulatory code is a set of rules enacted by federal or state agencies to implement a statutory code. Educational programs operate under the requirements of both types of codes.

Code of Federal Regulations: The regulations adopted by federal executive agencies in order to implement statutes. Educational regulations are designated as Title 45 of the Code of Federal Regulations and are developed by the Department of Education.

Communicative Disability: A general term that refers to any expressive or receptive language or speech problem.

Compliance Review: A study to determine whether or not a school agency is complying with compulsory school service laws and regulations. The review includes visits by an external review team.

Comprehensive System of Personnel Development: Each state education agency must submit to the office of Special Education a plan which defines the system for providing preservice and in-service education to the professional people who must provide the services required by P.L. 94–142.

Cooperative Program: A special education program or service provided, under formal or informal agreement, by two or more agencies that are unable or do not choose to provide all special services on a unilateral basis.

Disability: A physical, mental, or emotional problem that is sufficiently different from the norm as to cause functional problems. While not all disabilities make an individual *handicapped,* this book tends to use the terms synonymously. (*See also* Handicap.)

Due Process Hearing: (*see* Impartial due process hearing).

Due Process Procedure: A practice established by laws, regulations, court orders, or policies to ensure individuals (and their parents or guardians) that their constitutional or legal rights will not be violated.

Etiology: The cause or source of a particular disability.

Exceptional Individual: An individual who deviates from the norm in sensory, physical, emotional, or cognitive characteristics to such a degree that he/she meets certain defined criteria and/or needs special education services. The term *individual* rather than *child* is frequently used because services extend through twenty-one years of age.

Free Appropriate Public Education: A term used in P.L. 94–142 to declare the intent of Congress. *Free* means at no cost to parents. *"Appropriate"* refers to the ways in which the educational needs of handicapped individuals are met. *Public education* refers to the responsibility of the general public and the public education agencies to provide educational programs for the handicapped.

Full Service Agency: An agency (usually a local school district) that provides exceptional individuals with every service prescribed by law.

Functional Disorder: A disability that is not organically caused in which no structural abnormality exists.

Funding Appropriation: The amount of money provided in a budget. The funding appropriation is frequently less than the amount of money authorized in the legislative act that authorizes the program. (*See* Funding authorization.)

Funding Authorization: The amount of money designated by a legislative act as the maximum that can be provided for in the authorized budget appropriation.

Funding Formula: A factor utilized by federal and state government agencies to calculate or generate funds for local education agencies or for the operation of special education programs.

General Administrator: A person responsible for overall school programs (e.g., a superintendent, a principal, or a business manager).

Gifted and Talented Student: A student who has demonstrated potential ability in areas such as general intellectual functioning, academic learning, leadership, and the performing arts. Some states define giftedness primarily on the basis of intelligence test scores.

Handicap: Any physical, sensory, mental, or emotional condition that prevents an individual from achieving his/her desired goals. The extent of a handicap determines whether an individual needs special education services.

Impartial Due Process Hearing: A hearing conducted at the local and/or state level regarding differences of opinion between parents and the local education agency about assessment, identification, or services provided for handicapped individuals between the ages of three and twenty-one.

Individualized Education Program (IEP): A written plan (required by P.L. 94–142 and implementing federal regulations) that outlines every handicapped pupil's curriculum and provides for needed services.

Informed Consent: Parental consent that allows a school to evaluate an individual or place him/her in a special education program. The term informed indicates that the parent must understand the action to be taken.

Laws and Regulations: Law referes to statutory codes adopted by legislative bodies. Regulations are adopted by agencies of the executive branches of government (e.g., State Department of Education) to help implement laws.

Learning Disability: A disorder of one or more of the basic psychological processes that manifests itself in a severe discrepancy between ability and achievement in one or more of the following areas: (1) oral expression, (2) listening comprehension, (3) written expression, (4) basic reading skills, (5) reading comprehension, (6) mathematics calculation, or (7) mathematics reasoning. The severe discrepancy between ability and achievement cannot be primarily as a result of (1) visual, hearing, or motor handicap, (2) mental retardation, (3) emotional disturbance, or (4) environmental, cultural or economic disadvantage. (*Federal Register,* December 29, 1977.)

Least Restrictive Environment: The program that most closely resembles a regular class but still fulfills a handicapped individual's needs. For one pupil this may be a regular class with minor modifications; for another it may be a special school.

Low Incidence Handicap: A disability that is very uncommon in the general population (e.g., deaf-blind).

Mainstreaming: A controversial term generally used to mean education in the regular classroom to the maximum extent possible. Mainstreaming does not imply that special classes should be abandoned or that all pupils can be served in the regular classroom.

Mental Retardation: Significantly subaverage general intellectual functioning existing concurrently with deficits in adaptive behavior, and manifested during the developmental period, which adversely affects the child's educational performance. (From *Federal Register,* Aug. 23, 1977.)

Noncategorical Program: An educational program for exceptional individuals that is based on the type of service needed (e.g., special class, resource room) rather than on a categorical classification. (*See also* Categorical program.)

Nonpublic School: A school that is operated by an individual or private agency instead of being publicly funded and operated.

Organic Disorder: A disorder with known physical abnormality or pathology.

Organizational Model: A structure that verbally and/or graphically describes how an organization functions or is governed.

Parental Rights: A number of rights are guaranteed parents under provisions of federal and state codes. Included are items such as: a free appropriate public education for their children; confidentiality of their children's records; and the right to give or withhold permission for assessment and placement.

Physical Disability: A disability that affects motor functioning and/or places health-related limitations on an individual's ability to function in a given situation (e.g., cerebral palsy, epilepsy, severe diabetes). The term is sometimes used to include sensory disabilities, such as hearing and vision disabilities.

P.L. 93–112: Public Law No. 112, passed by the 93rd Congress. It is entitled The Vocational Rehabilitation Act of 1973.

P.L. 94–142: Public Law No. 142, passed by the 94th Congress. It is entitled The Education for All Handicapped Children Act of 1975.

Prevalence: The number of exceptional individuals within a given population.

Procedural Safeguards: Procedures established by an educational agency to protect the rights guaranteed to individuals and their parents in the Constitution and in various laws and regulations.

Program Evaluation: As used in this book, program evaluation involves gathering data describing programs, keeping records, improving programs, ensuring accountability, reporting, and decision making.

Related Service: A related service is defined in Section 121a.13 of the Code of Federal Regulations as follows: "transportation and such developmental, corrective and other supportive services as are required, to assist a handicapped child to benefit from special education, and includes speech pathology and audiology, psychological services, physical and occupational therapy, recreation, early identification and assessment of disabilities in children, counseling services, and medical services for diagnostic or evaluation purposes. The term also includes school health services and social work services in schools, parent counseling and training."

Sensory Disability: A serious impairment of one of the major senses that restricts input of information through that sensory channel. The most common sensory disabilities involve a hearing or vision loss.

Sheltered Workshop: A facility or program that trains and/or employs individuals who are not capable of working in competitive employment situations.

Site Administrator: An administrator whose responsibilities relate to a given school location (e.g., a principal, a vice principal, or a dean of girls).

Special Education: Programs and services (classes, instruction, materials, curricula, corrective services) designed to allow handicapped and gifted individuals to obtain an appropriate education and to develop to their fullest potential.

Special Education Administrator: An individual who has primary responsibility for a local school district's special education programs. The most commonly used titles are director, coordinator, and supervisor of special education. If other responsibilities are included, the title is frequently director of pupil personnel and special education services.

Special School: A school specifically designed for exceptional individuals and enrolling only these pupils. A special school usually serves only the more severely handicapped pupils.

Spectrum of Services: All the special education programs and services needed by different exceptional individuals if they are to receive an appropriate education (e.g., special classes, speech therapy, transportation).

State Education Agency: As used in federal codes, the term refers to the agency responsible for a state's public school programs. The SEA is most frequently called the state department of education. However, the state board of education may also be included in the definition.

Statute: A law passed by a legislative body (e.g., Congress, a state legislature).

Support Personnel: People who provide services (other than instructional services) so that an exceptional individual receives an appropriate education (e.g., transportation, assessment).

Syndrome: A group of signs or symptoms that indicate the presence of a particular condition or disorder (e.g., Down's Syndrome). Signs or symptoms may vary in number and degree of intensity.

Vocational Education: Courses and/or practical experiences designed to prepare individuals for particular occupations or a cluster of occupations.

Vocational Rehabilitation: Programs or services that provide assessment, training, medical treatment/therapy, counseling and/or job placement to help handicapped individuals enter or reenter the work force.

Author Index

Subject Index